# MINGEI
# /
# ART
# WITHOUT
# HEROES

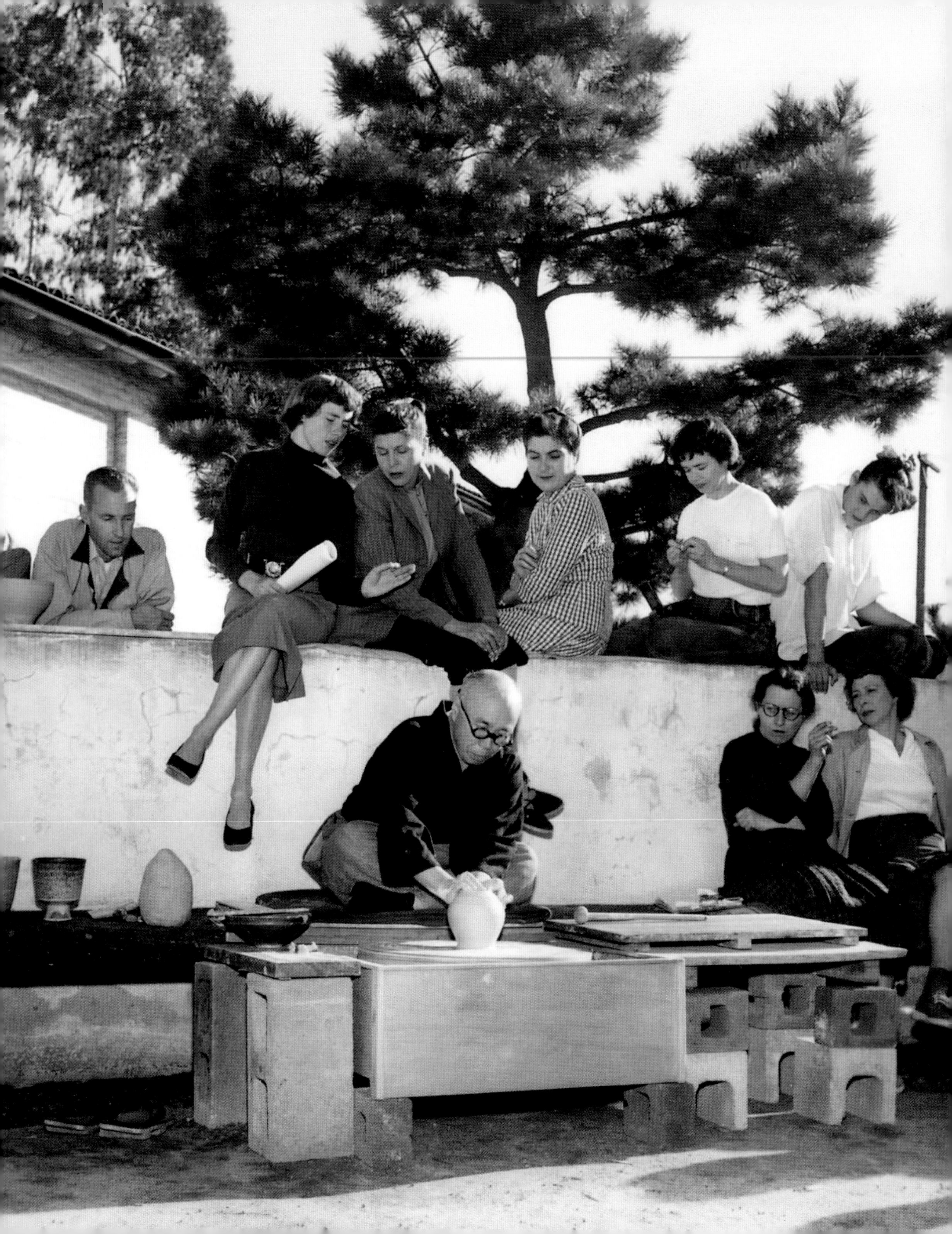

# MINGEI / ART WITHOUT HEROES

Edited by Róisín Inglesby

WILLIAM MORRIS GALLERY

YALE UNIVERSITY PRESS
New Haven and London
In Association with
William Morris Gallery

For information about this and other Yale University Press publications, please contact:
U.S. Office: sales.press@yale.edu yalebooks.com
Europe Office: sales@yaleup.co.uk yalebooks.co.uk

Project Editor: Daphne Fordham-Smith
Designer: Aniela Gil
Senior Production Controller: Leonie Kellman

Printed in Italy by Printer Trento

Library of Congress Control Number: 2023949268

ISBN 978-0-300-27428-8

A catalogue record for this book is available from the British Library.

All reasonable efforts have been made to provide accurate sources and clear permissions for all images that appear in this book. Any inaccuracies or omissions will be rectified in future editions.

10 9 8 7 6 5 4 3 2 1

MIX
Paper | Supporting responsible forestry
FSC® C015829

**PREVIOUS** Hamada Shōji throwing at Scripps College, California, 1952 | © Crafts Study Centre, University for the Creative Arts.

**FRONT COVER**
*Left to right from top left:*

**Butterfly Stool**, Yanagi Sōri, Rosewood-faced 5-ply plywood with brass cross-bar and metal fittings, 1956 © YMK Nagaoka Co., Ltd.

**Six-fold screen**, Serizawa Keisuke, Silk, stencil paste-resist dyeing (*bingata*), about 1940, Victoria and Albert Museum

**Bowl**, Tomimoto Kenkichi, Raku ware, pattern of plum blossoms with two nightingales, 1912, Victoria and Albert Museum

**Naruko kokeshi**, Okazaki Yasuo, date unknown © Okazaki Manami

**Water sprinkler**, porcelain with white glaze, Korea, Yi dynasty, 17th to 18th century © Crafts Study Centre, University for the Creative Arts

***Tsumugi* kimono**, Munehiro Rikizo, 1978 © Yoshizawa Tomo

**Faceted white porcelain square bottle**, unknown maker, Joseon, date unknown, National Museum of Korea

**Kimono**, unknown maker, Hemp (*asa*), tie-dyeing (*shibori*), 1870-1910, Karun Thakar Collection, London © Desmond Brambley

**Spoke Chair**, Toyoguchi Katsuhei, 1963, © Tendo Co., Ltd

**Somewake (separated glaze) dish**, Ushinoto kiln, design by Yoshida Shōya, 1931, Tottori Folk Crafts Museum

**Rice cooker**, Fukasawa Naoto for Muji, 2014

**Square vessel**, Hamada Shōji, stoneware with kaki glaze, c.1970–5, Royal Collection Trust © Hamada-gama Pottery Co. 2022

# Contents

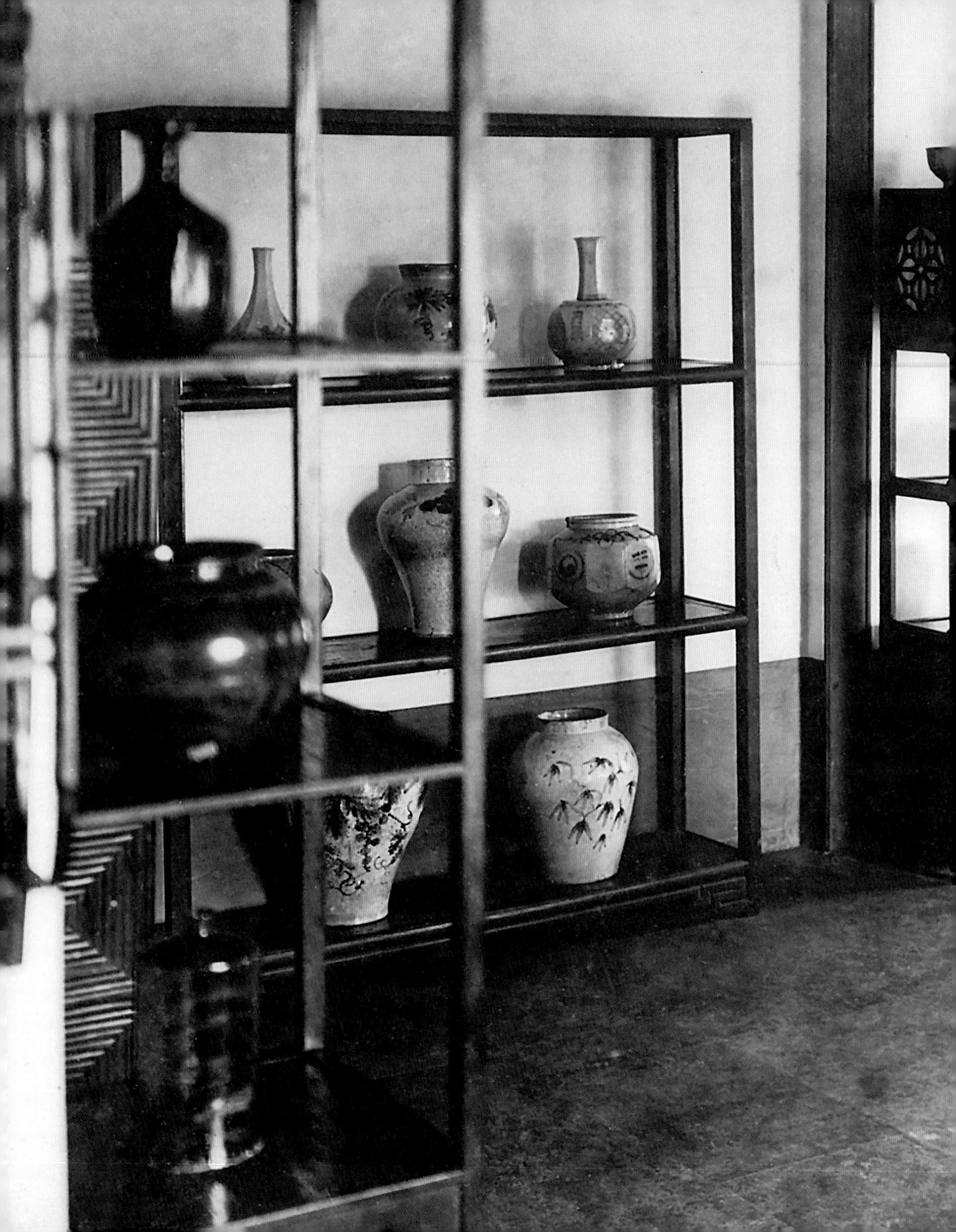

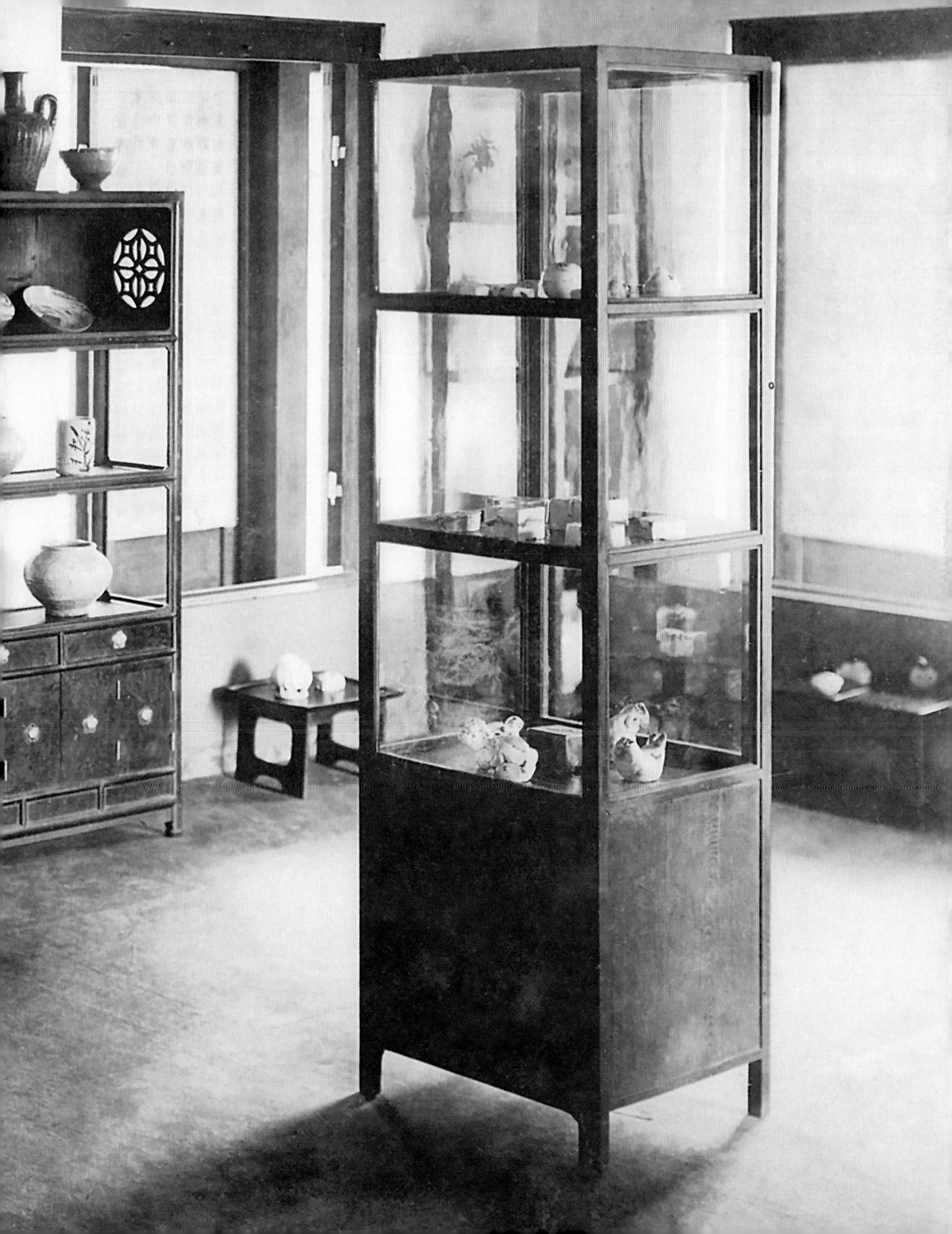

## A NOTE ON NAMES AND PRONUNCIATION

In this book Japanese and Korean names are given in their original order, i.e. with family name first, unless the subjects have specifically requested otherwise.

Macrons are used to denote a long vowel in Japanese, except where the word is commonly known in English (e.g. Tokyo), or where the subject chooses not to use a macron in Romanised form.

# Living with Mingei

It was summer 2012. The seminar room of the art university was packed and humid. At the front, three researchers were sitting at one large desk. Their fields of expertise ranged from religious studies to anthropology and folklore, with one underlying theme: the origin of these subjects dated back over a century. The Industrial Revolution started in Britain, bringing about economic and social change across Europe and the disappearance of historical cultures, including certain rituals, objects and stories. The study of these subjects was born in reaction to this situation.

Interestingly, similar trends were observed in Japan in the early twentieth century as it went through rapid industrialisation following the Meiji Restoration of 1868. The relationship between these geographically separate yet corresponding phenomena was the main theme of the seminar.

I listened keenly. The subject resonated strongly with me, as someone who grew up surrounded by Mingei culture. I knew about the Arts and Crafts movement in Britain in the nineteenth century. The topic seemed a perfect fit to explain the relationship between Mingei and the British movement. But the seminar ended without mention of the M-word.

I joined the next session, and the one after, hoping to hear the word.

It didn't happen.

Eventually, I asked one of the professors about it. He answered in a sympathetic manner, beginning 'Yes, I'm sure they are all related, but... Mingei is not an academic subject.'

---

I grew up in a small town in Japan, watching my father shave wood to make *koto*, a stringed musical instrument (fig. 1), and hearing the sound of my mother on her loom (fig. 2). Our vacations in the islands of Okinawa were as much about visiting a local weaver as going to the beautiful beaches.

After graduating from high school, I went to study in the UK. My uncle Munehiro Yosuke and his wife Kuniko, both weavers, came to stay, armed with a list of places they wanted to visit: Ditchling; St Ives. The names meant nothing to me. In Ditchling, we went to a small house where we were welcomed by a lady. I remember her saying 'Mashiko'. My uncle repeated the word, and they both nodded. I was the only bilingual person there, and

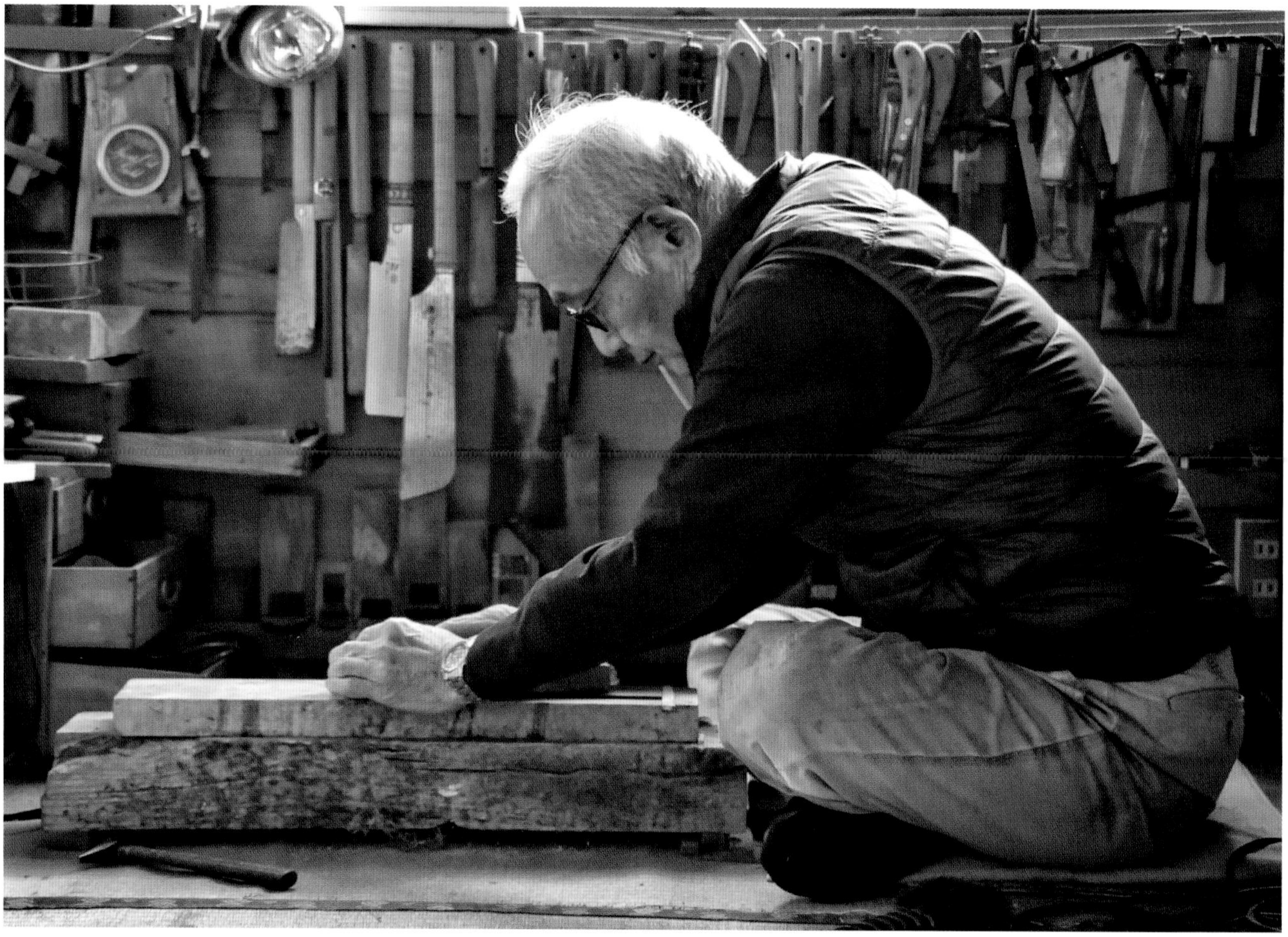

FIG 1 Yoshizawa Takeshi in his studio, 2021 | Credit: Takizawa Sayaka

the only one not getting the context, a situation that continued while visiting the Leach Pottery in St Ives.

On their last day in London, my uncle handed me a small book. 'It's for you. For you to understand what connoisseurship is.' The book was *Tea and Beauty* by Yanagi Sōetsu (1889–1961). I read the book over the rest of my time in the UK.

By the time I moved back to Japan, I had learned where Mashiko was. The dots were connecting into lines. I realised I had grown up surrounded by Mingei. I also learnt that the potter Kawai Kanjirō (1890–1966), one of the leading figures of the Mingei movement, was the one who encouraged my grandfather Munehiro Rikizo to pursue his path of *tsumugi* (pongee silk) weaving (fig. 3). Munehiro endeavoured to revive the *tsumugi* industry as a means for him and his village to survive after the Second World War. He started from zero, learning to cultivate the soil, grow plants and silkworms and use natural dye. In 1982, Munehiro was named a Living National Treasure; my uncle continued the weaving workshop until 2022.

---

Despite this family history, it was only after the Tōhoku Earthquake of 11 March 2011 that Yanagi's words revealed themselves to be much more than a way of seeing beauty. I was managing a shop that sold made-in-Japan products, run by a company with a mission to revive the nation's crafts industry. On the day following the earthquake and tsunami, I still opened the shop and sold an expensive scarf. I felt happy, but also a sting of guilt. What good does it do to sell scented candles and expensive chopsticks when there are people who have just lost their houses? The question whirled in my head.

The year 2011 was transformative even for those who didn't lose their homes or livelihoods. It taught that some basic matters should never be taken for granted. In need of answers to their own internal questions, some looked to wisdom from the past for answers. I did, too.

That's when I rediscovered Mingei. I went back to my collection of Yanagi's essays, including *Tea and Beauty*. As I read, I gained clarity: it felt as if I was peeling off a layer of words to connect with the meanings beneath. Yanagi looked at the process through which beautiful objects come into being and drew parallels to the human experience. He pointed to a way of being that was beyond the binary and free from ego. His words opened my eyes and lifted my heart.

A chapter in *Tea and Beauty* is dedicated to Kizaemon Ido, a masterpiece of a tea bowl. Yanagi describes its unparalleled quality as 'ordinary', then continues, 'but ordinary is good. Let me rephrase for the readers: it is good because it is ordinary. It has to be ordinary.'

The century-old term Mingei is a shortening of *minshūteki kōgei*, crafts for ordinary people. It was clear that Mingei was relevant to me today. But I had never explored the topic beyond my own personal experience. What are the crafts for ordinary people today? And does 'Mingei' mean anything to those who make and use those crafts? These are the questions I've asked makers, consumers and collectors and that form the basis for the short profiles in this book.

Yanagi praised Ido ware for being 'calm without any drama; no hidden intention; innocent and sincere. It is as it is and mindful. No arrogance; no pride. If these qualities aren't beauty, then what else is? The humble, plain, and honest; they naturally deserve admiration.'

His words could be used to describe some of the people I have met during the course of this project. Mingei is the people's art; it cannot help but change over time. Objects chosen by Yanagi remain, but everything else that surrounds them changes. In its ever-evolving nature, though, Mingei has been able to remain for the people – by being used, lived with and lived by. It is my wish to help illustrate the living Mingei of today.

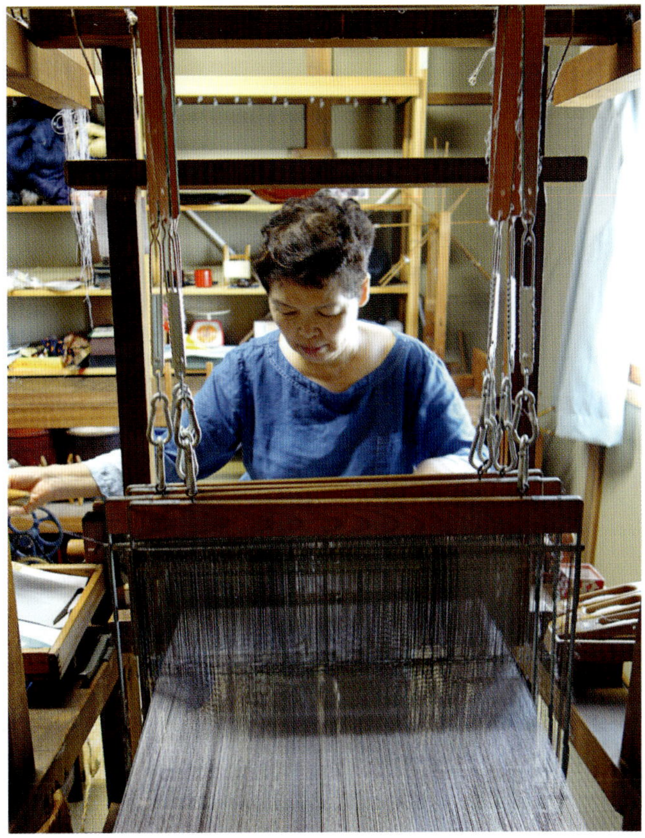

**FIG 2** Munehiro Yoshiko on her loom, c.2010

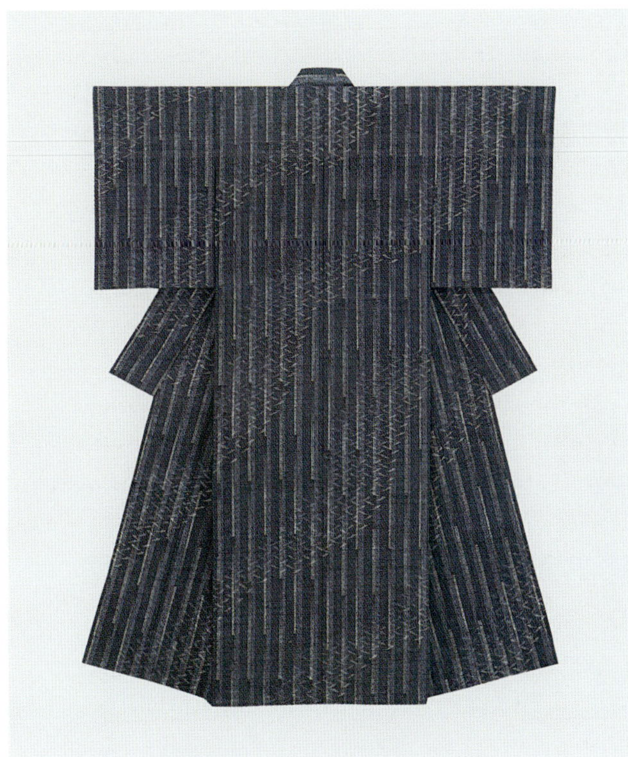

**FIG 3** Munehiro Rikizo, *tsumugi* kimono, 1978

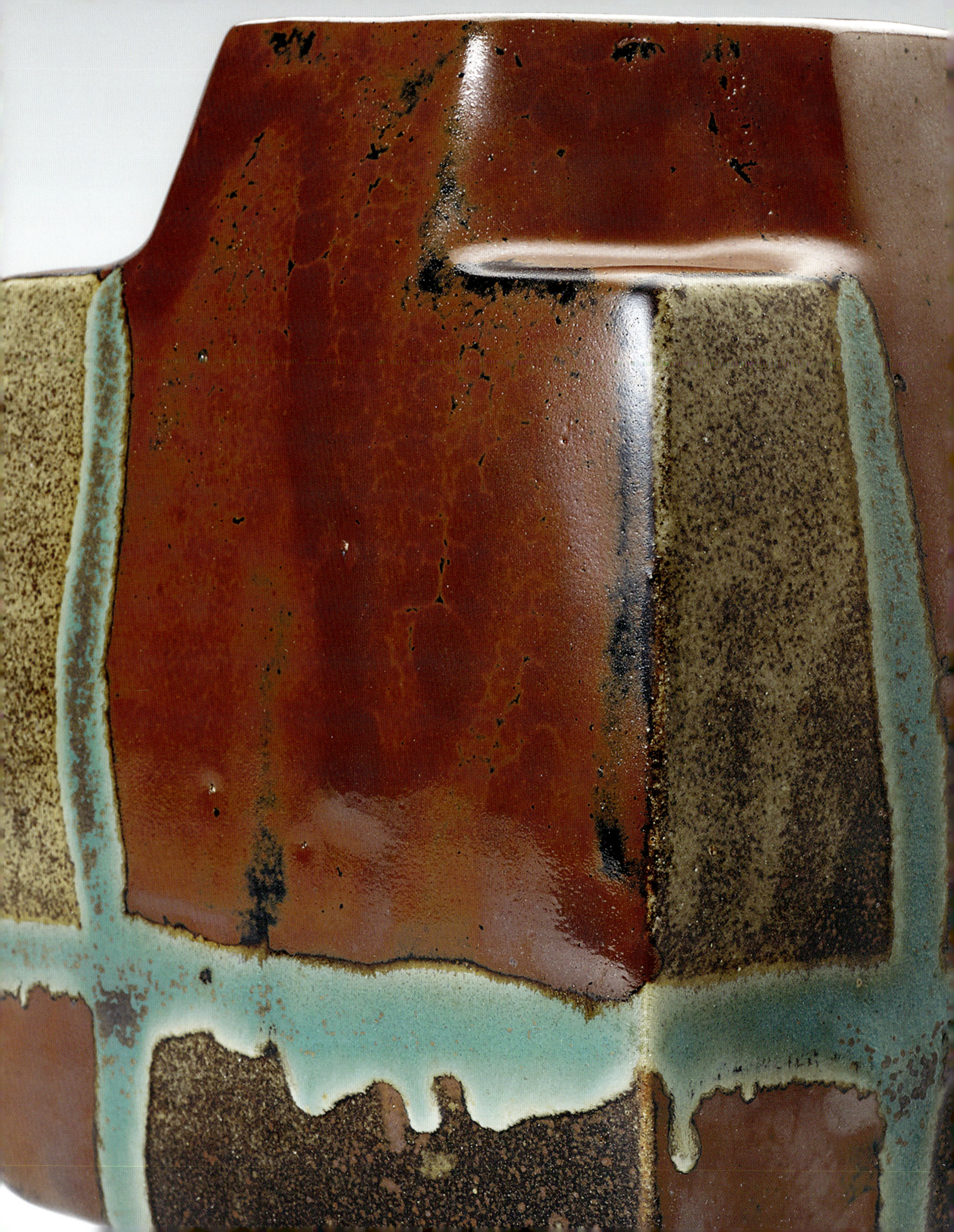

RÓISÍN INGLESBY

# Introduction

In July 1952, Yanagi Sōetsu[1] (1889–1961; fig. 1) delivered a speech at the International Conference of Craftsmen in Pottery and Textiles, held at Dartington Hall, Devon. A guest of honour, Yanagi was at the height of his powers as the de facto leader of the Japanese Mingei movement. Originally an aesthetic theory formulated by Yanagi in the 1920s, over the course of the following decades Mingei had evolved into a 'nationwide campaign for the recognition and creation of folkcraft' with an international reach.[2]

Addressing the audience in English, Yanagi spoke passionately of the urgent need for an artistic revival that would permeate all aspects of daily life. In conceptualizing this revival, Yanagi drew on the words of the ancient Chinese philosopher Lao Tze. 'When the Great Reason is obliterated,' Yanagi quoted, 'we have benevolence and justice. When wisdom and sagacity appear, we have much hypocrisy. When family relations are no longer harmonious, we have filial piety and paternal love. When a nation is in disorder, we have loyalty and allegiance.'[3]

At first sight paradoxical, Lao Tze's teaching, Yanagi explained, is that the overall condition of any society creates the opportunity for some people within it to act differently. Yet these laudable actions of the few are only necessary, or notable, when society as a whole is in disarray. For example, a world that in general has sufficient regard for the arts has no need of the individual artist: 'The artist brings light to darkness ... but the world which does not require him, [this] special individual artist, is a wonderful world, the world where the genius is merely a common individual.'

The influence of this genius-artist becomes, for Yanagi, an act of heroism, but again he warned:

> Hero worship may happen when the world is full of people who are not heroes and at such a time when the world would show no social happiness. Times when heroes are not needed, the times when they become ordinary people and their existence is not uncommon, then they are most admirable.[4]

Yanagi's message was unequivocal. In his estimation, the best society is that in which art is made by the everyday maker, unexceptional and unheroic. This idea is the key feature that runs throughout the Mingei movement: that beauty is inherent in the unselfconscious production of the anonymous craftsperson (fig. 2).[5]

Yanagi's plea for everyday arts was not unique, nor even an invention of the twentieth century. As Yuko Kikuchi

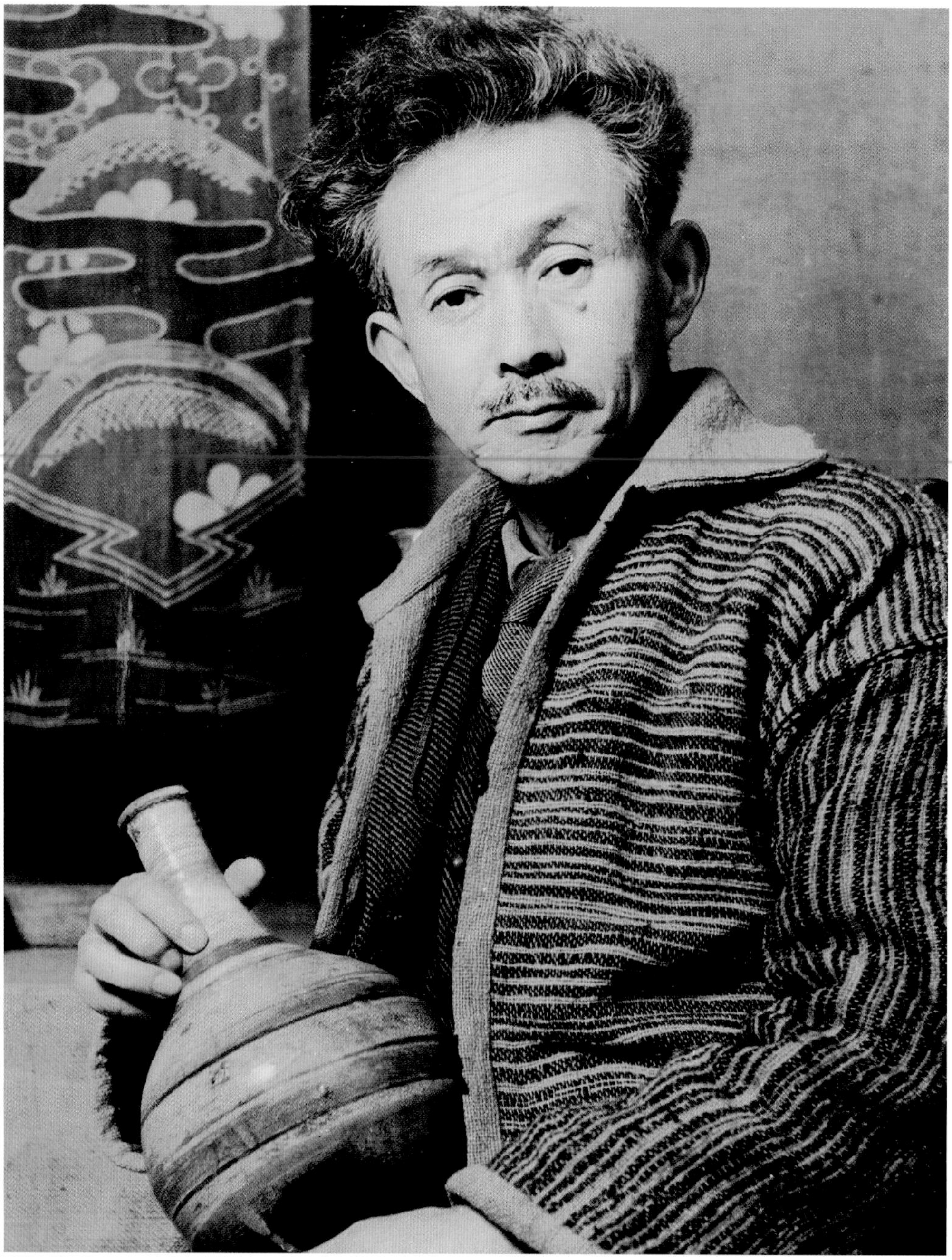

FIG 1 Yanagi Sōetsu at Nihon Mingeikan (Japan Folk Crafts Museum), February 1948 © Japan Folk Crafts Museum

explains (see p. 27), the concept of the 'art of the people' is a far-reaching idea that crosses temporal and geographical boundaries. As early as the 1870s William Morris (1834–1896) had articulated the historic importance of anonymous, commonplace craft production:

> Well, these things are just the common household goods of those past days, and that is one reason why they are so few and so carefully treasured. They were common things in their own day, used without fear of breaking or spoiling – no rarities then – and yet we have called them 'wonderful'.
>
> And how were they made? Did a great artist draw the designs for them – a man of cultivation, highly paid, daintily fed, carefully housed, wrapped up in cotton wool, in short, when he was not at work? By no means. Wonderful as these works are, they were made by 'common fellows', as the phrase goes, in the common course of their daily labour.[6]

Like Yanagi, Morris also saw exceptionality in the arts as symptomatic of a parlous situation, for in his own world, 'must there not be something wrong with a state of society which drives these into that bitter heroism, and the most part into shirking, into the depths often of half-conscious self-contempt and degradation?'[7]

The concept of an art without heroism runs throughout this book and the wider exhibition project of which it is a part. The Japanese term Mingei, written using the Chinese characters for 'people' and 'art', is an elision of *minshūteki kōgei*, which literally means 'ordinary people's craft'.[8] Implied in this 'ordinariness' is the sense of complete anonymity that subsumes any individual expression on the part of the maker; the maker becomes the conduit of the craft, but he or she does not leave their mark, nor self-consciously engage in the act of production. From a twenty-first-century, particularly Western, perspective, this sense of anonymity can be difficult to accept. In the context of Western art history, which attaches supreme importance to authorship and the signed work of art (particularly if that work is signed by a man),[9] there is an understandable urge to reinsert the personal identity of the maker into anonymous pieces, in order to create monetary value or place the object in a defined historical narrative. Anonymous objects are disproportionately made by women, the poor and other marginalised groups; attaching a name can therefore be an act of restitution, rescuing a maker from the unmarked grave of a forgotten attic or museum store.

Indeed, as Kikuchi points out in her discussion of Theaster Gates (b.1973; see pp. 34–7), signing work can be a deeply significant political act – there is a difference between the anonymous maker and those who have been *anonymised* by political and social oppression. It is hard to imagine a better example of the potency of authorship than the ceramics of the enslaved African American potter David Drake (c.1800–c.1870s; fig. 3), whose name is etched into pots he made in Old Edgefield District, South Carolina, a centre of stoneware production in the decades before the American Civil War (1861–5).[10] Through Drake's act of self-identification – one might say heroism – we can see an individual emerging from the past, and attach human experience to these silent objects, made under unthinkable circumstances. Yet perhaps Yanagi would argue that this undeniably forceful cry of selfhood – I Make Therefore I Am – should never be necessary, as no individual should ever be subjected to the attempted obliteration experienced by David Drake. The need for Drake's signature is therefore proportionate to the depravity of the society around him.

Moreover, within the framework of Yanagi's Buddhist ideal of beauty, the submission of the individual self into one's work, through a process that relies on the acceptance of grace, repetition and tradition, becomes a means of achieving

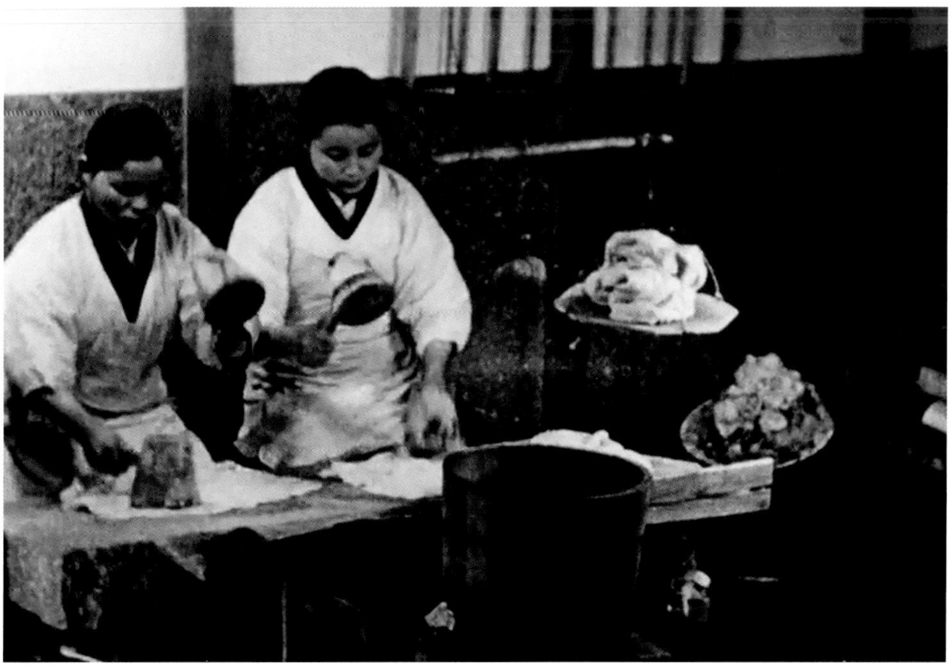

FIG 2 Women pounding fibres for papermaking, Mino, Japan, from *Japanese Paper* (film), 1938
Credit: Courtesy of the Mingei Film Archive Project/Marty Gross Film Productions Inc

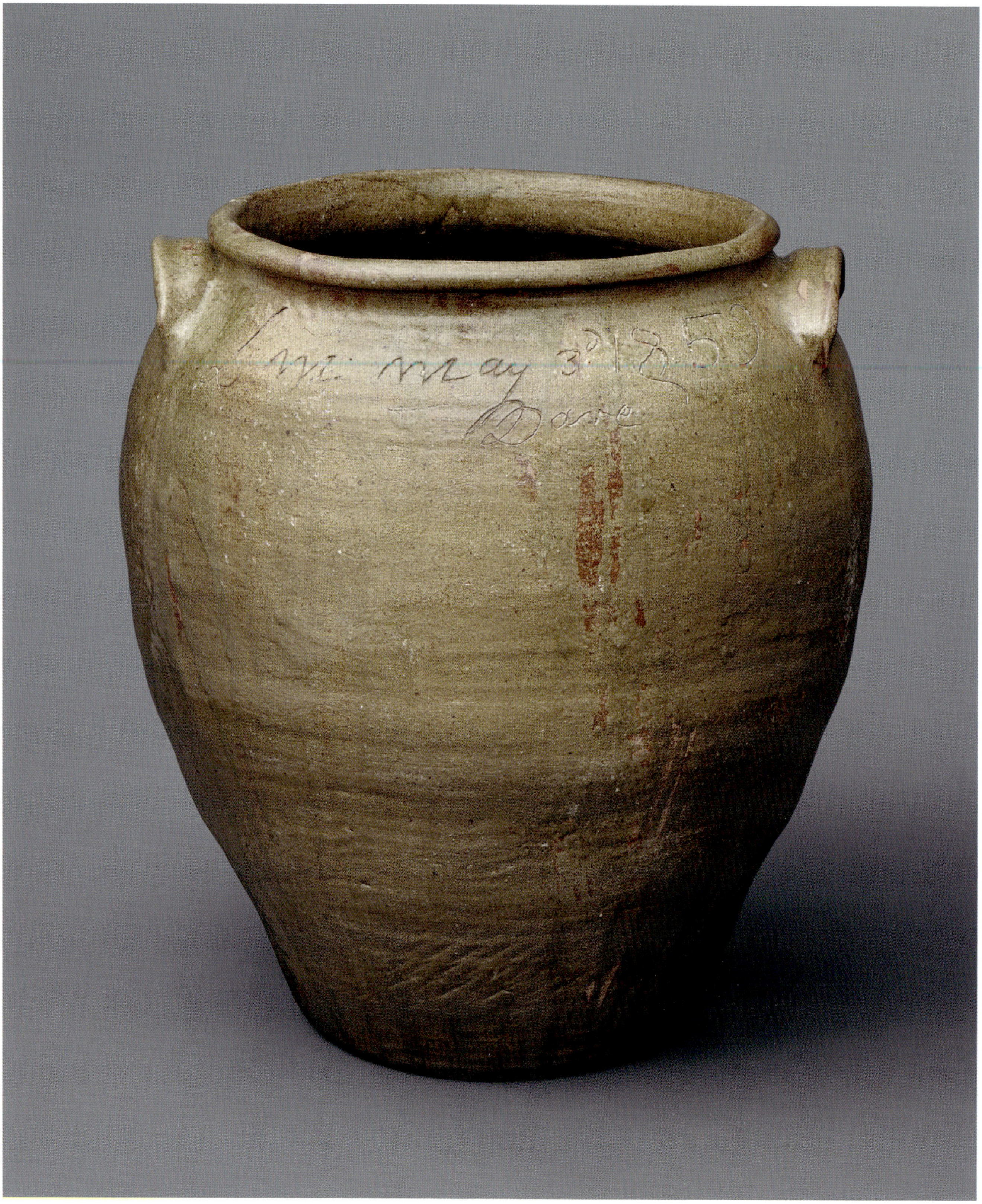

**FIG 3** David Drake (Dave the Potter), storage jar, alkaline-glazed stoneware, 1859, Philadelphia Museum of Art | Credit: 125th Anniversary Acquisition. Purchased with funds contributed by Keith and Lauren Morgan and with the gifts (by exchange) of John T. Morris, Mrs. John D. Wintersteen, and the bequest of Maurice J. Crean, and with the Baugh-Barber Fund, the Haas Community Fund, and other Museum funds (by exchange), 1997, 1997-35-1

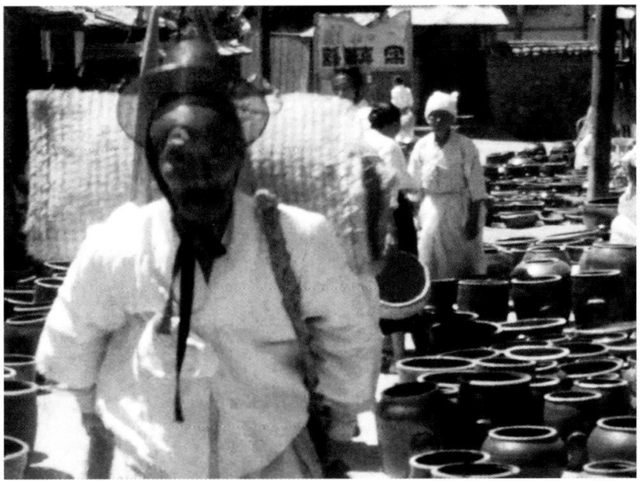

FIG 4 Market scene with Korean porter in *Bernard Leach Films Korea*, 1935 | Credit: Courtesy of the Mingei Film Archive Project/Marty Gross Film Productions Inc

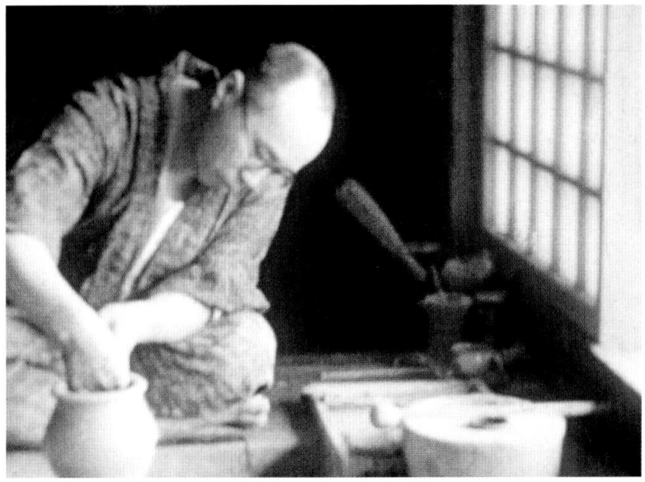

FIG 5 Hamada Shōji in *Pottery Making in Mashiko and Other Japanese Villages*, 1934, filmed by Bernard Leach | Credit: Courtesy of the Mingei Film Archive Project/Marty Gross Film Productions Inc

Oneness, and thus ultimate liberation.[11] The ability to accept the benefits of anonymity therefore in part depends on one's understanding of freedom and the role that craft can play in the liberation of the maker. In Morris's conception, while true beauty is the result of work created 'unconsciously and without effort',[12] a degree of variety in labour is essential: 'To compel a man to do day after day the same task, without any hope of escape or change, means nothing short of turning his life into a prison-torment.'[13] In Morris's utopian novel *News from Nowhere* (1890), this freedom is illustrated by the ability to choose, on any given day, what work to engage in. Yet while to some the 'repetitive monotony'[14] that Yanagi advocates may appear dehumanising, to many craftspeople a near-mechanical action born of endless repetition can be liberating: the thought process removed in order that one can 'think, talk, listen or sing'.[15] In the words of Samuel Gompers, a nineteenth-century cigar maker working in the tenements of New York City, in honing his craft 'I had earned the mind-freedom that accompanied skill as a craftsman'.[16] Similarly, many Japanese craftspeople interviewed as part of this exhibition project described a sense of *mushin*, a state of mental quietude translated by the Zen scholar D.T. Suzuki as 'being free from mind-attachment'.[17]

Nonetheless, Yanagi's aesthetic vision of beauty created through 'discarding of the self'[18] can certainly be accused of a disconnection with socio-political reality, particularly in the context of Japan's aggressive colonial expansion, effected from the mid-nineteenth century to the end of the Second World War. Inhabitants of these colonised areas whose work Yanagi admired, including the indigenous Ainu of Hokkaido and the people of Korea, were subjected to forced cultural assimilation and a loss of personal and political agency. Dasom Sung's chapter on Korea's relationship with the Mingei movement (pp. 41–9) explores the historic connection between Japanese Mingei protagonists and the folk craft of colonised Joseon, while also charting the ways in which Korean scholars have since reclaimed and disrupted Yanagi's infamous judgement of Korea's 'beauty of sorrow' (fig. 4). Anna Jackson's chapter on Mingei textiles (pp. 55–67) further problematises the development of Mingei as an aesthetic category isolated from social context, particularly in the case of Okinawan *bingata*, a type of brightly coloured stencil-dyed fabric. Lauded by Yanagi as an example of indigenous folk craft, *bingata* had, until the Japanese annexation of the region in 1879, been the exclusive preserve of the royal court and thus not 'popular' at all. Moreover, Jackson raises the point that the majority of textiles that Yanagi praised existed, even in the past, within a nexus of socio-economic relations, with skilled makers renowned for their work.[19] These craftspeople were therefore not actually anonymous: they are merely anonymous *to us*. This circumstantial anonymity is highlighted in Brian Moeran's study of Onta pottery – a craft form considered by many as emblematic of Mingei production – in which he argues that while members of the community can identify who has made

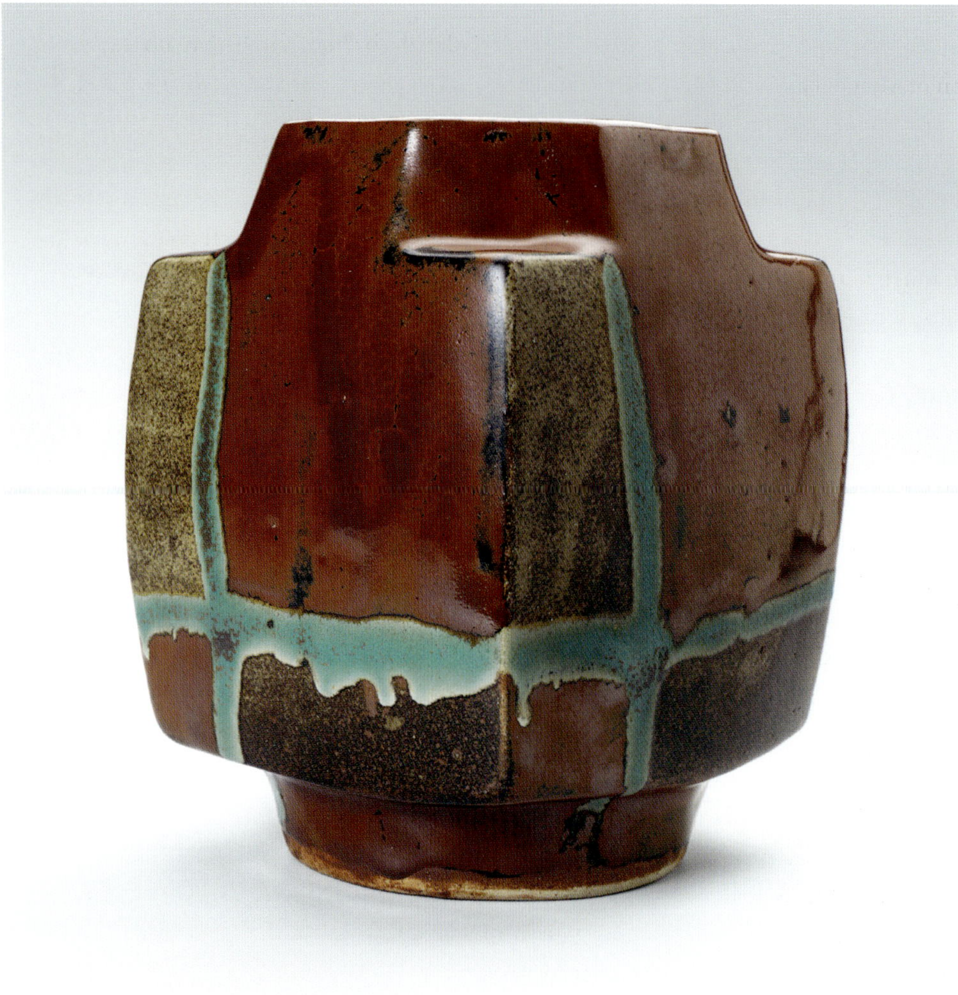

**FIG 6** Hamada Shōji, square vessel, stoneware with *kaki* glaze, c.1970–5, Royal Collection | Credit: Royal Collection Trust/© Hamada-gama Pottery Co. 2022

a piece of work, remaining anonymous to the outside world of consumers and critics has become a collective decision that exists within a complicated socio-economic framework.[20]

The paradoxes of anonymity were not lost on Yanagi, one of the 'Three Musketeers' along with the potters Bernard Leach (1887–1979) and Hamada Shōji (1894–1978) (fig. 5), who themselves came to be seen as the heroes of the Mingei movement. In Japan, Leach has tended to be replaced by Kawai Kanjirō (1890–1966) in the established Mingei holy trinity. Yet despite Yanagi's protestations that 'Mr Hamada and Mr Kawai, who are Japan's two greatest pottery artists, do not put their signature on their goods',[21] in reality this has had no effect on their identification, desirability and prices. Hamada was designated a 'Living National Treasure'[22] in 1955, and two decades later a vase by him was presented by Prime Minister Miki Takeo to Queen Elizabeth II during her state visit to Japan, a reflection of its elevated cultural significance (fig. 6). Hamada remains Japan's most celebrated ceramicist and his work commands extremely high prices, an inevitable situation in a world in which the major way of expressing value is financial.

---

The tortured relationship between craft and capitalism, of which Morris was so acutely aware, is a thread that runs through every chapter in this book. As Adam Sutherland points out in his chapter on everyday making (pp. 125–36), in today's society, craft is not necessary in any practical sense – machines can and do make everything we need. Since the Industrial Revolution craft has become economically marginal, with the costs of production placing the crafted object far above the reach of the average person. Even at the beginning of the Mingei movement, the situation was similar. As Sam Thorne explains in his chapter on the display and consumption of Mingei (pp. 87–97), the clientele for these objects in the 1930s were urban literati, purchasing their rustic pots and handmade textiles through fashionable Tokyo stores. In Kawabata Yasunari's 1948 novel *Snow Country*, Shimamura, the wealthy protagonist, consumes rural handcraft much in the same way as he consumes Komako, the young geisha whom he visits in the countryside, as a rustic tonic to rejuvenate his jaded urban existence. Shimamura owns a collection of nineteenth-century *chijimi* garments, which he 'still sent back for snow-bleaching' (fig. 7). 'It was', Kawabata continues,

> a great deal of trouble to return old kimono – that had touched the skin of he could not know whom – for rebleaching each year to the country that had produced them; but when he considered the labours of those mountain maidens, he wanted the bleaching to be done properly in the country where the maidens had lived. The thought of the white linen, spread out on the deep snow, the cloth and the snow glowing scarlet in the rising sun, was enough to make him feel that the dirt of the summer had been washed away, even that he himself had been bleached clean. It must be added, however, that a Tokyo shop took care of the details for him, and he had no way of knowing that the bleaching had really been done in the old manner. [23]

This concept of the handmade object being a signifier of genteel taste, even when authentic craft is lacking, is at the crux of Aaron Angell's chapter on the legacy of Mingei in ceramic art (pp. 113–121). In Angell's argument, the pretentions of fashionable craft fail to match their reality, in a form of 'failed seriousness' that Susan Sontag considered a defining feature of camp.[24] Indeed, as Mingei objects became desirable, fashion created another dimension to the skewed relationship between craft skill and capitalism, as discussed in Okazaki Manami's chapter on kokeshi (pp. 73–83), which charts the twentieth-century ascent of these humble wooden playthings to collectables for the literati. Such market forces naturally change the way in which makers perceive their products; to command a share of the profits, craftspeople must ensure that it is their work that is sold rather than that of their counterparts (or worse, their competitors), and therefore the mark of the individual enters their work in an attempt to ensure it is correctly attributed. The mercenary nature of our society thus translates into what Okamura Mihoko has described as 'greed in the object', an egotistical situation entirely

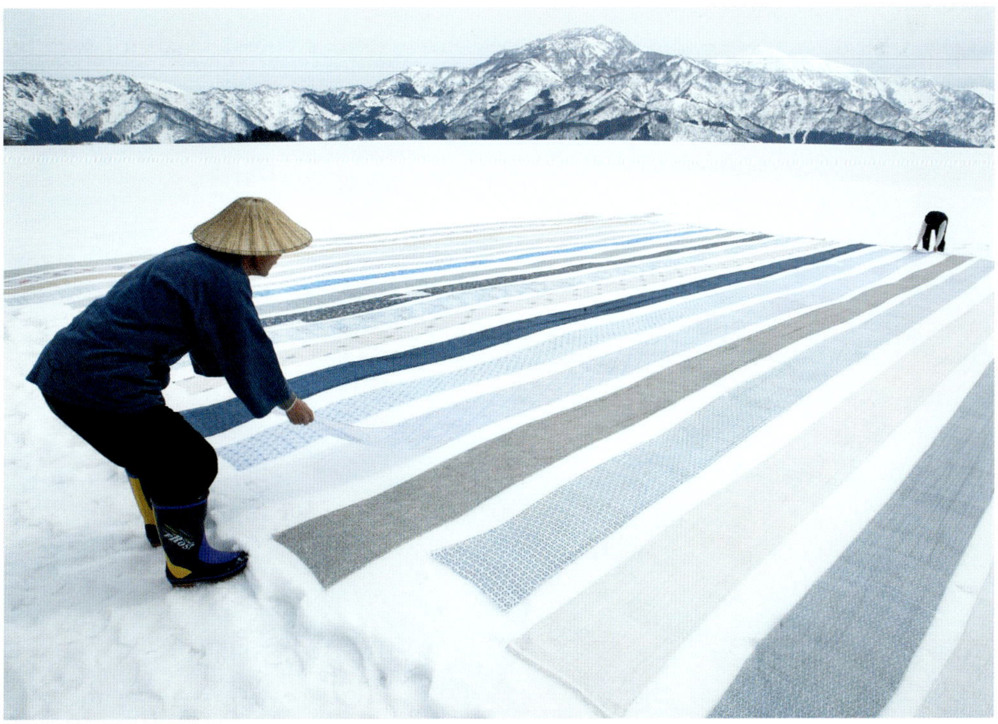

FIG 7 Nakajima Kiyoshi, fourth generation weaver, bleaching fabric on snow in the mountain village of Shiozawa, Niigata, 2005 Photograph © Everett Kennedy Brown

at odds with the production of beauty.[25] This greed is exacerbated by the inequalities in society that have increasingly rendered craft in the West the preserve of the educated amateur. Through financial security and leisure time, these makers create objects purely as a means of personal fulfilment, encroaching on the labour of the underprivileged in what Sutherland refers to as the 'identity theft of the vanquished' (p. 127).

From this perspective, any discussion of Mingei seems bleak: we have a situation in which ownership of the art of the people has become a mark of cultural elitism; a way of life has been commodified. The crafted object becomes a shortcut attempt to purchase a form of cultural authenticity that is lost through the very act of consumption, or a consumerist answer to far larger social, political and environmental problems. Yet there is also a more hopeful way of understanding interest in crafted objects and craft practices. Mingei's development is undeniably linked to the major shocks suffered by Japanese society in the past century: rapid industrialisation; the hardship of the Second World War; and the tragedy of the Tōhoku Earthquake in 2011, which is referenced by several authors in this book. Japan is not alone; since the Industrial Revolution, craft movements around the world have occurred as a response to social and political dislocation and the perceived division of the self that results in a fractured society.[26] In Morris's handwritten notes on Karl Marx's *Capital* (1867–94), he pays particular attention to Marx's understanding that 'when labour is divided ... *it is the man himself who is cut up*' (my emphasis; fig. 8). Yanagi was similarly preoccupied with the concept of separation, which he termed 'the divorce' between the body and mind and between the subjective and the objective brought about by consciousness. He sought to return, through craft, to a state before this separation began.[27] In today's world too, craft is often considered a way of returning to a fundamental state of integrity, in which craft skills, the objects they produce and the lifestyle that makes them possible are seen as tools for reunification – of body with mind, of people with nature (and perhaps, by extension, God), and of person with person. This concept of connectedness through craft is a striking feature of Okazaki's explanation of the popularity of kokeshi – consumers are emotionally affected by their 'warmth', of the security of human contact provided by the handmade (p. 73).

Can such values be transmitted in contemporary society? One route, which was already underway during Yanagi's lifetime, is through the development of product design and its desire to create high-quality, useful objects that are affordable to the masses. Naomi Pollock's chapter on the evolution of Japanese design charts the ways in which it oscillates in and out of the world of Mingei, addressing the new forms that Mingei – if we may still call it that – might take today (pp. 101–10). In the UK, too, there are examples of large-scale factory production that employ considerable manual skill and handcraft at every stage, that use locally sourced materials to create useful products, and whose individual workers remain anonymous to the end consumer.[28] In both contexts, there is significant support for the concept of a national craft, whether this be the UK's Made in Britain campaign or the Japanese *furusato nōzei* (hometown tax) scheme discussed by Kikuchi (p. 33). For reasons ranging from the economic to the cultural or the nationalistic, there is a popular recognition of the importance that *somebody* in the country is still making things, even if not every individual themselves.

A second alternative is through craft education, participatory projects and small start-ups, as discussed by Sutherland (himself a former student at Dartington Hall School) in his description of the work of Grizedale Arts in the Lake District (p. 130–2). In this conception, making is an everyday thing done by everyone, utilising local skills and resources to mould one's surroundings as an act of material self-determination and environmental and social sustainability.

Whichever route we follow it seems that as a society we must urgently increase our 'material intelligence', our understanding of how things are made.[29] Simply buying handmade objects is not enough to counteract the ills to which craft is posited – arguably incorrectly – as the cure.[30] Even more so than in Morris's time, 'We do not know how a piece of goods is made, what the difficulties are that beset its manufacture, what it ought to look like, feel like, smell like, or what it ought to cost apart from the profit of the middleman.'[31] As Morris understood, knowledge about making liberates the individual from a feeling of disconnection with the surrounding world of things. It also forces us to rethink the relative value we place on human labour and raw materials, which can only be a good thing for global social inequality and the environment.

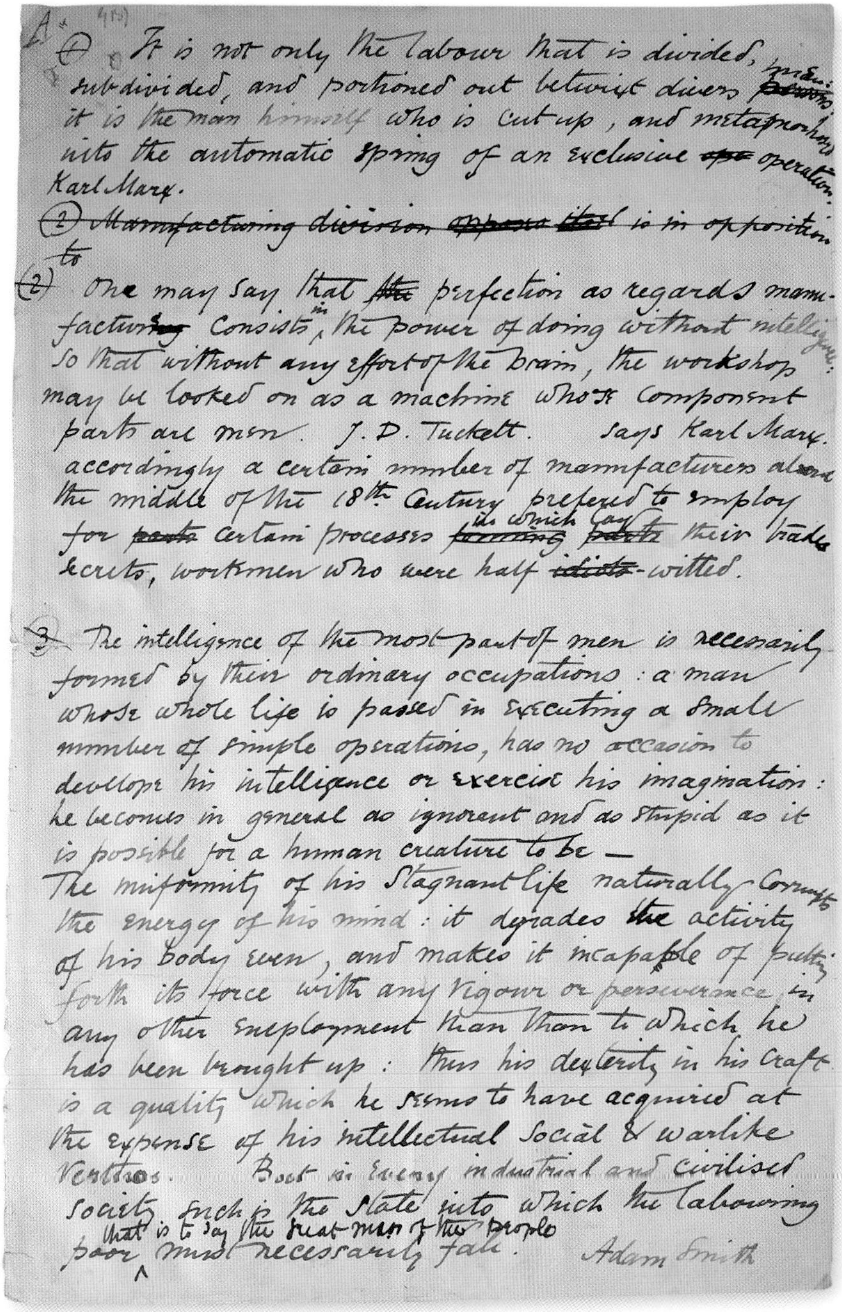
(1) It is not only the labour that is divided, subdivided, and portioned out betwixt divers men: it is the man himself who is cut up, and metamorphosed into the automatic spring of an exclusive operation. Karl Marx.

~~(2) Manufacturing division~~ is in opposition to

(2) One may say that perfection as regards manufacture consists in the power of doing without intelligence so that without any effort of the brain, the workshop may be looked on as a machine whose component parts are men. J. D. Tuckett. says Karl Marx. accordingly a certain number of manufacturers about the middle of the 18th Century preferred to employ for certain processes in which lay their trade secrets, workmen who were half-witted.

(3) The intelligence of the most part of men is necessarily formed by their ordinary occupations: a man whose whole life is passed in executing a small number of simple operations, has no occasion to develope his intelligence or exercise his imagination: he becomes in general as ignorant and as stupid as it is possible for a human creature to be — The uniformity of his stagnant life naturally corrupts the energy of his mind: it degrades the activity of his body even, and makes it incapable of putting forth its force with any vigour or perseverance in any other employment than that to which he has been brought up: thus his dexterity in his craft is a quality which he seems to have acquired at the expense of his intellectual social & warlike virtues. But in every industrial and civilised society such is the state into which the labouring poor that is to say the great mass of the people must necessarily fall. Adam Smith

**FIG 8** William Morris's notes on Karl Marx's *Capital*, 1883, William Morris Gallery, London Borough of Waltham Forest

The profiles of contemporary makers within this book demonstrate some of the approaches to everyday making being utilised in Japan today. As Yoshizawa Tomo discusses in her foreword (p. 11), whether or not practitioners actively consider themselves part of a Mingei tradition is to some extent irrelevant: one can be part of something without necessarily conceptualising it as such; equally one can be considered a 'Mingei' practitioner while actively objecting to the association. As a category, Mingei is a twentieth-century invention, but its manifestations and principles extend both backwards and forwards in time, with the word itself a nebulous concept, and one that is increasingly confused with 'craft' of any kind rather than specifically inexpensive crafts made for everyday use. The perspectives in this book, representing the views of curators, academics, makers and others involved in what can loosely be described as the 'Mingei world', are therefore by no means an attempt to define the boundaries of Mingei or 'solve' its many paradoxes. They do, however, all consider what is meant by an 'art without heroes', and what this concept can look like today.

## NOTES

1. In Japan, Yanagi is known as Yanagi Muneyoshi, but this book will refer to him by the alternative pronunciation of Sōetsu, by which he is more commonly known in the Anglophone world.
2. Kikuchi 2004, xv.
3. The quotations from this speech are taken from an audio recording held by the Mingei Film Archive. I am sincerely grateful to Marty Gross for his generosity in sharing material from the Archive.
4. Yanagi delivered this speech in English, so from the recording it is impossible to know whether his use of the word 'hero' bears a distinctly Western tinge of individualism and self-promotion. In Japanese, the English loanword 'hero' (ヒーロー) is frequently used, as is sometimes the case for vocabulary that has no adequate translation, or to connote foreign influence. The Japanese term *eiyuu* denoting a great person is subtly different from the Anglophone understanding of a 'hero'.
5. Yanagi 1972, 199–204.
6. Morris 1883; originally delivered as a speech before the Birmingham Society of Arts and School of Design, 19 February 1879.
7. Ibid.
8. The terms 'art' and 'craft' are used interchangeably in this publication to reflect the difficulties of precise translation, and both Morris's and Yanagi's belief that there should be no hierarchy between the two. Yanagi himself used both terms, speaking of 'artists' in his speech at Dartington, though the Japanese Mingei Museum that he founded translates mingei as 'folk-crafts'. For further information on the linguistic complexities, see Kikuchi 2004, 80–82.
9. See Gorrill 2020.
10. See Spinozzi 2022.
11. Yanagi 1972, 133–5.
12. Morris 1888.
13. Morris 1884.
14. Yanagi 1972, 137.
15. Adamson 2021, 135.
16. Cited in ibid.
17. Suzuki 1935, 80
18. Yanagi 1972, 153.
19. See Moeran 1997 and Guth 2021 for the ways in which Japanese craft existed within socio-economic networks, from the perspective of an anthropologist and a historian respectively.
20. Moeran 1997, 165–8.
21. Quoted from Yanagi's speech at Dartington Hall, 1952.
22. The popular term for those individuals certified as Preservers of Important Intangible Cultural Properties.
23. Kawabata 2022, 136–7.
24. The disconnection between the earnestness with which capitalist society consumes craft and its corresponding failure to be politically useful is also described by Leopold Kowolik as 'ripe for satire' (Kowolik 2021, 113).
25. Okamura Mihoko (1935–2023) was the personal assistant to the Buddhist scholar D.T. Suzuki from 1953 until Suzuki's death in 1966. A series of interviews between Okamura and Marty Gross that took place in 2013 is in the collection of the Mingei Film Archive; one of these is quoted here.
26. Some of the numerous examples include the Bauhaus school and the Młoda Polska (Young Poland) movement.
27. From Marty Gross's interview with Okamura Mihoko, 2013.
28. One notable example is the Ercol furniture factory in Princes Risborough, which exhibits a fascinating symbiosis between hand and machine production.
29. See Adamson 2018.
30. For a discussion of the political claims, limits and possibilities of craft, see Black and Burisch 2021.
31. Morris 1888.

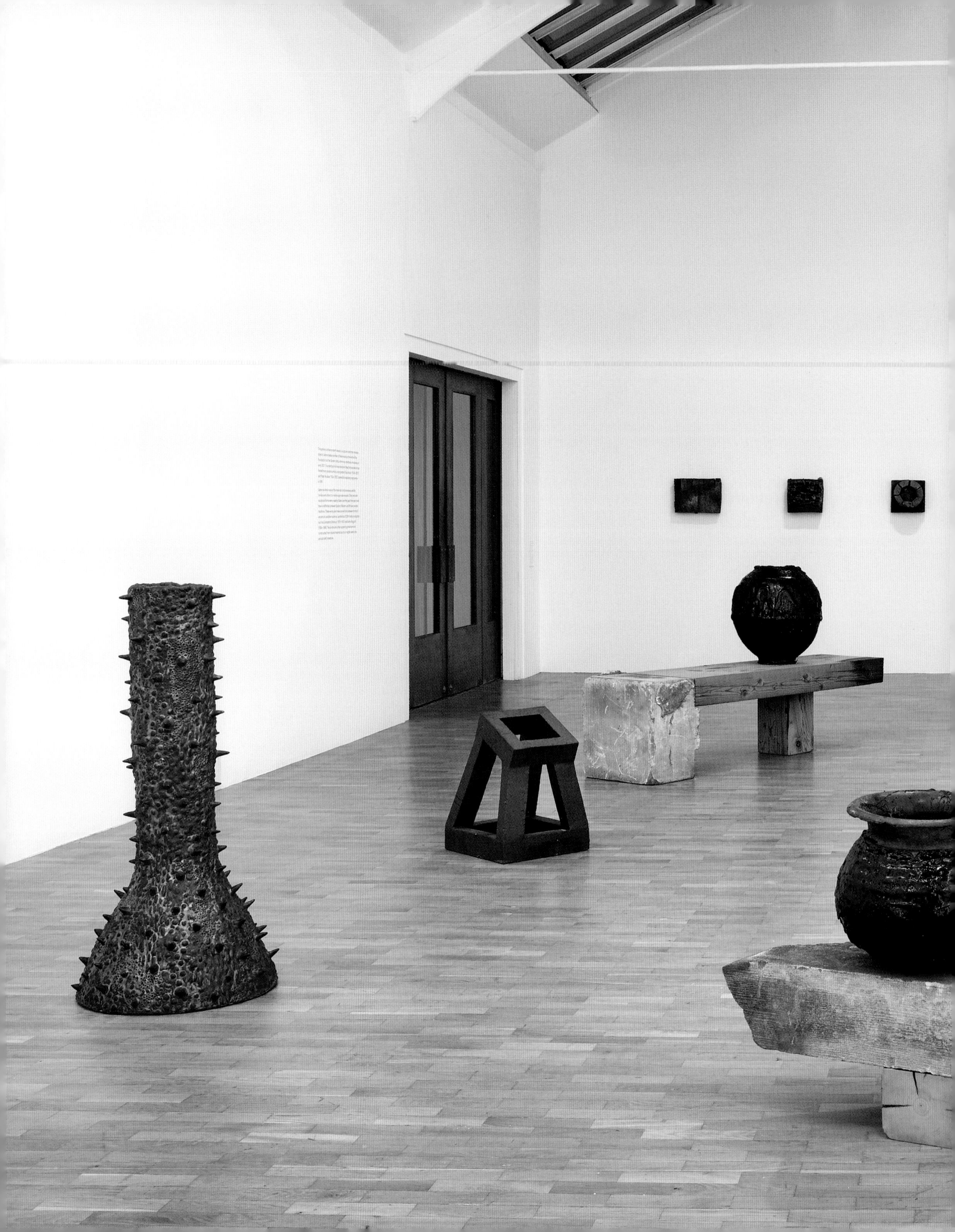

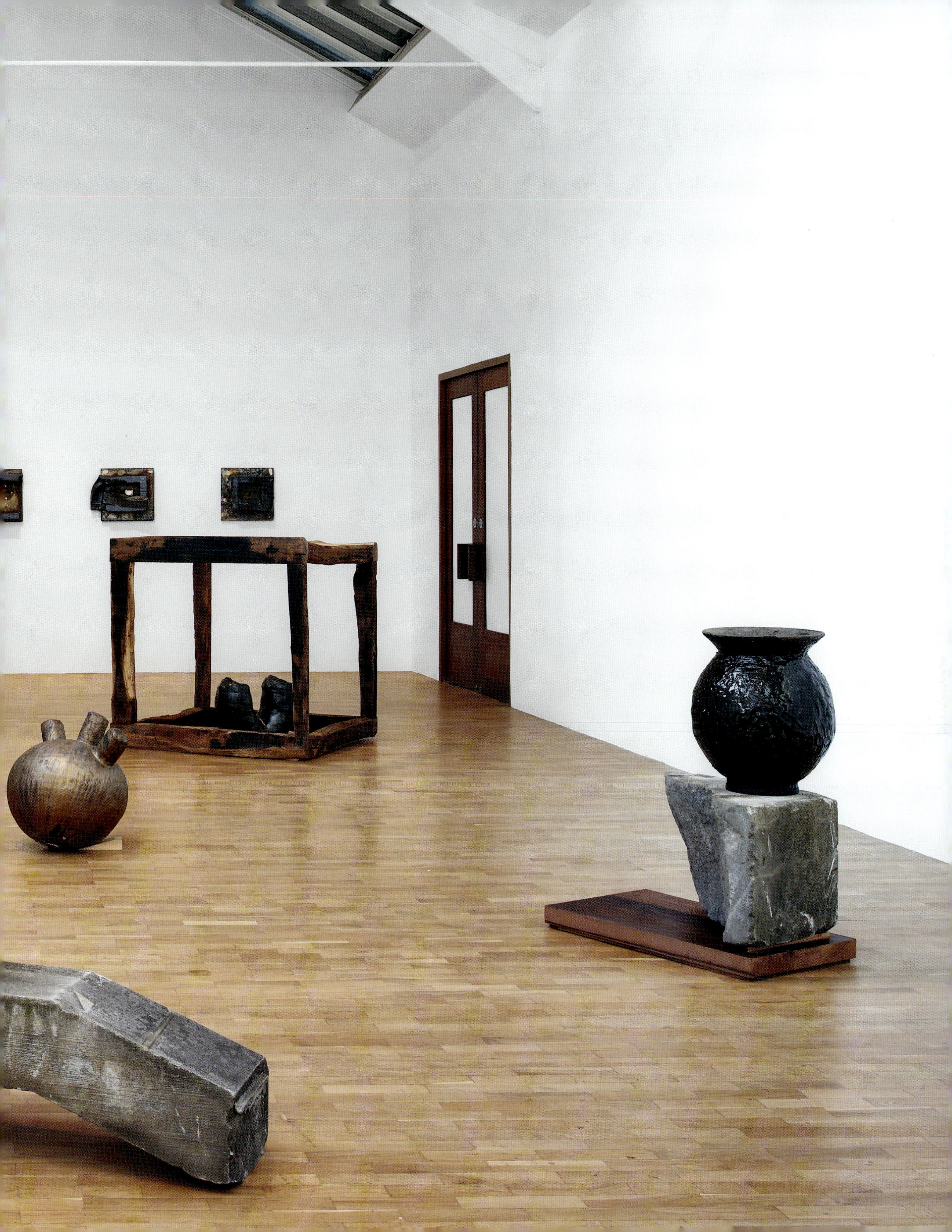

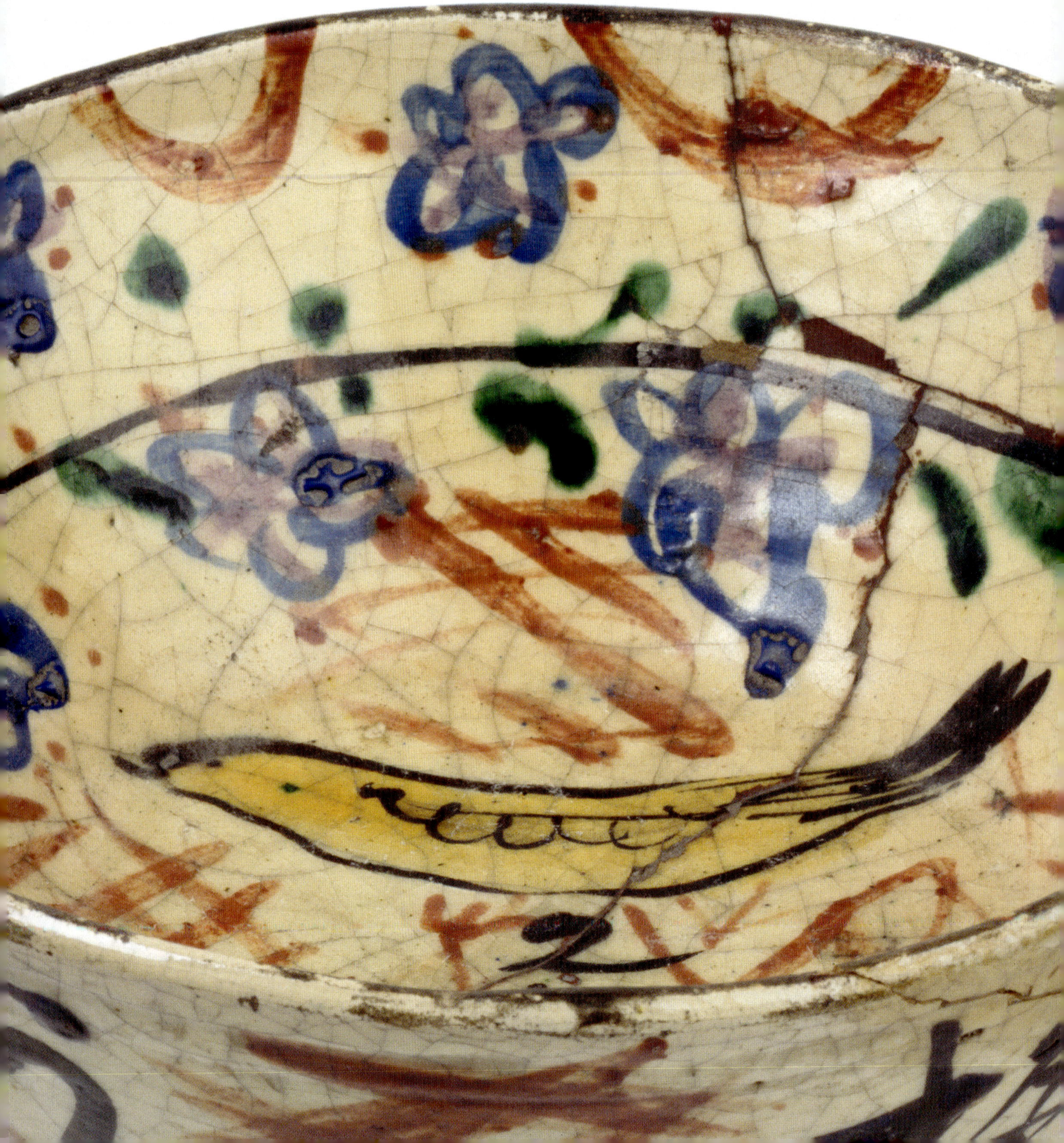

YUKO KIKUCHI

# Morris, Mingei and Studio Crafts

## The transformative idea of the art of the people

As a term and an idea, Mingei (usually translated as 'the art of the people') is both a twentieth-century Japanese invention and a modern concept that has developed in multiple cultural centres worldwide. In the nineteenth century, William Morris shaped the English Arts and Crafts movement around the idea of the art of the people in theory and practice.[1] The concept was widely disseminated, including via the Mingei movement in Japan. However, its translation into regionally specific cultures, and the objects produced by makers who are part of those cultures, created something beyond what has conventionally been described as Morris's 'influence', as the Mingei movement clearly shows. In the latter half of the twentieth century, we can identify a multi-directional evolution of the idea of the art of the people, while in the twenty-first century we can observe its revival alongside our contemporary interest in community.

Transnationality and the capacity to be transformative are key requirements for imagining and visualising our current goal for a sustainable world underpinned by diversity and inclusivity. Postcolonial thinkers question the concept of 'culture' in different ways and problematise it as neither reflecting lived reality, nor providing equal opportunities because of the retention of old power relations and institutional systems. In order to make multiple 'cultures' visible, some useful ways of looking at them have been suggested. For example, Édouard Glissant proposes the idea of 'creolisation' as a token for understanding the whole world.[2] Jean Fisher argues for the term 'syncretic turn' as a normative state of culture in which there are continual 'altering relations' between the powerful and less powerful.[3] This contrasts with Homi Bhabha and Néstor García Canclini's 'hybrid',[4] which Fisher regards as pointing to a binary power relation between original culture and that which it influences. Meanwhile, James Clifford, Edward Said, Paul Gilroy, Françoise Lionnet and Shu-mei Shih and many others have investigated the situation of diaspora and proposed theories of travelling, translation and transnationalism.[5] The world they propose is imbued with commonalities but also has many differences between, ruptures with, and resistance to retaining specific, local values. This postcolonial condition of multiple cultures is also described as a 'chaos-world' and a 'jungle' in a complex, positive and creative sense, in order to reject the idea of totality implied by globalisation.[6] It recognises unpredictable, under-represented new creations with elements of untranslatability. Informed by these

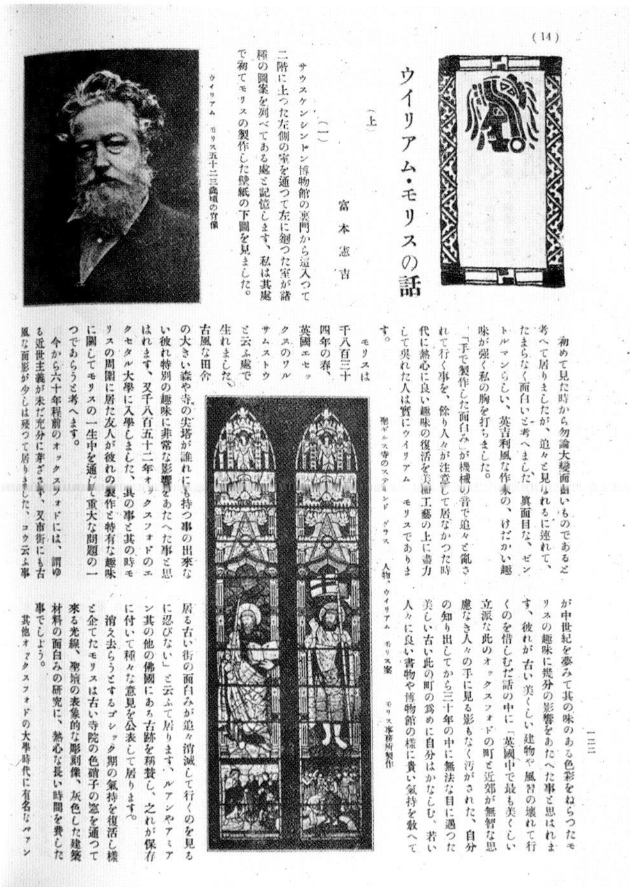

(14)

ウイリアム・モリスの話

（上）

富本憲吉

（一）

サウスケンシントン博物館の裏門から這入つて二階に上つた左側の室を通つて左に廻つた室が諸種の圖案を列べてある處と記憶します、私は其處で初てモリスの製作した壁紙の下圖を見ました。

ウイリアム　モリス五十二三歳頃の肖像

初めて見た時から勿論大變面白いものであると考へて居りましたが、追々と見なれるに連れて、たまらなく面白いと考へました眞面目な、ゼントルマンらしい、英吉利風な作家の、けだかい趣味が強く私の胸を打ちました。

「手で製作した面白み」が機械の音で追々と亂されて行く事を、餘り人々が注意して居なかつた時代に熱心に良い趣味の復活を美術工藝の上に盡力して與れた人は實にウイリアム　モリスであります。

聖ポルス寺のステインド　グラス　人物、ウイリアム　モリス案　モリス事務所製作

モリスは千八百三十四年の春、英國エセックスのワルサムストウと云ふ處で生れました。古風な田舍の大きい森や寺の尖塔が誰れにも持つ事の出來ない彼れ特別の趣味に非常な影響をあたへた事と思はれます、又千八百五十二年オックスフォドのエクセタル大學に入學しました、其の事と其の時モリスの周圍に居た友人が彼れの製作と特有な趣味に關してモリスの一生中を通じて重大な問題の一つであらうと考へます。

今から六十年程前のオックスフォドには、謂ゆる近世主義が未だ充分に芽ざさず、又市街にも古風な面影が少しは殘つて居りました、コウ云ふ事が中世紀を夢みて其の味のある色彩をねらつたモリスの趣味に幾分の影響をあたへた事と思はれます、彼れが古い美くしい建物や風習の壊れて行くのを惜しむだ話の中に『英國中で最も美くしい立派な此のオックスフォドの町と近郊が無智な思慮なき人々の手に見る影もなく汚がされた、自分の知り出してから三十年の中に無法な目に遇つた美しい古い此の町の爲めに自分はかなしむ、若い人々に良い書物や博物館の樣に貴い氣持を敎へて居る古い街の面白みが追々消滅して行くのを見るに忍びない」と云ふて居ります、ルアンやアミアン其の他の佛國にある古跡を稱賛し、之れが保存に付いて種々な意見を公表して居ります。

消え去らうとするゴシック期の氣持を復活し樣と企てたモリスは古い寺院の色硝子の窓を通つて來る光線、聖壇の表象的な彫刻像、灰色した建築材料の面白みの研究に、熱心な長い時間を費した事でしよう。

其他オックスフォドの大學時代に有名なバァン

一三三

FIG 1　Tomimoto Kenkichi, 'William Morris no Hanashi' ('The Story of William Morris'), *Bijutsu Shinpō* [*Art News*], 1912

postcolonial perspectives on cultures, this chapter will discuss the transformative and transnational aspect of the Mingei movement. It shifts the perspective from the prevailing understanding of the Mingei movement as a Japanese 'authentic tradition', or a derivative of the English Arts and Crafts movement, to a constantly evolving creative movement sharing many commonalities and contemporaneous cultural interests.

The Arts and Crafts movement and its core idea of 'art of the people' developed in reaction to industrialisation and the radical change characteristic of the modern world. It is a modern idea that finds 'modernity' in repositioning the past. Among the multiple forms of this modernity, William Morris was one of the most successful examples in that he expressed himself philosophically as well as aesthetically. Known in Japan since the 1890s, Morris's ideas were introduced among modern socialist thinkers whose political vision of a democratic world brought about by transforming feudal society represents only one aspect of Morris's thought. In 1912 Tomimoto Kenkichi (1886–1963) first articulated the aesthetic idea of the 'art of the people' from an art practitioner's point of view, publishing 'The Story of William Morris' in the leading art magazine *Bijutsu Shinpō* (fig. 1).[7] This was written after Tomimoto's period of study in Britain (1908–10), his introduction to Bernard Leach and their shared discovery of Raku pottery, which resulted in Tomimoto's first piece of Raku ware (fig. 2). As is well known, these two potters were later joined by the younger Hamada Shōji, and subsequently developed the studio pottery movements in Britain and Japan.

Tomimoto was not a potter at that stage, rather an amateur who had started to become interested in pottery, yet he was equipped with training in *zuan* (design) for crafts and architectural decoration at the Tokyo School of Art. His article introduces the life of Morris and his works, including wallpaper designs in the collection of the Victoria and Albert Museum, stained glass, wallpapers, tiles, tapestries, carpets and Kelmscott Press book design, alongside the overall interior design of Red House and Kelmscott Manor. Tomimoto was 'profoundly impressed' by Morris's strong determination, his self-belief, the judgement of what is beautiful and good, and his 'courage to break bad conventions'.[8] He praises Morris's amateurship, his tireless self-guided study from scratch, and the approaches he took. Following Morris, Tomimoto went on learning about design by making sketches from collections of medieval, Middle Eastern and other objects at the Victoria and Albert Museum, which he visited frequently, learning and experimenting with materials and techniques using self-taught handmade methods. Morris's entrepreneurship in managing his business was another refreshing model for artists. Tomimoto describes how Morris's 'artist's individual originality' was combined with 'eternal beauty' in crafts.[9]

Tomimoto's writing demonstrates that the most appealing aspect of Morris's example was the liberation modern artists can take from self-awareness, individuality and management of the complete process of designing, making and selling. Morris's experimentation with natural dyes rather than industrial aniline dyes made Tomimoto reflect on Japan's situation of modernisation, whereby the market was flooded with inexpensive summer kimono (*yukata*) made with cheap chemical dyes that would

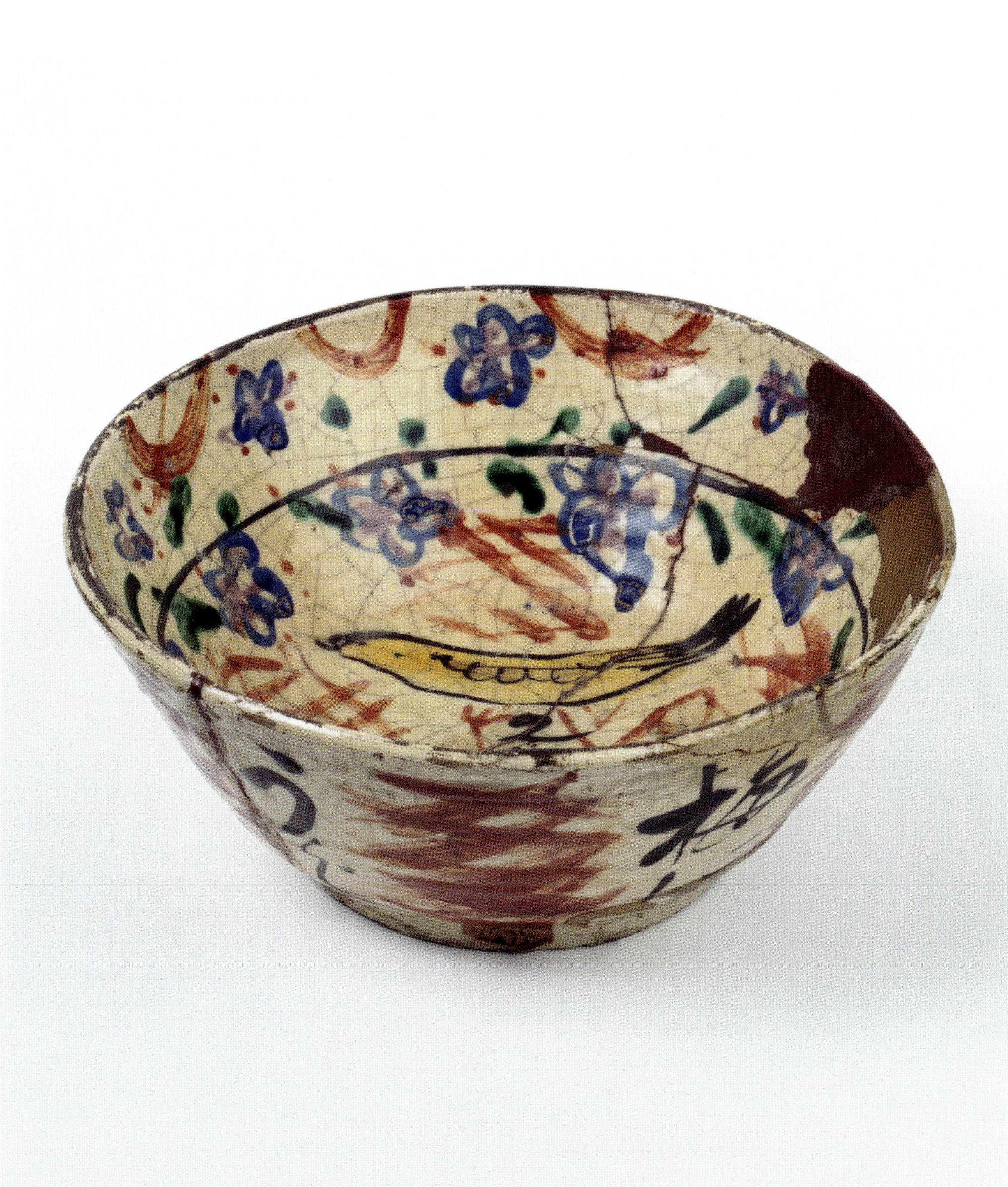

**FIG 2** Tomimoto Kenkichi, bowl, Raku ware, pattern of plum blossoms with two nightingales, 1912, Victoria and Albert Museum

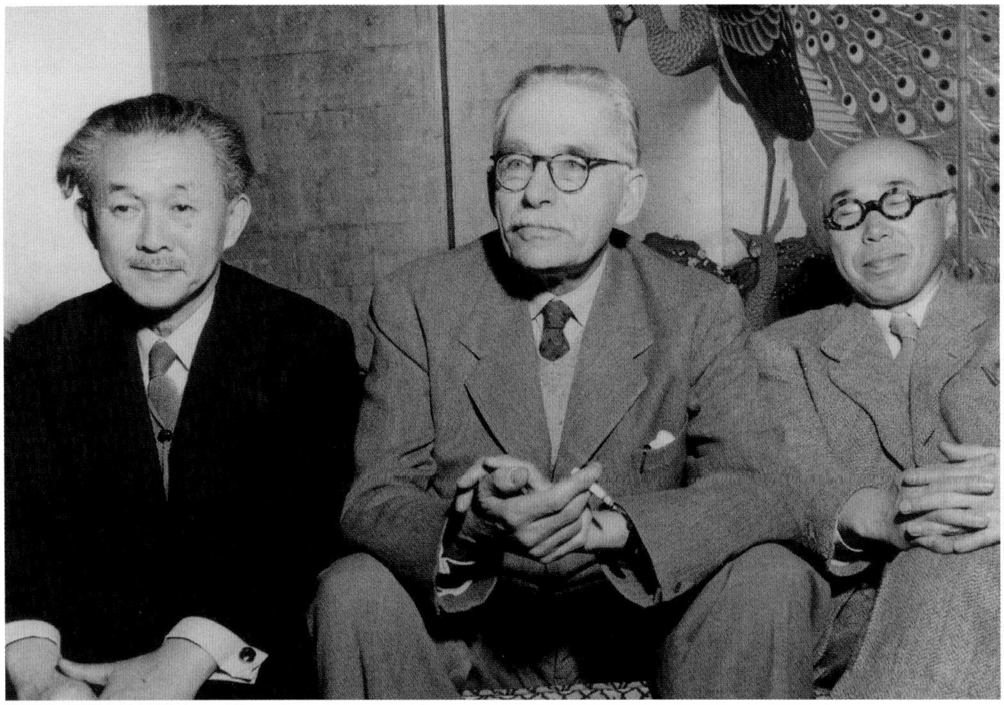

FIG 3 Yanagi, Leach and Hamada, c.1952 © Crafts Study Centre, University for the Creative Arts

quickly fade. Tomimoto was also critical of the convention of craftsmanship in Japan whereby only technical skills and intricacy were appreciated and valued. He quotes Morris's criticism of Japanese embroidery, which he saw as highly technical but without originality and creativity.[10] Tomimoto's article can thus be read as a manifesto by which he presents his determination to be an individual studio potter by breaking the old conventions of craftsmanship and embracing artistic creativity. While he maintained his personal friendship with Leach, Tomimoto had dissociated himself from the Mingei movement by 1929, as his idea of the 'art of the people' clashed with that of Yanagi. Tomimoto criticised Yanagi for preserving objects from the past just because they were handmade by unknown makers when they included items that had no contemporary relevance to the 'art of the people'. Tomimoto felt this especially keenly in respect of creative artists (perhaps like himself) who derive inspiration and evolve their ideas from their local environment.

After the legendary International Conference of Craftsmen in Pottery and Textiles at Dartington Hall in 1952, the 'Three Musketeers'[11] – Yanagi, Leach and Hamada – spent five months in the United States (fig. 3). Their tour triggered a North American regional Mingei movement, including Alix and Warren MacKenzie's 'Mingeisota' group in Minnesota, and the war veterans who took pottery education and careers through the GI Bill, a government initiative to provide financial assistance for former servicemen, including to attend university or vocational schools.[12] In Santa Fe, an extraordinary synergy between the Anglo-Japanese Mingei movement and Indigenous American Pueblo pottery was created by the encounter between the Three Musketeers and Maria Martinez (c.1887-1980), a Pueblo potter, her husband Julian and her son Popovi Da.[13]

This transnational dissemination of the Mingei movement in the United States informs us about the scalability and translatability of the 'art of the people'. This phenomenon no longer requires the idea of 'influence' that characterises a binary framework based on an imperial/colonial power as an originator-influencer, and the marginal/colonised as a passive receiver. Rather, this Mingei phenomenon is a creative and multi-directional syncretic cultural mix, as argued by Lionnet and Shih when they propose the idea of 'minor transnationalism'.[14] Based on postcolonial theories that challenge the supposition that culture is transmitted from powerful (major) to subordinate (minor) groups, this understanding focuses on the idea that all cultures are created in a syncretic state based on simultaneous exchanges. Minor-to-minor transmission and exchanges are always in the process of happening in the creative arena. For example, Sinophone cultures of diaspora are not defined by their relation to mainland China, but rather emerge from within each region as original creations from fragmented local elements and contemporary globality. The Mingei movement in the United States shows a similar trajectory: many original Mingei movements have emerged, each with their own regional and contemporary relevance.

The Mingei movement similarly spread and became localised through the Commonwealth network. For example, John Reeve (1929–2012), who was apprenticed at the Leach Pottery in St Ives, Cornwall, created a community of Mingei-style potters who contributed to the studio pottery movement and modern art in Canada. The Mingei movement spread as far as New Zealand through Len Castle (1924–2011), who was also apprenticed in the Leach Pottery and worked with Hamada Shōji in Japan. Castle set up his pottery in the artist colony of Titirangi near Auckland and pioneered the studio pottery movement in New Zealand. At first his style was Anglo-Oriental, similar to Leach and Hamada, but gradually his work transformed into something unique and distinctly characteristic of his own, which can be interpreted as a reflection of the dynamic nature of volcanoes and lakes in New Zealand (fig. 4).

A more recent and fascinating discovery for Mingei researchers is that of Sardar Gurcharan Singh (1898–1995), known in India as 'the father of studio pottery' (fig. 5).[15] Although his existence in the Mingei movement was known to some Mingei scholars, the main narrative of the Mingei story, which has also shaped its study, has long been fixated on the relationship between East and West only. Research outside this narrative, such as, for example, the cultural relation between India and Japan, has been neglected.[16] One of the interesting focal points that has emerged is a collection of some 300 pieces of pottery Singh accumulated during his stay in Japan and bequeathed to the Government Museum and Art Gallery in Chandigarh, which offers significant insight into Singh's perspective during the early and formative part of his career.

Between 1919 and 1921, Singh studied ceramic technology at the Tokyo Higher Technical School, a renowned progressive technical college. Kawai Kanjirō and Hamada Shōji had attended the same school some years earlier. Singh studied maiolica (tin-glazed pottery originally developed in Italy) and underglaze techniques developed by the hired German chemical engineer Gottfried Wagener (1831–1892) and a modern potter,

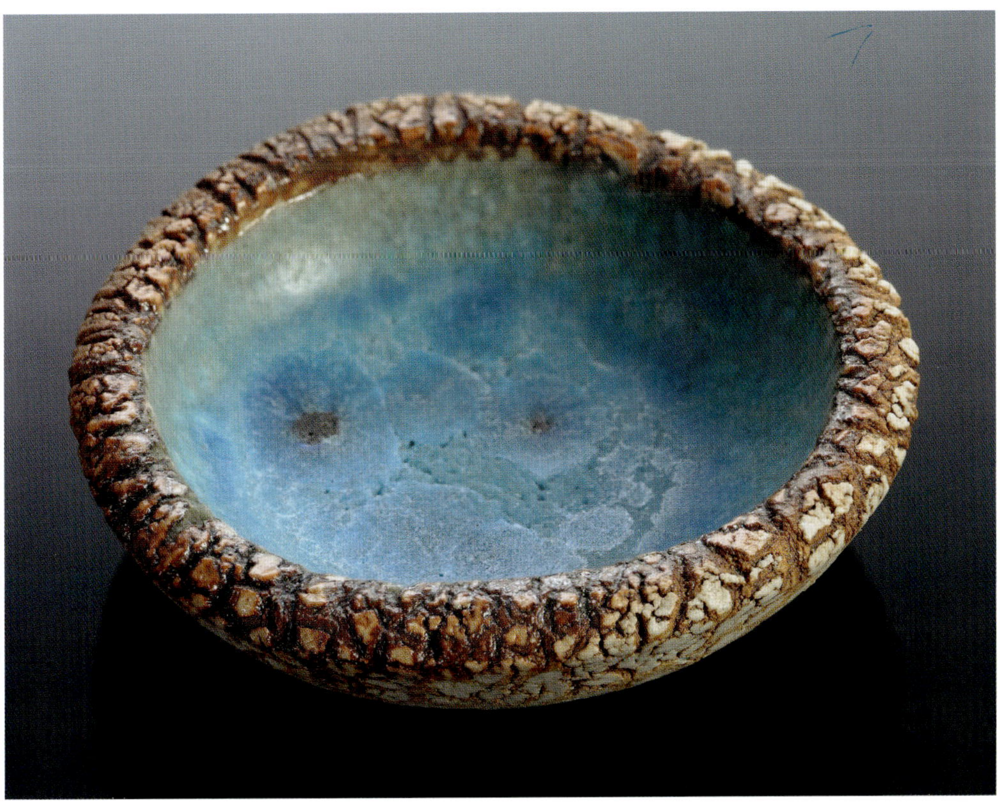

**FIG 4** Len Castle, bowl, from the group *The Ocean*, from the series *The Magma Flows, the Magma Cools on Its Way to the Ocean*, 1991 Credit: Commissioned 1991, in partnership with Expo NZ 1992 Ltd and the Queen Elizabeth II Arts Council of New Zealand. Te Papa. CC BY-NC-ND 4.0. Te Papa (1996-0033-9/20)

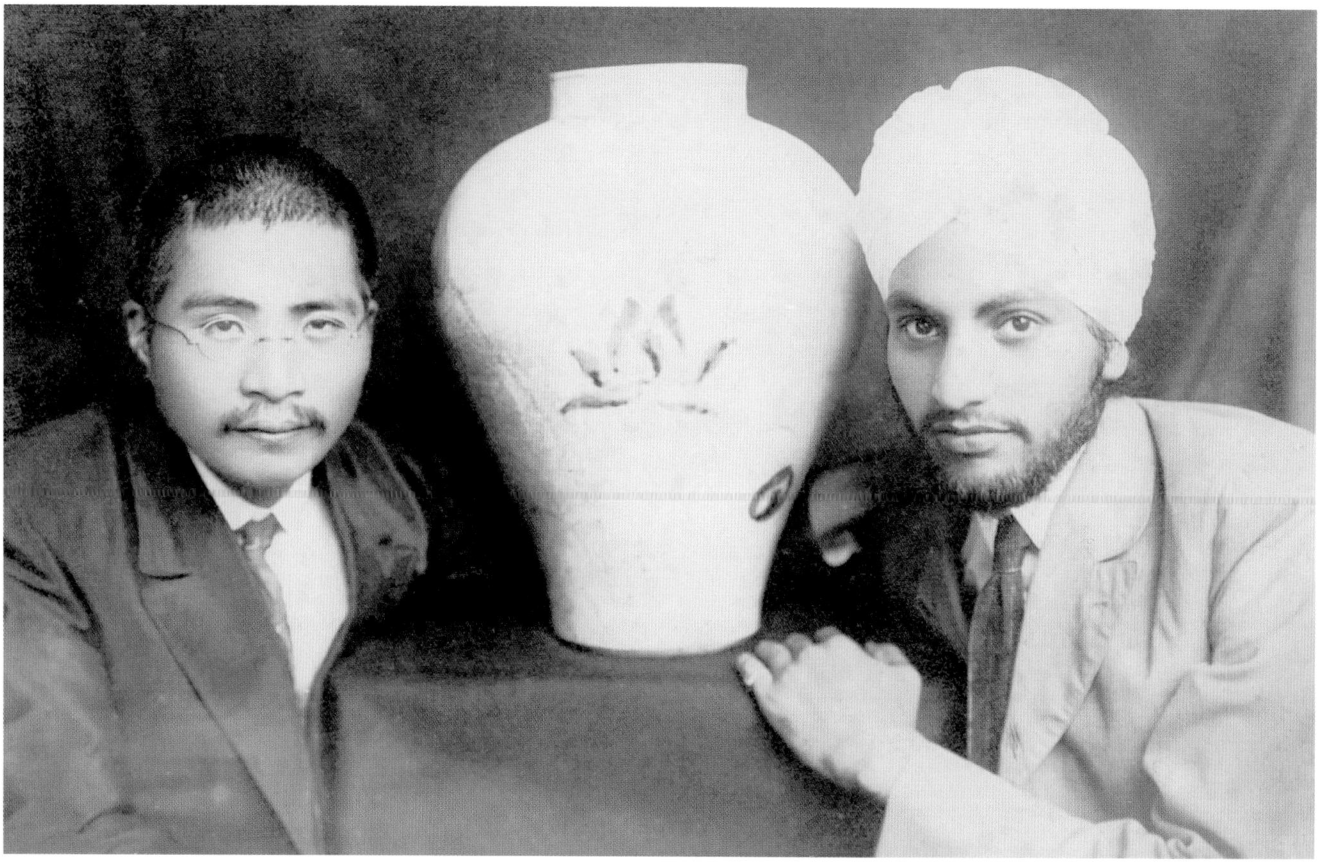

FIG 5 Sardar Gurcharan Singh and Asakawa Takumi with a white porcelain Joseon period vase collected by Yanagi and the Asakawa brothers, 1919–21 | Credit: Delhi Blue Pottery Trust

Itaya Hazan (1872–1963). Singh mingled with Yanagi and Tomimoto as the Mingei movement burgeoned, and formed part of a network of cosmopolitan intellectuals and expatriate artists living in Tokyo. On his return to India, Singh founded the Delhi Blue Pottery, leading the studio pottery movement in India. Singh's direct involvement in the early Mingei movement in Tokyo reveals an important East–East relationship between India and Japan, revising the familiar East–West account, and poses questions of how multiple narratives and untold stories and objects from the Global South can be integrated into contemporary understandings of the Mingei movement. Singh's involvement also presents a new perspective on Japanese colonisation. He visited Korea on the advice of Leach, Yanagi and Tomimoto, and developed considerable sympathy for colonised Koreans because of the parallels to the situation in India, then under British rule. However, he also looked at Korean craft through the biased lens of Yanagi, who had spoken of Korean pottery as representing the 'beauty of sadness' in Korean culture.[17] Singh adopted a version of Mingei theory that incorporated Japano-centric views of colonial Korea, yet his empathy was for the Korean people under colonial rule which he linked with the colonised Indian people and his support was for Gandhi's anti-colonial, craft-centred Khadi movement. Singh's case points to the importance of further investigation into Mingei's complexity with respect to colonial modernity within Asia.

---

After Yanagi's death in 1961, a second wave of interest in the Mingei movement swept through Japan. As the sociologist Hamada Takuji (grandson of Hamada Shōji) has noted, the 1960s–70s saw the rise of the 'Mingei boom' as a reaction to rapid economic growth, a nostalgic yearning for pastoral Japan, which was also encouraged by the National Railway's tourist campaign 'Discover Japan' (fig. 6).[18] Hamada's fieldwork on ceramic production centres including Mashiko, Onta and Koishihara reveals how outsider tourists' gaze drove producers' consciousness of their local identity and created an industry of cultural consumption.[19] Legendary studio potters such as Leach and Hamada were re-situated in this context, and the model of the individual studio potter with an idealised Mingei-inspired lifestyle was revived. However, this second wave did not last long and the idea of Mingei could not compete with Japan's subsequent financial upswing. By the turn of the twenty-first century, Mingei had become synonymous with touristy 'craft village' products and the 'unknown craftsman' ceased to exist in any authentic way.

However, there is evidence to suggest we may be seeing a further, third ghostly revival, particularly after the unprecedented natural and man-made disaster of the Tōhoku Earthquake in 2011. This revival manifests itself in terms of the rediscovery of rural areas of Tōhoku, and values such as provision of mutual aid and cohabitation.[20] Currently, Japan's economy is stagnant, having been further affected by the COVID-19 pandemic. The social mood is one of scepticism, not only of the central government, but also of economic growth, progress and urbanisation. The younger generation in particular is in search of fundamental and humanistic values again, in a similar way to the original studio craft movement, which pursued modernity by breaking from the past. So in contemporary Japan, the Mingei movement has resurfaced and captures people's interest yet again. In 2021–2 the National Museum of Modern Art, Tokyo (MOMAT) organised *100 Years of Mingei: The Folk Crafts Movement*, an exhibition that re-evaluated Mingei as an activist movement that opposed modern art by being outside any institution (rather than part of one), by being regional (rather than urban), by being craft (not art) and by being made within a collective (not by an individual). Through this activism and opposition, the exhibition argued, the Mingei movement is ultimately modern (fig. 7). It also highlighted the process by which the Mingei movement made Mingei part of the 'culture industry' for mass consumption. The irony of the choice of venue – MOMAT, the shrine of modernist art – was not lost on the curators who directly quoted Yanagi's own criticism of the museum as 'bureaucratic', 'modern' and the place of 'fine art', and hence a thoroughly inappropriate place in which to appreciate Mingei.[21]

Such exhibitions and the messages they convey do not take place without context. Local culture has been at the centre of interest again in recent years, as a place in which a real and tangible community can thrive, but also as a place to which

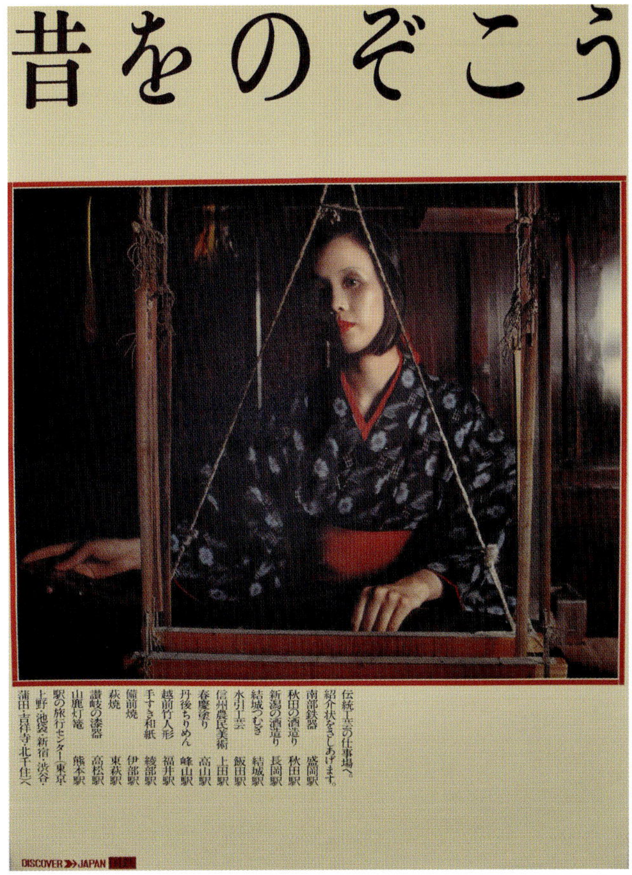


**FIG 6** Discover Japan Poster 'Mukashi o Nozokō' (Let's look at the Past – visit studios of traditional crafts), 1972, The Railway Museum collection Credit: Dentsu (design), JRTT (formerly the National Railway office)

one can relocate from crowded cities where life is expensive and depersonalised. Many remote areas in Japan suffer from an ageing society and depopulation; thus, local governments use subsidies to encourage urban dwellers to relocate with the purpose of regenerating these dying communities. In 2008 the central government also created a scheme called *furusato nōzei* (hometown tax) to entice people to make gifts and donations in order to support the regions that are laden with shrinking tax revenues due to depopulation.[22] The concept of *furusato* (native place) has been a historically recurring notion since the nineteenth century. As the historian Jennifer Robertson argues, it is a dialectical idea reacting to external forces such as internationalisation and urbanisation. Often politically motivated and helped by tourism promotion, this native place-making within an imagined countryside evokes nostalgia for primal landscape and family roots.[23] The idea is also a reminder of the romanticisation of the countryside in the English Arts and Crafts movement, and of the rural

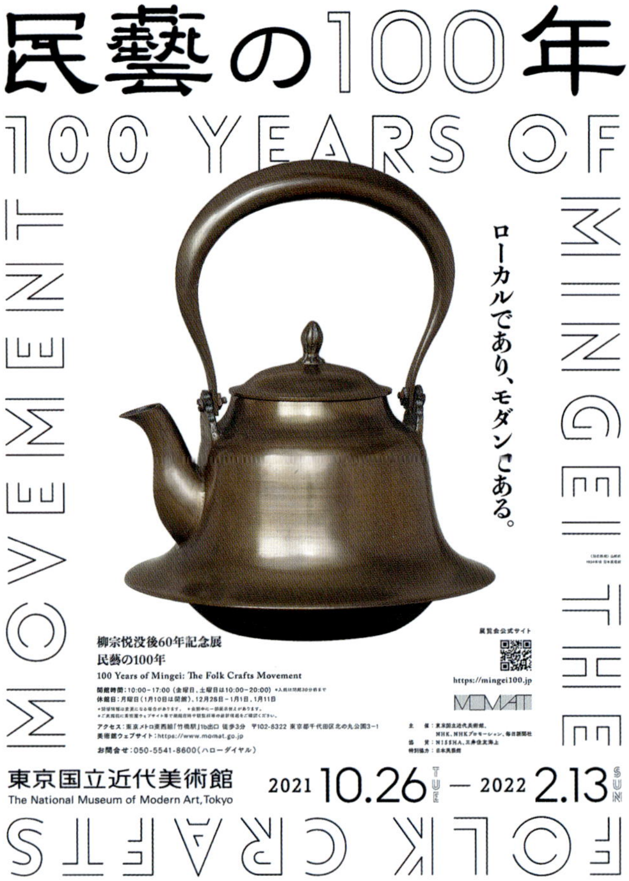


FIG 7 Poster from the exhibition *100 Years of Mingei: The Folk Crafts Movement*, at the National Museum of Modern Art, Toyko (MOMAT), 2021–2

backcountries in the Mingei movement. Contributors of *furusato nōzei* are offered local gifts, including regional food, travel coupons and items of so-called 'Mingei'.[24] These products are not entirely what Yanagi might have categorised as 'Mingei', but include many overlaps such as Mashiko pottery reminiscent of Hamada's work and the iconic Onta ware in the same style that Yanagi and Leach admired.

The term *seikatsu kōgei* (crafts for everyday life), coined in the 1950s in association with Mingei, was revived in the 1970s,[27] and is again being used as part of the third resurgence of the movement. The term has connotations of usefulness for everyday life: craft items that are affordable and beautiful, not decorative or ornamental luxuries, but characteristically situated somewhere in between objects of mass production and handmade crafts. This term *seikatsu kōgei* and the idea of handmade originality and 'warmth' to bring quality to everyday life has been revived again in the twenty-first century in the context of a new studio crafts movement, exemplified by the *Seikatsu Kōgei* exhibition at the 21st Century Museum of Contemporary Art in Kanazawa (October 2010), which featured active studio craft artists such as the glass artist Tsukamoto Kazumi, and Mitani Ryūji, who works in wood and lacquer.[28] Similarly, the aesthetic value of 'everyday life', particularly as conveyed by a section curated by the trendsetting couple Terry Ellis and Kitamura Keiko, who now own a shop selling folk art in Tokyo, came through clearly in the *MINGEI: Bi wa Kurashino naka ni aru* (*The Beauty of Everyday Things*) exhibition at the Nakanoshima Museum of Art, Osaka (July–September 2023).[29] Given that Mingei now extends over a full century, one can observe the consistent recurrence of the term *seikatsu* to represent Japanese taste and appreciation of the small details of everyday life, from the time Tomimoto Kenkichi introduced William Morris, up to the present. It continues to capture studio artists' and designers' interest alongside that of consumers. Students coming to craft departments in art colleges across Japan predominantly harbour ambitions to become makers of contemporary *seikatsu kōgei*.

This current curious resurgence of interest in hand making and 'everydayness' has been analysed as something extraordinary in Japan: a sympathetically shared feeling of amateurish endeavour and resetting of life from the bottom up.[30] In parallel, sociologists and cultural theorists such as Michel de Certeau and Ben Highmore have articulated 'everyday' practice as the site of activism with a transformative nature, thus making the invisible visible through subjective creativity and subversion by the marginalised invisibles in a controlled society.[31] Such postmodern and postcolonial contemporary interest in 'everydayness' appears to be a common underlying current of this third wave of revived interest in the idea of Mingei in Japan.

The twenty-first-century interest in the 'everyday' is also driving international studio craft artists to explicitly engage with the Mingei movement. The British artist Grayson Perry (b. 1960) challenges Euro-American modernism and hierarchy in art whereby 'craft' and its associated qualities, such as 'decoration', are undervalued. In order to centre the marginalised, Perry used the idea of anonymous crafts in his exhibition *The Tomb of the Unknown Craftsman* at the British Museum in 2011 (fig. 8).[32] A homage to unknown and under-represented craftsmen across the world, the project sought to evaluate the extraordinary beauty and spirituality of their objects.[33]

Meanwhile, the American artist Theaster Gates (b. 1973) connects Mingei with regeneration of the local community.[34] His 'Rebuild Foundation' project is involved in the regeneration of Chicago's South Side through art projects in urban space and creative reuse of abandoned houses and derelict buildings.[35] Gates is also a studio potter interested in Japanese culture and ceramics, and has spent time at the International Workshop of Ceramic Art in Tokoname. He has also closely examined the North American Mingei movement that developed after the Three Musketeers' visit. In his words, 'Mingei found me, in advance of my arrival to Tokoname. In some ways, my imagination of Japanese traditions via the books on Mingei made me want to be present even more.'

Gates developed the concept of 'Afro Mingei', which uniquely connects his pottery practice, Black activism and the regeneration of marginalised communities. He understands 'Mingei' as Japan's response to Westernisation, claiming that 'Japan is beautiful – Our crafts matter' overlaps with 'Black is beautiful – Black Lives Matter'.[36] This in essence pays homage to unknown and marginalised makers whose creations constitute our daily, familial and domestic lives. Conscious of Mingei's 'tremendous faults and the lack of representation and oversight in identifying the presence and full nationality of some of the great makers', Gates also alludes to a lack of representation of women and ethnic minorities. For him, colonialism had obliterated the identity of Korean craftspeople, making them unknowable and using a coloniser's system of evaluation to define what is 'known' and what is 'unknown', what is 'beautiful' and what is not. While he believes that this requires revision and correction when viewed from the twenty-first-century postcolonial perspective, Gates nevertheless concludes that 'the core values of Mingei' lie in 'a belief in hand ability and its connection to cultural specificity', and so it continues to appeal to him.

Gates's practice is political, and as such can be captured by the term 'craftivism'. 'Craftivism' is a neology coined by Betsy Greer in 2003, and Sarah Corbett, the founder of the global Craftivist Collective, who has created a platform for critical debate and exchanges among activists. Gates's craftivism proclaims that 'hand matters'. He cuts across current trends for Artificial Intelligence replacing what humans have been doing, and the focus on STEM learning (science, technology, engineering and maths), underpinned by propaganda celebrating economic efficiency. Gates argues:

> To choose clay, or any craft, is to choose the body, the hand, the personal, the slow, the restrained; it is to remember that when we celebrate what the body can do, we are also celebrating what the mind can do. This act is wonderfully political, and we do need movements that insist that the hand matters and that people have a right to understand deeply their capacities, limits and abilities.

In Gates's practice, pottery is both political and a metaphor of identity. He believes that 'clay is a channel', enabling connection – with slavery, with unknown potters and with Black activism – in that the materials and techniques of clay are based on local and personal knowledge and the makers' individual bodies.[37] As a result of white, Euro-American-centric knowledge, pottery has been marginalised because it has been classified as a 'minor' art within an art history that excludes non-white people, women, the poor and Indigenous groups. Thus it functions as a metaphor for

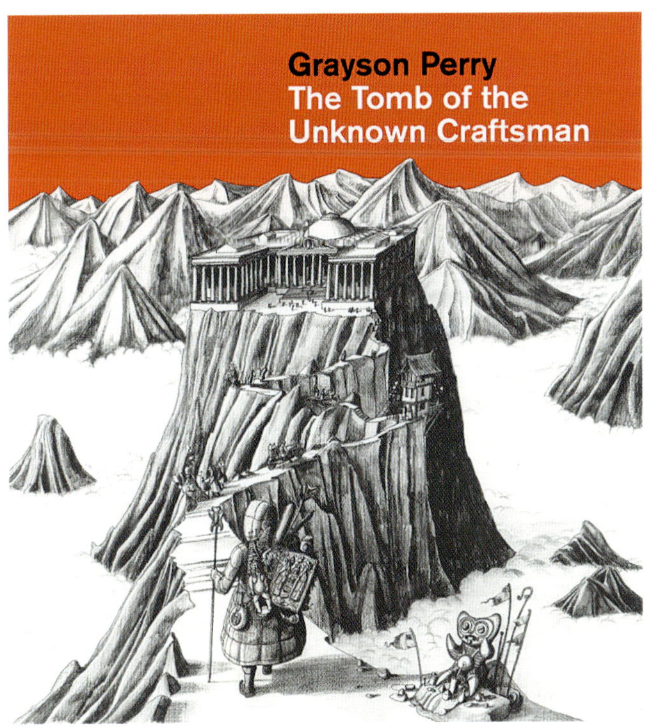


FIG 8 Grayson Perry, *The Tomb of the Unknown Craftsman*, at the British Museum, 2011

unknowable, unrecorded individuals' lives and creativity. In the same way that 'Black' is not a fixed identity as represented and stereotyped by white-dominated society, pottery involves constant changes in clay and glazes that occur during the creative process. For Gates, the alchemy of pottery is a visual demonstration of transformative identity, liberated from a Euro-American view of a monolithic 'Black' and thus a means of decentralising and decolonising Euro-American white-centred knowledge.

Pottery's metaphoric value is well explained in Gates's use of Hamada Shōji's favourite *nuka* glaze, which is a silica-rich glaze that creates what Gates calls a 'suspended state'.[38]

> The vessel is mature in body and surface, but within the surface remains raw material, semi-changed and affected by fire but nonetheless a portion of its mineral-/material-/energy-based potential is withheld. In surface, it is in a state of both resolve and becoming.

Gates's recent *nuka* glazed work embodies this 'suspended state'. A white matt vessel with a foot at the bottom rises to become a human body, a double decker of 'craft' and 'fine art' resolved in one (fig. 9). The pot is an elongated metamorphosis of the iconic moon jar made by an 'unknown craftsman' in Joseon Korea and championed by Bernard Leach (see p. 129). In referencing this Mingei object, Gates makes visible the technical and material quality specific to pottery, while at the same time providing a metaphor that layers 'marginal suspended identity' with creative potential. This is precisely the 'suspended state' of identity in creolisation which Édouard Glissant describes as 'never fixed, or stopped, or inscribed in essence or absolutes of identity'.[39]

Together with recognition of this postcolonial identity, Gates's 'Afro Mingei' practice works towards decolonisation and addresses marginalised 'unknown' people's rights. This does not mean making 'unknown' people into individual artists, but recognising the potential for creativity in everybody, including 'unknown' people, in particular those marginalised Black people who have been made 'unknowable' through racist power structures. Yanagi argued for the extraordinary beauty of the 'unknown' people's work as an antidote to a modernism that championed individual artists of the powerful West. The work of Perry and Gates is another scalable transformative aspect of the Mingei movement, the spirit of which is also found in recent craftivism and community-based design history projects.

The idea of the 'art of the people' as it relates to the Mingei movement is transnational and transformative, and thus holds a limitless potential for creative evolution. It formed the basis for nurturing studio craft artists to open their creative channels and identity. It has triggered the creativity of individuals in different cultures by sharing commonalities and articulating differences. In Japan, over the span of a century, the Mingei movement has been through several waves of revival. It has become a creative industry in the dynamic of the global and local, in particular being promoted by tourism and the external 'gaze' onto others. The movement is currently evolving again in line with the global interest in social equality and inclusiveness as captured in the United Nations' Sustainable Development Goals. More specifically, 'art of the people' has become relevant once again in a broad postcolonial context of democracy and collective activism. The Mingei movement, which has maintained a capacity for transformation in the transnational context of a creolised and syncretic contemporary world, presents us with a compelling expressive framework that encapsulates the interdependency of people and communities, in pursuit of the very human desire to make and create.

## NOTES

1. Morris 1883.
2. Glissant 2020.
3. Fisher 2005.
4. Bhabha 1994; Canclini 1995.
5. Clifford 1992; Said 1983; Gilroy 1993; Lionnet and Shih 2005.
6. Mercer 1994.
7. Kikuchi 2004, 17–25.
8. Tomimoto 1912, part 1, 124.
9. Ibid., 167.
10. Ibid., 163.
11. Leach's letter to Lucie Rie dated 4 November 1952, in Cooper 2003, 250; also see Ajioka 2015, 1–12 for the details of their tour.
12. A notable example of this is Peter Voulkos, who led work in radical abstract clay in California, encouraged by Hamada.
13. Peterson 1977.
14. Lionnet and Shih 2005.

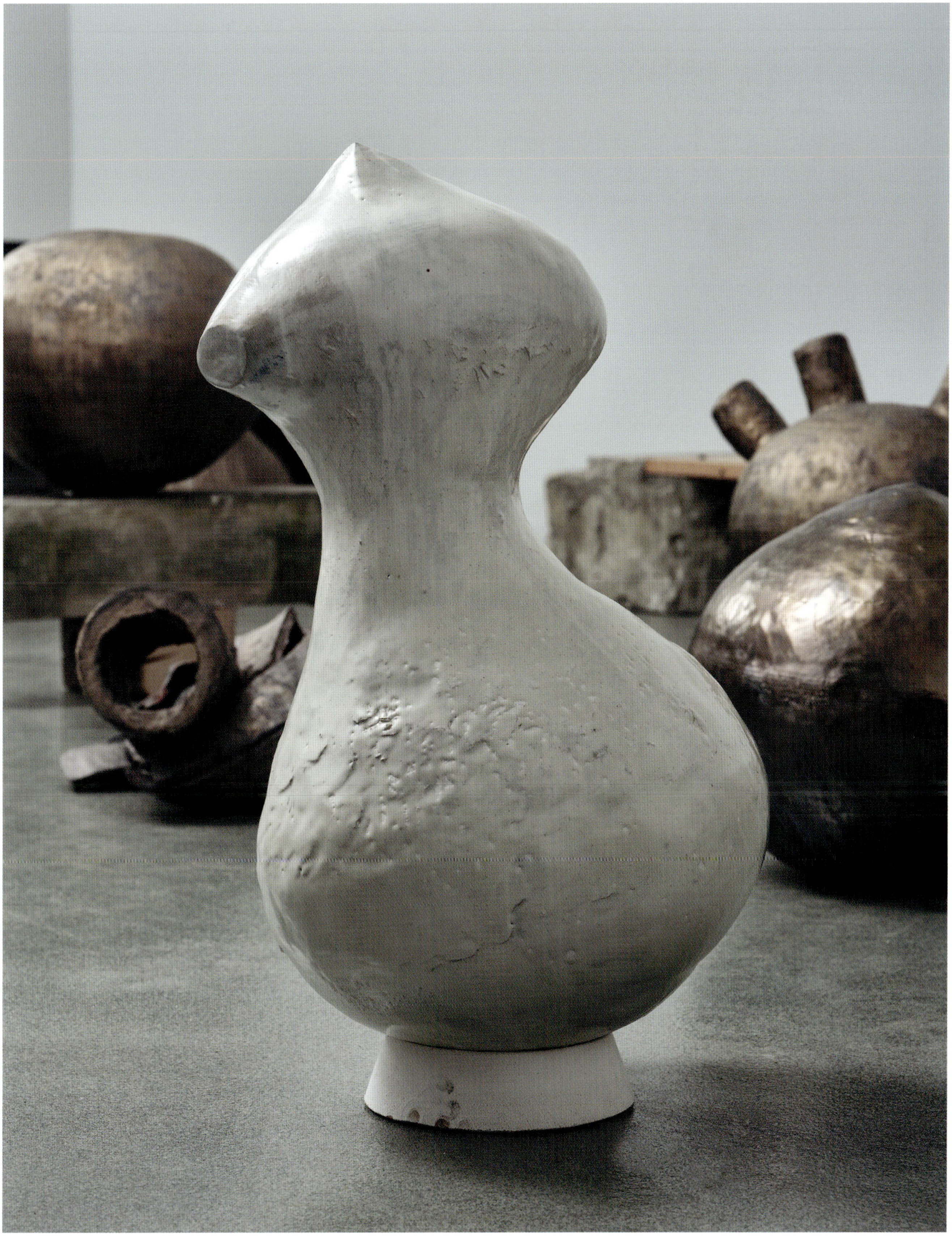

**FIG 9** Theaster Gates, white *nuka* glazed vessel | Credit: © Chris Strong. Courtesy of Theaster Gates Studio

15. Mago 1995.
16. This particular case came to light initially through Brij Tankha's interest in modernity as shared between India and Japan which he developed into a symposium, from which a group of scholars interested in transnationalism started to collaborate and share ideas. These included Helena Čapková (Singh's involvement with Garakutashū cosmopolitan network in Tokyo), Hashimoto Yorimitsu (Singh's involvement in colonial Korea, and the meaning of Singh's lotus in colonial India and colonial Korea), Takuya Kida (Singh's collection at the Government Museum and Art Gallery in Chandigarh) and myself (Singh's work in Japan and his involvement in the Mingei movement and colonial Korea).
17. See Kikuchi 2004, 131. The story of Singh's involvement in the Mingei movement has been made into a documentary, *The Lotus and the Swan*, by Nirmal Chander for Delhi Blue Pottery Trust in 2023. See https://ualresearchonline.arts.ac.uk/id/eprint/11748 (accessed 4 September 2023).
18. Hamada 2006.
19. Hamada 2006; see also Urry 1990.
20. Kurata 2012, 22–38.
21. Yanagi 1981, 282–8.
22. Kazuaki Nagata, 'Tax Breaks, Local Specialites: What to Know about Japan's *Furusato Nōzei*. Program', *Japan Times*, 2 October 2022, https://www.japantimes.co.jp/news/2022/10/02/national/tax-breaks-furusato-nozei-program (accessed 26 July 2023).
23. Robertson 1998, 110–29.
24. https://www.furusato-tax.jp/search?q=%E6%B0%91%E8%8A%B8%E5%93%81&header=1&target=1&sst=A (accessed 26 July 2023).
25. https://www.furusato-tax.jp/search?q=%E7%9B%8A%E5%AD%90%E7%84%BC&sst=A&header=1 (accessed 26 July 2023).
26. https://www.furusato-tax.jp/product/detail/44204/4514320 (accessed 26 July 2023).
27. Maeda 1975, 21–2, 43–4.
28. *Seikatsu kōgei* is also called *kurafuto* ('craft' in Japanese romanisation), but the idea is specifically modern functional crafts inspired by Scandinavian design of the 1950s.
29. https://artscape.jp/report/curator/1223877_1634.html. For the work of these artists, see https://factory-zoomer.com/about and http://www.mitaniryuji.com (all accessed 26 July 2023).
30. Kurata 2012, 22–38.
31. Certeau 1984.
32. This title is taken from Leach's adaptation of Yanagi's writing, published in English as 'The Unknown Craftsman'.
33. Kikuchi 2015, 87–115.
34. Quotes from Theaster Gates in this section are extracted from my interview with him on 18 February 2023.
35. Crawford 2022, 44.
36. See the comment transcribed in Yee and Foote 2022, 205–11.
37. Interview with Gates conducted by the author, 18 February 2023.
38. Yee and Foote 2022, 20.
39. Glissant 2020, 14.

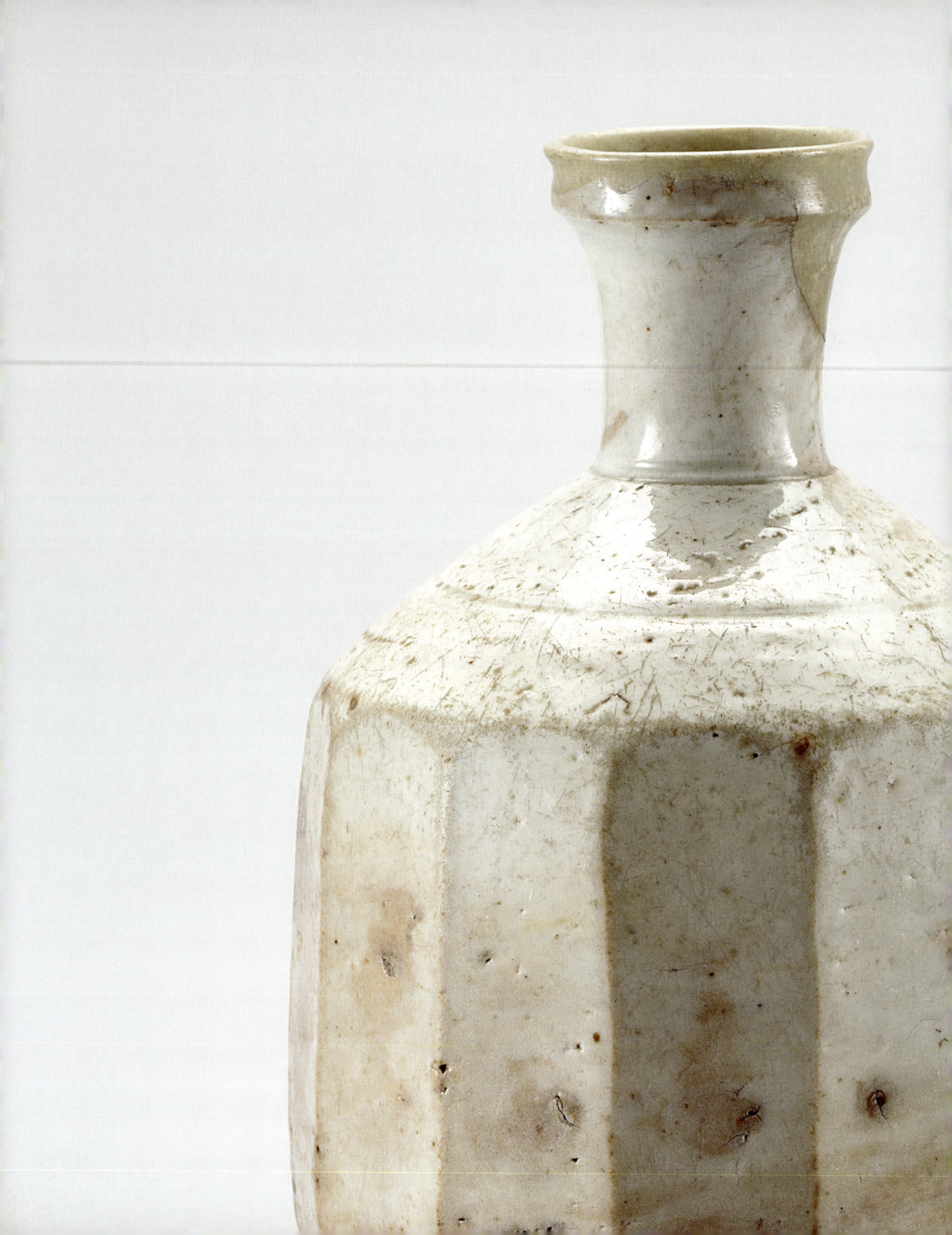

DASOM SUNG

# The Role of Joseon in the Early Mingei Movement

Korean crafts played an important role in the early stages of formulating Mingei theory, at a time when the movement's key figures were working towards the goal of finding an alternative aesthetic to overcome the increasing modernisation and Westernisation of Japanese crafts. Further, each of the key figures associated with the early Mingei movement – including Yanagi Sōetsu (1889–1961), Bernard Leach (1887–1979), Asakawa Noritaka (1884–1964), Asakawa Takumi (1891–1931), Tomimoto Kenkichi (1886–1963), Hamada Shōji (1894–1978) and Kawai Kanjirō (1890–1966) – had different perceptions of Korea. Their ideas were formulated in the context of Japanese colonial occupation of Korea, which lasted from 1910 until 1945. The Joseon dynasty (1392–1897) was briefly renamed the Korean Empire (1897–1910), but after the country was annexed by Japan in 1910, the country's name was changed back to Joseon to signify its status as a province of the Japanese Empire rather than a nation in its own right.

It is widely known that Yanagi came to value the traditions of folk culture and the beauty of daily objects through his encounter with Joseon ceramics, and that he used them as key concepts in developing Mingei theory.[1] Yanagi's appreciation for Joseon art began in 1914, when he received a gift of a Joseon white porcelain jar (fig. 1) from Asakawa Noritaka,[2] who, alongside his brother Takumi, pioneered the Japanese study of Korean ceramics. Yanagi made his first visit to Joseon in 1916, and started collecting and studying the everyday objects he found there. Yanagi's exposure to the beauty of everyday objects in Joseon redirected his ideological, artistic interest from the West to his native Japan and its neighbouring countries, leading him to explore the folk arts of East Asia and laying the foundation for Mingei theory. In 1924 he founded the Korean Folk Arts Gallery[3] in Gyeongbokgung Palace in Seoul, as a small museum showcasing practical items created by anonymous Joseon craftsmen that were widely used by the people (fig. 2).

Yanagi loved the art of Joseon and opposed the violent suppression and assimilation of Joseon culture by the Japanese. However, he did not question the injustice of colonialism itself, and his early perception of Joseon was more a romantic, sentimentalised appreciation of the colony than one based in political reality. In Korea, there have been a few studies that praise Yanagi for promoting Joseon's beauty through his writing and collecting activities,[4] but many contemporary writers now critically analyse Yanagi's attitudes towards Joseon.

In the 1920s, Yanagi famously depicted Joseon aesthetics as a 'beauty of sorrow', due to the nation's history of being invaded. For Yanagi, the white of the Joseon porcelain was the

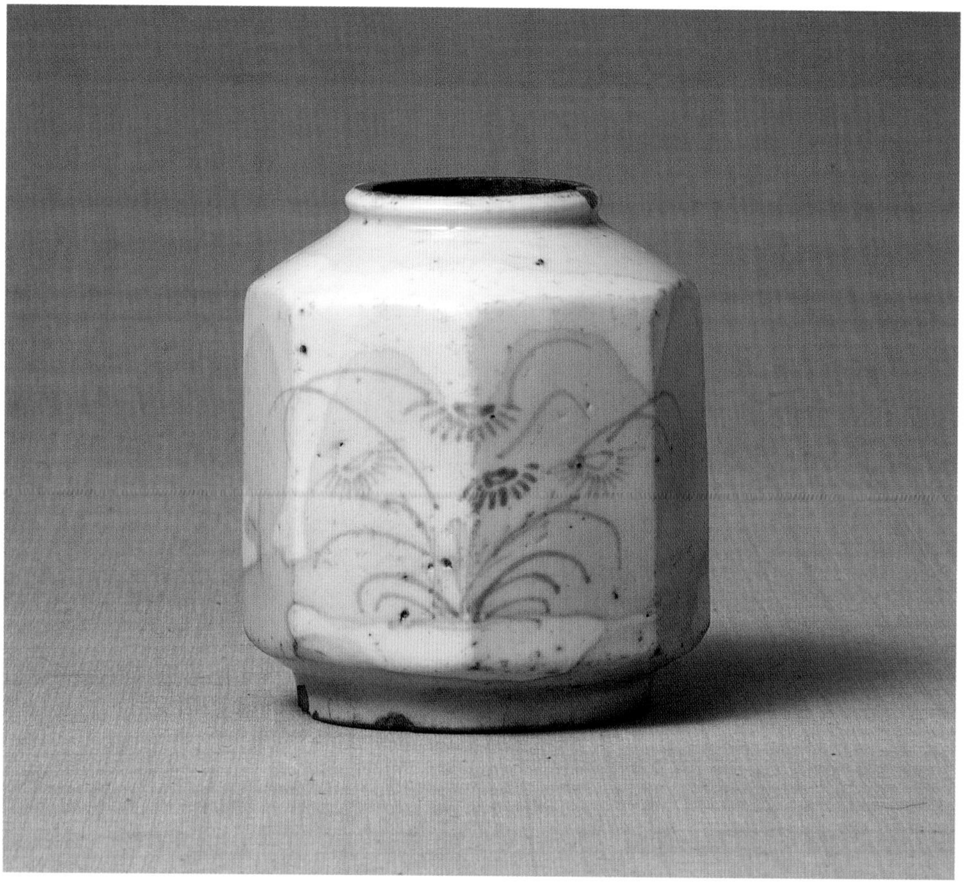

FIG 1 Faceted blue and white porcelain jar with flowering plant design, white porcelain, underglaze cobalt blue, Joseon, eighteenth century, Japan Folk Crafts Museum

same colour as the country's traditional white clothing and appeared like mourning dress, attesting to the fateful sorrow of the Joseon people, while the delicate and fluid lines of the porcelain were sad lines of seeking eternity, leaving earth behind.[5] However, many scholars have pointed out that this is an expression of the overly poetic sympathy of an individual, which is never enough to be considered as an aesthetic, and indeed cannot be regarded as the characteristics of the nation.[6] Furthermore, Yanagi's appreciation of Joseon was a Japanese form of Orientalism, exoticising it as an 'other' relative to his native Japan.[7] This was in line with a wider strategic move by Japan to strengthen its own cultural identity by centring Japan within the East and distancing itself from its periphery, as well as expanding its colonies. Yanagi similarly 'othered' the art of Japan's periphery to create a vision of a pure Japan separated from the rest of Asia, while developing a fictional communal beauty of the Orient into his wider Mingei theory.[8] A further criticism is that Yanagi's work in Korea ultimately helped to consolidate Japan's colonial control of the country. While he criticised Japan's violent response to the March 1 movement in 1919 – a major series of demonstrations by Korean people that called for independence from imperial Japan and a stop to the forced assimilation into Japanese culture – and expressed his love and respect for the Korean people,[9] a deeper analysis of his writing reveals that Yanagi's seemingly anti-Japan texts are not meant to support Korean independence, but to discourage resistance to colonial rule.[10] In addition, Yanagi's activities in Korea were tacitly supported by the colonial government,[11] which shifted its governing policy from one of total suppression, to policies that included more cultural lenience to placate Korean resistance following the March 1 movement. Yanagi and his colleagues had a desire to protect Korean art and culture, but whether they intended it or not, their engagement with Joseon was used as a means of reproducing Japanese colonial power.[12]

The Asakawa brothers acted as a bridge between Joseon and figures in the Mingei movement.[13] In 1913, Asakawa Noritaka moved to Korea; between 1922 and 1946 he travelled to more than 700 kiln sites across the country, studying Korean ceramics.

In 1914, Noritaka's brother, Takumi, also emigrated to Korea to work as a forestry research engineer. Takumi, in particular, was instrumental in establishing the aforementioned Korean Folk Arts Gallery. While Yanagi travelled frequently between Japan and Korea, it was Takumi, residing in Joseon and fluent in Korean, who was responsible for the museum's operation until his sudden death in 1931. Unlike many collectors who took Korean objects abroad, the Asakawa brothers kept the majority of their collections in Korea. After Japan's defeat and Korea's liberation in 1945, Noritaka incorporated the museum's collection into the National Museum of Anthropology established by Song Seok Ha (1904–1948), one of Korea's early folklorists and originator of the Korean Folklore Society,[14] before his eventual return to Japan in 1946.[15] These objects were later integrated into the National Museum of Korea.

For Takumi, Japan's oppressive colonial policy was to make the beautiful everyday life of Korea disappear in the name of modernisation. Takumi became committed to preserving the daily life of Joseon, and valued the utilitarian beauty of the country's crafts. Takumi's intentions were reflected in the museum's display and its collections. Noritaka's close friend, the Japanese artist Katō Shōrinjin (1898–1983), who visited the museum often, said of the collection:

> It's a collection of all the everyday objects of Korean people. Today, the folk objects in department stores and art shops are quite elaborate and much more expensive than the real thing, but the objects in this museum were not deliberately made like that. They were actually used by the people of Korea, so many of them were broken or chipped, and they were stained with the marks of daily life.[16]

Because the Asakawa brothers had lived in Joseon and directly witnessed its vivid lifestyle, they understood the country in a fundamentally different way from Yanagi. In contrast to Yanagi's evaluation of Joseon as a culture of sadness, the Asakawa brothers depicted Koreans as always

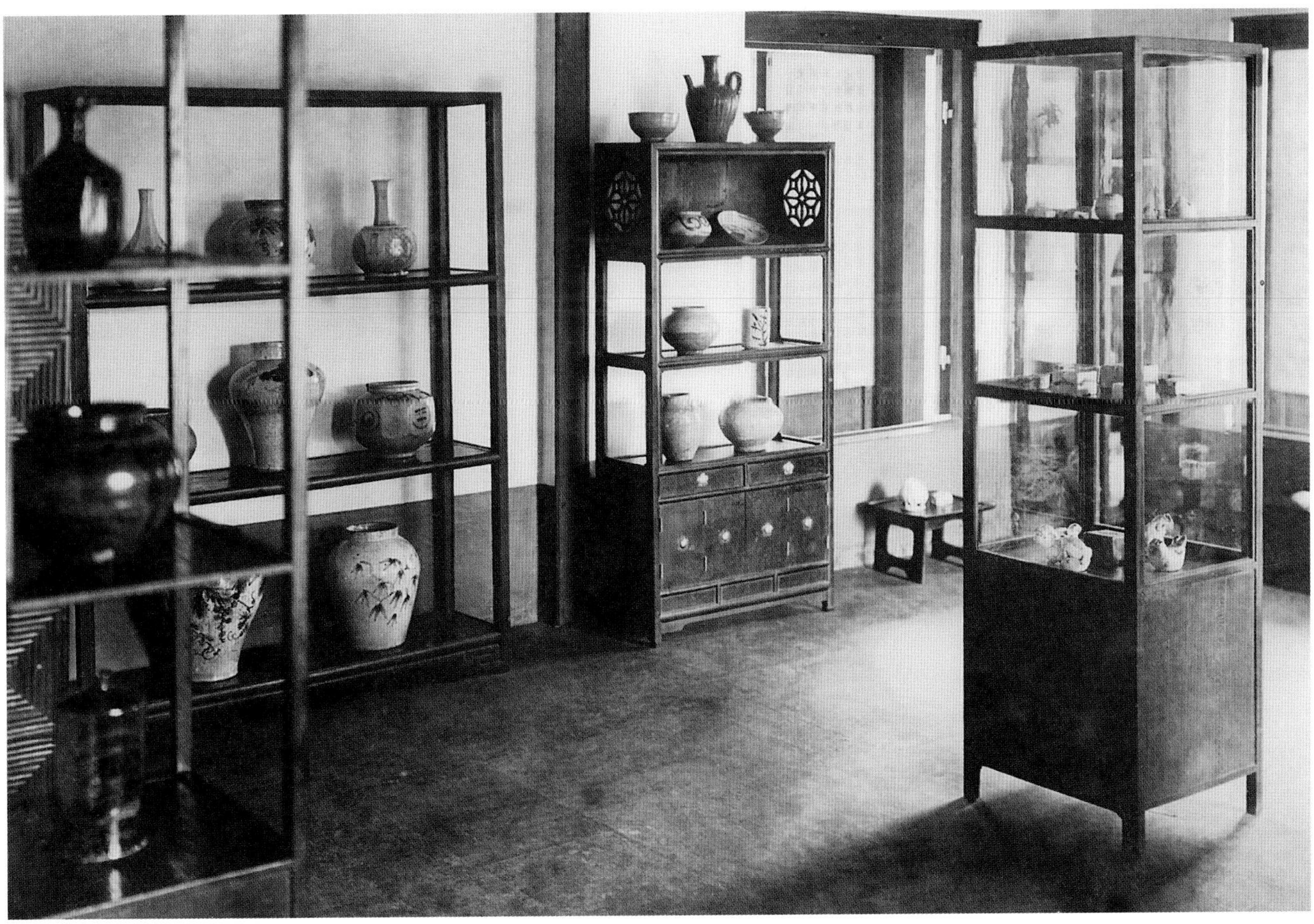

**FIG 2** Display of the Korean Folk Arts Gallery, 1924, Japan Folk Crafts Museum

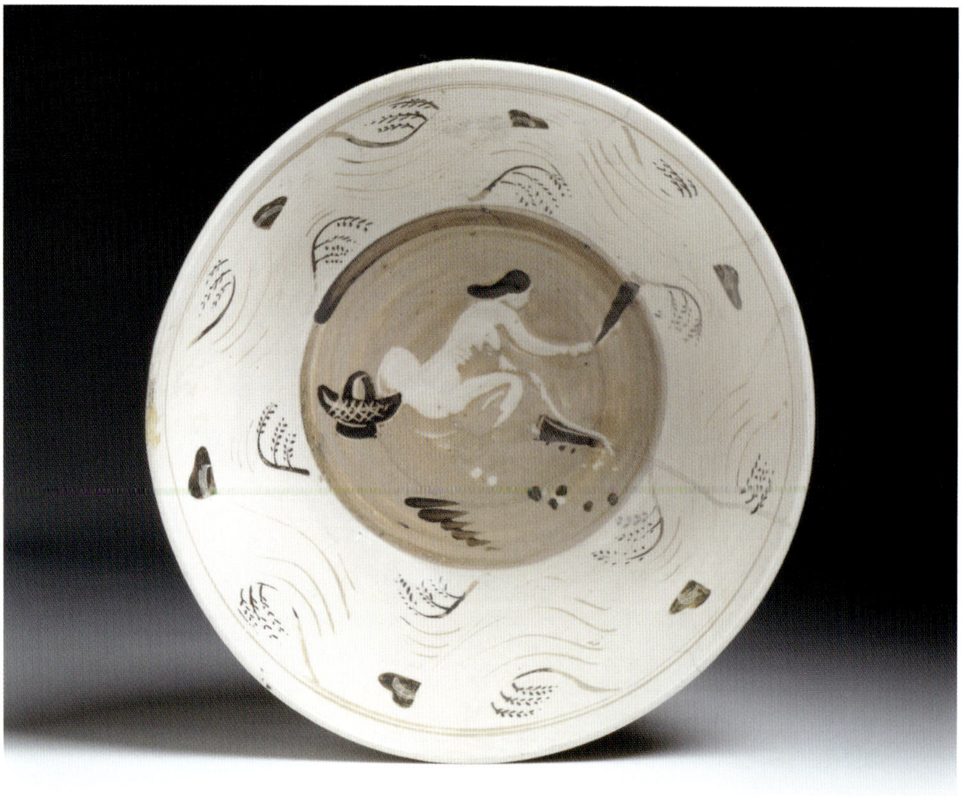

FIG 3 Bernard Leach, bowl showing a Korean washerwoman, earthenware, 1940, Victoria and Albert Museum

optimistic and cheerful people, as they travelled throughout Joseon and experienced its humorous and energetic local culture, watching dance, music and acrobatic performances.[17] In addition to the Joseon ceramics that had already attracted the attention of the Japanese, Takumi studied Joseon's wooden furniture to assert the uniqueness of its culture. In Takumi's *Soban* [a one-person dining table] *of Joseon*, published in 1929, he utilises his expertise as a forestry research engineer to list objective facts about the Joseon crafts that he observed, such as the wood species of the furniture and the unique design features of each region. Takumi mentions that 'Joseon's *soban*, with its honest beauty in a decent shape, can be called an example of righteous craftsmanship, as it serves our daily lives with familiarity and gaining elegance with age',[18] which epitomises his understanding of the values of Joseon. Rather than romanticising colonial Joseon, Takumi sought to comprehend the country and its art based on his lived experiences.

---

In October 1912, Bernard Leach and Tomimoto Kenkichi first encountered Korean ceramics through a collection of Yi dynasty porcelain at the first Colonisation Exposition (*takushoku hakurankai*) in Tokyo's Ueno Park. Leach, who was studying pottery at the time, was highly impressed by the Korean ceramics on display. This encounter sparked his interest in creating similar ceramics, and he sought out materials to make them.[19]

It is noteworthy that while Leach initially influenced Yanagi by introducing him to the ideas of the British Arts and Crafts movement, Leach's perception of East Asia, including Korea, was significantly informed by Yanagi and his fellow Mingei enthusiasts during the Japanese colonial period. This colonial context played a role in shaping Leach's understanding and interpretation of East Asian art and culture. Before turning to ceramics, Leach was a specialist in etching prints and was naturally drawn to the beauty of lines. After visiting Korea in 1920, Leach wrote a letter to Yanagi, saying, 'The unique and excellent lines of Joseon flowed everywhere,' and 'I have loved the beauty of lines all my life, so why have I not visited Joseon before?'[20] Leach's perception of Korea echoes that of Yanagi, who, alongside the 'beauty of sorrow' and 'the beauty of whiteness', categorised the beauty of Joseon as 'the beauty of lines'.[21] Later, Leach wrote about his impressions of the Joseon people during this visit and drew images of scenes he saw on his ceramics (fig. 3).[22]

At first glance, Leach and Yanagi's attitudes towards Joseon may seem similar, in that they both 'othered' Joseon with romantic attitudes that projected their personal feelings. Yet the two men had different objectives. If Yanagi used Joseon crafts as objects to crystallise his development of the concept of Mingei, then for Leach, the crafts of East Asia, especially Joseon and Chinese Song dynasty objects, were considered as visual representations of pre-modern art offering alternatives to industrial production, countering Western modernisation and mechanisation, and bridging the gap between the East and West. Leach believed that East Asian crafts embodied the European values of the pre-modern era, which were championed by William Morris's Arts and Crafts movement with its resistance against the advancements of modernity. Although Leach spent many years in East Asia, and directly experienced the arts of the East, he did not escape the Orientalist perspective that viewed the East as an exotic 'other'. Leach perceived and favoured Joseon ceramics as a pre-modern form, exhibiting the virtues that were already lost in the West through dehumanised mechanical manufacturing, but in so doing reinforced colonial perceptions of what constituted modernity. His analysis – 'The Coreans [sic] and their pots are childlike, spontaneous and trusting. We had something akin to this in Europe up to about the thirteenth century'[23] – plays into a rationale for Japan's colonial rule over Joseon, in suggesting that Korea was an undeveloped nation that required colonisation in order to modernise. Leach's fondness for the medieval, anti-industrial and pre-modern qualities of the Arts and Crafts movement led him to consider the aesthetics of Korean ceramics as pre-modern attributes, rather than as characteristics in their own right within an alternative framework for defining 'modernity'. Nonetheless, Leach's works often combined Western patterns with Eastern vessel shapes or incorporated Eastern drawings on Western-style ceramics, creating a unique aesthetic that he referred to as a 'marriage of the East and the West'.[24]

---

With the introduction of new machinery and technology from the West in the seventeenth century and the start of mass production, modern Japanese ceramics split into two streams. One was handmade, one-of-a-kind wares for appreciation, in the vein of traditional wares, and the other was machine-made, mass-produced ceramics for export to Europe. Against this backdrop, Kawai, Hamada and Tomimoto became involved in the Mingei movement, seeking alternative visual references in the folk crafts of Japan's neighbour in East Asia. There are many other prominent figures in the Mingei movement, but here I focus on the early companions who helped develop the notion of Mingei in relation to Korea.

Kawai and Hamada first visited Joseon in 1919. At the time, they were producing highly decorative ceramics and were intrigued by the exquisite techniques of Goryeo celadon and buncheong wares, but had little interest in Joseon's everyday objects made by unknown potters.[25] In 1921, Kawai's debut solo exhibition focused on decorative and figurative ceramics, and was well received by the critics. However, Yanagi criticised Kawai's work, arguing that it was mere imitation.[26] In the same year, Yanagi organised a Joseon crafts exhibition in Tokyo, showcasing Korean objects made for utilitarian purposes,[27] rather than what was considered 'fine art' in Japan at the time. Kawai visited the exhibition and was impressed by the Joseon ceramics and Yanagi's insights, which sparked his interest in practical folk crafts.[28] Following Hamada's introduction to Yanagi in 1924, Kawai became actively involved in the Mingei movement. Not content with simply collecting Korean crafts, he hired Sohn Doo-chang (1888–?), a Korean

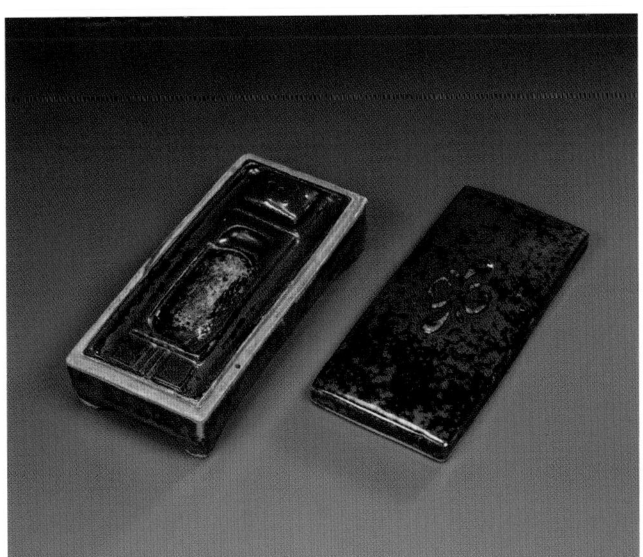

**FIG 4** Kawai Kanjirō, lidded ceramic inkstone, stoneware with iron underglaze, 1936, National Museum of Modern Art, Kyoto

living in Japan, to explore the rustic beauty of the Korean straw crafts Sohn made in his spare time while working as a woodcutter.[29] Kawai was fascinated by the intricate weaving of straw becoming fine crafts, and Sohn made straw mats, cushions, baskets and more at Kawai's home, while Kawai observed without giving any special orders or instructions.[30] Kawai valued the beauty of use in Korean everyday objects,[31] which were simple in form and used techniques that were easy to repeat. During the late Joseon period, water droppers, inkstones and nests of boxes were largely produced as everyday objects, and Kawai studied them in depth to produce similar forms, especially focusing on making ceramic inkstones between 1935 and 1936 (fig. 4).[32] However, he did not completely switch to making utilitarian crafts, and continued to produce sculptural pottery based on his artistic creativity.

Hamada remained an active collaborator in the Mingei movement until the end of his life and is considered the person who best exemplified the values of Mingei theory through his work. In addition to being a potter, he was an avid collector. In 1936, 1937 and 1941, Hamada travelled to Joseon with Yanagi and Kawai to collect Joseon crafts. In 1932, he wrote about the forms and patterns of Yi dynasty wares, in which he found 'a special beauty that comes from lively complexity and natural inequality'.[33] He also mentions that Joseon's faceted wares are 'really lively and have a deep taste', elements which he integrated into his own creations (figs 5, 6).[34] Hamada was captivated by Joseon ware's natural and authentic beauty made through free-flowing patterns drawn with fluid brushstrokes, which he reflected in his own work.[35] Kawai, Hamada and Leach were also all fascinated by faceted Joseon ceramic forms and the white slip brushing (*gwiyal*) and underglaze iron painting (*cheolwha*) techniques found in buncheong ware, and incorporated them into their works.

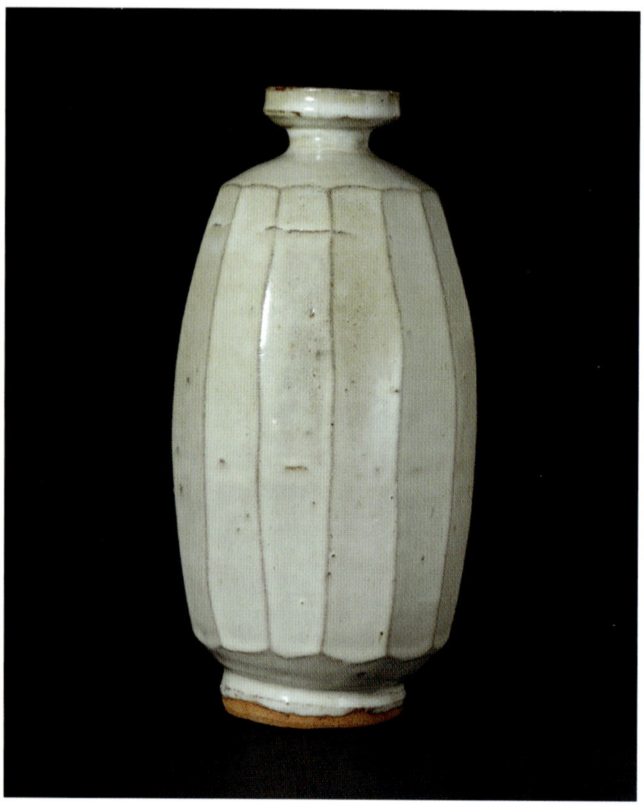

FIG 5 Hamada Shōji, vase, stoneware, 1931, Victoria and Albert Museum

Tomimoto, who studied architecture and interior design at Tokyo Arts University and was exposed to Western craft design during his period of study in England, held a different set of educational values from the Japanese potters who were traditionally apprenticed to a master. He aimed to reintegrate ceramics into people's everyday lives, challenging the prevailing notion of ceramics as one-of-a-kind artworks. He had an early interest in 'art for the people', and sketched William Morris's work at the Victoria and Albert Museum. After returning to Japan and helping Leach with Japanese translation, Tomimoto began studying ceramics in 1913 and subsequently travelled to Korea in 1922. During the same year, he wrote an essay titled 'Water Droppers of Joseon' discussing a Joseon water dropper that harmoniously combined the shape of white porcelain with the blue patterns of cobalt pigment. Furthermore, he studied Joseon blue and white porcelain styles, incorporating these aesthetics into his own works (figs 7, 8).[37] He aspired to create crafts that were practical, affordable and accessible to a wide range of people, aligning with the principles of practicality and affordability found in Mingei theory. However, Tomimoto's idea of making affordable objects through large-scale production did not resonate with Mingei principles, eventually leading him to leave the movement. White porcelain was of particular interest to Tomimoto due to its unadorned colour and shape (fig. 9). He drew inspiration from Korean white porcelain, Chinese dingyao and French white porcelain in his work. Further, in 1940, Tomimoto visited kilns in the region of Ogeum-ri in Yeoju-si, south-east of Seoul, in search of the right white clay to produce the porcelain he

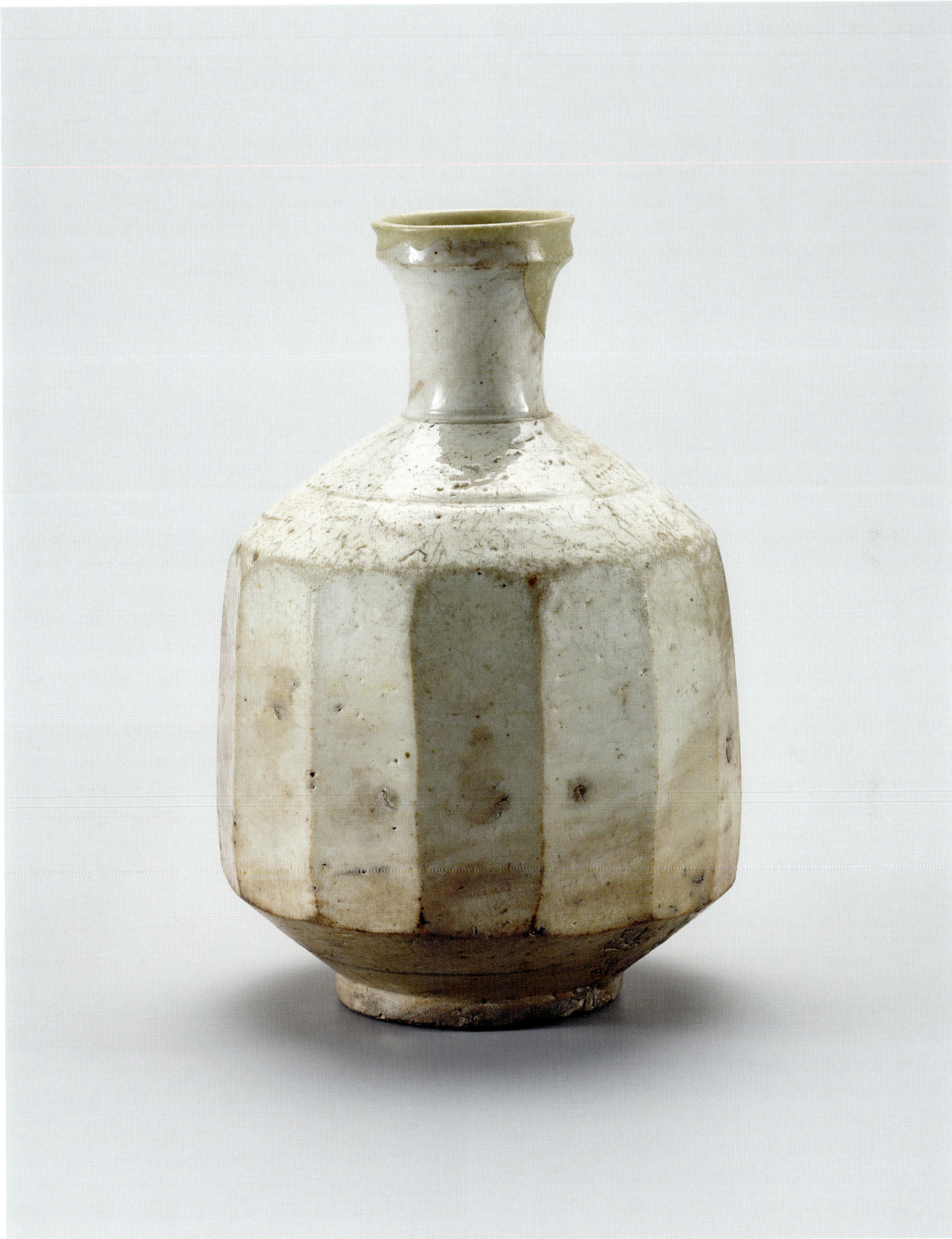

**FIG 6** Faceted white porcelain square bottle, Joseon, date unknown, National Museum of Korea

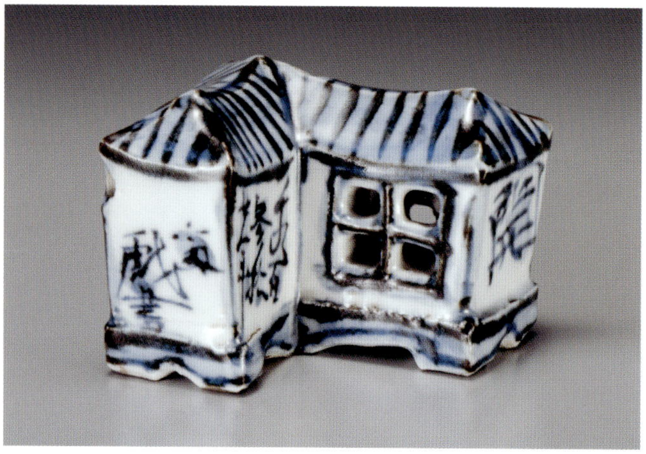

FIG 7 Tomimoto Kenkichi, Chinese house design water dropper, white porcelain with underglaze blue, 1937, National Crafts Museum, Japan

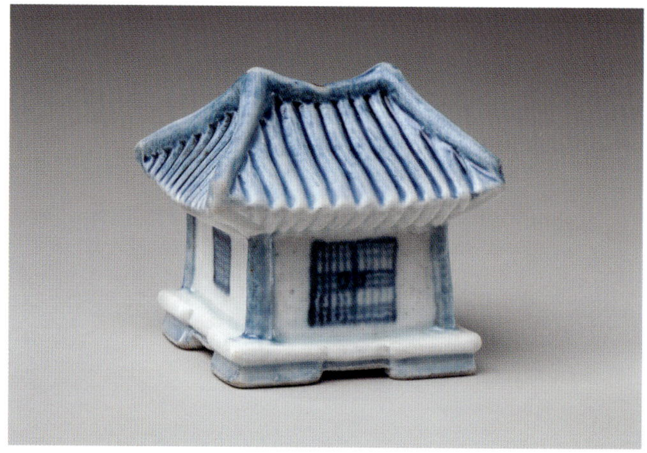

FIG 8 Water dropper in the shape of a house, porcelain with underglaze blue, Joseon, nineteenth century, Metropolitan Museum of Art, New York

envisioned. However, he was unable to find the suitable materials and consequently abandoned his plan to stay in Korea and make white porcelain, instead returning to Japan to continue his practice (fig. 10).[38]

---

Criticising both the Meiji (1868–1912) period's decorative crafts and the Taisho (1912–26) period's emphasis on the aesthetics of an individual artist, Mingei artists aimed to find beauty in the everyday objects used by the common people. Yanagi crystallised his Mingei theory through the crafts of Joseon, seeking to unite Japan and Korea through art, but his methodology was not free from colonial and Orientalist influences. The Asakawa brothers, who lived in Joseon, devoted their lives to understanding Joseon arts and culture, experiencing the reality of the country at first hand. Leach drew on Eastern references in creating his own aesthetic to resist Western modernism, while the masters of modern Japanese ceramics Kawai, Hamada and Tomimoto, were interested in Korean ceramics as a means to address their own interests in practicality, aesthetic 'health', and the art of the people, in the search for an alternative to the modern reality of Japanese ceramics, which was then dichotomised between artistic ceramics that were made for appreciation, and machine-made ceramics for export purposes.

In addition to his interest in everyday objects from the Joseon period, Yanagi left extensive writings about a variety of Korean art, including Buddhist sculpture at the Seokguram Grotto from the Unified Silla period (696–935), celadons from the Goryeo period (918–1392), and architecture and paintings from the Joseon period (1392–1897). Regrettably, despite his exposure to such a wide range of Korean culture, Yanagi overly simplified Korean art in his early aesthetic theory as the 'beauty of sorrow'. From the 1930s, Yanagi mainly described Korean art as embodying a natural, unselfconscious beauty, and he did not explicitly refer to Korea as a sorrowful nation. However, this still implies the

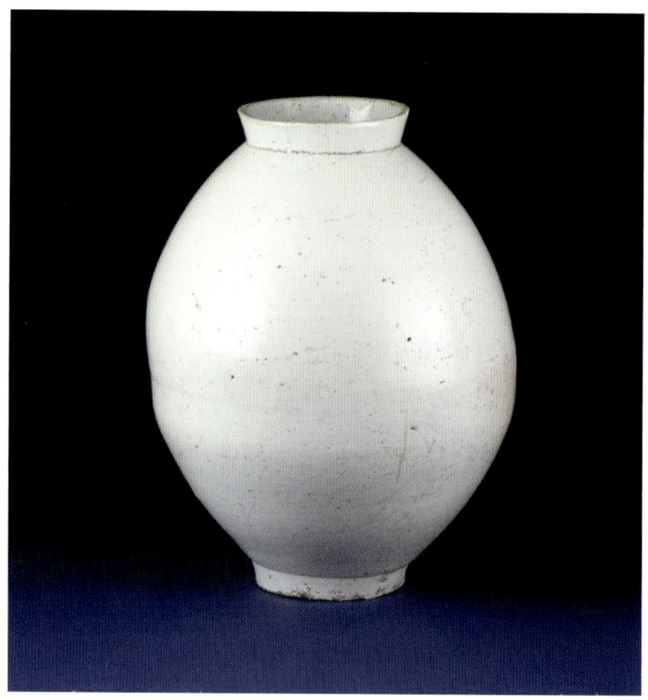

FIG 9 Moon jar, glazed white porcelain, Joseon, nineteenth century, Victoria and Albert Museum

FIG 10 Tomimoto Kenkichi, round vessel, glazed white porcelain, 1933, National Museum of Modern Art, Kyoto

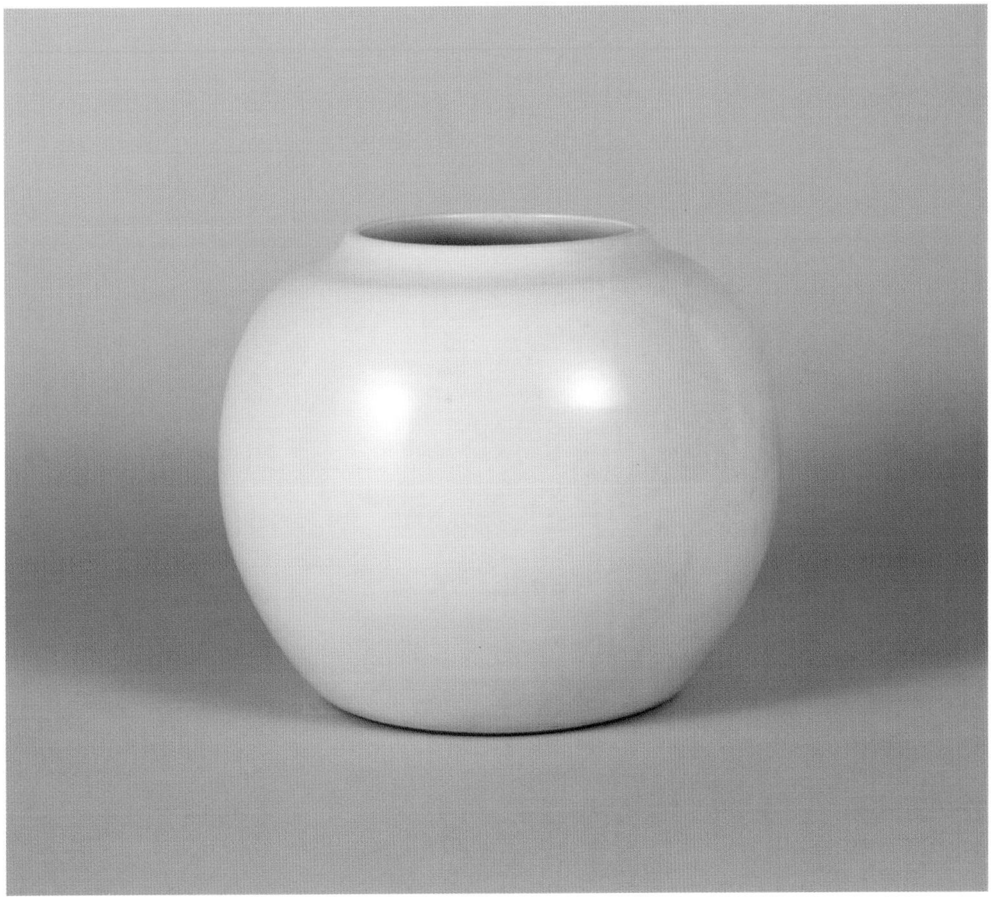

perspective of colonisers, portraying Korea as underdeveloped and remaining in a more primitive state than Japan.

As Yanagi was one of the few foreigners to comment on Korea's distinct art, his discourse not only became part of Japan's cultural landscape, developed through the Mingei movement, but also held significant influence in colonial Korea itself. Furthermore, his ideas reached a worldwide audience through his lectures and exhibitions abroad, as well as his writings in English translation. Given the extensive scope of Yanagi's involvement in Korea, his outsider's perspective on Korean art exerted a profound impact on twentieth-century debates surrounding the identification of Korean art. For Korean art historians, the endeavour to rectify Yanagi's widely distributed yet distorted ideas about the attributes of Korean art has been viewed as a challenge, and evading its influence was not straightforward. The free and natural beauty of Joseon craft, which Yanagi, Hamada and other Mingei artists assessed in the 1930s from a romantic, anti-modernist perspective, has been imbued with terms such as 'earthy', 'unconcerned' and 'unintentional finesse' by Korea's first art historian, Ko Yu-seop (1906–1944).[39] This early identification of Korean art was subsequently embraced and developed by other leading Korean art historians, such as Kim Won-ryong (1922–1993) and Choi Soon-woo (1916–1984).[40] Their efforts to overcome colonial discourses and establish a foundation for Korean art history have prompted a deeper examination of how to evaluate the distinct features of Korean art from a Korean perspective, which played a pivotal role in shaping the development of Korean art discourses as they stand today.

Today, in the realm of Yanagi and the Mingei movement, about 30 books and more than 200 academic articles have been published in Korea. These cover diverse subjects, extending beyond the exploration of Yanagi's Korean aesthetics within Mingei theory to encompass areas such as the Shirakaba group, Korean literary figures, the Mingei movement after the 1930s and the religious discourses and mysticism woven into Mingei theory. However, there has been a noticeable lack of discourse regarding the utilitarian beauty that initially prompted Yanagi's interest in Korean art. A deeper exploration of the practical aspects of Korean arts will open up a new realm of discussion on the intersection between Mingei and Korea.

## NOTES

1. Kikuchi 2004, 124–40; Brandt 2007, 7–37; Lee 1999.
2. Yanagi 2006c, 298–311.
3. The original English translation of the museum's name by Yanagi was 'Korea Folk Arts Gallery', but the direct translation from Japanese would be 'Joseon Folk Arts Gallery'.
4. Kim 2011. However, Kim is also critical of Yanagi's appreciation of Korea as a beauty of sorrow.
5. Yanagi 2006a.
6. Early evaluations are from Park Jonghong (1922), Ko Yu-seop (1931), and the extensive criticism towards Yanagi's 'beauty of sorrow' concept came in the late 1960s and mid-1970s. In 1968 the Korean-Japanese novelist Kim Dal-soo noted that white beauty is immortal beauty, not tragic beauty, and in 1974, Choi Ha-rim pointed out the problems with the colonial perspective on which the idea of 'beauty of sorrow' is based. This was followed by critical evaluations by many scholars, including Lee Man-yeol (1974), Moon Myung-dae (1977) and Kim Yanggi (1977). See further critical Korean studies of Yanagi's view on Korea, e.g. Kato 2012, 6–27.
7. Kikuchi 2004, 123–4, 131–7.
8. Yeom 2007, 235–52.
9. Yanagi 2006d.
10. Jung 2007.
11. Brandt 2007, 25–6.
12. Brandt 2000, 711–46.
13. Noritaka sent fragments of celadons to Bernard Leach, who was interested in Joseon ceramics and eager to investigate how celadon was produced. He also offered Kenkichi Tomimoto ceramic samples and knowledge. Yanagi visited Korea for the first time in 1916, Leach in 1920 and Tomimoto in 1922, at the suggestion of the Asakawa brothers.
14. Janelli 1986, 39–40.
15. Takasaki 2005, 112–13.
16. Ibid.
17. Takasaki 2005, 62, 171.
18. Asakawa 1996, 19.
19. Tomita 2014, 191–2.
20. Yanagi 2006b.
21. Yanagi 2006a.
22. 'Woman beating washing on flat stones in the clear flowing water of river-beds, the lovely line of dark hair resting on the napes of their necks' (Leach 1978, 200).
23. Leach 1960, 161.
24. Leach 1978, 310.
25. Bae 2018, 399–400.
26. Idekawa 2002, 224–5. Regarding the fact that Kawai was deeply immersed in the study of Chinese traditional ceramics and their techniques at that time, Yanagi implied that Kawai's works were mere imitations of Chinese traditional decorative ceramics.
27. Roh 2014, 103.
28. Bae 2018, 394–5.
29. Kawai 1935.
30. Han 1997, 190–2.
31. Kim 2015, 293.
32. Kim 2020, 55.
33. 'Inequality' here refers to aesthetic imbalance, not inequality of a social or cultural kind.
34. Quoted by Matsuzaki 2020, 139.
35. Bae 2019, 41–2.
36. Park 2010, 152.
37. Han 1997, 149; Tomita 2014, 191–2.
38. Tomita 2014, 194–5.
39. Ko 2007.
40. Kim 1973, Choi 1993.

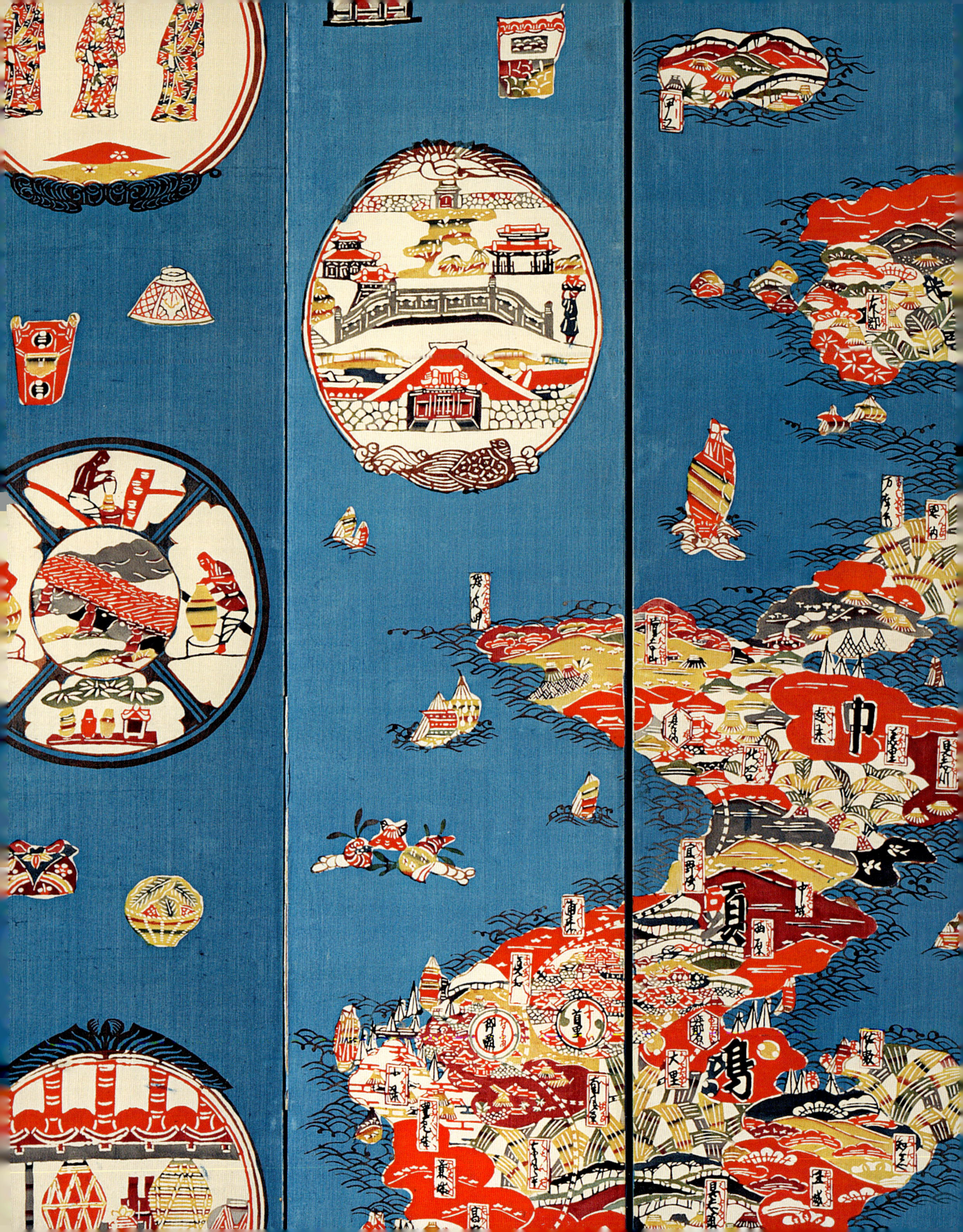
中
頭
嶋

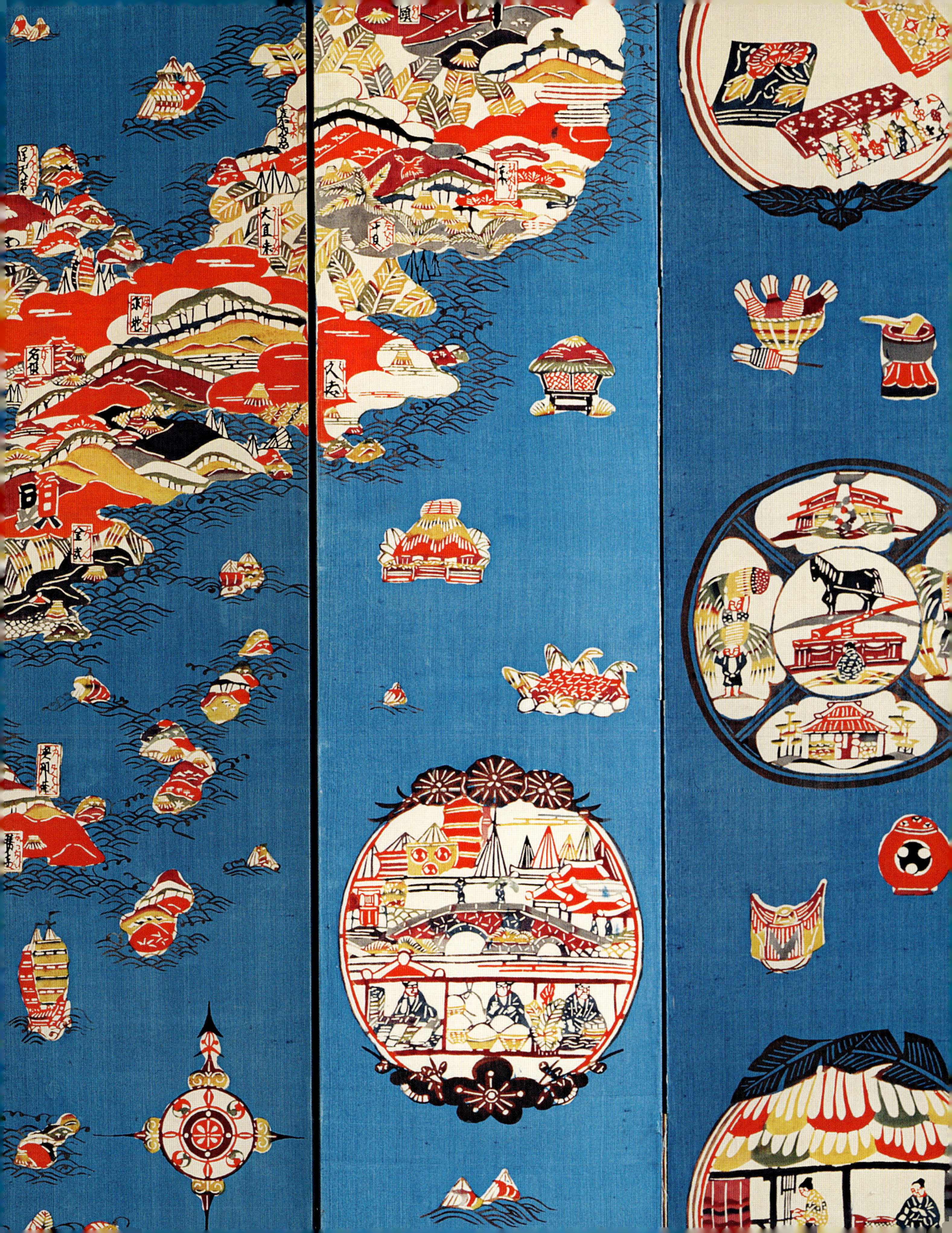

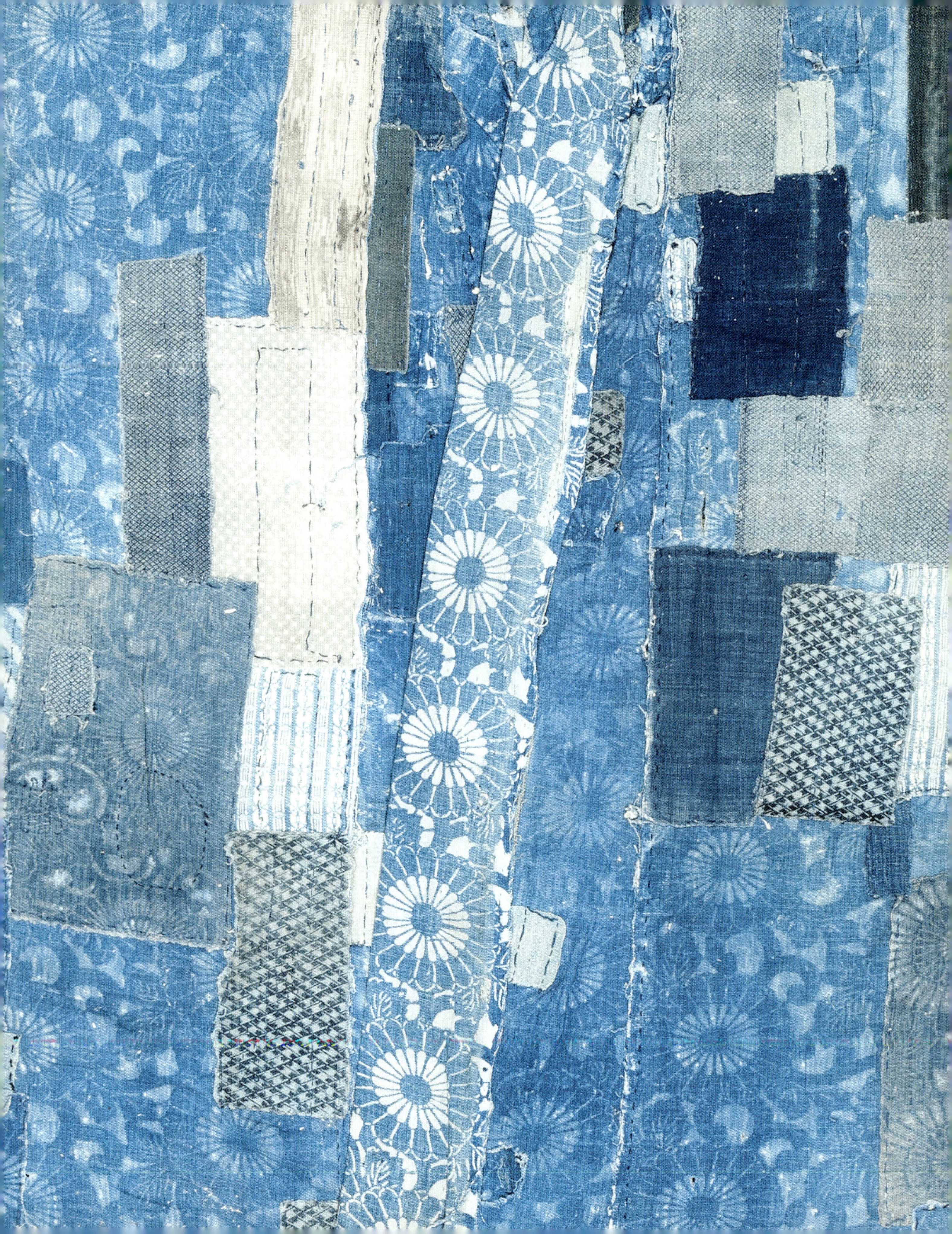

ANNA JACKSON

# Appropriate Charm and Fundamental Honesty

## Textiles and the Mingei aesthetic

In one of his celebrated landscape prints, Hokusai Katsushika (1760–1849) depicts women returning home to their village after a day in the fields (fig. 1).[1] Their work baskets are on their backs and their indigo-blue garments are hitched up to aid walking. On their heads are small blue and white towels (*tenugui*) that keep their hair out of the way and protect them from the sun. This idyllic scene evokes a romantic image of life in the countryside in nineteenth-century Japan. It is one in keeping with Yanagi Sōetsu's (1889–1961) utopian vision of rural communities in which anonymous craftsmen and women worked in harmony with nature, making simple, functional objects for use solely by themselves and their village, with no concern for monetary gain.

The woodblock print, however, is a product of the city of Edo (Tokyo), much as Mingei itself is an urban movement. Hokusai's subject matter may seem far removed from that often depicted in *ukiyo-e*, the 'pictures of the floating world', which focus on the fabulous fashions of the pleasure districts. The artists and publishers of landscape prints and the customers who bought them were, however, often the same as for those depicting courtesans in silk kimono.[2] Similarly, many of the textiles so admired by Yanagi were also a feature of metropolitan life, even when made in rural areas.

Although comparable to a lavish kimono in basic cut, this work coat (*noragi*) is different in character and purpose (fig. 2).[3] It was probably made in Tōhoku, the northern region of Japan's main island, far from the centre of luxury textile production in Kyoto. It is highly functional: the sleeves are tapered to allow for ease of movement and the fabric is quilted to provide extra comfort and durability. It is made of cotton, not silk; it is dyed with just one colour; and the patterning is achieved through a simple stitching technique rather than elaborate embroidery. Called *sashiko*, literally 'little stabs', this method of sewing together one or more layers of cloth with running stitch was initially used as a way of making fabric last longer or to recycle old pieces of cloth. Clothing that was made in this way was strong and warm and thus suitable as working apparel. On this coat three different patterns have been used on the main body and sleeves and around the neck. Of a *sashiko* garment such as this, Yanagi said, 'This needlework looks like added decoration, but it is nothing of the sort. Its charm is in its appropriateness to use and the strength of its stitching. The delightful patterning is incidental and utterly suitable. There is no concept of décor for its own sake.'[4]

Yet Mingei garments such as this reveal the inherent flaws in Yanagi's theories. All textiles are functional; they

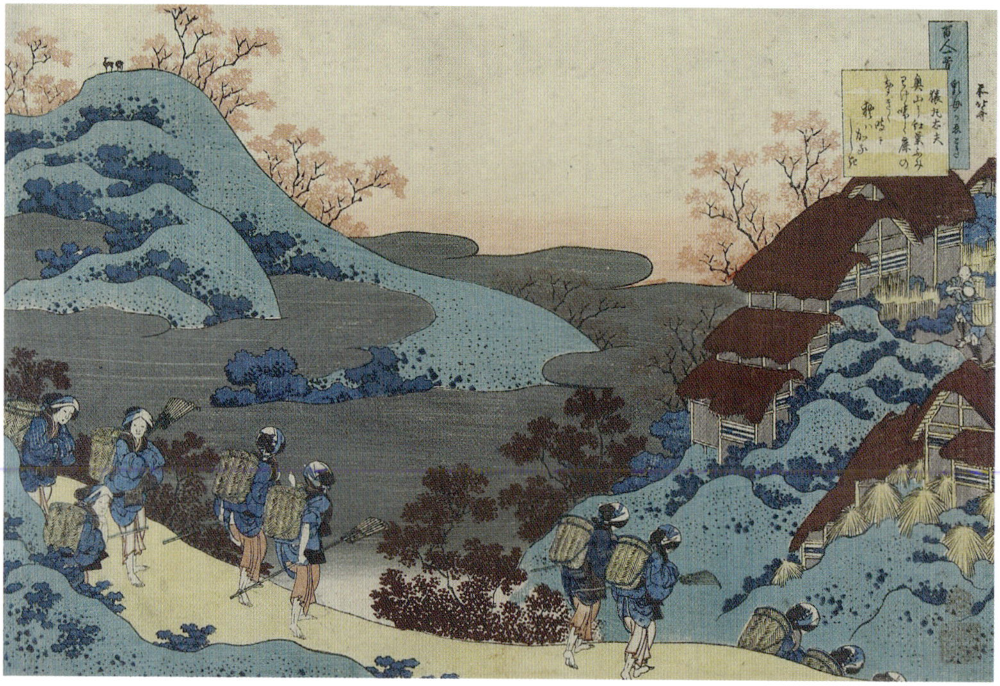

**FIG 1** Hokusai Katsushika, 'Women Returning Home at Sunset,' from the series *One Hundred Poems Explained by the Nurse*, woodblock print on paper, Edo (Tokyo), 1835–6, Victoria and Albert Museum

are all made to be used or worn regardless of their social context. This coat is a unique item and while its maker is indeed unknown, so are those who made luxurious silks for the wealthy elite. In pre-industrial Japan all objects were made by hand from natural materials. The patterning may appear simple, but the techniques employed are not and require a great deal of skill to execute, while the resulting design suggests a love of decoration for its own sake. Yanagi believed that commerce destroyed good craftsmanship, yet in the Edo period (1603–1868) Japan witnessed the growth of an extensive network of trade and the wide distribution of a large volume of goods. Many farming communities turned to textile production because it provided a better source of income than rice cultivation. Fabrics were woven and dyed to be used by immediate community members, but many were also sold to city merchants and even to samurai, the ruling military elite.

Indeed, when the objects that Yanagi admired were originally created and consumed there was no strict dichotomy between rural and urban, high art and folk craft. A great range of textiles was made for diverse groups of people with varying lifestyles, tastes and income levels. Prints of city life reveal that blue-patterned garments were as ubiquitous there as in rural areas (fig. 3). Such clothes and other textiles were part of the everyday world of virtually everyone, even those who could afford silk for special occasions. What is significant about most Mingei textiles is not that they separated groups of producers and consumers, but that they bound them together.

The *sashiko* coat might be an example of work attire, but its excellent condition suggests it was not worn by a farmer toiling in the fields. It is not possible to know who wore it, where or for what purpose, but it does share some of the chief material characteristics of Mingei textiles, being of indigo-dyed cotton. Indigo (*ai*) is the name given to a group of plants containing indican, a colourless substance that turns blue when exposed to oxygen. Indigo is an immersion dye and repeated dipping in a dye bath creates the shade required. Indigo also has medicinal properties. Leaves from indigo plants were used in Japan to treat insect and snake bites. The wearing of indigo-dyed clothing was believed to give protection against such creatures, while the depth of the colour concealed dirt and stains. Both practically and aesthetically, indigo was an ideal dye and by the nineteenth century indigo-dyed fabrics were synonymous with everyday life in Japan.

Indigo was used to colour silk, hemp and ramie, but it is most commonly associated with cotton, which takes the dye very successfully. Cotton was initially imported from Korea and China and was an expensive fabric, but in the sixteenth century it began to be successfully cultivated in the more southerly and westerly areas of Japan. The increasingly widespread production and use of cotton transformed the clothing and household textiles of the common populace. It was much softer, warmer and more comfortable than the bast fibres that had been used previously, and much easier to process.[5] The development of an extensive trade network in the Edo period, fostered by the growth of towns and cities, meant cotton was available even in areas where it was not grown. In response to the increased demand, many farmers turned their land over to the cultivation of the lucrative plant. It was a risky business, however, highly dependent on good weather, and prices fluctuated widely. Cotton farmers could become very wealthy, but they could also be forced to sell their land and become tenants of richer landowners. Long-established social hierarchies in rural villages were often broken down as the successful production of cotton became the guarantee of social status and wealth. All this was rather a long way from Yanagi's folkcraft ideals, in which thoughts of personal profit played no part.

Most textiles classified as Mingei are patterned, not with stitching techniques such as *sashiko* but with resist-dyeing methods.[6] Some of these use a starch paste made from rice flour, lime and water as a resisting agent. Rice paste can be applied to fabric through stencils, a technique called *katazome*. Stencils (*katagami*) are made from two or three sheets of mulberry (*kōzo*) paper laminated together with persimmon juice, which, apart from its adhesive qualities, serves to strengthen the paper and makes it water-resistant. Various tools and methods are used to cut different kinds of designs, from the small and intricate to the large and bold. To pattern the cloth the stencil is placed on the fabric and the paste applied through it with a wooden or bamboo spatula. The stencil is then removed and carefully repositioned on the next section of fabric and the process repeated along the length of the cloth. The colour does not penetrate the pasted areas when the cloth is dyed. Once the dye has dried, the paste is washed off. *Katazome* is distinguished by repeat patterns which create a sense of rhythm across the textile surface.

*Katazome* can be seen to conform to the basic principles of Mingei, in that it does not reflect the individualism that Yanagi felt sullied good craftsmanship, as the dyer relies on a pattern that has already been cut. The stencils themselves can also be reused, allowing for many copies of the same design to be created. Yet the realities of production and consumption do not fit folkcraft ideology.

The stencil-cutting industry was centred on Shiroko and Jike, two small towns in Ise (modern-day Mie prefecture), whose merchants and artisans exercised a virtual monopoly on the trade because of the support and influence of the powerful Kishū-Tokugawa samurai clan who controlled the region.[7] The formal attire of samurai men throughout Japan was patterned using stencils with small-scale designs, known as *komon*. These were also used for the garments of wealthy townsmen. Larger designs, *chūgata*, came in a great variety of patterns and were popular across all classes, and genders, of society. Among the crowds in the print by Utagawa Toyokuni (1769–1825; fig. 3), a number of figures are wearing cotton *katazome* kimono, including the woman seen from behind in the middle of the bridge and, below, two of the women standing in the boats, the one on the left with a toothpick and the one holding out her arm to steady herself. The kimono of these city dwellers are highly fashionable garments, worn with elaborate *obi* (waist sash), but the

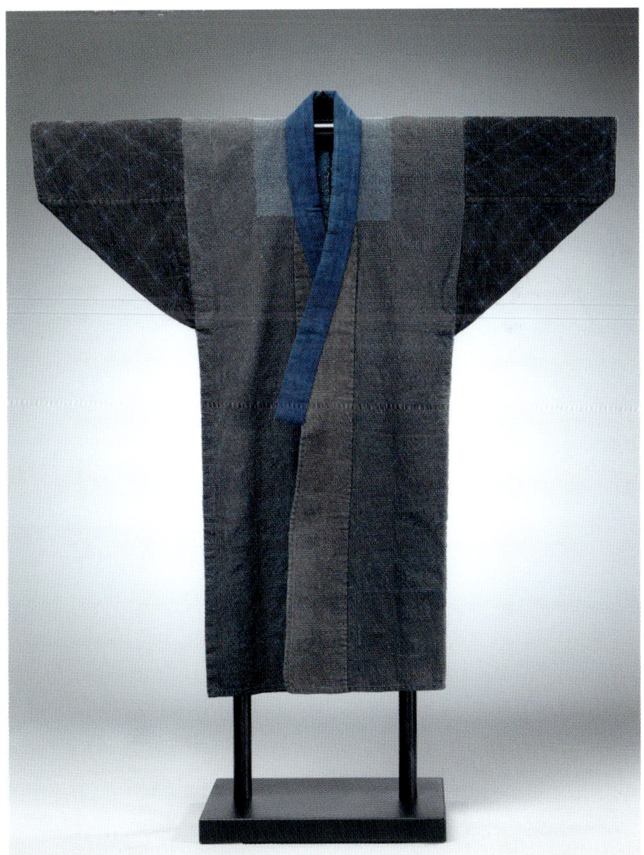

FIG 2 Work coat (*noragi*), cotton, quilting with cotton thread (*sashiko*), probably Tōhoku, 1850–1900, Victoria and Albert Museum

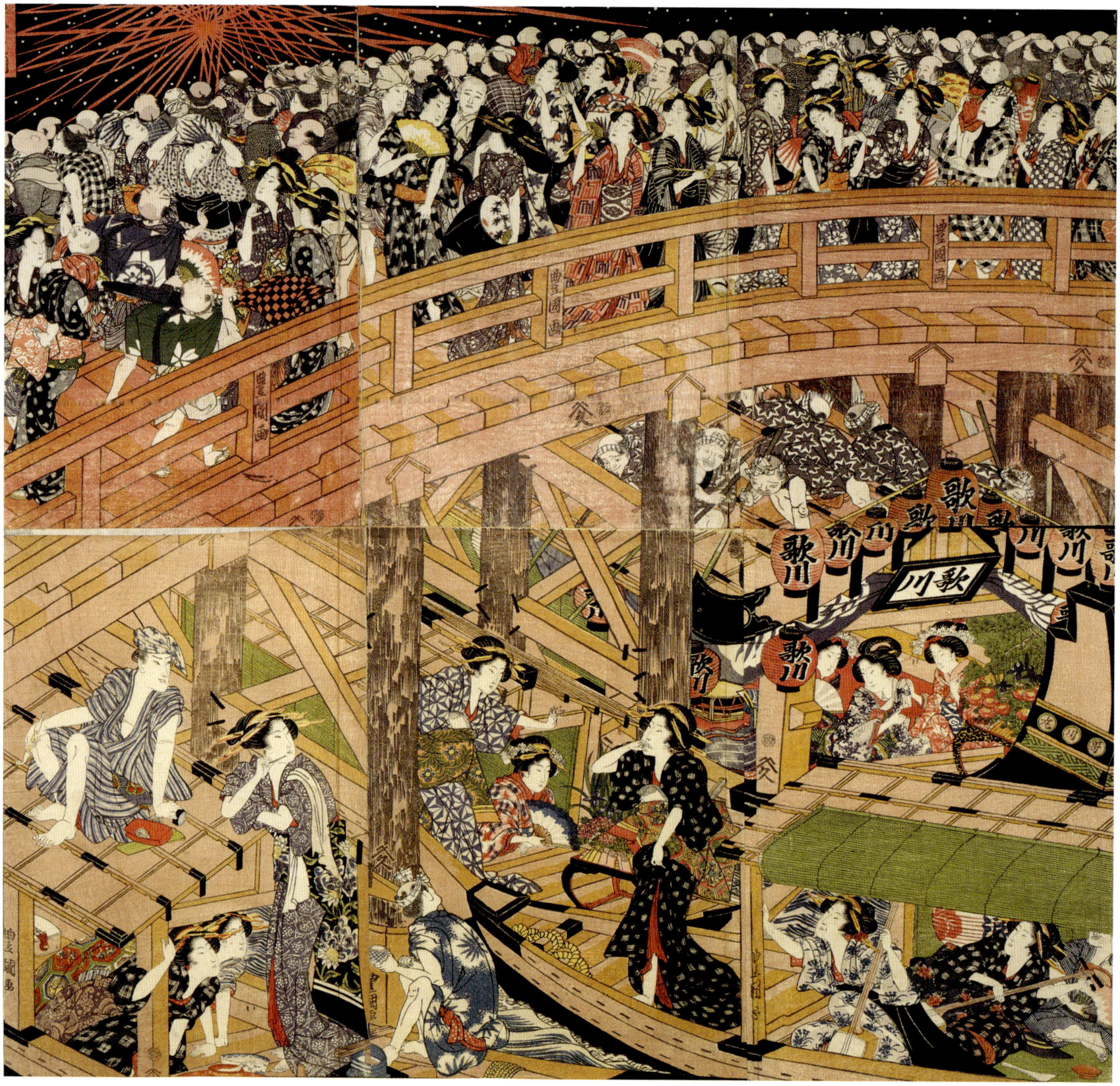


FIG 3 Utagawa Toyokuni, *Fireworks at Ryōgoku Bridge*, woodblock print on paper, Edo (Tokyo), 1820–5, Victoria and Albert Museum

clothing and textiles of the less affluent also reveal the popularity of *katazome*. Cotton fabric stencil-dyed with a motif of chrysanthemums and scrolling vines forms the basis of this sleeping coverlet (*yogi*; fig. 4). Shaped like an oversize kimono, it was originally stuffed with raw cotton and would have wrapped around the sleeper to provide extra warmth on a cold night. The *yogi* reveals how, for poorer members of society, every textile was a highly valued possession to be endlessly repaired, patched and re-stitched with fragments of fabric, resulting in a layered, patchwork collage. This type of textile is known as *boro*, meaning 'rags'.

The paste used with stencils was also employed freehand, a technique called *tsutsugaki*. In this method, a design is drawn on the cloth with rice paste squeezed from a paper tube (*tsutsu*). As with *katazome*, the paste forms a protective coating that prevents the colour penetrating when the cloth is dyed. While the use of

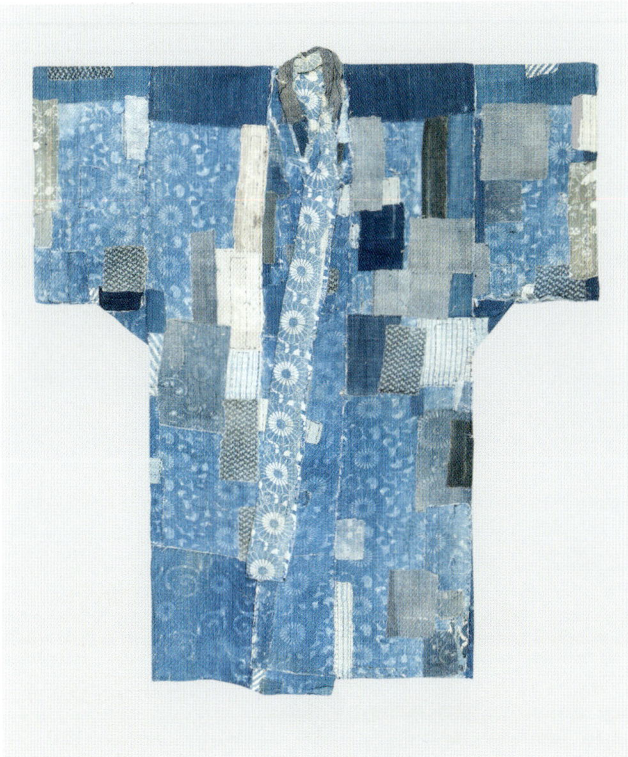

FIG 4 Sleeping coverlet (*yogi*), recycled and stitched cotton (*boro*), Japan, 1850–1900 | Credit: Karun Thakar Collection, London/ © Desmond Brambley

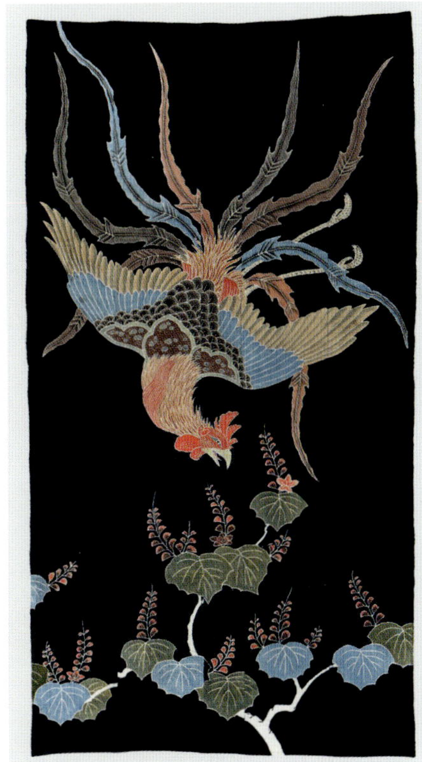

FIG 5 Bedding cover (*futonji*), cotton, freehand paste-resist dyeing (*tsutsugaki*), Japan, 1870–1910, Ashmolean Museum, Oxford

stencils allows for repeat production, *tsutsugaki* designs are unique and thus more expensive. As a result, this technique tended to be used on textiles made for special occasions such as festivals and other celebrations that marked important stages of life. Many are associated with weddings. Brides would be accompanied to their new home with a trousseau of gifts that would include many textiles, one of the most important being a richly decorated bedding cover, or *futonji* (fig. 5).[8] Square or rectangular in shape, in contrast to *yogi*, *futonji* were particularly suited to bold, pictorial imagery. Marriage covers featured auspicious motifs designed to bring good fortune to the couple in their new life together. This example depicts the mythical *hōō* bird, symbolic of peace and prosperity and the female counterpart of the dragon. Its many feathers represent the virtues of truthfulness, propriety, righteousness, benevolence and sincerity. *Hōō* are generally depicted, as here, with a paulownia tree, which, according to legend, is the only plant on which the bird will alight. As well as indigo blue, this *futonji* features other dyes, which would have been obtained from common plants.[9] These would have been brushed on first, within the paste boundaries. These areas would have then been completely covered with paste before the fabric was dipped in the indigo vat. Once the desired blue shade of the feathers was attained, they would be covered with paste. More immersions would have created the blue leaves, which again would then be resisted with the paste, and the fabric dipped again and again until the dark blue of the ground was achieved. Celebratory *futonji* would be used on the wedding night, after which they would be carefully stored and used only on special occasions or for important guests. The survival of so many *tsutsugaki futonji* is due to their being treasured in this way.

As *tsutsugaki* was a freehand method of drawing on fabric, the range and style of designs was limited only by the talents of the dyer. Despite the individualism inherent in this process, the recurrent use of popular motifs places them within the Mingei canon, and they tend to be associated specifically with rural communities. Yet *tsutsugaki futonji* and other textiles were also a feature of city households, of the lives of rich merchants as well as farmers. *Tsutsugaki* is essentially the same technique as *yūzen*, named after the

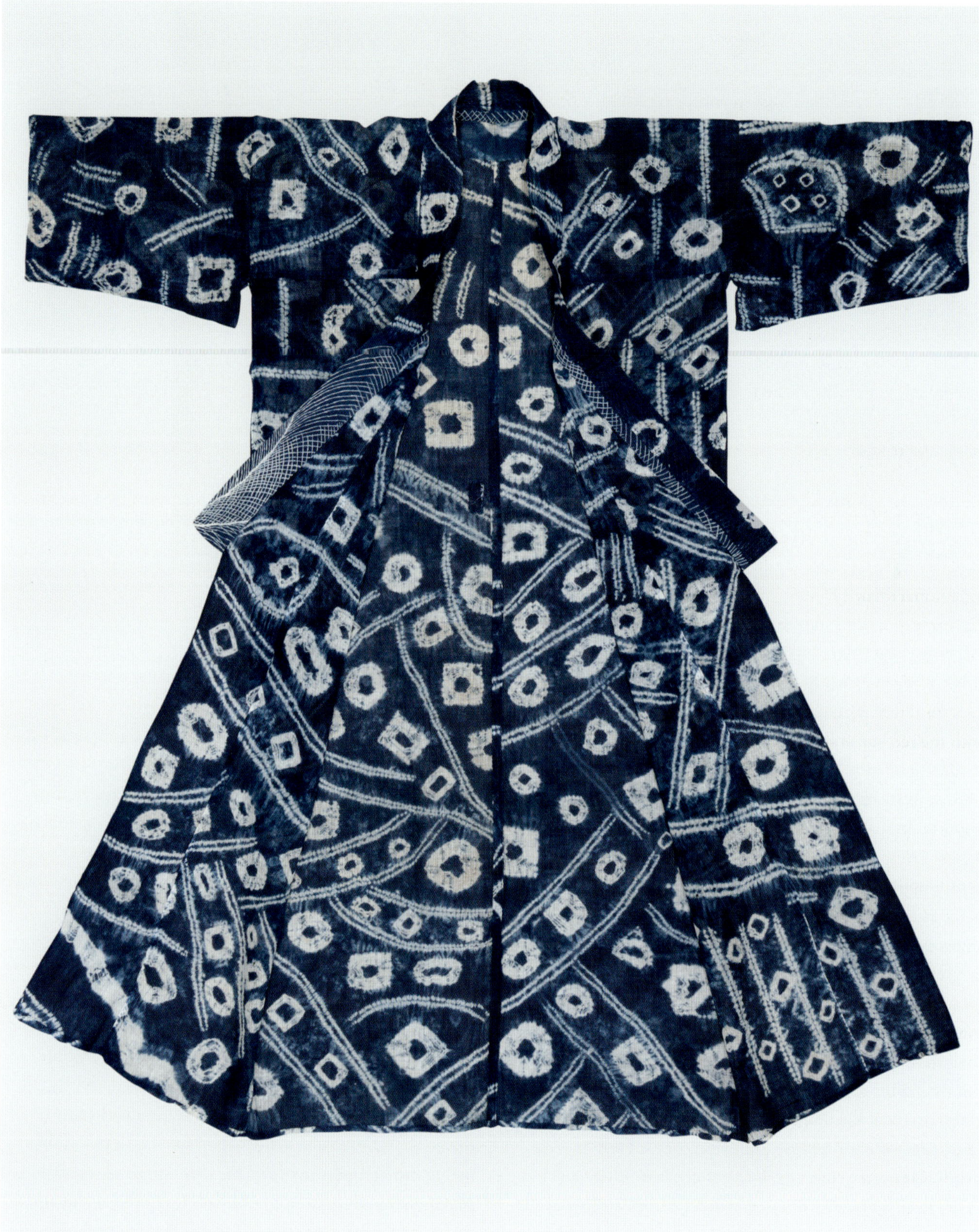

**FIG 6** Kimono, hemp (*asa*), tie-dyeing (*shibori*), Japan, 1870–1910
Credit: Karun Thakar Collection, London/© Desmond Brambley

artist Miyazaki Yūzen (1654?–1736), who, already famous for his elegant fan paintings, began to design motifs for kimono in the late seventeenth century. *Yūzen* patterning is associated with silk and high-quality ramie garments of the elite and is generally finer and more detailed than *tsutsugaki*, but the divide between the two is blurred, defined only by the dichotomies of Mingei classification.

*Shibori* is another resist-dyeing technique, usually translated as tie-dyeing (fig. 6). In this method fabric is bound, stitched or clamped before being placed in the dye bath. The most famous centre of *shibori* production was Arimatsu near Nagoya. It was next to Narumi, one of the post stations on the Tōkaidō, the great coastal road that linked Edo (Tokyo) with Kyoto. There were 53 of these stations and each became known for its natural features, particular restaurants or local products, such as Arimatsu *shibori*. The fabric was thus not only transported along the major highway, but travellers passing through Narumi would buy Arimatsu *shibori* as a souvenir. Such promotion of local craft products, as with Ise *katagami*, was important to regional identity and prosperity in the Edo period. *Shibori* was used to pattern silk but was also a popular method to pattern cotton or hemp garments, particularly *yukata*, informal kimono worn in summer. The man depicted right at the bottom of Toyokuni's print (fig. 3), with the red *obi*, is wearing such a garment.

*Sashiko*, *katazome*, *tsutsugaki* and *shibori* are all methods of patterning cloth after it has been woven. *Kasuri*, in contrast, is a thread-resist technique in which sections of yarn are tightly bound or compressed to prevent the colour penetrating when the skein is dipped in the dye bath. The binding is then carefully removed, leaving a yarn that is partly white and partly coloured. This is then used as the warp or weft or sometimes both; a pattern emerges as the cloth is woven. The slight mismatching of the resisted threads merging as the cloth is woven gives the patterns on *kasuri* fabric their characteristic blurred outline. *Kasuri* was used for household items such as *futonji* and on garments such as kimono (fig. 7). The strong association of *kasuri* with the Mingei aesthetic has obscured the fact that it was used to pattern the clothing of fashionable town dwellers as well as those of rural areas. Echigo, a mountainous region in the north-west of Japan, was famed for the production of fine-quality ramie characteristically patterned with small, hatched designs using the *kasuri*

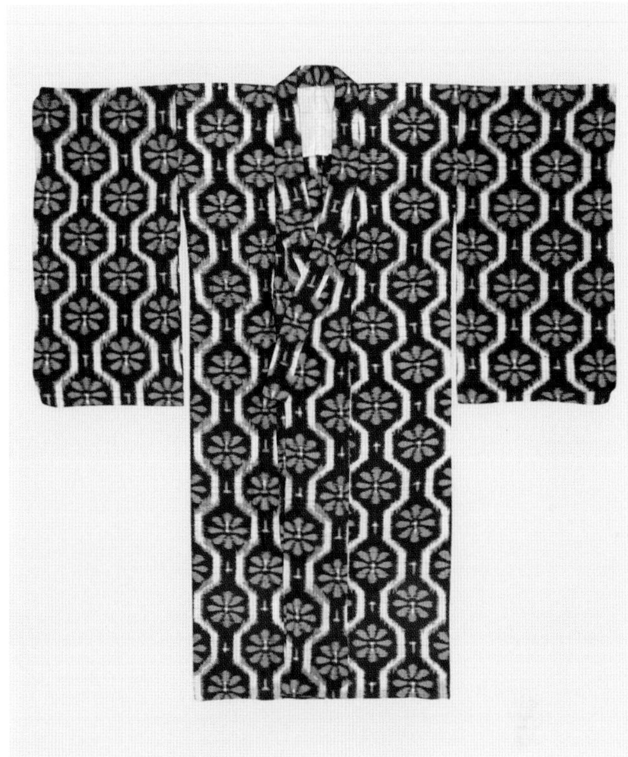

FIG 7 Kimono, cotton, woven with selectively pre-dyed yarns (*kasuri*), Japan, 1870–1910 | Credit: Karun Thakar Collection, London/© Desmond Brambley

technique. It was a luxury fabric, the creation of which involved highly specialised skills. Echigo *kasuri* was woven by women working under contract to a producer who supplied the yarn, and was so expensive that the weavers could not afford to wear it themselves. It was all sold to the cities, where it was worn by wealthy merchants and samurai.

Several of the people shown enjoying the summer fireworks in fig. 3 are wearing Echigo *kasuri*, including the elegant man with the fan flirting with the *katazome*-clad young woman on the bridge, and further to the left the woman with the checkerboard *obi* and the one carrying a child on her back. Some of the women in the boats wear fine *kasuri* also, most conspicuously the one standing in the centre. She has caught the eye of the rather rakish-looking man in a striped kimono and a jauntily tied *tenugui* on the neighbouring boat, and raises her hem provocatively to reveal the bright red of her undergarment. Virtually everyone in this spectacular print is wearing a fabric that could be classified as Mingei, but this is a world away from Yanagi's perception of the past and of folkcraft production and consumption.

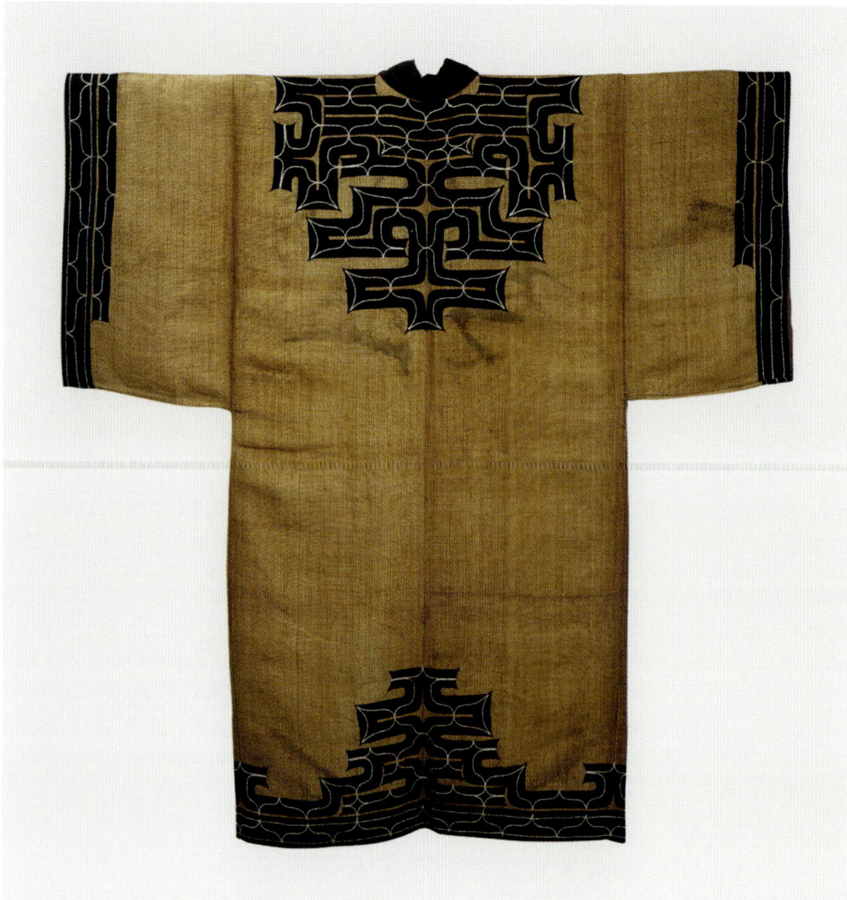

**FIG 8** Robe (*attush*), elm-bark fibre (*ohyō*), cotton cloth appliqué and cotton thread embroidery, Hokkaido, 1850–1900, Victoria and Albert Museum, given by Bernard Leach

Far from the fashions of the city, and from each other, are two other groups of textiles admired by Yanagi. In the 1930s and early 1940s he became interested in the country's peripheral cultures, those of the Ainu in Hokkaido in the north and Okinawa in the south.[10] The Ainu are an indigenous people whose language, religious beliefs and material culture are distinct from those of the mainland Japanese. One distinctive type of Ainu garment, known as *attush* (or *attus* in the Ainu language), is made from fibres taken from the inner bark of the elm tree (*ohyō*; fig. 8). Using an appliqué method known as *kirifuse* ('cut and lay down'), pieces of indigo-dyed cotton cloth imported from the mainland have here been stitched down in a pre-determined design. This has been embellished with an embroidery technique known as *oki-nui* ('placing and sewing'), with thick white threads couched down to create the thorn-like motifs which are believed to protect the wearer from harm.[11] Decoration is focused on the hem, upper back, and front and sleeve openings to prevent evil spirits from entering at vulnerable points.

The Ainu suffered economic and social discrimination and were subject to a policy of forced assimilation from the late nineteenth century.[12] As they were ethnically different and regarded as barbarians, their crafts did not fit into the theoretical framework that defined Mingei objects as expressing an 'innate and original Japaneseness'.[13] Yanagi nevertheless admired what he saw as the spiritual power of objects made by the Ainu, a view informed by European notions of romantic primitivism introduced to him by Bernard Leach (1887–1979). Ainu textiles were considered 'too ethnographic to be of more than marginal interest' to the Victoria and Albert Museum, but it acquired its one *attush* robe as a gift from Leach in 1963.[14]

By contrast, Yanagi saw Okinawa, the largest of the islands that form the Ryūkyū archipelago, as a vital cultural archive that had retained the original qualities of ancient Japan. He eulogised Okinawa's beauty, calling it a 'heaven with miracles'.[15] He particularly praised the stencil-dyed fabric known as *bingata* (fig. 9). The basic techniques of *bingata* are the same as *katazome*, but what distinguishes it is the brilliance of colour. This vivid palette derives from the use of mineral pigments, which are applied with a stubby brush in a number of layers to achieve the intensity required.[16] While many *bingata* motifs are similar to those of Japan, as in this example depicting maple leaves, the patterning is often very dense. This garment is also wider and shorter than a kimono, the sleeves are sewn completely to the body, the sleeve ends are open from top to bottom, and there is a gusset under the arm. *Bingata* robes are often lined with fabrics of a different design. This example has two, one for the body and the other around the collar, the latter being rolled over to form a neckband that stands out in contrast to the body.

Yanagi declared that 'greater homage' should be paid to *bingata* than *yūzen* 'because of its more fundamental honesty', by which he meant that the dyeing technique was not augmented by hand-painting and embroidery and was thus more 'faithful to the dictates of material and method'. He also observed that *bingata* was executed on cotton rather than silk and thus 'these textiles were available to all, and were not for the upper classes alone'.[17] In this Yanagi was fundamentally mistaken. Until it was annexed by Japan in 1879, Ryūkyū was an independent kingdom and *bingata* was reserved exclusively for the use of the royal court. It was made to order in the workshops of Shuri, the capital, and – unlike on mainland Japan – the entire process, from the making of the stencils to the final finishing of the garments, was carried out within one household workshop. Yanagi's misunderstanding may have stemmed from the fact that restrictions on the use of *bingata* had been abolished along with the royal family in 1879. *Bingata* workshops had been forced to seek a popular audience, but commoners were either unable to afford the prized fabric or were reluctant to wear something that had previously been the sole prerogative of royalty. As Yanagi observed, production had seriously declined by the time of his visit in the late 1930s.

On his second trip to Okinawa in 1939, Yanagi was accompanied by the artist Serizawa Keisuke (1895–1984).

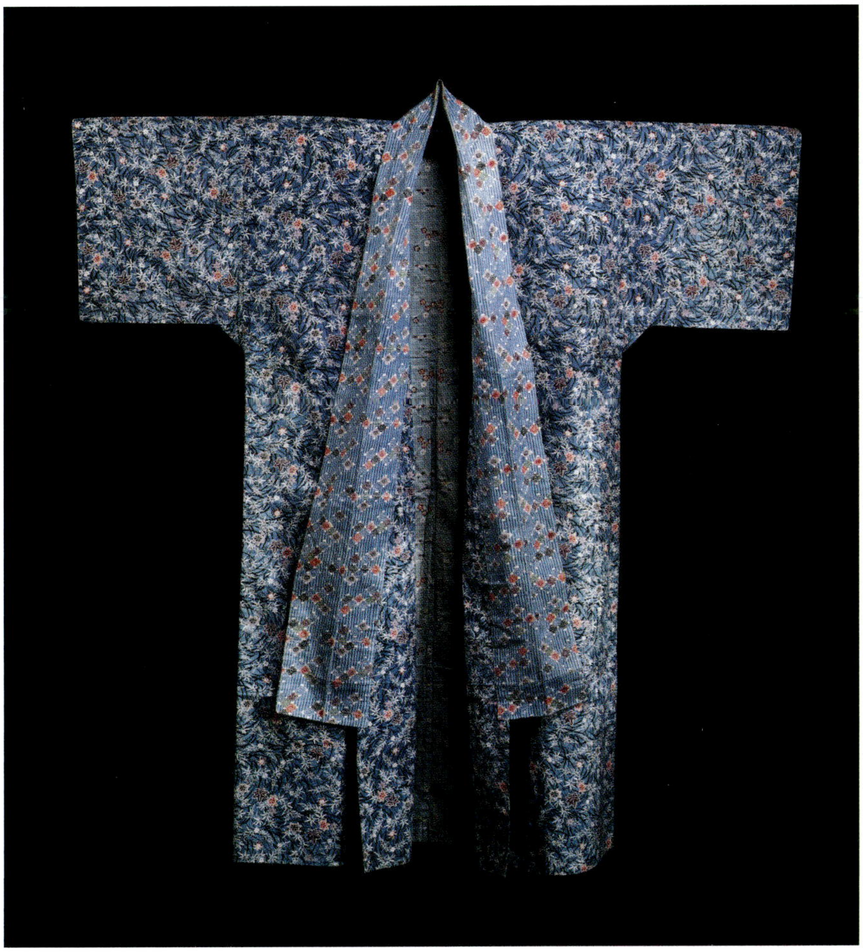

**FIG 9** Robe, cotton, stencil paste-resist dyeing (*bingata*), Shuri, Okinawa, 1800–80, Victoria and Albert Museum

Originally trained as a graphic artist, Serizawa first met Yanagi in 1927, which marked the beginning of a lifelong involvement with the Japanese Mingei movement. An encounter with *bingata* textiles in an exhibition the following year provided the inspirational spark that set Serizawa on the path of his future career and creativity. On this, his first actual trip to Okinawa, he was able to study *bingata* techniques in depth with the few workshops that had survived the loss of royal patronage. During his lifetime Serizawa created a great diversity of stencil-dyed textiles in a wide range of formats, including kimono, *noren* (doorway curtains), book illustrations and screens. In one way this appropriation of an Okinawan technique by a Japanese artist may be viewed as indicative of the submission of the islands not only to political but also to cultural control by the mainland. Yet as one of the most important and influential textile artists of the twentieth century, Serizawa did much to ensure the continuing survival and appreciation of *bingata*. In this screen (fig. 10) he used the technique to create the most direct and powerful image of Okinawan identity possible, a map of the island itself. In vignettes around the map, Serizawa depicted various images of Okinawan life and cultural activity. One of these shows *bingata* fabrics, another the cloth being worn.

As an acclaimed Mingei artist-craftsman, with the contradiction this implies, Serizawa was able to transcend cultural and ideological complexities.[18] In 1956 he was honoured as the Holder of an Important Intangible Cultural Property, popularly known as a Living National Treasure. This system had been introduced by the Japanese government the previous year as part of their efforts to ensure that historic practices, including dyeing and weaving, were preserved in the face of the increased Americanisation of Japan following the war. The Committee for the Preservation of Cultural Property created a special category for Serizawa, that of *kataezome*, or stencil-picture dyeing. This recognised the rich pictorial expression of his work, although the techniques Serizawa employed were no different to *katazome*, other than that he undertook all the stages, including the cutting of the stencils, himself.

The Okinawan weaver Taira Toshiko (1921–2022) was made a Living National Treasure in 2000 for the creation of *bashōfu*, cloth woven from the fibres of the thread-banana plant (fig. 11).[19] The processing of the fibre is

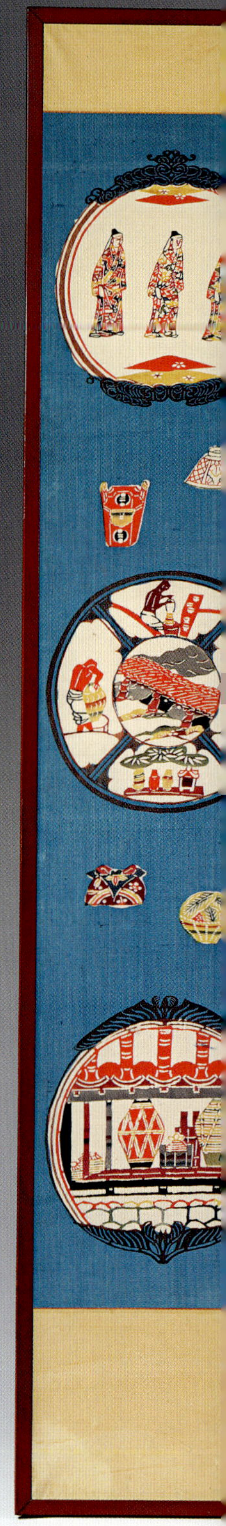

**FIG 10** Serizawa Keisuke, six-fold screen, silk, stencil paste-resist dyeing (*bingata*), Tokyo, c.1940, Victoria and Albert Museum

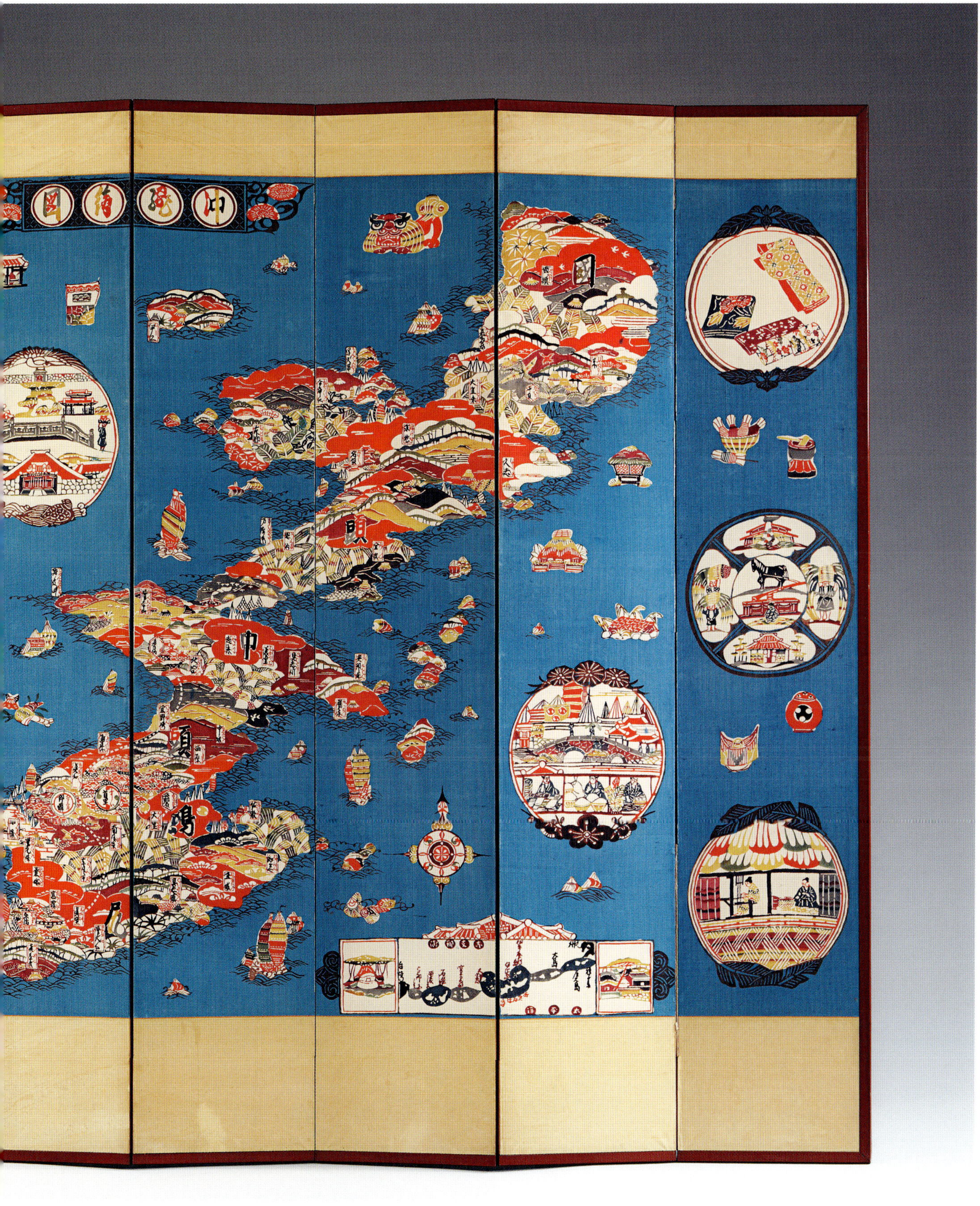

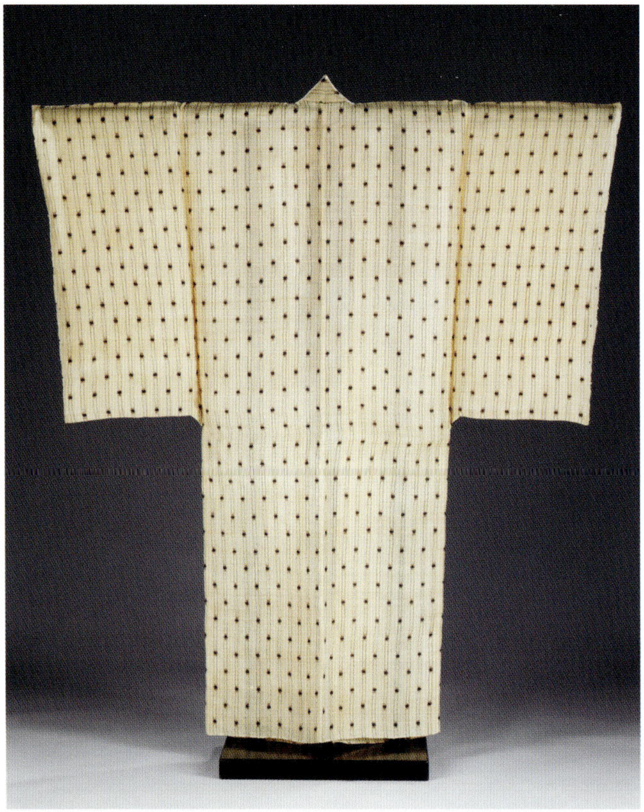

FIG 11 Taira Toshiko, kimono, banana fibre (*bashōfu*), woven with selectively pre-dyed yarns (*kasuri*), Kijōka, Okinawa, 2016, Victoria and Albert Museum, gift of the artist

labour-intensive and highly skilled, but the resulting light, crisp cloth is ideal for the semi-tropical Ryūkyūan climate. Historically, all sections of Ryūkyū society wore *bashōfu* garments, although quality of cloth and design varied according to social status. Commoners wore plain or striped cloth, while that worn by members of the aristocracy was often woven with pre-dyed yarns. Taira was sent to work in mainland Japan during the war, where she was introduced to the Mingei movement and to Yanagi's 1943 publication *Bashōfu Monogatari* (Tales of Bashōfu), in which he praised the beauty and authenticity of the textile. In 1946 Taira returned to her native village of Kijōka, in the north of Okinawa, determined to revitalise the production of *bashōfu*. As a result of her efforts, *Kijōka bashōfu* was registered as an Important Intangible Cultural Property in 1974, two years after Okinawa was returned to Japanese control following the post-war American occupation.

Mingei textiles and garments acquired meaning not so much in contrast with fashionable silk kimono worn by a wealthy elite, but in the face of increasingly mass-produced, global commodities. To Yanagi and his adherents, the vernacular symbolised stability and continuity in the face of an uncertain future. For similar reasons these works resonate with us in the present. *Boro* is one type of Japanese textile now much admired (fig. 4). Born of necessity rather than philosophy, *boro* has nevertheless come to exemplify certain principles of Japanese ethics and aesthetics, such as the regret over anything wasted (*mottainai*), the preference for subtle, modest beauty (*shibui*) and the admiration for imperfection and intransience expressed in the concepts *wabi* and *sabi*. Objects of utility, of poverty, *boro* textiles have been appropriated as art and are now sold internationally for very high prices. The visual abstraction of these textiles gives them a quality that chimes with modern sensibilities, while the variety of their textured surfaces appeals to our sense of touch. More significantly perhaps, at a time of growing environmental and social responsibility, *boro* speaks to the present, rather than of the past, ever more forcefully. In the face of fast, superficial and unrestrained consumption, it stands as an exemplar of slowness, sincerity and sustainability.

The aesthetic and ethical resonance of *boro* is reaffirmed in the creative practices and productions of the Nuno Corporation, whose artistic director, Sudo Reiko (b.1953), is one of Japan's most highly regarded and innovative makers. Sudo is committed to preserving historical techniques while experimenting with materials and methods drawn from beyond the normal textile world. She supports the many small textile workshops across Japan with whom Nuno works, and ensures that nothing is wasted in the production process. Nuno has long made use of leftover scraps, such as in the puzzle-like cotton and linen collage of *tsunagi* ('patching or cobbling together') in which no lengths are ever the same (fig. 12).

Sudo is on the advisory board of the Japanese retail company Muji, and collaborated with them on the Re-Muji collection, which utilises recycled materials. The company, whose name is an abbreviation of *Mujirushi Ryōhin* (no brand, quality goods), was established in 1980 with a focus on low-cost, good-quality products sold with minimal packaging. Muji is popular the world over for its stylish minimalism; few would associate it with Mingei. Yet the emphasis on natural materials, simplicity, functionality and anonymity resonates with the ethos of the movement, and in 2021 Muji collaborated with the Japan Folk Crafts Museum on an exhibition that toured Japan.[20] More recently the company

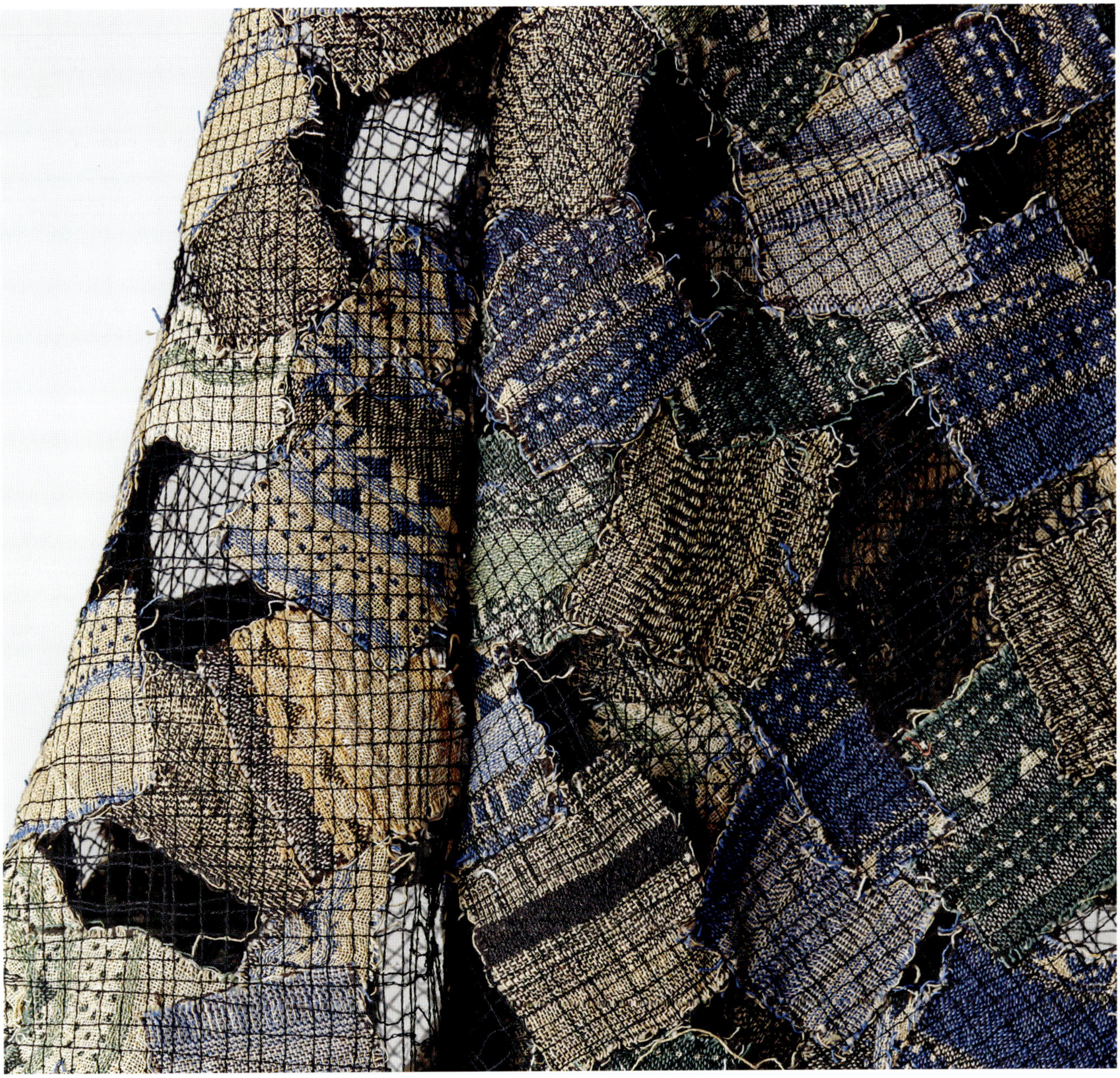

**FIG 12** *Tsugihagi* fabric, designed by Sudo Reiko and Ueno Kazuhiro, 2009 | Credit: Masayuki Hayashi

has launched Found Muji, which promotes pre-existing ('found' rather than created by the company) products of daily life that reflect the region in which they were created. These items come from more than 30 countries, including Britain, but there is a strong emphasis on textiles and other crafts from different parts of Japan. Regionalism, with the promotion of noted craft products as a marker of local identity, is as significant in Japan today as it was in the Edo period, and forms part of the political and economic strategy of many prefectural governments.

These endeavours, at individual, company and administrative level, are aimed at sustaining and in some cases reviving Japan's craft skills, techniques and culture. There is no rigid adherence to historical precedents, however, and the pieces being produced do not echo nostalgia for an irretrievable past. Whether weaving, dyeing or stitching, makers in Japan today are creating work of enormous diversity, but what continues to bind them together is a strong awareness of the country's incredibly rich textile heritage.

## NOTES

1. The title of the print is an adopted one, rather than one ascribed by the artist. It is one of a series of works by Hokusai that relate to poems in a thirteenth-century anthology. This print is the fifth in the series and refers to a poem by the early eighth-century writer Sarumara Dayū which appears in the large cartouche on the upper right (the smaller cartouche behind gives the series title). The poem can be translated as:

   In the mountain depths,
   Treading through the crimson leaves,
   Cries the wandering stag.
   When I hear the lonely cry,
   Sad – how sad – the autumn is.
   (Translation from Forrer 1992, cat. 77.)
2. Artists such as Hokusai and Hiroshige both designed Kabuki and *bijin* (beautiful women) prints in their earlier years and became known particularly for landscape prints in later years. Thus, *ukiyo-e* genres were produced by the same people, but not necessarily at the same time. This is also the case with publishers who would work with particular artists and respond to particular trends. As for their clientele, landscape prints had a great appeal to those who had visited specific places, but all the genres seem to have been enjoyed by the same type of customer.
3. *Noragi* translates as 'rural clothing' and is a term that can be applied to a range of robes and jackets.
4. Yanagi 1972, 117.
5. Bast fibres are obtained from the phloem, the tissue that conducts the sap, located in the inner bark of the stems of dicotyledon plants. Processing of these fibres is difficult and time-consuming. They are very stiff and cannot be spun, so have to be split and joined end to end by tying or twisting. Many of the textiles used by the rural classes in Japan were made from fibres gathered from various wild plants. These included *kōzo* and *kaji*, from the paper mulberry tree family, and the vines wisteria (*fuji*) and *kuzu*. The grass fibres ramie and hemp, known collectively in Japan as *asa*, were cultivated. They could be lightly spun or twisted in a continuous thread and were easier to weave than other bast fibres. In Hokkaido the Ainu used fibres from the bark of trees such as linden (*shinanoki*) and, most commonly, elm (*ohyō*). In Okinawa, the thread banana plant (*bashō*) was used.
6. Resist-dyeing is a collective term for a variety of techniques by which parts of the threads to be used in weaving or the already woven cloth are protected in some way to 'resist' the dye.
7. In the Edo period, Japan was divided into *han*, the estates of the individual *daimyō* (samurai regional lords) who governed them as personal property but as vassals to the Tokugawa shogun (military ruler). The Kishū-Tokugawa family were a branch of the main Tokugawa clan. They ruled Kii (present day Wakayama prefecture and the southern part of Mie prefecture). This territory did not include Shiroko and Jike but they had control over the area. The samurai were the ruling military class during the Edo period. In 1868, the shogun was overthrown and the authority of the emperor restored. The samurai class was abolished.
8. *Futon* consist of two sections, a mattress and a coverlet, both of which were stuffed with raw cotton. The top section was more patterned. *Futon* were introduced in the seventeenth century and brought unimaginable luxury to the commoner classes, who had hitherto slept on straw on the floor.
9. Browns and greys were derived from the bark of oak, chestnut and walnut trees. Phellodendron and miscanthus plants produced yellow dyes. Common pigments included mercuric sulphide (*shu*), which produced bright red, and iron oxide (*bengara*), for red-brown. Organic pigments were also used, particularly black calligraphy ink (*sumi*) derived from pine soot.
10. See Kikuchi 2004, 140–63.
11. Couching is the term used to describe the technique of placing threads on the surface of the fabric and attaching them with small stitches.
12. The Ainu were an independent community until 1669, when they came under the governance of the Matsumae clan, who ruled the southern part of what was then called Ezo. In the Meiji period (1868–1912), the island officially became part of Japan and was renamed Hokkaido.
13. This expression appears frequently in Yanagi's work: see Kikuchi 2004, 153.
14. V&A Archives, Bernard Leach nominal file, MA/1/L627.
15. Quoted in Kikuchi 2004, 143.
16. Dyes are soluble in water and penetrate the fibres of the fabric, while pigments are insoluble and adhere to the surface. On the whole, dyes are extracted from vegetable sources and pigments derive from minerals. Pigments can also be created from vegetables dyes. For a list of the pigments used in *bingata* see Amanda Mayer in Rathbun 1993, 82.
17. Yanagi 1972, 166–7. The main difference between *yūzen* and *bingata* is that the former is a freehand technique. Yanagi was incorrect in assuming it was always augmented with hand painting or embroidery. This is not necessarily the case with *yūzen* created in Kyoto and never the case with that made in Kanazawa, the other major *yūzen* dyeing centre.
18. See Terry Satsuki Milhaupt in Earle 2009, 97–100.
19. A tree-like plantain in the banana family, distinct from fruit- or flower-bearing plants and known as *ito-bashō* in Japanese.
20. See https://www.ryohin-keikaku.jp/eng/about-muji/whatismuji and https://www.muji.com/jp/feature/mingei/en (both accessed 31 July 2023).

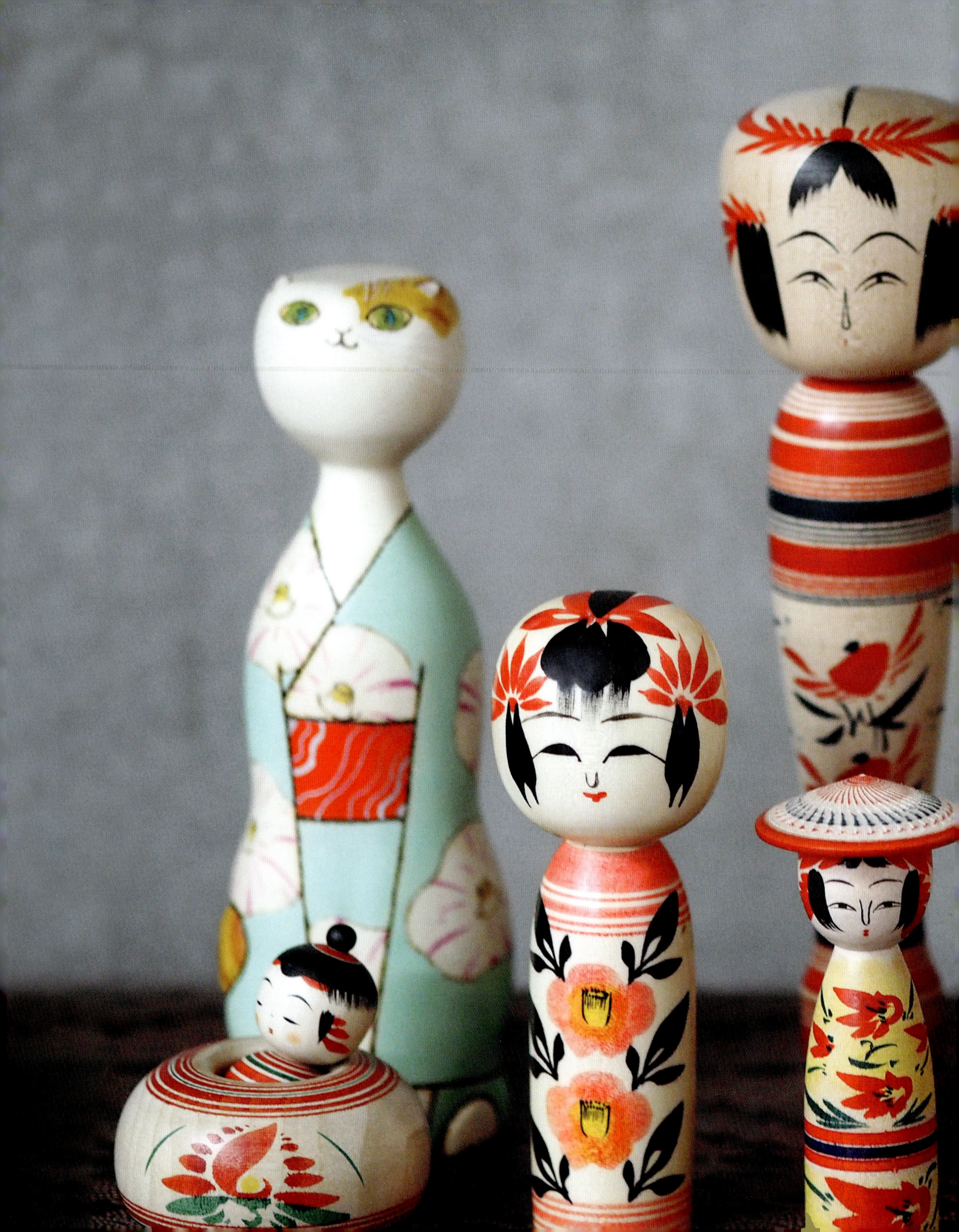

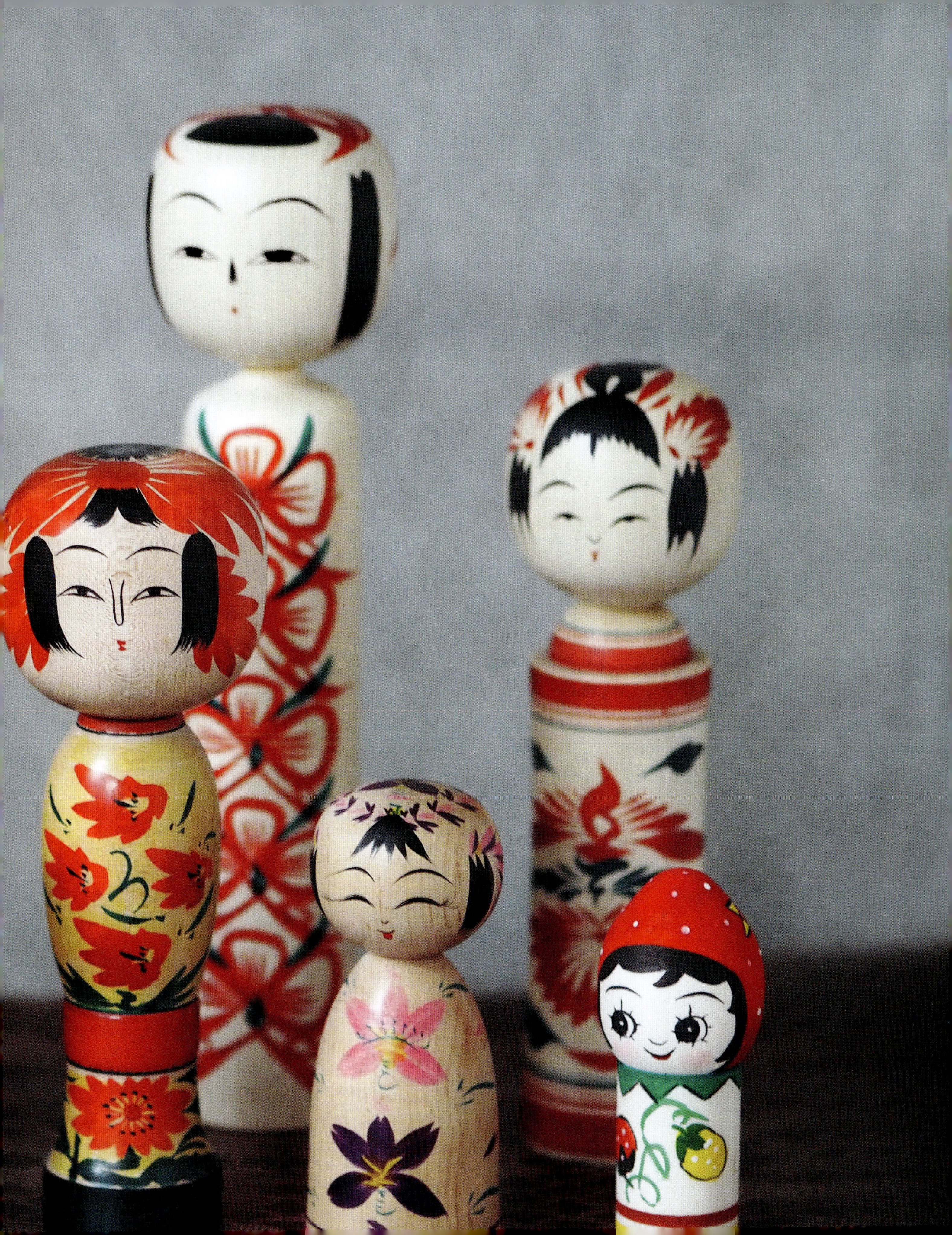

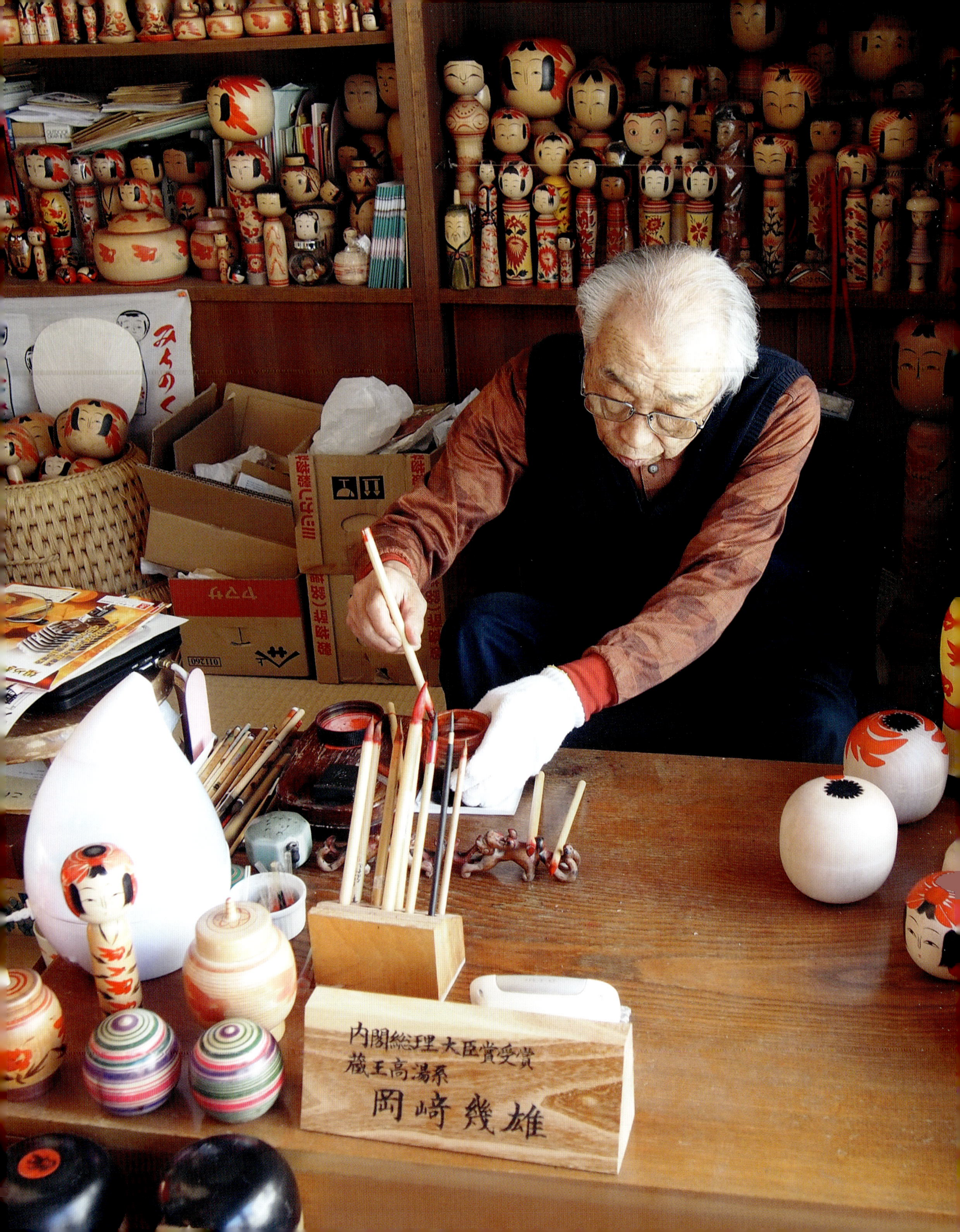
みちのく
内閣総理大臣賞受賞
蔵王高湯系
岡崎幾雄

OKAZAKI MANAMI

# Kokeshi

## *Kawaii* Mingei and the consumption of Japanese popular culture

Kokeshi are simple wooden dolls crafted in the Tōhoku region of northern Honshu island since the Edo period (1603–1868). Loved for their unassuming charm and rustic appearance and characterised by their rudimentary form, kokeshi consist of a round head on top of a long cylindrical torso, and lack arms and legs. They are usually embellished with floral motifs painted with calligraphic precision on the torso. Over time, kokeshi have taken on various identities, from an exemplar of Mingei austerity, to minimalist design object, to a souvenir epitomising the pinnacle of kitsch and back again.

*Dentō*, or traditional, kokeshi are made in Tōhoku by artisans who adhere to craft lineages and undergo an apprenticeship with a recognised practitioner. They are classified into 12 strains according to their shape, bodily decoration and facial features. The most common strain is the Naruko kokeshi, which typically have tranquil-looking facial expressions and are adorned with abstract chrysanthemum patterns (fig. 1). The other 11 types are the Yajiro, Kijiyama, Zao, Tsuchiyu, Nakanosawa, Togatta, Nanbu, Tsugaru, Yamagata, Sakunami and Hijiori (fig. 2).

Kokeshi were originally made from scraps of wood in Tōhoku *onsen* hot spring villages, by *kijishi* woodworkers, and were intended as children's toys. They were sold to farmers who visited for *tōji*, a practice where agricultural workers would stay at *onsen* inns for several weeks to recuperate over the snowy winter season. These farmers gave these dolls to their children and grandchildren, who played with kokeshi much in the same way that people play with modern dolls now. Even today, it is rare to find a traditional kokeshi artisan who is not in a remote mountain village in Tōhoku. Turned on a lathe, the dolls are made from local wood types such as dogwood and zelkova; stacked lumber piles outside the ateliers are an indicator that a woodworker is inside.

Nowadays, kokeshi are admired as interior design items, and passionate collectors around the world gather at conventions and on social media platforms. Much like members of the British Arts and Crafts movement who advocated for a 'simplicity in design and manufacture and a need to allow the quality of materials to speak for themselves',[1] fans often talk of the materiality of kokeshi and the affective qualities inherent in the wood, such as the 'warmth'. The dolls are often described as having a 'comforting' presence and described in terms 'beyond visuality', where the item is given agency and a perceived ability to 'heal'.[2] Artisan Shiratori Yasuko (b.1961) describes the appeal of kokeshi for adult women as 'stemming from the wood itself. People like that it has an earthiness and

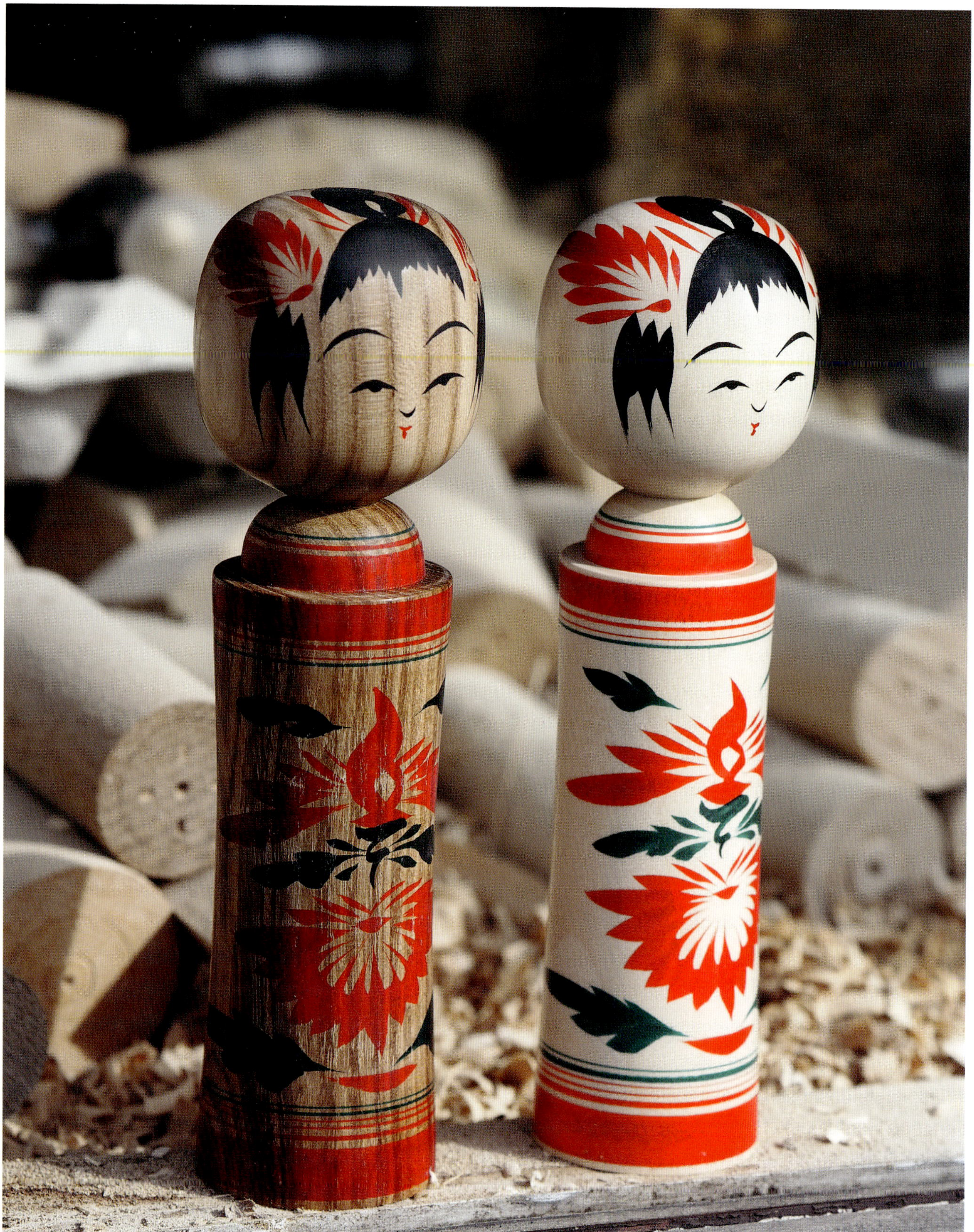

FIG 1 Naruko kokeshi by Okazaki Yasuo | Credit: Okazaki Manami

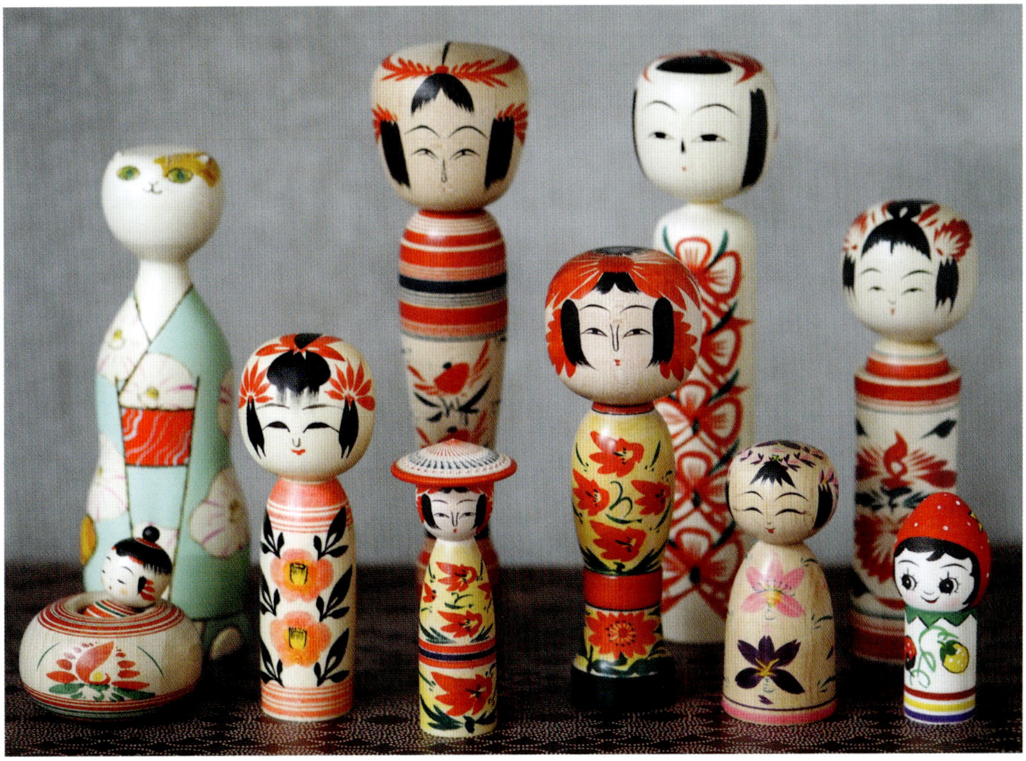

FIG 2 A group of kokeshi in traditional and modern styles
Credit: Okazaki Manami

it is soothing as it is something from nature, the wood was once a tree that was alive.'[3]

The history of kokeshi is sparsely documented, but the Iwamatsu Naosuke manuscript, an invaluable document from 1860, records the activities of woodworkers in the Sakunami district, Miyagi prefecture. This document by the woodworker Iwamatsu was passed down through the generations of his family and describes his professional activities, including the making of kokeshi. It is the first known written record of kokeshi and states that they were made in the region from the late Edo period. They were already commodified as goods sold by *kijishi* rather than simple domestic playthings, when the document was written.

During the Meiji era (1868–1912), when Japan underwent rapid industrialisation, mass-produced goods such as kitchenware and toys flourished. While the proliferation of celluloid and vinyl figures saw the demise of kokeshi as a children's doll, in the early twentieth century they acquired a new set of adult fans fuelled by an interest in folk crafts driven by the Mingei movement. Academics of the time such as Shibusawa Keizō (1896–1963), Arisaka Yotarō (1896–1955) and Yamanouchi Kinzaburō (1886–1966), who established Gohachi, a folk toy shop that opened in Ginza in 1937, espoused the beauty of Tōhoku's *getemono*, or utilitarian, unrefined items. The Mingei movement itself was 'radical, modern and progressive', and it was mostly educated urbanites who turned their gaze to Tōhoku and its wares.[4]

The Mingei movement founder Yanagi Sōetsu (1889–1961) and designer Serizawa Keisuke (1895–1984), alongside architect Bruno Taut (1880–1938) and Modernist designer Charlotte Perriand (1903–1999), visited the Tōhoku region multiple times to research the folk architecture and items used in daily life. As advocates, they also brought awareness of the cultural richness of Tōhoku, which was often 'regarded as a backward and marginal region', and promoted the notion that 'activities of the people and life in Tōhoku are connected to the present'.[5] Rather than being redundant, these European designers saw rural crafts as applicable to contemporary sensibilities and Japan's drive to modernise. Yanagi himself went to Tōhoku more than twenty times between 1927 and 1944; his trips fed into his work as a curator for major department stores such as Matsuzakaya and Takashimaya, which hosted exhibitions of folk craft. Although kokeshi were not a major part of Yanagi's (admittedly highly subjective) categorisation of 'Mingei', there is one doll in the collection he created for the Japanese Mingei Museum, a Zao kokeshi likely from the late nineteenth century, blackened with use and age. Yanagi was also employed by the Research Institute

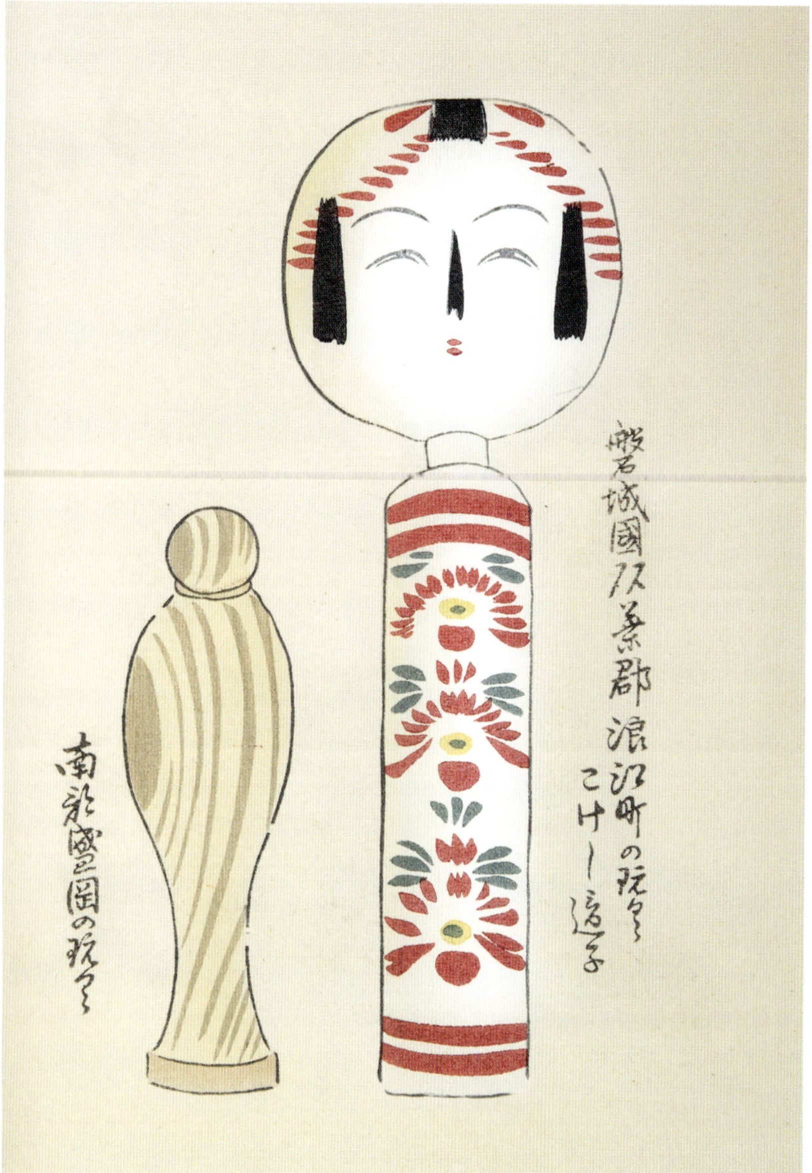

FIG 3 Kokeshi illustrated in *Unai no Tomo* [*A Child's Companion*] by Shimizu Seifū, 1891–1923 Credit: Metropolitan Museum of Art, New York

of Agrarian Economy in Snowbound Districts to research and host exhibitions of work produced in the region. Bruno Taut visited Tōhoku three times in the 1930s; the latter two of his visits are recorded in his memoir, *Nihonbi no Saihakken* (*Rediscovering the Beauty of Japan*).

In 1930 the illustrator Takei Takeo (1894–1983) published *Nihon Kyōdo Gangu* (*The Collection of Japanese Folk Toys*), in which he shared illustrations of his personal collection that he had amassed from individuals and shops around Japan. A hugely successful picture artist, printmaker and author, Takei was part of a children's culture movement during which many luminaries worked on books and art for children. Aimed at an adult audience, *The Collection of Japanese Folk Toys* was extremely popular and helped spark a highbrow interest in the subject. Many people interested in folk toys went on their own hunting expeditions around rural Japan, an activity that still continues today. Some of these aficionados become researchers, curators and authors creating self-published books in order to share their discoveries. This enthusiasm coalesced with urban communities of toy collectors who had created organisations as early as 1896 with the foundation of Shuko Kai. Established by one of the pioneers of anthropology in Japan, Tsuboi Shōgorō (1863–1913), a professor at the Imperial University of Tokyo, the association originally focused on archaeological artefacts and books. The group's interests broadened due to the influence of Shimizu Seifū (1851–1913), a famed folk toy researcher and collector whose publication *Unai no Tomo* (*A Child's Companion*) marked a seminal moment in the adult appreciation of traditional toys (fig. 3).

Thereafter Odomo Kai – a toy connoisseur's club celebrating *tomo* (companions or playfellows) – was formed in 1909 and Ningyo Ippin Kai (Rare Dolls Association) in 1911, as well as kokeshi organisations such as the Sendai Kokeshi Kai, established in 1923, and the Tokyo Kokeshi Friends Association in 1952. These communities were responsible for giving the wooden dolls the name 'kokeshi' in 1940; previously they were called a variety of disparate names, such as *kina kina*. They also hosted events and competitions, and evaluated items.

Inevitably as a result of these connoisseurial organisations rare and vintage kokeshi became more esteemed, and historical kokeshi were seen as aesthetically improving with time: the wood picks up a caramel patina and the green and yellow lines fade, leaving behind the red and black details, which gives the kokeshi a rustic, understated appearance. By the 1950s, kokeshi crafted by certain makers – such as Mori Hidetaro (1896–1986), an Aomori-based craftsman whose work was praised by Munakata Shikō (1903–1975), a woodblock artisan associated with the Mingei movement – became incredibly coveted (fig. 4).[6] In the post-war period, urban department stores hosted kokeshi events, and sold both new and high-priced vintage kokeshi. Kokeshi artisan Arakawa Yoichi (b.1938), based in Aizuwakamatsu, recalls his bewilderment when he first learnt about the concept of folk antiques and vintage collecting, calling it a 'weird world'; the urban concept of aged kokeshi as valued antiques is completely alien to the small-scale rural production that constitutes his livelihood.[7] Even now, Mori kokeshi are sought after by collectors and reach high prices – an example of the way in which many crafts we associate with Mingei are not made by anonymous craftsmen, but by named creators whom consumers actively seek out.

As the interest in these dolls began to boom, *kijishi* who made wooden domestic products such as trays and bowls slowly switched to making kokeshi as their main occupation. Tsuchiyu kokeshi artisan Watanabe Tadao (b.1938) describes the people who bought kokeshi as the same as 'scholars' who were 'drawn to the fact that they all had different faces and facial expressions. Suddenly, these kids' toys became something for urban intellectuals.'[8]

Following Japan's economic ascent and a subsequent spike in domestic travel in the 1960s, the middle class began to collect folk toys, alongside the intelligentsia. The concept of travel for pleasure started to spread from the early Shōwa period (1926–89). While travel was espoused as an 'alternative method for knowledge production and political education' by intellectuals such as the 'legendary traveler' folklorist Yanagita Kunio (1875–1962), it was the advent of transport infrastructure such as train lines to remote areas including Aomori and Naruko Onsen that saw these regions flourish as leisure-orientated spa destinations.[9] Kokeshi therefore became souvenirs for people on vacation, creating such demand that artisans' wives also started making kokeshi during busy periods.[10]

During this domestic travel boom, a completely separate type of kokeshi was born to cater to a growing market of middle-class tourists, that of *sosaku* or contemporary kokeshi. While they also originated in Tōhoku, being made by

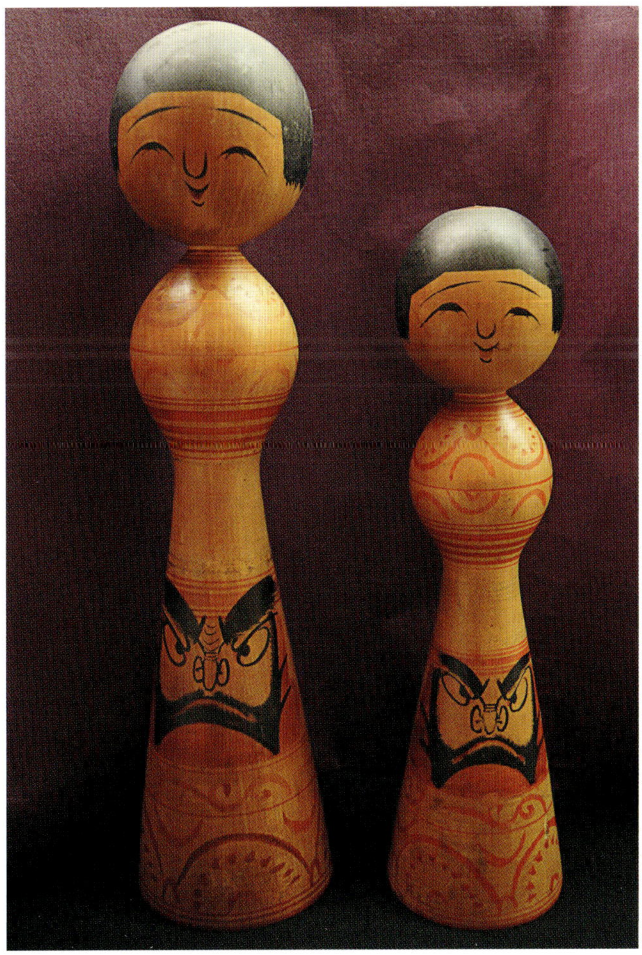

**FIG 4** Two kokeshi by Mori Hidetaro | Credit: Okazaki Manami

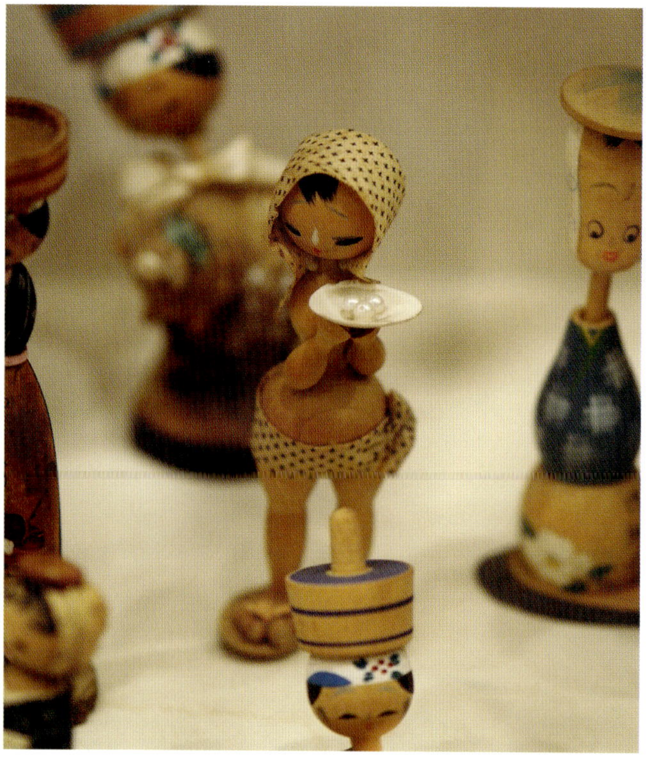

FIG 5 A souvenir kokeshi depicting a Mie prefecture *ama* pearl diver, Usaburo factory, Gunma Prefecture, 1960s | Credit: Okazaki Manami

woodworkers in Shiroishi in Miyagi prefecture, these new styles of kokeshi were unrelated to the traditional kinds. Rather than signifying Tōhoku, they had themes from across Japan, with dolls relating to nationwide attractions such as Tokyo Tower or *ama* pearl divers from Mie in central Honshu (fig. 5).

The huge popularity of *sosaku* kokeshi resulted in production being spread to other areas such as Gunma prefecture, just north of Tokyo. The region had an existing toy and woodworking industry so the infrastructure was already in place to make enormous quantities of kokeshi, completely overwhelming traditional kokeshi culture in terms of output. At the peak of kokeshi production in Gunma from the mid-1960s, there were more than 100 woodworking studios, many of which utilised a process of division of labour, rather than the traditional method by which the same artisan would cut the wood, turn the doll's shape and paint its decoration. These studios also employed traditional *nihonga* painters rather than those specifically trained in painting kokeshi. While quite charming in appearance, and crafted meticulously as the embellishments were decorated by classically trained painters, souvenir kokeshi often employ incredibly kitsch themes. The Usaburo factory in Gunma has a museum showcasing the dolls they made from the 1950s through to the 1970s, which range from Kyoto geisha to air stewardesses (fig. 6). Contemporary *shingata* (new form) kokeshi were akin to many of the food *meibutsu* (famed local products) that are 'central to the travel experience in contemporary Japan' and have become 'part of the national collective memory', though in fact they rarely had any authentic connection to the region.[11] Souvenirs such as wooden Ainu dolls in traditional dress were completely unrelated to indigenous Hokkaido culture and were made by woodworkers in Gunma.

From the later twentieth century, social changes in Japan led to the demise of kokeshi culture, in both traditional *dentō* and contemporary *sosaku* form. International travel became accessible to the masses, decreasing interest in the bucolic *onsen* villages in rural areas of Japan. Kokeshi became a thing of the past, while urban myths arose suggesting that they represent aborted children in their visual similarity to Buddhist *jizo*, small statues that protect the souls of unborn babies and children who have died before their parents, a confusion compounded by phonetic pronunciation: *ko* is a homonym of the Japanese for 'child', and *keshi* is a homonym of the word for 'erase'. Slowly, kokeshi fell out of popular culture.

In March 2011 the Tōhoku Earthquake triggered a devastating tsunami that hit the coast of Tōhoku. In the

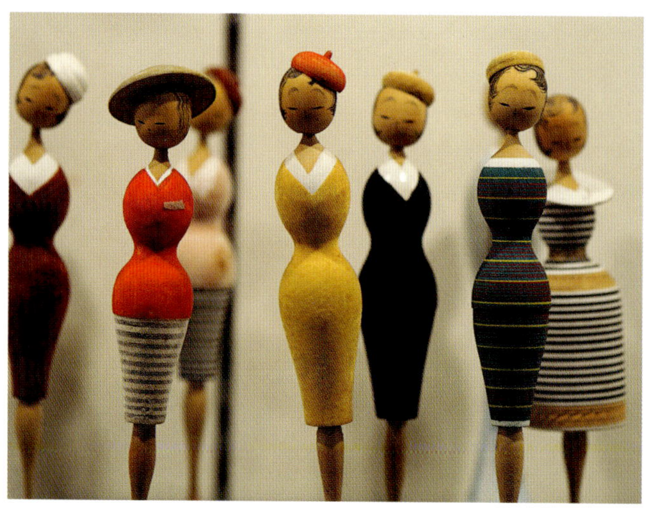

FIG 6 Stewardess kokeshi, Usaburo factory, Gunma Prefecture, 1960s–70s | Credit: Okazaki Manami

worst-affected prefectures of Iwate, Miyagi and Fukushima, more than 20,000 people died or are still missing. Rural *onsen* resort villages became refugee shelters of sorts, where people made homeless were relocated for months on end. The crafts of Tōhoku, including kokeshi, were suddenly back in the public eye as the media flocked to the region. Recovery efforts sought to promote regional products from the devastated area, and Tokyo art spaces such as Claska Hotel Gallery and Parco Museum held popular kokeshi shows. The architect Kuma Kengo (b.1954) worked on a kokeshi during the time, as did famed fashion designers Koshino Michiko (b.1943), Hiroko (b.1937) and Junko (b.1939).

Fennica, a folk craft shop that is part of the popular Tokyo lifestyle and fashion brand BEAMS, also made collaboration kokeshi as a way to promote local Miyagi prefecture crafts. Much like the Mingei pioneers, Fennica's then creative director and founder, Terry Ellis, placed emphasis on demonstrating how Mingei could be a part of modern living by publishing books with stylish interiors that featured traditional crafts. From 2014 Ellis produced several kokeshi projects, such as a Rastafari culture-themed kokeshi, and an indigo-coloured kokeshi crafted by artisan Satō Yasuhiro, dubbed the 'denim head' (fig. 7). The latter proved incredibly popular with fashionable young men interested in urban street culture – a demographic not hitherto associated with Mingei – who lined up for hours to purchase one. Beyond the appeal of BEAMS as a trendsetting brand, this interest in kokeshi spoke to a more general interest in crafts, particularly among socially conscious youth. In contrast to an oblique and anonymous factory process, the elemental craftsmanship and human connection of folk toys speaks to a desire to experience – however remotely – the comfort and quietude of manual skills. A video of Naruko Onsen kokeshi artisan Okazaki Yasuo (b.1935) working the lathe on the streaming service Vimeo has had more than 1.5 million views, with comments such as 'This is so calming and relaxing', 'hypnotizing' and 'satisfying'.[12] Young consumers find the notion of supporting local purveyors appealing, as well as the accessibility of the items' backstory – where they came from, how they were made and by whom (fig. 8).

While kokeshi are seen as exemplars of rustic minimalism for many fans, in reality, the aesthetic

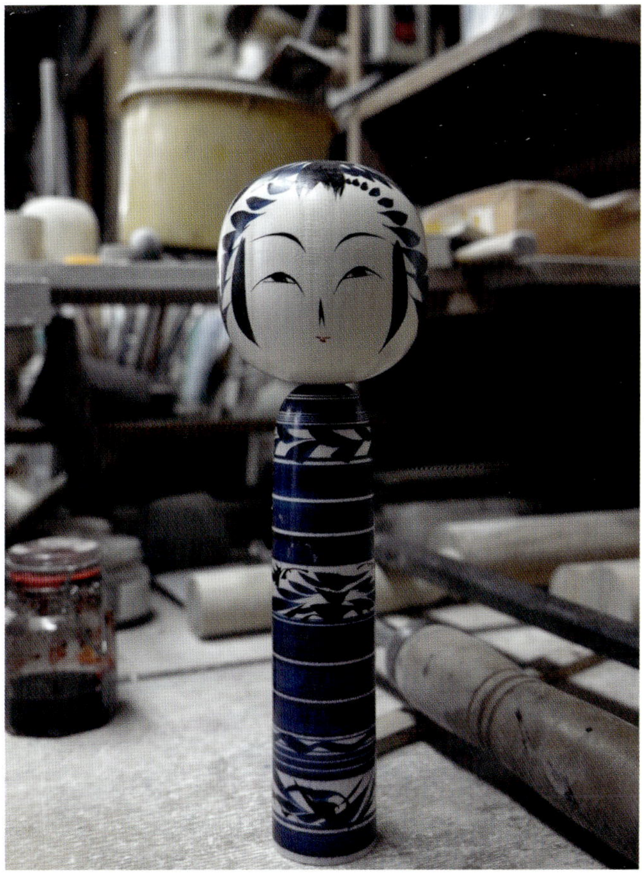

FIG 7 Fennica's indigo kokeshi, crafted by Satō Yasuhiro, 2014
Credit: Okazaki Manami

sensibility of *kawaii* is as prevalent in the kokeshi world as it is in mainstream popular culture. Roughly translating as 'cute', *kawaii* is a multi-faceted aesthetic quality that describes the physical traits of children and baby animals. *Kawaii* things are usually 'small, delicate, and immature', round in shape and pastel coloured.[13] The term itself was popularised by illustrator Naitō Rune (1932–2007) and describes affective things that are thought to 'produce positive feelings', such as adoration and love.[14] It is a ubiquitous pop cultural aesthetic, and as a design and art sensibility it crosses the gamut from anime and games to fashion and art.

*Kawaii* culture has been cultivated over the centuries by a wide range of creators and as an aesthetic it has been prevalent throughout history. *Chōjū-jinbutsu-giga*, four scrolls from the twelfth and thirteenth century, feature anthropomorphic frogs and rabbits that are *kawaii* even by today's standards. The Edo period (1603–1868) was rife with cute depictions. Fashionable *bijinga* woodblock

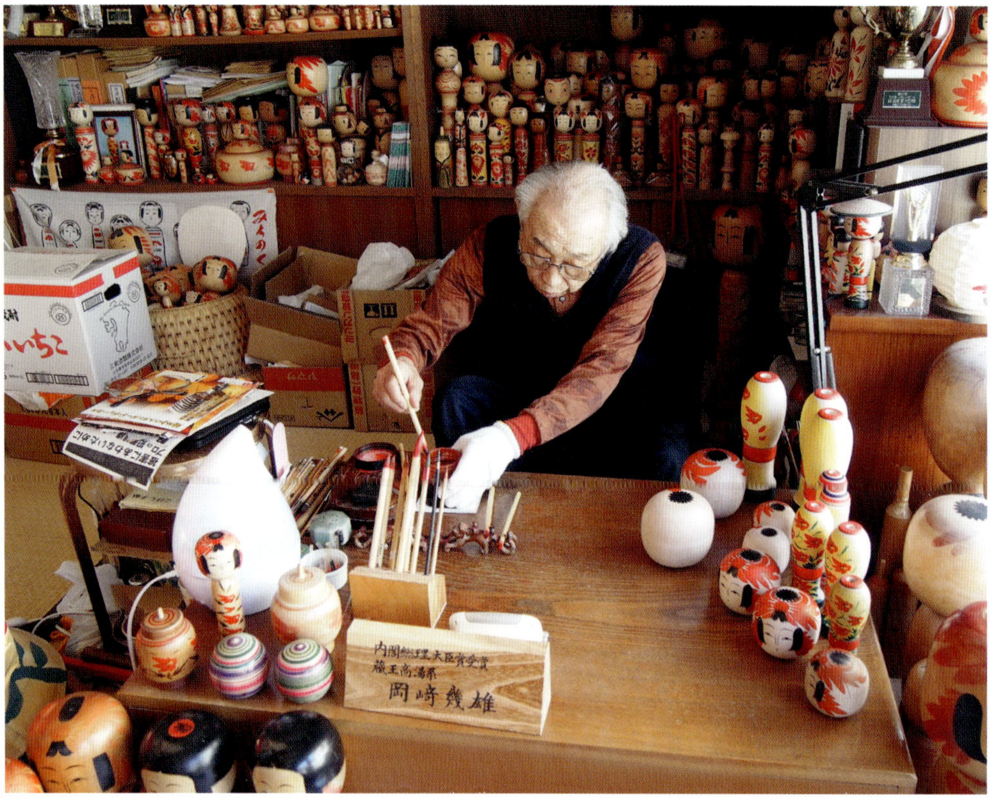

FIG 8 Zao-style kokeshi artisan Okazaki Ikuo paints the head of a large kokeshi doll in his studio at Zao Onsen, Yamagata prefecture
Credit: Okazaki Manami

prints illustrate stylish women wearing kimono, while other woodblock prints are laden with adorable cat protagonists.

Girls' illustrations, *shojo* (girls') manga and the merchandising of cute goods contributed to what is considered *kawaii* culture today. Nakamura Keiko, a curator at the Yayoi Yumeji Museum in Tokyo, considers 1914 to be the birth year of *kawaii* in Japan: that is when illustrator Takehisa Yumeji (1884–1934) opened his shop selling items such as stationery for educated girls. 'Takehisa placed importance on the cuteness of his designs and referred to them as *kawaii*. However, this is a rare example of the word being used at the time, as it wasn't a commonly used word, as it is now.'[15]

Around the time of the 'oil shock' (the 1973 Arab oil embargo), the manufacturing landscape transformed, as the escalating price of fuel caused Japanese producers to look towards the domestic market, rather than focusing on goods for export. The birth and subsequent success of Hello Kitty – an anthropomorphised white cartoon cat created by the entertainment goods company Sanrio – meant that cuteness became associated with far-reaching sales and spawned a culture in Japan where *kawaii* characters are emblazoned on everything from bank cards to police cars. In this context it is perhaps inevitable that *kawaii* culture would also impact kokeshi design. Many kokeshi (and folk toys more broadly) enthusiasts are those who embrace *kawaii* items in general. Kokeshi are often described as *shibu-kawaii* (subdued cute), and are part of a modern trend for Shōwa period nostalgic goods, cafés and retro travel spots. Yokoo Yukiko (b.1971), a gaming designer best known for *Taiko no Tatsujin*, an extremely *kawaii* taiko drumming game in which the drums sport cute faces, says, 'Kokeshi are really influential on me and I think they are the roots of *kawaii* design. The vague expressions mean people of any emotional state can feel close with these characters.'[16] In this way, kokeshi are similar to the mouthless Hello Kitty and many other popular characters who have ambiguous faces and thus offer a blank slate for people in need of empathy.

Since the 1960s, young people, rather than living with their extended family, have been far more likely to live in city apartments. Whereas in the past large kokeshi that were akin to wooden sculptures were popular, nowadays miniature types are the most common, simply because collectors do not have much living space. Browsing any

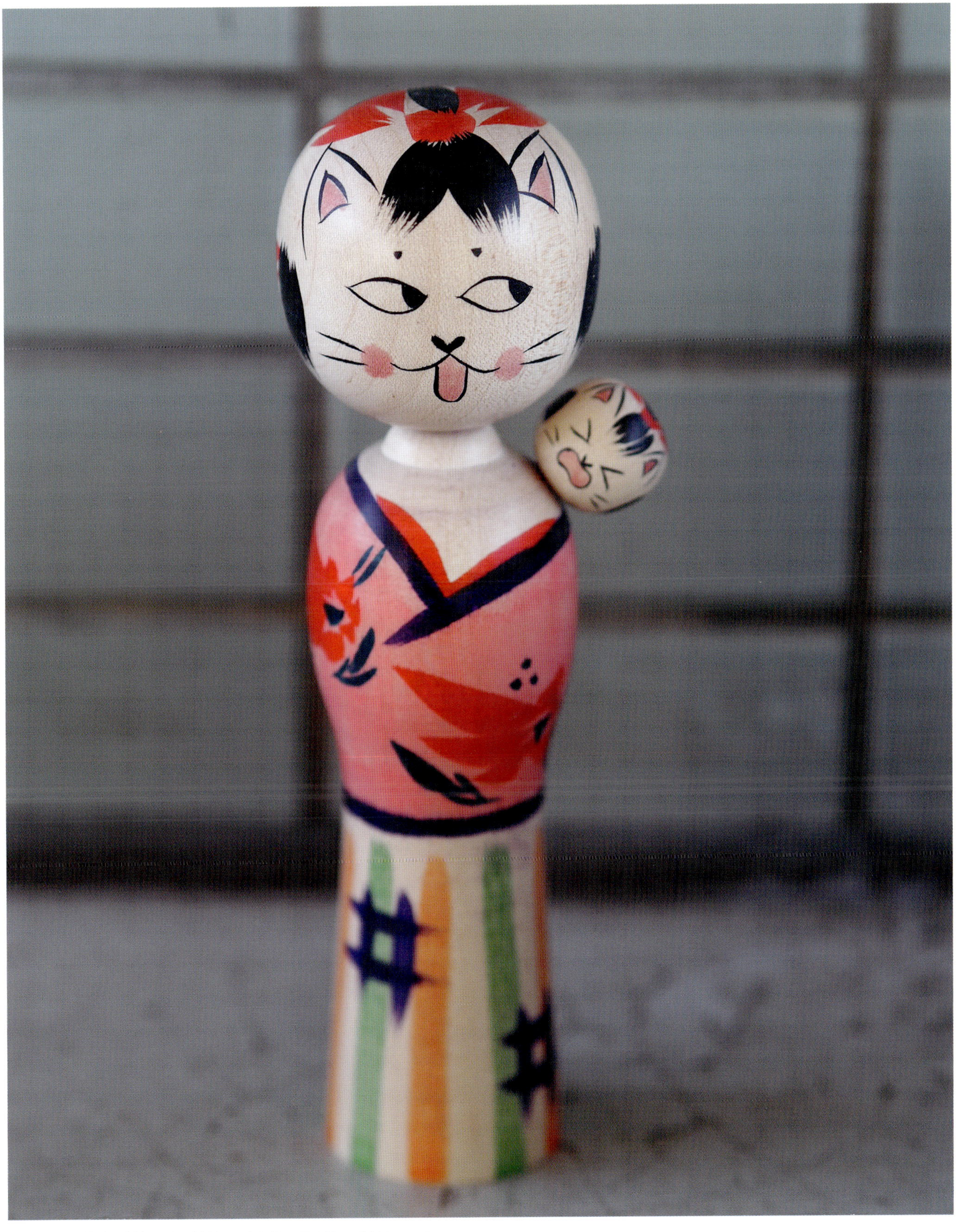

**FIG 9** Cat kokeshi by Umeki Naomi | Credit: Okazaki Manami

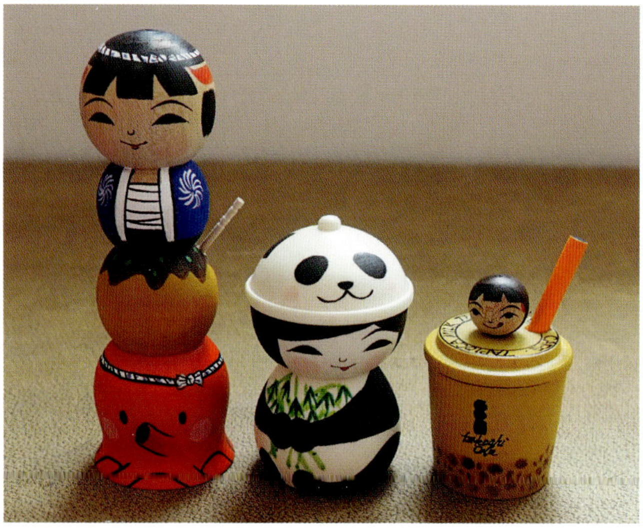

FIG 10 *Kawaii* kokeshi by Abo Masafumi | Credit: Okazaki Manami

kokeshi convention, it is apparent that almost all the kokeshi artisans make small, *kawaii* types to attract the largest current demographic of kokeshi fans – young to middle-aged females.

Dubbed *kokejo* (an elision of kokeshi and *joshi* – 'girl'), these women collect dolls by artisans such as Umeki Naomi (b.1968), known for her kokeshi cats (fig. 9), Hiraga Teruyuki (b.1972), who makes a variety of sweet dolls, such as those in the likeness of rainbow-coloured ice cream cones, and Abo Masafumi (b.1983), who makes shaved ice and pudding-shaped kokeshi, where the face emerges from the bowl of food (fig. 10). *Kokejo* also travel around Tōhoku, enjoying hot springs and hunting for rare kokeshi on the same trip, much like male Mingei enthusiasts did before them.

In broader pop culture, cute designer toys are also incredibly popular. Figures such as *sofubi* (soft vinyl) toys are trending among young people, with conventions such as Wonderfest – a semi-annual exhibition of models of anime, manga and video game characters – attended by more than 50,000 people. *Sofubi* are limited-edition collectible items and are made by artisans in small lots (albeit not with natural materials). Apart from the fact that toy collectors often buy both kokeshi and *sofubi*, the two genres overlap in numerous ways. Collectors use both *sofubi* and kokeshi as social media photo props, putting them in travel photos; another reason people prefer smaller kokeshi is that they are portable. As with all pop culture trends, showing off on the internet is now a part of kokeshi culture, and the hashtag #kokeshi has hundreds of thousands of results on Instagram.

Designer toy makers such as Katsumata Hideyuki (b.1974), Izumonster (b.1974) and Chiba Teresa (b.1980) make *sofubi* in the likeness of traditional folk toys such as kokeshi, *akabeko*, a talisman cow from Aizu, and *daruma*, a roly-poly doll based on the likeness of Bodhidharma, the founder of Zen Buddhism (fig. 11). Chiba says that *sofubi* are similar to folk toys in that there is an 'aesthetic looseness. For example, *inuhariko* [a talisman dog made of paper mâché] does not really look like a dog. *Akabeko* is bright red and looks so absent-minded.'[17] Both Chiba and Katsumata suggest that toy culture developed in Japan due to the Shinto culture of animism: the belief that everything has a soul lends itself to a spiritual identification with these seemingly inanimate objects.

*Sofubi* makers themselves consider their production process a form of craftsmanship. Chiba says, 'As an artist who produces things, I want to make things locally in Japan and communicate directly with artisans. This narrative is important. Things like capsule toys are made in China because they are just a mass-produced product.'[18] Katsumata adds, 'With toy culture, as a design or decorative form of art, the product itself is superior, they are made really well.'[19] Fans often refer to *sofubi* as 'neo folk toys', and see collecting designer figures as a contemporary extension of going on pilgrimages to find rare folk toys.

Kokeshi, particularly the kitsch types, are also one of the most popular souvenirs for international tourists visiting Japan. In fact, the easiest place to find them outside the production bases themselves are the shops at Tokyo's international airports, Narita and Haneda, as well as in areas heavily populated by tourists, such as Nakamise street in Asakusa.

Usaburo is still the most popular *sosaku* kokeshi maker and the only company making kokeshi on a mass scale, although it continues to use local wood types, found in the mountainous regions of Gunma. Usaburo's output capacity is 15,000 dolls a month using specifically designed machinery, including a laser-cutting machine for the details; the firm also uses a handheld lathe for some of its products (fig. 12). Usaburo started to focus predominantly on international tourists in the 1990s, when the initial drop in kokeshi popularity after the bubble era coincided with Japan's ascent as a tourist destination. Seizing that opportunity, they made kokeshi with designs that capitalise on clichés such as a round face with bobbed black hair, slender eyes and kimono with cherry blossoms. Usaburo also collaborated with one of Japan's best-known contemporary artists, Murakami Takashi (b.1962), who made a kokeshi with Murakami's famous flower designs alongside a smiling Mount Fuji, which came with an $800 price tag. While Usaburo's dolls appear to be a manifestation of Orientalist tropes in wooden form (ninja, samurai and geisha galore), made specifically for tourists, they are in fact an extension of the souvenir kokeshi designs the company made in the 1960s and 1970s for Japanese domestic travellers.

While Yanagi might consider recently popular forms of kokeshi as succumbing to 'bad taste, overburdened with needless decoration and meaningless frivolity',[20] today's reality is that most folk toy makers are adopting a strategy in order to survive, and their products are anything but meaningless. Daruma Land, in Shirakawa, Fukushima, is a *daruma* entertainment facility where papier mâché dolls are made into every iteration possible, such as in the likeness of bowls of ramen. *Akabeko* cows are café au lait-themed. Sasano *ittōbori* craftsmen carve incredibly cute, rotund puppies and Seto artisans make an overwhelming amount of *kawaii* cat figurines doing things like taking a bath. Even *wara* straw craftsmen in remote villages in Nagano make cat-shaped ornaments rather than their traditional protective amulets that are meant to invoke

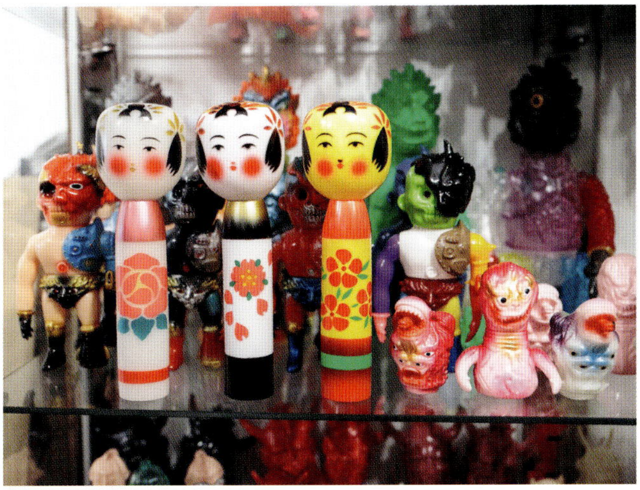

**FIG 11** Kokeshi *sofubi* by Izumonster | Credit: Okazaki Manami

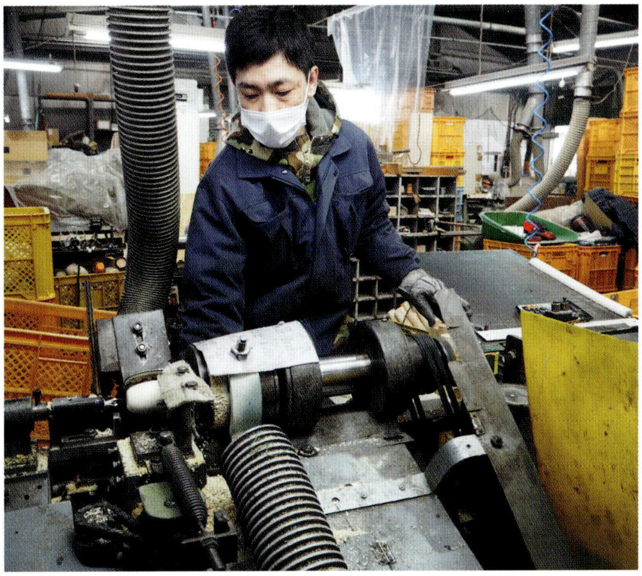

**FIG 12** Usaburo use a number of custom-made machines to produce dolls | Credit: Okazaki Manami

the gods. While artisans make these accessible types out of necessity, many admit that they hope the consumers of their new products will become interested in traditional wares as well. It is not an exaggeration to say that many Mingei artisans are in fact living off *kawaii* kitsch, yet nonetheless, their meticulous craft skills remain. The cat kokeshi of Umeki Naomi (b.1968), while painted in shocking pink hues, are also embellished with traditional Zao motifs, such as chrysanthemums on the torso that resemble firework blooms, and sophisticated flourishes on the head. While the cats are irresistibly *kawaii*, there is no doubt Umeki is a master craftsperson: her brushwork is elegant and, having trained under her father, Umeki Shūichi (b.1929), she has an eye for composition and balanced works.

While other types of folk craft are nearing extinction, kokeshi remain perennially popular, riding waves of both Mingei and kitsch with apparent ease, and this flexibility and adaptability has meant that they have remained relevant. While there is a demographic of kokeshi lovers who enjoy the classic, subdued types of kokeshi that comply with Yanagi's aesthetic ideals that 'reject technical ostentation in favor of a more restrained and robust aesthetic',[21] the humble kokeshi doll has in fact always oscillated between Mingei and kitsch. In straddling both worlds, they have managed not just to survive the tides of time, but to thrive.

## NOTES

1. Livingstone 2008, 242.
2. Thielemans 2015, 1.
3. Interview with Shiratori Yasuko conducted by the author, 2019.
4. Livingstone 2008, 249.
5. *Eyes on Tōhoku* 2022, Introduction.
6. A video of Mori making kokeshi is available online at https://www.youtube.com/watch?v=mvKFjeX4ERw (accessed 31 July 2023).
7. Interview with Arakawa Yoichi conducted by the author, 2019.
8. Interview with Watanabe Tadao conducted by the author , 2012.
9. Kojima 2011, vii, 20.
10. Prior to this, women did not make kokeshi as they were part of the male-dominated world of woodworking. Today, however, some of the most successful kokeshi artisans are women.
11. The phenomenon of fabricated *meibutsu* is described in Cwiertka 2020.
12. https://vimeo.com/79369173 (accessed 31 July 2023).
13. Burdelski and Mitsuhashi 2010, 65.
14. Nittono et al 2012, 1.
15. Interview with Nakamura Keiko conducted by the author, 2012.
16. Interview with Yokoo Yukiko conducted by the author, 2012.
17. Interview with Chiba Teresa conducted by the author, 2022.
18. Ibid.
19. Interview with Katsumata Hideyuki by the author, 2022.
20. Yanagi 2018, 5.
21. Faulkner in Livingstone 2008, 255.

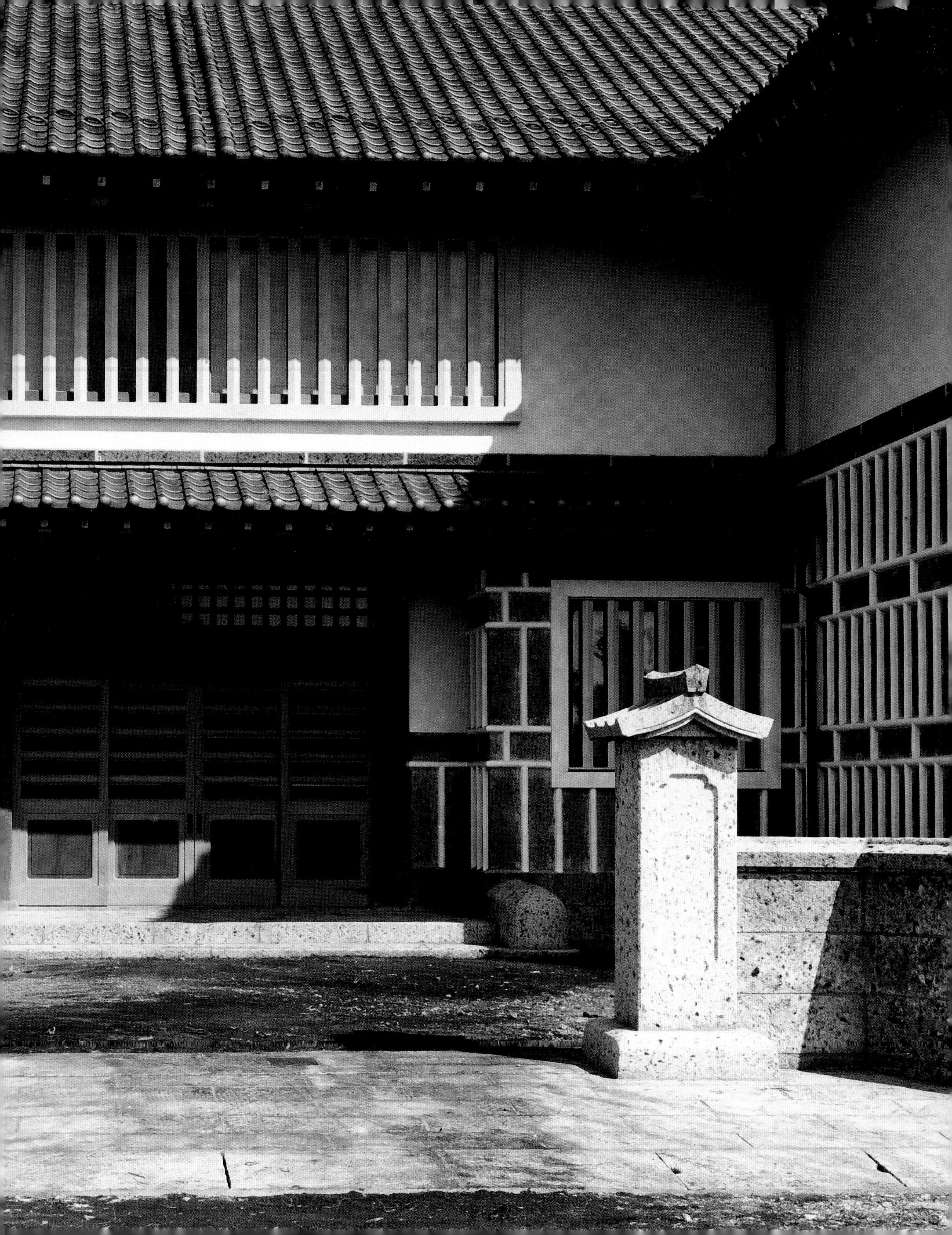

SAM THORNE

# Objects on Display

## Mingei, museums and department stores

In Yanagi Sōetsu's 1947 essay 'The Japan Folk Crafts Museum', he recounts the genesis of the institution that he had co-founded a decade before.[1] This telling is one among several of how the Japan Folk Crafts Museum, or the Mingeikan, came into being. The setting is rural, wintry, suggestively secluded. It is January 1926, and Yanagi – accompanied by a group of friends – is spending a night on the slopes of Mount Koya, reached via the ancient pilgrimage routes that crisscross Wakayama prefecture. These comrades had been drawn together, Yanagi writes, by a shared sense of finding 'incomparable beauty in myriad things that had previously been ignored ... What we were strongly drawn to were the utilitarian things that were generally overlooked in the hustle and bustle of daily life.'[2] It was here, he claims, that he had an epiphany. Just a few months later, Yanagi would publish 'Prospectus for the Establishment of a Mingei Art Museum', the pamphlet-manifesto often said to mark the beginning of the Mingei movement.

The Mount Koya episode is a keystone in the Mingeikan's origin story. Its remote location, some 350 miles south-west of Tokyo, is part of its rhetorical potency: it is set at a distance – aesthetically as well as geographically – from the imperial metropole.

Yet as Mingei grew in public visibility in the decade that followed, West Honshu and Tokyo continued to be intertwined in a multitude of ways. A year and a half after Yanagi and his associates were travelling through Wakayama, they held their first folk crafts exhibition in Japan, gathering together works by anonymous craftspeople, which they had been busily collecting from around the country. But this presentation was neither in some bucolic idyll nor in a gallery, but in the commercial heart of Tokyo, 'on the top floor of the Kyūkyodō speciality store in Ginza.'[3] How did presentations such as these lay the ground for the Mingeikan? More broadly, what were the relations between the display strategies developed during the interwar period – across an 'exhibitionary complex'[4] of department stores, boutiques and trade fairs – and emergent approaches to museum design?

Following that inaugural display in Ginza, Yanagi and his collaborators went on to organise a series of exhibitions in department stores across Tokyo, Kyoto and Osaka.[5] Their promotional activities were dependent upon a wide-ranging social network, as well as the support of major publications and corporations. For example, a number of department-store displays were enabled by sponsorship from the likes of the *Osaka Mainichi* newspaper and the cosmetics retailer Shiseido.[6]

Over the course of several years, their efforts began to pay off, as Mingei gained increasing public recognition and popularity. The affordable and decorative wares of rural artists became fashionable with metropolitan and suburban elites as well as with the bourgeoisie.

A number of these exhibitions were installed in the Nihombashi Takashimaya department store in Tokyo, whose general director was a friend of the Mingei potter Kawai Kanjirō (1890–1966).[7] When Takashimaya opened in 1933, its air-conditioned building was seen as the height of early Showa-period sophistication (fig. 1). Takashimaya's sales strategy was to install home furnishings and household items in carefully staged 'model rooms'.[8] In 1934, Bernard Leach – who had recently returned to Japan after a 14-year absence – was invited to organise a week-long 'model room' exhibition there.[9] Leach had been documenting his travels with a 16mm camera, and made a short film documenting the display. In the somewhat wobbly handheld footage, we see vases of flowers and fans; a dish and a paper lamp; and fabric draped casually over the back of a wooden chair, while clothes made from bark and grass hang from the ceiling. The atmosphere is homely but also sparse, almost spartan, notably less cluttered than Takashimaya's typical display.

This is a reconstruction of rural living transposed to an urban context, a facsimile of a traditional space installed in a Tokyo department store that had only been open for a year. There was a clearly didactic intent to these 'model rooms', as assembled by Yanagi, Leach and Kawai. A hybrid of a show home and history lesson (or what we might think of today as a mood board), their educational purpose was to introduce potential customers to how these long-neglected wares might be used or displayed in their own homes. Provenance was always insisted on. In one installation shot, we can see a large wall-mounted map of the Japanese archipelago (notably excluding Hokkaido and Okinawa). To give an overview of this presentation's regional diversity, strings and ribbons connect particular regions to specific objects or vessels (fig. 2).[10] The metropolitan site of display and the rural site of origin have, commercially and even literally, become entangled.

In parallel with these department-store displays, the early 1930s also saw the emergence of several dedicated Mingei shops across Tokyo. The short-lived Mizusawa opened in 1931, followed by Minatoya later that year. Both were firmly within Yanagi's social and aesthetic orbit, being regular advertisers in *Kōgei* (*Crafts*, 1931–41), the monthly publication that he co-founded at the beginning of that year. The most significant of these new shops, however, was Takumi, which opened its doors in Ginza in 1933,[11] still three years before the opening of the Japan Folk Crafts Museum. A few months later, Takumi's upper floor was converted into a dedicated gallery space, showing wares including handmade *washi*, textiles by Serizawa Keisuke (1895–1984), and potters such as Leach and Funaki Michitada (1900–1963).[12] Takumi was to become

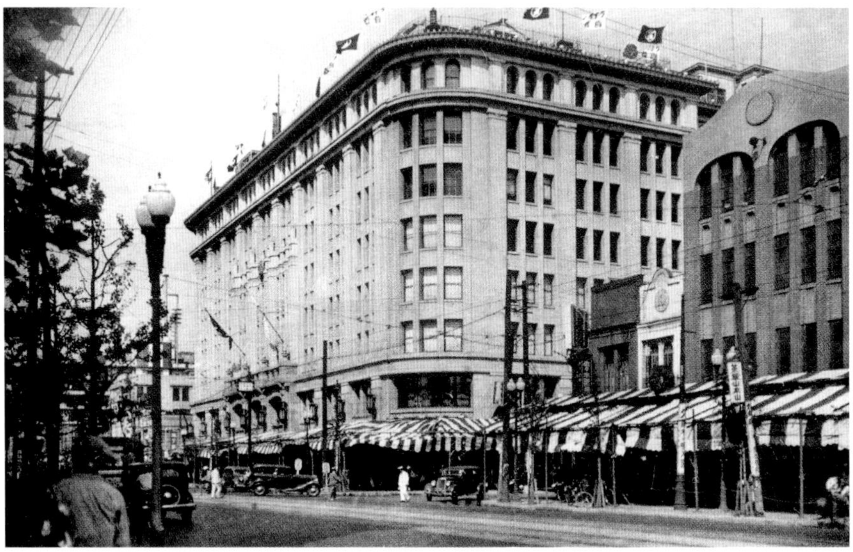

**FIG 1** Takashimaya Department Store, c.1940
Credit: From the collection of Steve Sundberg, OldTokyo.com

FIG 2 Map showing places of origin of Mingei objects on display at Takashimaya Department Store, 1934
Credit: Courtesy of the Mingei Film Archive Project/Marty Gross Film Productions Inc.

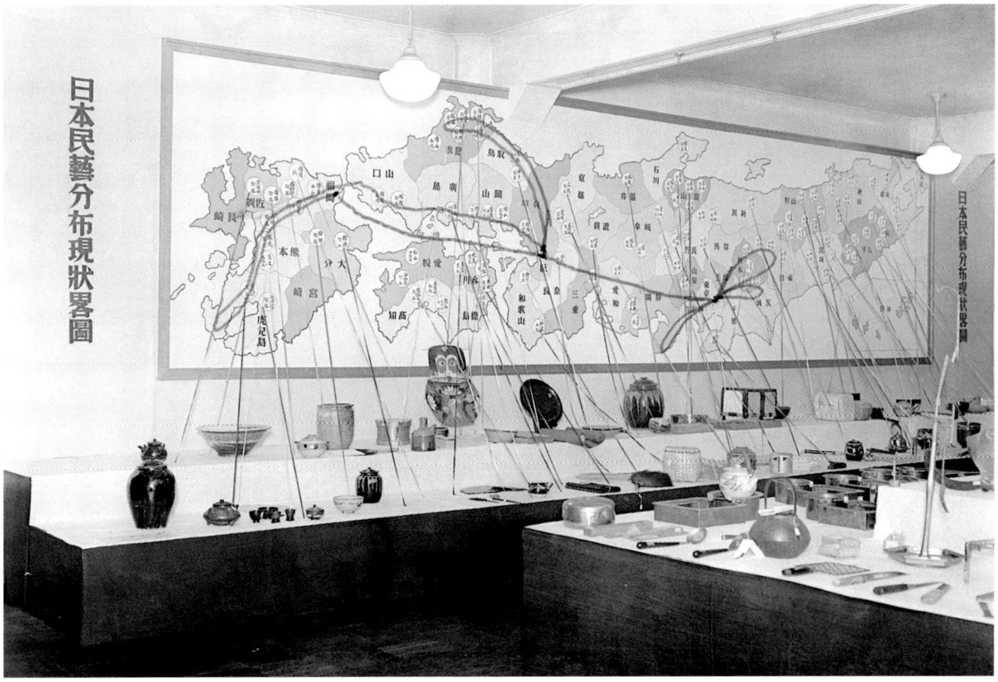


the official outlet for the Mingei movement, akin to a satellite museum shop for a museum that had yet to be built (fig. 3).

This was in fact Takumi's second branch, the first having been established a year earlier in Tottori prefecture, West Honshu, by Yoshida Shōya (1898–1972), a physician and folk arts advocate. Yoshida was a keen follower of Yanagi, and had made his acquaintance in early 1931, when Yanagi and friends visited the area (later that year, a special edition of *Kōgei* was dedicated to the crafts of the region). Yoshida had begun to work directly with local producers, supervising their work and giving them models to follow.[13]
To some extent, this strategy precipitated the Mingei movement's move from an essentially antiquarian endeavour, sourcing and selecting pre-modern crafts and curios, towards specially commissioning new products. Yoshida clearly understood the potential of expanding his enterprise from Tottori to Ginza. As the designer Jasper Morrison has written, his ambition was 'to establish a shop in the city to promote and sell Japanese rural crafts to sophisticated Tokyoites in order to make people aware of the quality and beauty of such goods'.[14]

Yanagi dedicated an article in *Kōgei* to the opening of Takumi's Ginza branch. In this piece, he strikes a cautionary, even pious note of censure: 'Business is connected to worldly matters in many ways, and it is dangerous for scholars and hobbyists to engage in.' This position may have been surprising to readers who had visited the department-store presentations that Yanagi had been involving himself with in recent months. Perhaps this is why he quickly shifts to a more accommodating tone: 'It is important to widely introduce proper utilitarian objects into the ordinary household. This store is to bear the role of bridge builder; and therefore, it will focus not on what will sell, but on what is authentic.'[15]

The saleable and the authentic were not, in the end, mutually exclusive. Indeed, what was sold in these first Mingei shops was marketed according to a nebulously defined idea of authenticity, with rural provenance acting as guarantor. The products at Takumi included men's clothing and accessories, such as hand-woven neckties, which proved particularly popular, alongside Panama hats and walking canes. Smaller objects, such as bookends and inkstands, were intended for home display in studies, while women's clothing included straw handbags, shawls and *obi* (kimono sashes). It could be said that, without the spaces of Takumi and Takashimaya, the passion for folk crafts may well never have reached much beyond Yanagi's own circle of middle-class intellectuals.[16]

In 1935, Yanagi and his group finally found a patron who could support their decade-long dream of establishing a Folk Crafts Museum in Tokyo (fig. 4). The businessman

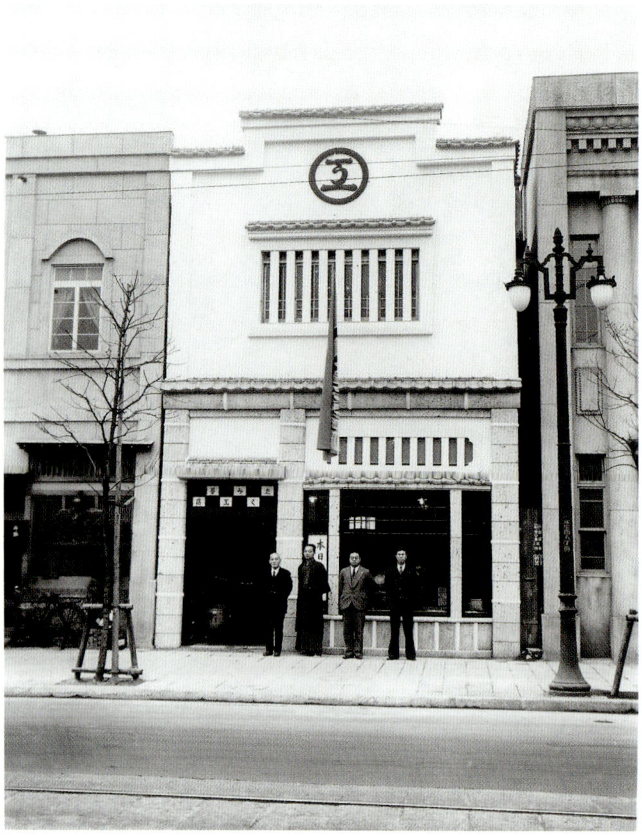

FIG 3 Takumi Folk Crafts Shop, Ginza, 1933, Tottori Folk Crafts Museum

and philanthropist Ōhara Magosaburō (1880–1943), who in 1930 had founded the Ōhara Museum of Art in Kurashiki, the first museum of Western art in Japan, offered to cover the costs of the construction, and a site in the affluent suburb of Meguro was identified. When the Mingeikan opened its doors to the public in late 1936, it encompassed 14 rooms and eight alcoves, with lighting provided through sliding paper screens. At the heart of the collection were the examples of folk art found and purchased by Yanagi and his associates on their excursions around Japan.

During the museum's first decade, its temporary exhibitions were wide-ranging in terms of geography: handicrafts from Korea and Okinawa; *akae* porcelain; Ainu works from Hokkaido. It was not long before these presentations developed a more commercial logic. Within a year of opening, Yanagi announced in the pages of *Kōgei* that the Mingeikan would present twice-yearly selling shows. He clearly appreciated the role of these commercial presentations and Takumi itself as critical to cultivating a broader – not to mention more commercially dependable – audience of informed consumers. The inaugural issue of *Gekkan Mingei* (*Folk Crafts Monthly*), in April 1939, included an illustration of a three-branched 'Tree of Mingei' (fig. 5). This triumvirate comprised a museum, a publishing house and a shop, Takumi. Indeed, Takumi would coordinate its displays and advertising with Mingeikan exhibitions, just as it did with selling shows in department stores.[17]

Throughout Yanagi's 1947 essay on the formation of the Mingeikan, he attempts to delineate the terms and priorities of institutional presentation versus commercial display, disentangling the museum from the store. He stakes a claim for rigorous selection, sharpened by didactic purpose. At one point, he states, 'Our museum is not simply a place for putting objects on display.'[18] There is nothing simple about putting objects on display, of course, as Yanagi was well aware; in Europe and North America, many of the most influential curators and museum directors of his generation were engaged with questioning conventional modes of display and spectatorship.[19] That said, Yanagi's essay pays curiously little attention to the actual design of the Mingeikan's spaces or to the conditions of its display. His remarks are limited to the penultimate paragraph, and remain vague, saying little more than that this should be done with care, that display shapes a work's reception, that light and backdrop should be considered. He goes on to conclude: 'The way objects are arrayed is an art in its own right, and I would like to see our museum come to be viewed as a work of art.'

Yanagi's essay implicitly recognises that the exhibitionary logic and spatial practices of museums and commercial retail spaces have close associations. (Indeed, as the anthropologist Yamaguchi Masao has noted, toy shops – rather than museums – 'may have been one of the first spaces of exhibition many of us encountered'.)[20] Writing contemporaneously with Yanagi, Walter Benjamin argued:

> There is a relationship between the department store and the museum ... The massing of artworks in the museum moves them closer to the character of commodities, which, where they are offered en masse to the passer-by, arouse the idea that a share in them must be his due.[21]

Central to this reading, modernity was synonymous with a new way of seeing, a revisioning of vision itself, which was manifested in the museum and the department store as much as in the casino and the garden.

The world's first modern department store opened in Paris in 1852, when a textile merchant named Aristide Boucicaut (1810–1877) gathered together a multitude of shops under one roof. (This was a year after the Great Exhibition in London, which itself birthed what became the Victoria and Albert Museum.) Named Le Bon Marché, this was followed a decade later by *grands magasins* such as La Samaritaine and Au Printemps. The modes of display and consumption in these new emporiums are compellingly evoked in an 1893 woodcut by the Swiss painter Félix Vallotton (1865–1925) titled *Le Bon Marché* (fig. 6).[22] Consumers, sellers and products have become pleasurably entangled, wrapped together by skeins of lush fabric. It is a chaotic portrait of commodity fetishism as a form of collective seduction, even eroticism.

Both in Japan and beyond, the first decades of the twentieth century saw significant shifts in approaches to display and circulation. The crowded presentations of mid-nineteenth-century department stores such as Le Bon Marché, not to mention imperial world's fairs, became less dense, less cacophonous. Just as the imagined community of the urban crowd began to be replaced by the more sharply defined figure of the viewer-consumer (each with their own individuated desires), cluttered displays gave way to more precise arrangements. In both

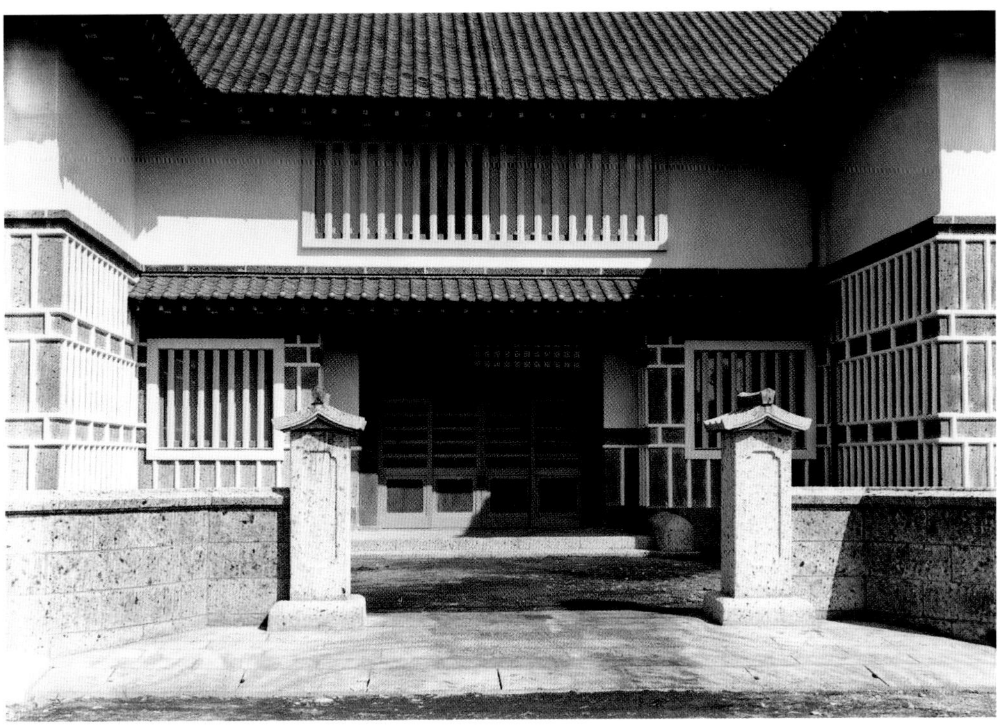

**FIG 4** Japan Folk Crafts Museum (Nihon Mingeikan), 1936, Japanese Folk Crafts Museum

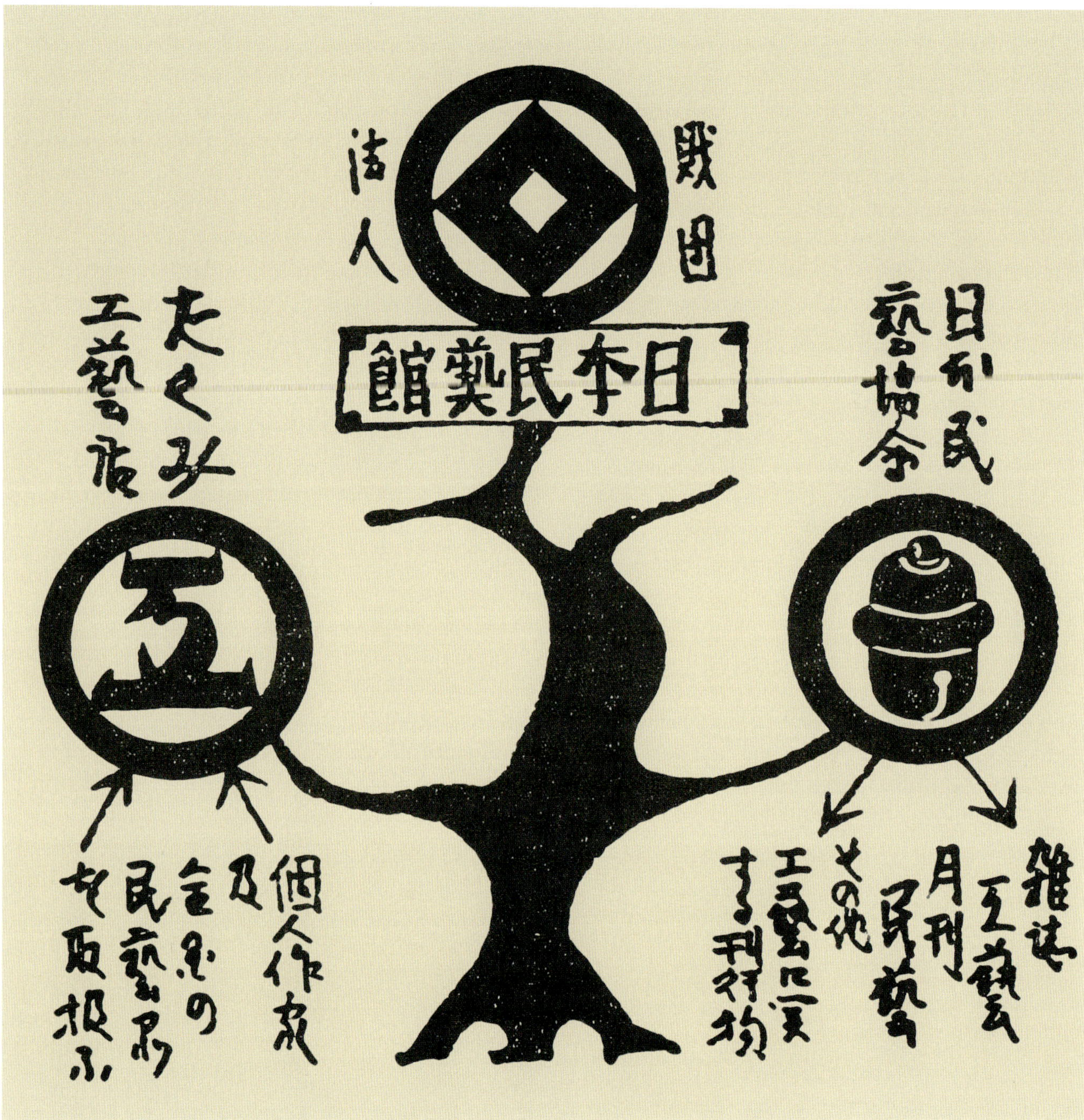


**FIG 5** 'The Tree of Mingei', *Gekkan Mingei* [*Folk Crafts Monthly*], 1939, Japanese Folk Crafts Museum

FIG 6 Félix Vallotton, *Le Bon Marché*, woodcut, 1893, Credit: Musées d'Art et d'Histoire, Ville de Genève

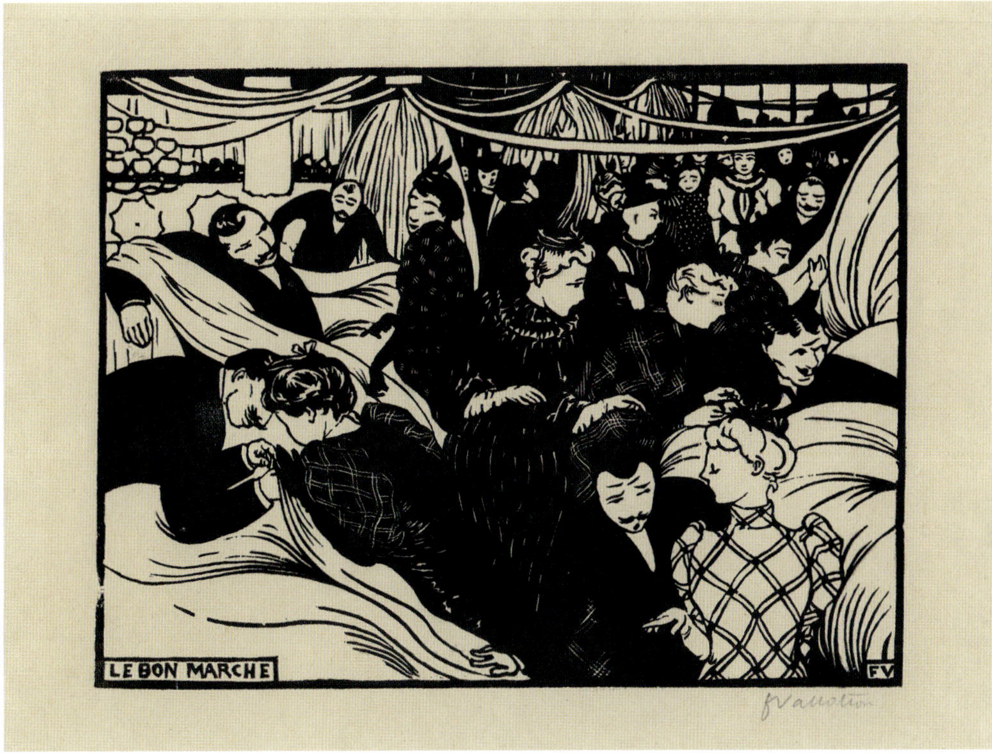


the department store and the museum, this period saw an increasing distance between objects and images on display.[23] Whether intended for contemplation or purchase, commodities and artworks were increasingly presented not in configurations but individually, against either monochrome or graphic backdrops.

In many exhibition histories of the last two decades, it has become familiar for museums and commercial spaces to be interpreted as being in conversation or competition.[24] During the 1920s and 30s in Europe and the United States, where this phenomenon was most advanced, the attraction between museum and department store was very much mutual. Many émigré artists and architects associated with breakthroughs in exhibition design found work in department stores. For example, in London, the former Bauhaus master László Moholy-Nagy (1895–1946) developed marketing materials and displays for Simpsons of Piccadilly (fig. 7),[25] which opened in 1936, the same year that Salvador Dalí (1904–1989) could be found dreaming up window arrangements for the Bonwit Teller department store in New York. In 1930, the architect Frederick Kiesler (1890–1965) published *Contemporary Art Applied to the Store in Its Display*, a treatise on circulation and flow, in which he argued that the department store was the agent responsible for introducing a reluctant American public to modernism.

In 1927, the same year as the first Mingei exhibition in Tokyo, the Metropolitan Museum of Art in New York collaborated with Macy's department store on a series of exhibitions spanning both venues, titled 'Art-in-Trade'.[26] These presentations saw contemporary rooms installed and furnished by designers, with each edition visited by up to 250,000 people. Also in 1927, Alfred H. Barr, Jr – the founding director of MoMA, the Museum of Modern Art in New York, which opened in 1929[27] – contributed a regular 'Modern Art Questionnaire' to *Vanity Fair*. This quiz posed the question, 'What is the significance of each of the following in relation to modern artistic expression?'[28] Among the 50 prompts were Saks Fifth Avenue and Alexander Archipenko (1887–1964), the Soviet émigré artist who two years later would actually install one of his own sculptures in the window of Saks. A decade on, in 1939, when MoMA inaugurated its new home, its revolving doors, reception desk, terrazzo flooring and marble-clad elevators struck some observers as resembling nothing so much as a department store.[29]

In the two decades after the war, innovations in display largely shifted from the site of the department store to an

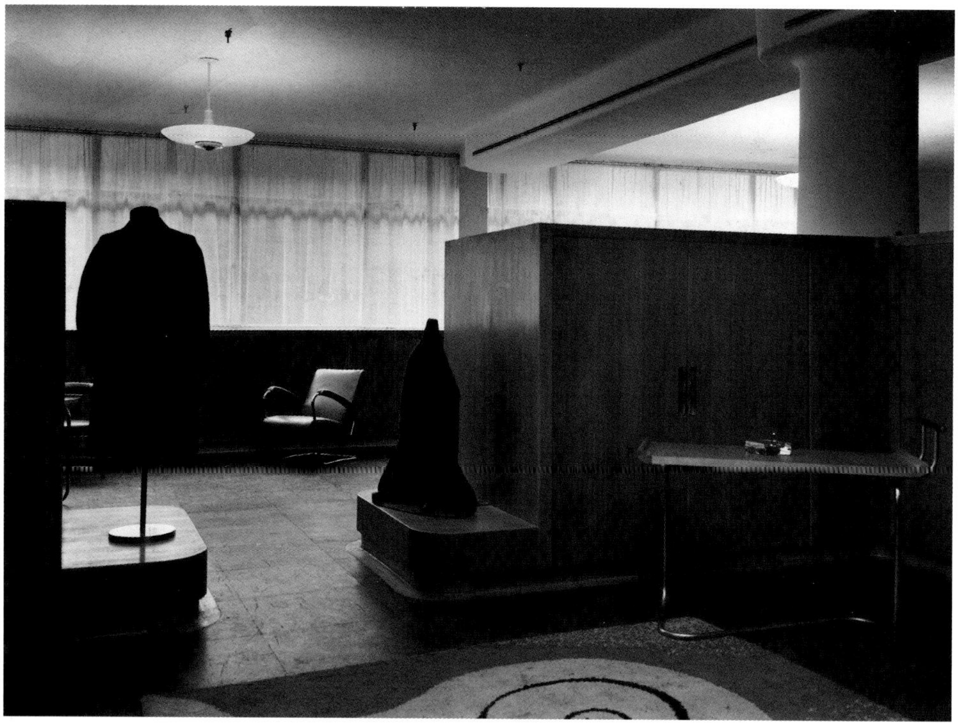

FIG 7 Display designed by László Moholy-Nagy for Simpsons of Piccadilly, 1936 Credit: Architectural Press Archive/RIBA Collections

international circuit of expos and trade fairs, enabled by a combination of corporate and state support.[30] In 1957, Japan's inaugural presentation at the XI Triennale di Milano was titled 'Traditional and Modern Ceramics'. Designed by Sakakura Junzō (1901–1969) and Seike Kiyoshi (1918–2005), the display juxtaposed handmade ceramics with mass-produced goods, shown on cypress tables in a low-lit space resembling a traditional Japanese garden, complete with a tiled walkway.[31] This approach was also evident in another display of 1957, the Japanese government's stand at the First United States World Trade Fair, hosted in the New York Coliseum. Ceramics and wicker baskets were displayed on ankle-height tables and in open-frame lacquer showcases; a suspended ceiling was made from *shōji* sliding doors. While there is clearly a genealogical link to the Mingei 'model rooms' that Yanagi and others were installing in Takashimaya two decades before, the context is markedly international. Those display strategies refined in Tokyo's shops, department stores and museums had been thoroughly absorbed into how a resurgent Japan – newly pacifist and no longer occupied – was now selling itself on the world stage: as a home of traditional craft skills but also modern, industrially competitive and outward-facing.

The proximity between consumerism and museums reached its zenith at the turn of the millennium. In 2001, architect Rem Koolhaas (b.1944) published a notably ambiguous critique of this relationship, titled *Harvard Design School Guide to Shopping*. At the same time, many architects of Koolhaas's generation, best known for their museums, were also commissioned by high-end fashion retailers to design boutiques and department stores. This can be seen by walking through the high-end retail district of Omotesandō in Tokyo. You will see SunnyHills by Kuma Kengo (who designed the nearby Nezu Museum, among many others), the Dior Building by SANAA (architects of the 21st Century Museum of Contemporary Art, Kanazawa), buildings for Prada and Miu Miu by Herzog & de Meuron (fig. 8) and the AO Building by Nihon Sekkei (architects of the Ghibli Museum), among many others.

Reflecting on the history of design exhibitions, MoMA's senior curator of architecture and design, Paola Antonelli (b.1963), has noted that curators 'have to make sure that the context is not a shopping context . . . What I usually try to do is to set up a really amazing scenography so people can distinguish between a museum and a trade fair or a normal store.'[34] However, a trade fair or 'normal store' aesthetic permeated many exhibitions of art and design at the turn of the twenty-first century (also the last period before shopping moved online, with the high street usurped by out-of-town logistics centres). Indeed, this tendency can be observed in a number of Antonelli's own exhibitions of the early 2000s. *Humble Masterpieces* (2004) brought together 120 affordable objects, from Post-its and white T-shirts to scissors and Frisbees. Another of Antonelli's exhibitions was titled *Workspheres* (2001), and examined the changing nature of the workplace, by way of contemporary designers such as Fukasawa Naoto (b.1956), who would go on to become closely associated with the Japanese retail company Muji.

Muji was founded in 1980, its name a contraction of four Chinese characters typically translated into English as 'no brand, quality goods'. Originally a spin-off of the Seiyu supermarket chain, Muji went independent in 1983, focusing on low-cost household items, as pithily summarised by its first slogan, 'Lower Priced for a Reason'. This phrase was coined by Koike Kazuko (b.1936), a curator and art director who was at the time working as a copywriter for Muji, implying that the company took, from the outset, a curatorially informed approach to its brand strategy.[35]

Since 2002, Muji's art direction has been overseen by the curator and designer Hara Kenya (b.1958), who has proposed that the guiding principle of its house style can be defined as 'editing'.[36] The sense is that a living space could be 'edited' according to personal preference (it is worth noting that this principle was concurrent with the word 'curated' entering common parlance). Exemplifying this 'edited' approach is Muji's 2004 advertising campaign 'House', when the retail chain expanded from selling household objects to selling actual homes (figs 9, 10). The campaign photographs, taken by Katagiri Asuka (b.1971), show a

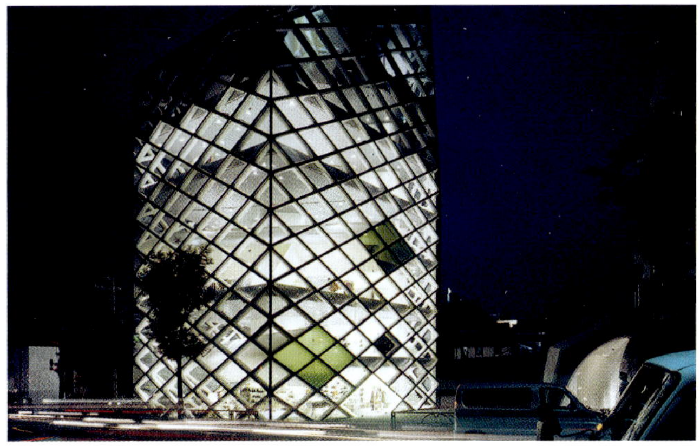

FIG 8 The Prada store in Aoyama, Tokyo, designed by Herzog & de Meuron, 2000 | Credit: © Christian Richters/Herzog & de Meuron

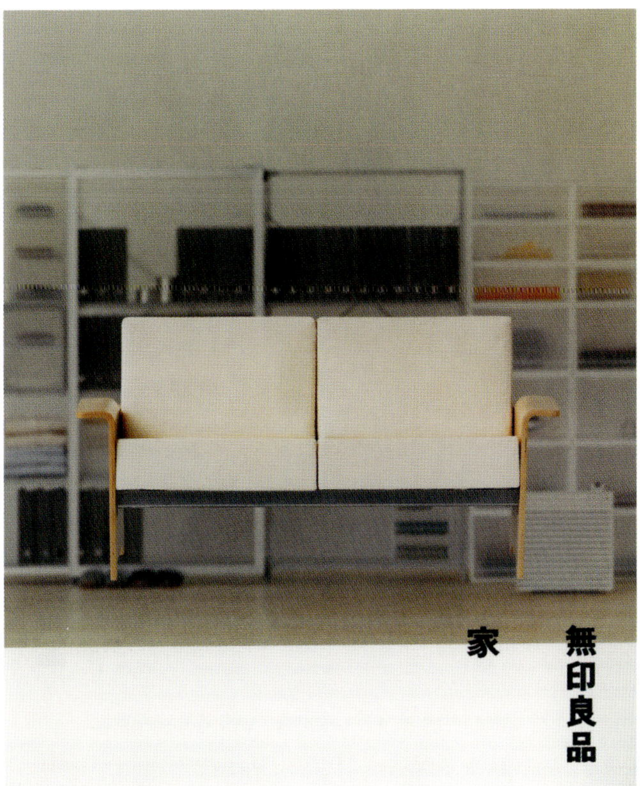


FIG 9 Katagiri Asuka for Muji, 'House' campaign, 2004

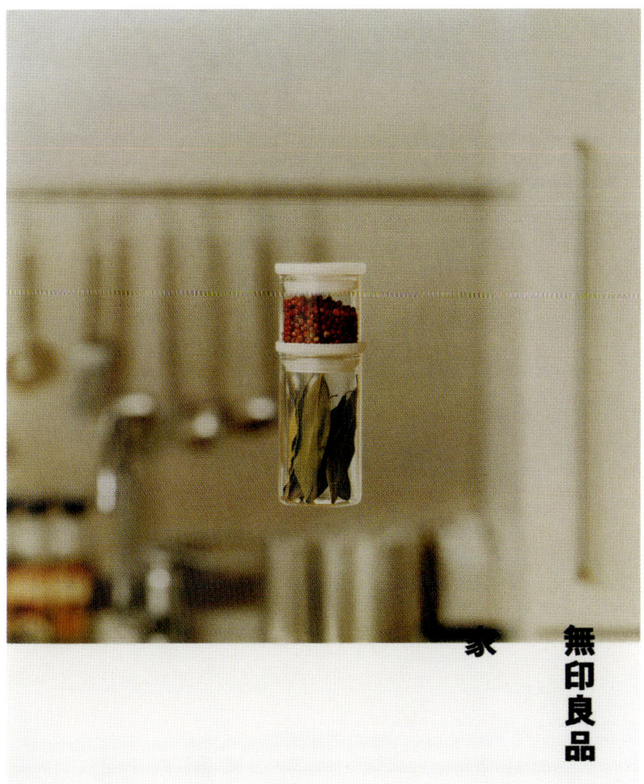


FIG 10 Katagiri Asuka for Muji, 'House' campaign, 2004

range of products – spice jars, a bent plywood sofa, a Perspex tissue dispenser –seemingly floating in midair, against a blurred backdrop of well-ordered domestic environments. These weightless objects typify design at the turn of the new millennium: unbranded, practical, the quintessence of living lightly, perhaps even ethically.

Hara has written that the guiding concept for Muji is one of 'emptiness' – no advertising copy, no ornament, only one unchanging logo.[37] He has even argued that this concept lies at the core of Japanese aesthetics, tracing it back to the void that lies at the centre of the Shinto shrine, to be filled by the enshrined *kami*, or deity.[38] In this reading, Japanese design and architecture is, in essence, one of framing; it is about the act of display as much as, perhaps more than, the thing in itself.

A year after Muji's 'House' campaign came the next promotional series: black-and-white photographs, taken by Ueda Yoshihiko (b.1957), of temples and teahouses (fig. 11). One of these images is an interior shot of the famous Ginkaku-ji (or Silver Pavilion) in Kyoto, commissioned as a retirement villa by the shogun Ashikaga Yoshimi in the late fifteenth century. Dating from the period when the tea ceremony was first being formalised, the pavilion is one origin of both the teahouse and what has come to be regarded as a traditional Japanese-style room. Its interior architecture influenced emergent approaches to study and to contemplation, by way of its *shoin* (a built-in writing desk) and *tokonoma* (a recessed display space). In Ueda's photograph, in front of partially drawn *shōji* opening out onto a garden, we see a lone porcelain rice bowl placed on tatami. A century on from Vallotton's Parisian crowd, this unpeopled and intimate world is one of quietude as well as of commerce. An architectural national treasure houses a single piece of mass-produced porcelain. What is on sale here? The bowl or the temple? Muji or Japan? In this meditative study, the line between craft and commodity, between shop and museum, between object and display, has all but disappeared.

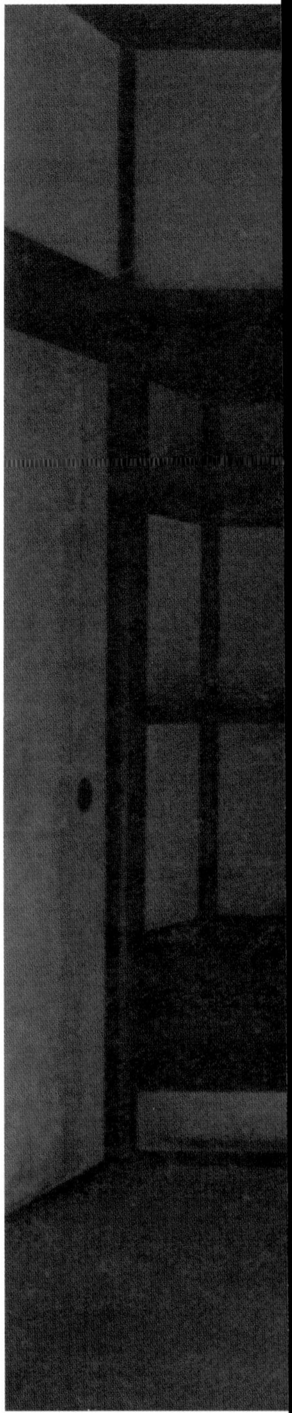

FIG 11 Ueda Yoshihiko for Muji, 'Teahouse' campaign, 2005

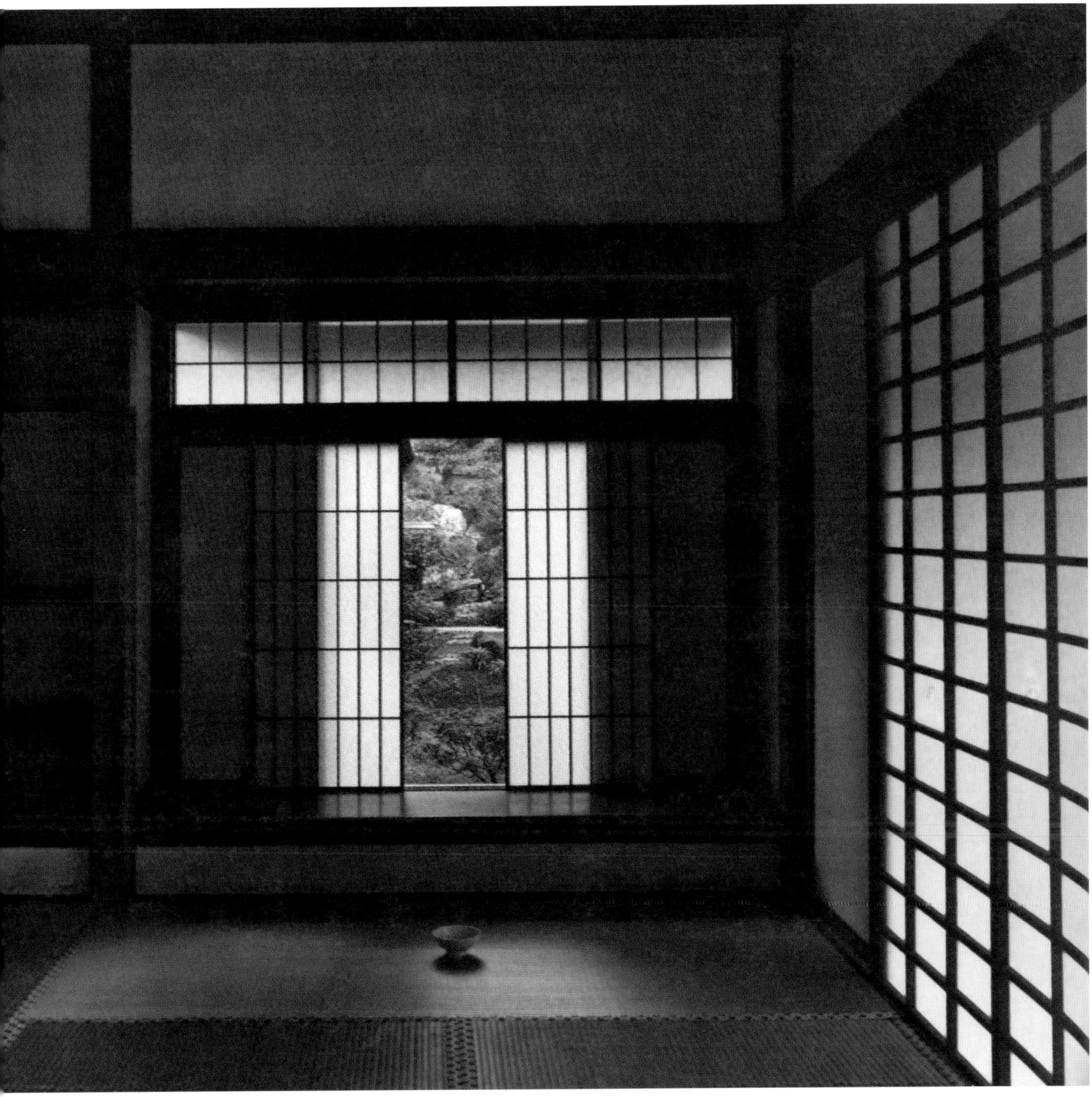

## NOTES

1. Yanagi 2018, 325–46.
2. Ibid., 327.
3. Ibid., 331.
4. This influential term was coined in Bennett 1995.
5. In the early decades of the twentieth century, it was not uncommon for avant-garde exhibitions to be installed in shops. The contents of these displays would often run in striking opposition to their site. For example, *The First Brücke Exhibition* was installed in the showroom of the Seifert lamp factory in Dresden (1906); in 1916, Vladimir Tatlin organised a group exhibition titled *Magazin* (*The Shop*) in a rented shop in Moscow. In many cases, these sites were about necessity as much as a critique of 'capitalist realism', to use a phrase used half a century later by four young German artists – Manfred Kuttner, Konrad Lueg, Sigmar Polke and Gerhard Richter – to describe their own exhibitions and happenings, one of which occurred in the furniture store Möbelhaus Berges, Düsseldorf, in 1963.
6. Yanagi 2018, 337.
7. Moeran 1981, 90.
8. These might be compared to the 'atmosphere rooms' pioneered in Hanover in the mid-1920s by the German curator Alexander Dorner (1893–1957), and which spread to other museums in Europe and North America.
9. Kikuchi 1994, 247.
10. Indeed, it is possible to make out a hand broom that was made in Wakayama, close to Yanagi's formative conversation on Mount Koya.
11. Almost a century later, Takumi remains in business.
12. Brandt 2007, 95.
13. Ibid.
14. Jasper Morrison, 'The In and Outs of a Woven Table', *Japan Times*, 6 May 2016, https://www.japantimes.co.jp/life/2016/05/06/food/bamboo-table-wove-way-back-us (accessed 4 August 2023).
15. Quoted in Ginbura Hyakunen, 'The King of Mingei on Nishiginza-dori', 25 September 2020, https://www.ginza.jp/en/column/15884 (accessed 4 August 2023).
16. Kunik 2012, 16.
17. Brandt 2007, 114.
18. Yanagi 2018, 344.
19. Most notably, at the Provinzial-Museum in Hanover, Alexander Dorner commissioned artists to produce what he termed 'atmosphere rooms'. Best known among these was the contribution of the pioneering Russian constructivist El Lissitzky (1890–1941), whose contribution *PROUN* is one of the most singular and influential installations of the twentieth century.
20. Yamaguchi 1991, 57
21. Benjamin 1982, 522.
22. Fischli, Olsen and Jasper 2021, 90.
23. Von Hantelmann 2019, 257.
24. As Andrew McClellan has suggested: 'When it comes to molding public taste with respect to domestic products, museums were soon surpassed by department stores, which by the 1920s had assumed a central place in the life and economy of North American and European cities' (McClellan 2008, 203).
25. The space of commerce was clearly enticing for Moholy-Nagy. In the same year, he contributed photographs to a book titled *The Street Markets of London*. In his foreword, he describes darting around with his Leica: 'This method of studying a fragment of present-day reality from a social and economic point of view has a wide general appeal' (Benedetta 1936, vii).
26. McClellan 2008, 205.
27. Yanagi visited the United States this same year, delivering a lecture series at Harvard University titled 'The Criterion of Beauty in Japanese Art', which he went on to publish in 1931.
28. Meyer 2013, 54.
29. Klonk 2009, 148.
30. This development was perhaps most strikingly exemplified by a remarkable generation of Italian architects and designers, such as Gae Aulenti, Carlo Scarpa, Franca Helg and Franco Albini, among others, whose clients encompassed museums as well as Fiat and Olivetti.
31. Franck 1961, 104.
32. Ibid., 150.
33. This question is explored extensively in Jones 2017.
34. Antonelli 2007, 87.
35. Hara 2018, 232.
36. Ibid., 258.
37. Ibid., 241.
38. Hara 2014, 14.

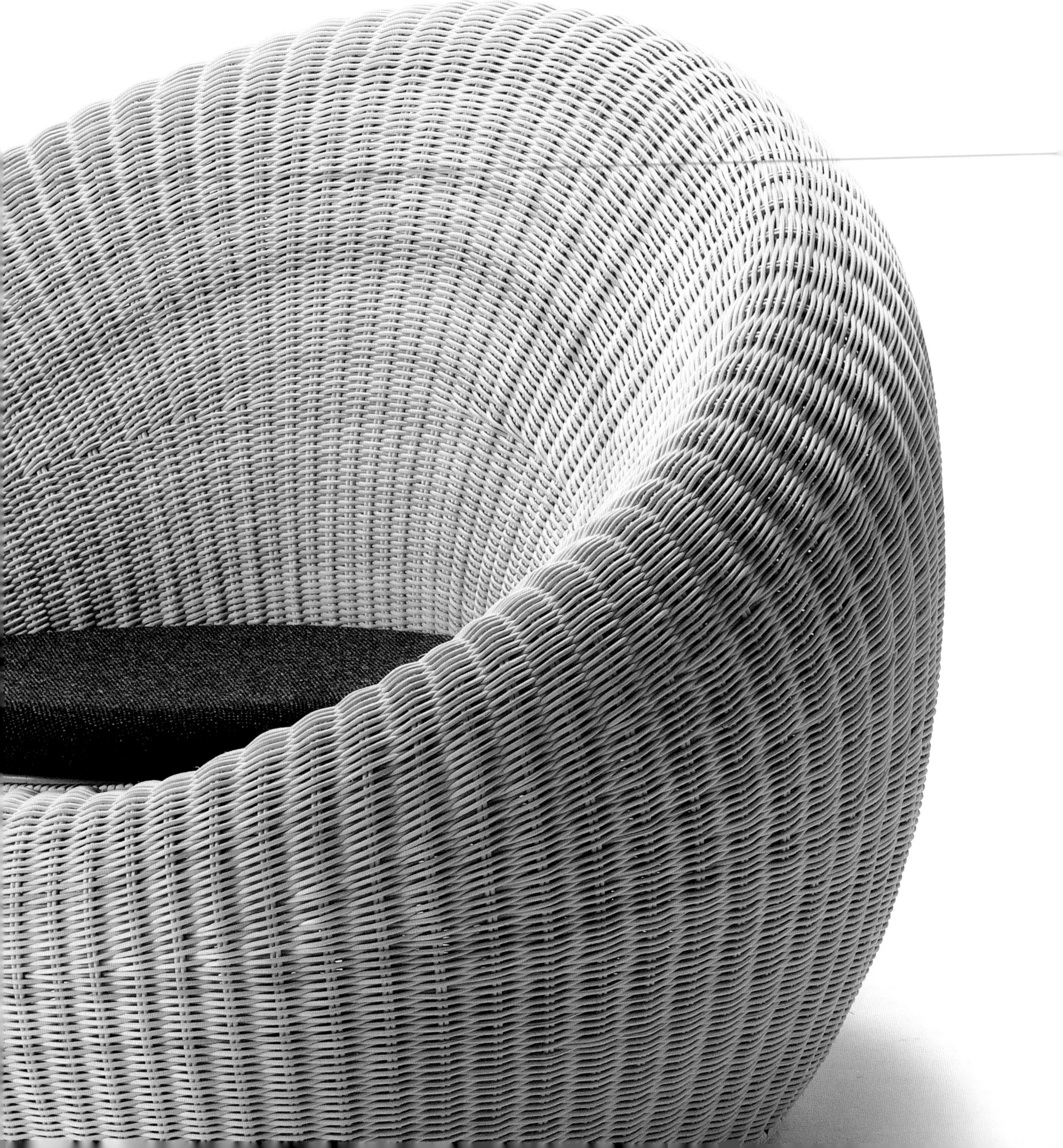

NAOMI POLLOCK

# From Mingei to Modern

## The growth of Japanese design

Consider a striking ceramic plate glazed half green and half black (fig. 1). And then consider a soy sauce pot whose tailored form can be easily cupped by the hand (fig. 2). Fashioned from clay, each one is an elegant, functional and modestly priced piece of tableware created with the end user in mind. The former came out of the climbing kiln at a Tottori prefecture pottery workshop founded by the medical doctor and Mingei protagonist Yoshida Shōya (1898–1972) in 1931. Still made today, the plate with its two-tone surface epitomised Yoshida's New-Design Mingei movement, which designed new products while keeping to the spirit of Mingei, blending the conscious aesthetics of design with the unconscious beauty of everyday, handmade objects. The soy sauce pot, awarded both the Japanese government's Good Design Prize in 1960 and the Long Life Design Prize in 1977, was manufactured at Hakusan Porcelain Co.'s Kyushu factory, where designer Mori Masahiro (1927–2005) was hired in 1956. At that time, the company president wanted to differentiate Hakusan's product line from those of its competitors. Introducing the clean lines and elegant forms promoted by contemporary design was a way to modernise as well as reach a broad customer base. Despite their different origins, the two vessels appear like distant cousins who share common traits. Yet the former is labelled as Mingei and the latter is not. In Japan, where modern design history is tightly intertwined with the country's deeply ingrained craft culture, it can be hard to differentiate between the two. In concept as well as concrete form, there are many overlaps between the Western idea of design, adopted by Japan from the mid-twentieth century, and the home-grown, Japanese idea of Mingei. Historically, Mingei has been used to describe hand-crafted goods intended for daily use, yet aspects of Mingei can also be present in modern, factory-made objects. Either explicitly or not, these qualities have distinguished the work of many Japanese designers and continue to do so today.

In part, the determination of whether something is Mingei or not stems from an inherent subjectivity. In many respects, this designation is in the eye of the beholder. No one knew this better than Yanagi Sōetsu (1889–1961), who conceived of the idea and coined the term Mingei while on a trip to Mount Koya with his friends, the potters Kawai Kanjirō (1890–1966) and Hamada Shōji (1894–1978) (see p. 87). Yanagi broadly defined the term as 'artifacts created from and for the daily lives of common people'.[1] According to his son Sōri (1915–2011), Sōetsu regularly patronised antique markets where he sought out ordinary objects crafted from clay, cloth, wood and other natural materials. Ultimately, his selected ceramics,

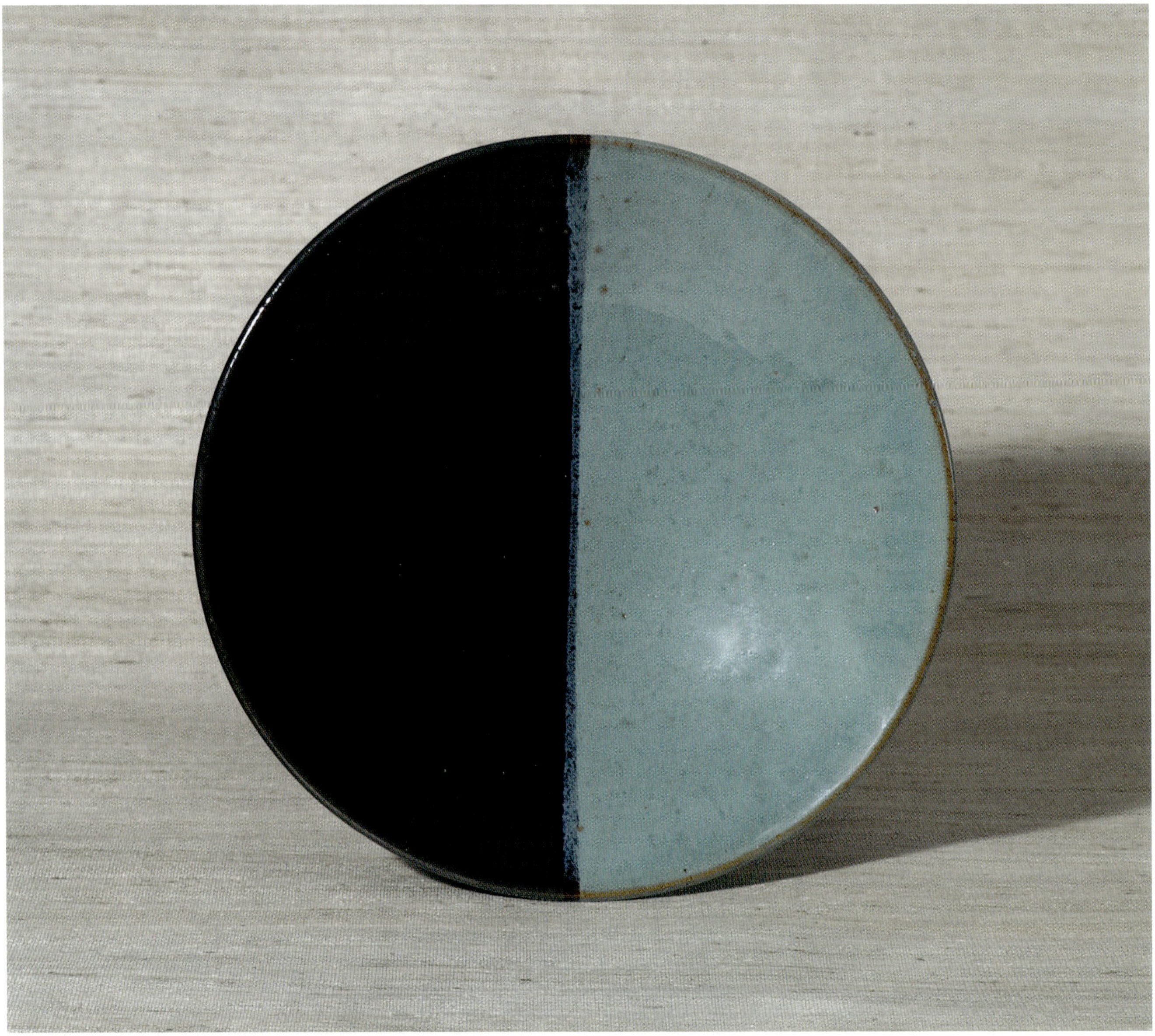

**FIG 1** *Somewake* (separated glaze) dish, Ushinoto kiln, design by Yoshida Shōya, 1931, Tottori Folk Crafts Museum

agricultural tools and woven goods became the starter collection of Tokyo's Japan Folk Crafts Museum, or Mingeikan, which he founded in 1936.

At about the same time that the museum was established, the Western idea of design, which separated the processes of product conception and manufacture, began developing in Japan. Though handmade, utilitarian goods had a centuries-long history, their recognition by Yanagi coincided temporally with the birth of Japan's design industry, which dovetailed with a push towards large-scale manufacturing. As explained by Sōri, 'Yanagi's theory on Mingei is a reaction against the poor quality of mechanized mass production.'[2] In turn, the development of design in Japan emerged partly from the country's rich craft heritage. Driven by a push to produce exports, the Japanese government initially sought the guidance of design experts from Europe, where ideas promulgated by the Deutscher Werkbund and the Bauhaus had propagated and the field as a whole was more developed. The goal for these imported designers was to advise on ways to convert traditional Japanese materials and methods into household goods that could be made in the country but sold successfully abroad. Among the earliest invitees was the German architect and designer Bruno Taut (1880–1938), who arrived in 1933.

Shortly after landing in Japan, Taut began consulting at the Industrial Arts Research Institute (IARI), a government facility established to promote product development. The centre stood in the city of Sendai, a location within easy reach of the many craft workshops in northern Japan. Impressed by the beauty and sophistication of their works, Taut shunned making simple imitations of Western objects and urged his advisees to blend traditional Japanese knowhow with contemporary consumerism: in other words, to utilise the same materials and techniques employed by craftspeople to create items suitable for a modern lifestyle. He stressed the importance of high quality, which he defined as the 'correct choice of material; correct use of materials; correct treatment of materials; and function'.[3] The sensitivity to materials about which he spoke was intrinsic to Japan's artisanal objects. In many ways, he overlaid basic tenets of modern design on top of the handcraft culture he encountered in Japan.

As if setting an example, Taut spent two years following his stint at the IARI designing tableware, furniture and other items which were sold at Miratesu, a Tokyo-based crafts shop.[4] In the store's displays and shelves, his modern pieces were in proximity to those authored by potters and weavers, underscoring the relationship between the two.

Following in Taut's footsteps, the French architect-interior designer Charlotte Perriand (1903–1999) came to Japan in 1940 under the auspices of the Japan Export Craft Association, a government agency where Yanagi Sōri, a recent art school graduate, was then affiliated. The younger Yanagi was captivated by the brand of

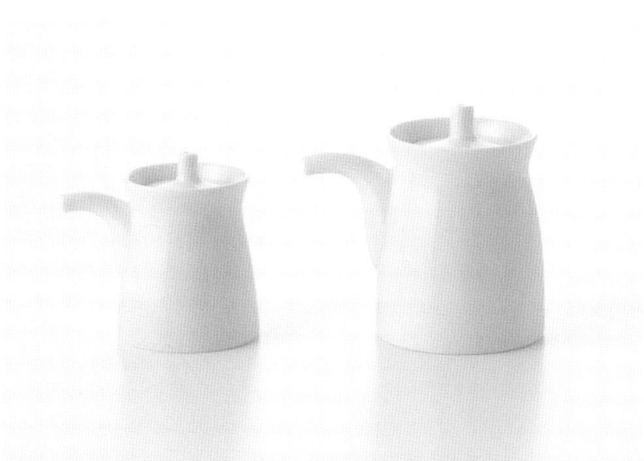

FIG 2 Soy sauce dispenser, Hakusan Porcelain Co., design by Mori Masahiro, 1958 | Credit: Hakusan Porcelain Co., Ltd.

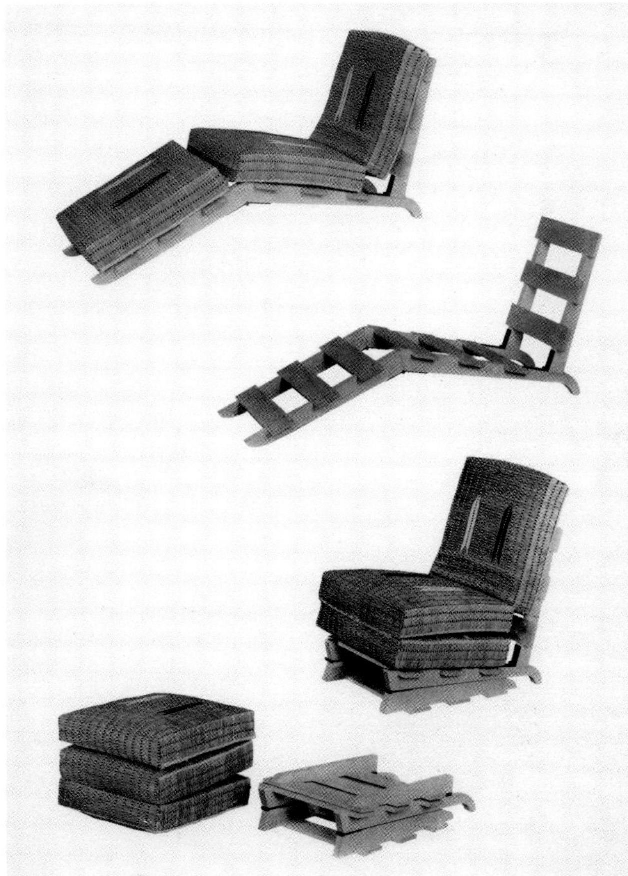

FIG 3 Charlotte Perriand, Chaise longue, 1941
Credit: © ADAGP, Paris and DACS, London 2023.

modernism espoused by the Swiss architect Le Corbusier (1887–1965), and suggested inviting Perriand, the architect's colleague, to advise Japan on export product development. To get up to speed, Perriand toured the country, acquainting herself with craft workshops as well as traditional Japanese homes and their furnishings. Accompanying her on many of these expeditions, Yanagi Sōri observed Perriand interacting directly with artisans as she familiarised herself with their ways of working. '[She] felt joy in discovering the purity that emanated from the "Mingei" wares used in everyday life in local areas,' he noted.[5] Perriand's aim was to merge her own design sensibility with Mingei. No doubt exposure to her process impacted Yanagi Sōri's own approach in his subsequent career as one of Japan's most important product designers.

In watching mentors sharing their techniques with apprentices, Perriand comprehended the meaning of tradition in Japan. According to Yanagi Sōri she often reiterated the idea that 'to invigorate and bring out the

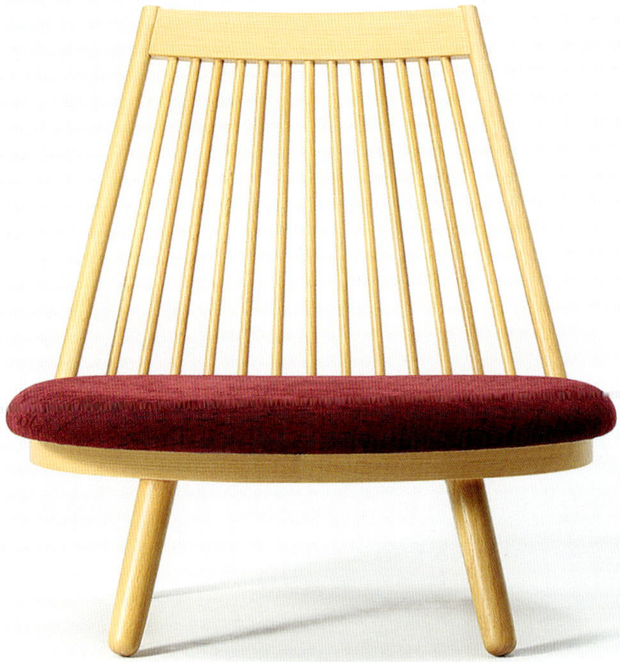

**FIG 4** Toyoguchi Katsuhei
Spoke Chair, 1963
Credit: Tendo Co., Ltd

best of true tradition, does not imply dutifully copying something. It is creating something new in accordance with the eternal principles of tradition.'[6] Even today, tradition in Japan is revered but viewed as a continually evolving concept. Yanagi Sōri's term for this was 'living Mingei'.[7] With the passing of information from one generation to the next, change occurs bit by bit, be it a subtle difference in shape, colour or texture. A connection to the past can be evident even in a cup or cushion that seems entirely new.

Though Perriand's aim was to create contemporary household goods, tradition was the starting point for the works she authored while in Japan. Instead of separating herself, Perriand sat alongside artisans, using rough sketches and simple models to communicate and repeatedly refine her ideas. In her hands, bamboo became frames for chairs and chaises and woven straw, historically used for raincoats, their upholstery (fig. 3). For the French designer, the Japanese craftsperson's materials became her palette, their assembly methods her scaffolding. Despite the visible connection to Mingei, Perriand's forms were decidedly modern and her products were intended to have broad, international appeal. In 1941, a collection of her works was displayed in an exhibition titled *Selection, Tradition, Creation* held at the Tokyo department store Takashimaya, enabling the Japanese public to view her experimental pieces.[8]

While Taut, Perriand and others demonstrated ways that craft could be transformed and repurposed, the task of converting the methods and materials used by Mingei makers into mass-market products filtered down to local creators. Those first home-grown designers included Yanagi Sōri, who created a wide range of products over the course of his career, Toyoguchi Katsuhei (1905–1991), known for innovative furniture (fig. 4), Yoshitake Mosuke (1909–1993), who specialised in cast metal, and Kenmochi Isamu (1912–1971), who pioneered the field of interior design in Japan.

Like many of the country's early practitioners, Kenmochi launched his career at the IARI. During his tenure there, Kenmochi developed the concept of 'Japanese Modern', which became an institute initiative in 1953.[9] Integrating Mingei and modern design, this term referred to a wide range of new furnishings whose materials and construction evoked tradition. 'In this continuous search for "Japaneseness", "modern" and "good design" in design, Mingei stood out as a point of reference', explains Yuko Kikuchi.[10] In keeping with the Japanese lifestyle that emerged after the Second

World War, the goods that exemplified Japanese Modern – chairs, ashtrays, lamps, glassware and the like – were familiar but fresh.

Kenmochi's quest led to collaborations with numerous factories, workshops and creators, both foreign and local. This included the Japanese American sculptor Isamu Noguchi (1904–1988), who had a stint of his own at the IARI. Together the two designed the Bamboo Basket Chair. Reminiscent of an *ikebana* flower basket, it consisted of woven bamboo cushions supported by a steel frame (fig. 5). While visiting the United States, Kenmochi also interacted with American designers, such as Charles and Ray Eames and George Nelson. In 1954, Kenmochi left the IARI and launched his Tokyo practice soon after. Blending his knowledge of the design world and Japanese craft culture, Kenmochi was well positioned to help his country move forward after the devastation of the Second World War.

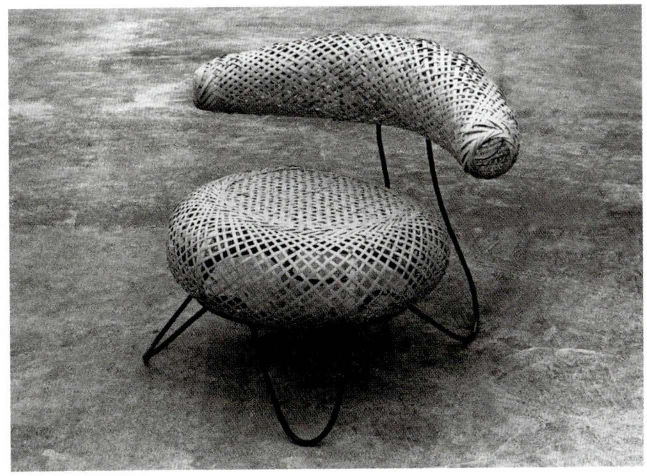

**FIG 5** Isamu Noguchi and Kenmochi Isamu, Bamboo Basket Chair, 1950 | Credit: Noguchi Museum Archives, 02244. Photo: Isamu Noguchi. ©The Isamu Noguchi Foundation and Garden Museum, New York/ARS–DACS

With the war receding and its economy growing, Japan modernised rapidly from the mid-1950s . As new offices, hotels and government buildings were built, the need for interior design grew too. Engaged in many of these large-scale projects, Kenmochi created comprehensive schemes whose elements – everything from sofas to silverware – embraced the abstract lines and planar surfaces of contemporary aesthetics while evoking the elegant simplicity of Japanese forms and natural materials. Designed in 1960 for the lounge of the Hotel New Japan, Kenmochi's

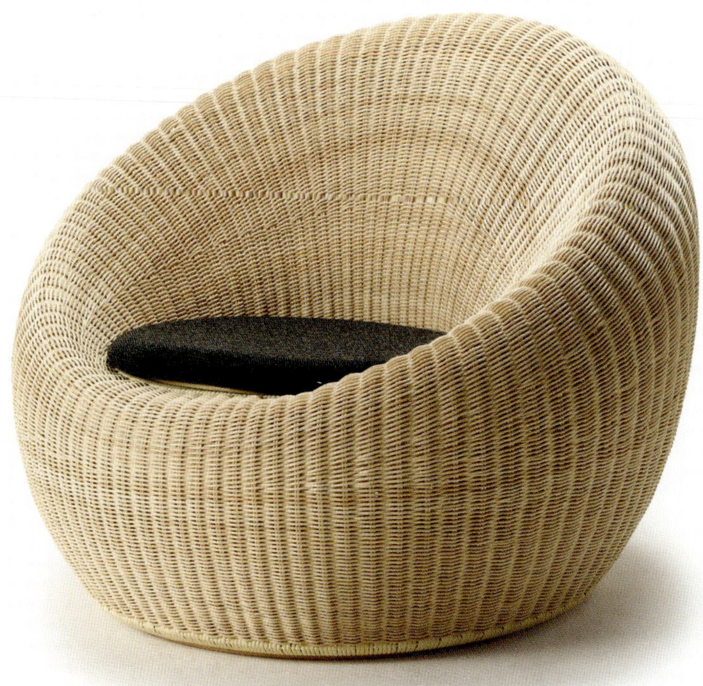

**FIG 6** Kenmochi Isamu, Rattan Chair, 1960
Credit: YMK Nagaoka Co

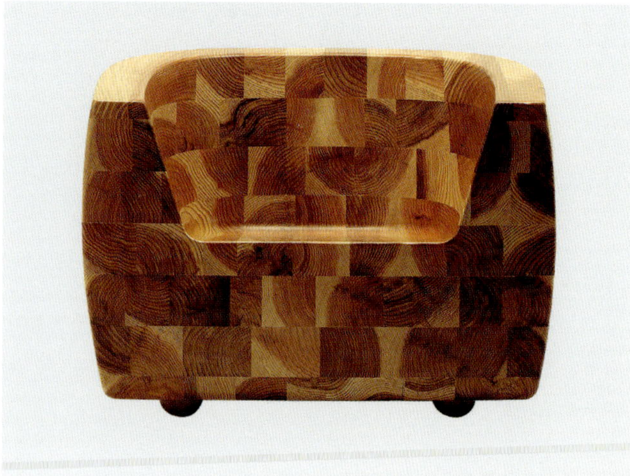

FIG 7 Kenmochi Isamu, Kashiwado Chair, 1961 | Credit: Tendo Co., Ltd

Rattan Chair, an orb of woven cane indented in the middle for a colourful seat cushion, has a timeless appearance yet bows politely to Japan's long history with the material (fig. 6). Similarly, the Kashiwado Chair, created in 1961 for the Atami Garden Hotel, consists of layered wood slabs shaped and smoothly sanded to form an integrated seat, back and arm rests (fig. 7). Taking its name and bulky size from a then-popular sumo wrestler (fig. 8), the chair is still made by the furniture manufacturer Tendo Co., Ltd. It employs the *uzukuri* woodworking technique that was historically used to bring out the grain of decorative pillars in *tatami* mat rooms.

Located not far from the IARI in Yamagata prefecture, Tendo started out as a guild of *miyadaiku* shrine and temple carpenters, *tategushi* woodworkers skilled at making frames for *shōji* and other sliding panels without nails or screws, and *sashimonoshi* cabinetmakers able to construct *tansu* chests with intricate wood joinery. In 1942, the group formed a company but its focus did not return to furniture until after the Second World War. Like manufacturers up and down the Japanese archipelago, the firm's capabilities were corralled by the army during the war. This included producing wooden boxes to transport munitions. Another assignment was devising decoy aeroplanes made of wood under the aegis of Kenmochi and his IARI colleagues. According to Motohashi Naoko, Tendo's current sales division chief, the furniture fabricator used this as a chance to test out a new technology: moulded wood.[11] The bending of thin layers of laminated plywood into curved shapes went on to become a Tendo speciality.

After the war ended, Tendo was asked to make furnishings for the homes of Allied Occupation Force families, a task undertaken once again with guidance from Kenmochi and the IARI. Following that, the company turned its attention to Japanese consumers who needed both Japanese- and Western-style furniture that fit the country's rapidly modernising lifestyle. Utilising moulded plywood not only differentiated the company from competitors who relied on solid wood construction, it also enabled the construction of light, strong and mass-produced furniture that suited Japan's post-war homes and offices. While the company had its own in-house design capability, many projects were collaborations with independent practitioners.

Working with Kenmochi and others provided important stimuli for developing techniques and material experimentation – company goals that continue today. Even as the use of machines and scale of production changes, the craftsperson remains present in their process and products. Hearkening back to the firm's founders, new employees start by training their hands as well as their eyes. As in the mentor–apprentice system of a potter or weaver's workshop, knowledge is passed from the seasoned worker to the young hire. Learning to sand wood is among the first skills acquired. 'The hand is taught to remember the texture of the finished surface by feel', comments Kato Naoki, vice manager of the planning division at Tendo.

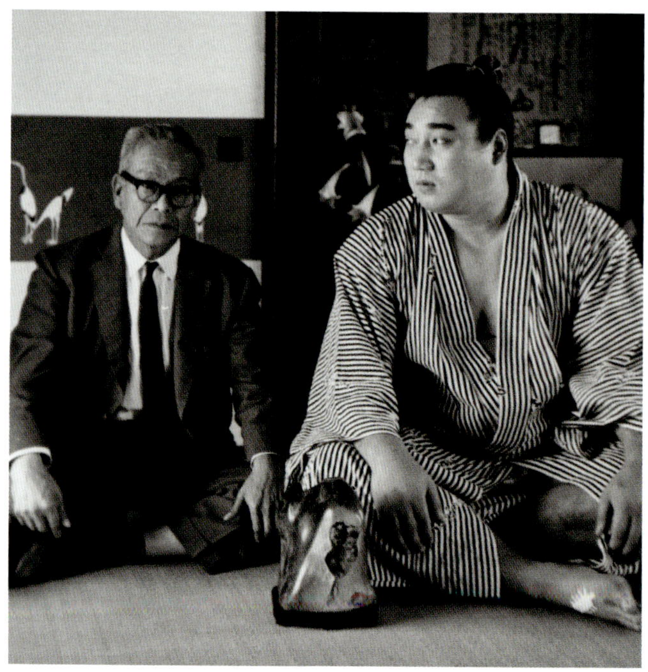

FIG 8 Kashiwado Tsuyoshi, after whom the chair (fig. 7) was named, and Ōyama Fujitaro, the second president of Tendo Co., 1961
Credit: Tendo Co., Ltd

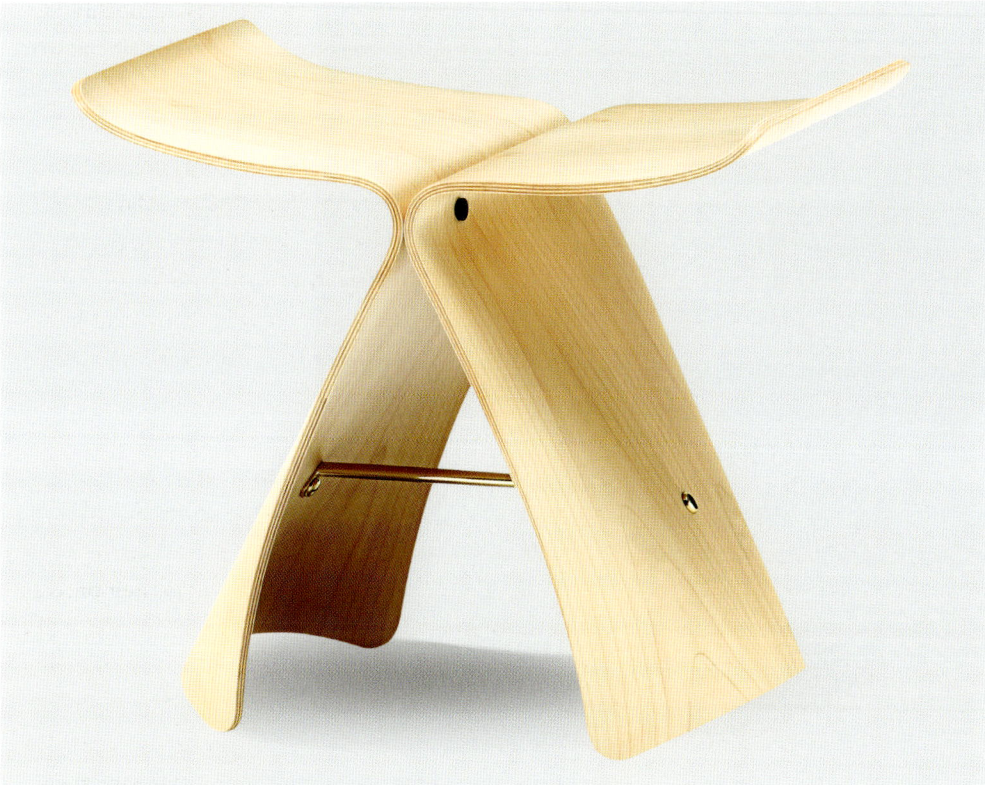

FIG 9 Yanagi Sōri, Butterfly Stool, 1956
Credit: Tendo Co., Ltd

The initial cutting of wood may be guided by computer data, but the finishing – an essential feature of Tendo furniture – is done by hand. Nothing can replace the touch and sensitivity of the human hand. 'Machines are just there to help', explains Motohashi, echoing a philosophy of making articulated by Mingei protagonists decades earlier.

Among the most impactful of Tendo's partnerships was that with Yanagi Sōri. It began in 1954 when the young designer brought them a model of a unique stool he had devised with guidance from Inui Saburō (1911–1991), then an engineer at the IARI and later Tendo's technical director after he joined the company in 1956. Likened to a traditional *torii* shrine gate in miniature, its splayed, sculptural form looked as much like an abstract artwork as a seating element. The simple scheme consisted of a pair of pinned, wooden plates. Since both curved in three directions, figuring out how to construct the complex geometry was a challenge. Working together, designer and fabricator found their solution in moulded plywood. Titled the Butterfly Stool, the final design went into production in 1956, becoming one of the company's most popular pieces and one of Yanagi Sōri's early successes (fig. 9).

Yanagi began his design career shortly after the end of the Second World War, when clay was one of the only available raw materials. To familiarise himself with the medium, he learned how to make moulds and other ceramic techniques at a factory in Nagoya. With the diligence of a workshop apprentice, he gleaned his knowledge from company experts. Acquiring this information laid the groundwork for generating high-quality design. Among Yanagi's first works was a plain white teapot, whose lack of ornament initially met with a lukewarm response (fig. 10).

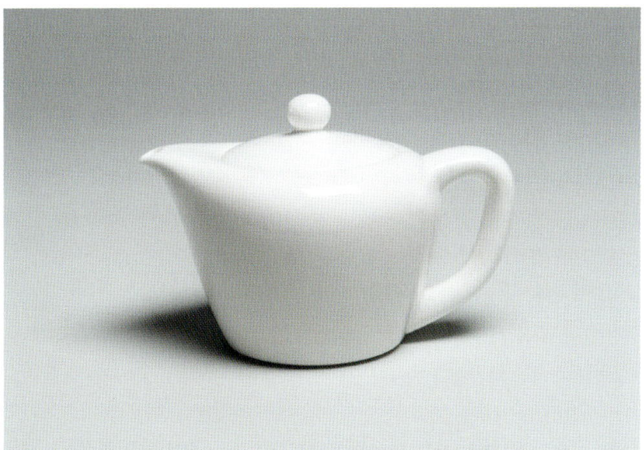

FIG 10 Teapot, porcelain, designed by Yanagi Sōri and manufactured by Nikon Company, 1948 | Credit: M+, Hong Kong

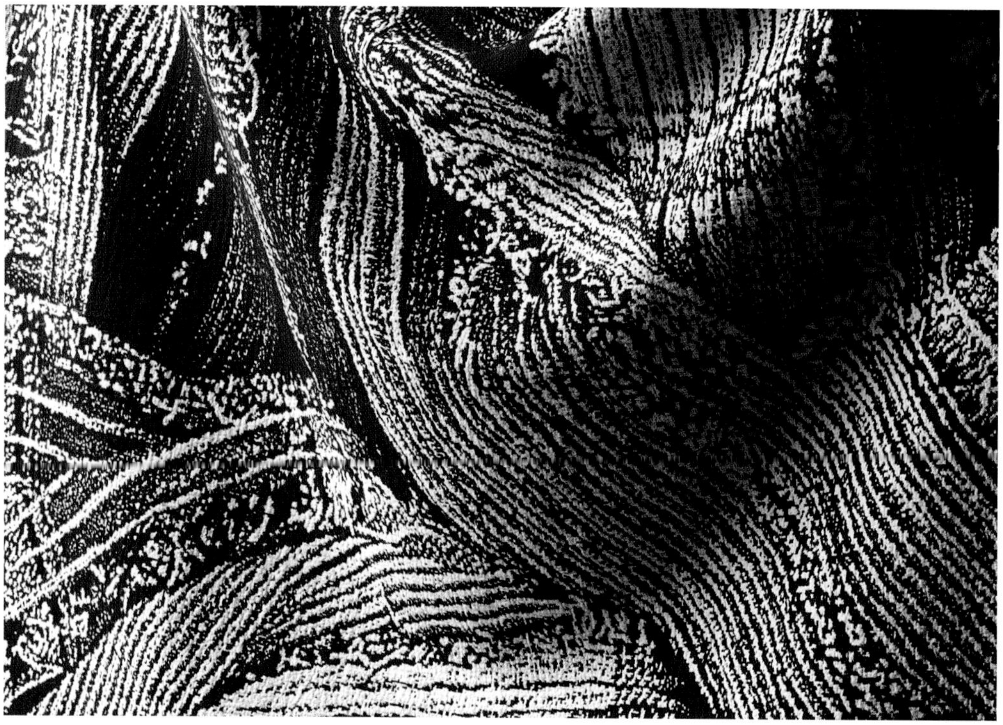

**FIG 11** Arai Junichi for Nuno, *Woven Structure* fabric, 1981
Credit: Hayashi Masayuki (photographer), 2019

Echoing the simplicity of Bauhaus design, the scheme derived its beauty from a graceful shape and a purity of form. These qualities contrasted sharply with then-popular merchandise featuring decorative floral motifs and colourful patterns, but in due course, the teapot was well received by customers.

Historically, the same person both conceived and created many of the things that Yanagi Sōetsu classified as Mingei, often for the maker's own use. In the design world, these functions are usually separated, since most designer ideas are realised at a factory by trained workers using mass production methods. But for Yanagi Sōri and many others, learning how something is made is an essential component of the design process. One needs hands-on experience with materials and machines, as well as a close relationship with the factory workers who operate them. Analogous to craftsmanship, Yanagi Sōri termed this knowledge 'productsmanship'.[12] He believed that good 'productsmanship' would enable the manufactured to mirror the quality of the handmade.

Among Yanagi's many goods still in production are the stainless-steel kettles made at Nihon Yoshokki Co., a kitchenware factory in Tsubame city in Niigata prefecture where metalworking has been the local speciality for centuries. A series of connected, shed-like spaces, the factory appears not to have changed much since its 1955 founding. Streaming down from above, muted daylight illuminates rows of machines. Emitting a clank or hiss, they transform metal sheets into flatware, kettles and other cooking utensils under the workers' watchful eyes. As each piece comes onto the conveyor belt, it is closely inspected. With the care of the craftsman, the machine operator runs his hand over the kettle's curved metal surface, checking for dings or scratches before sending it onto the next station. Yanagi's kettles are assembled by machines, but, evoking the artisan's workshop, the human hand deems them complete.

For Yanagi the importance of the hand began in the design studio. Located at the base of a building fittingly designed by Le Corbusier's protégé Maekawa Kunio (1905–1986), the space remains today much as he left it. Lining the main room, shelves hold Yanagi's collection of shells, dolls and folk art – inspirational objects, no doubt. Rolls of drawings are stashed overhead. Though the studio is still active, it feels like a place frozen in time. In lieu of computers, worktables occupy the middle of the room, where staff members meticulously carve models as their mentor did. He reasoned that a three-dimensional prototype revealed more about the object and how it will sit in the user's hand than a drawing. A means to develop and refine ideas, the act of model-making is like thinking with the hands. 'You do not so much as design and then create, but create and then a design emerges', said Yanagi of this process.[13]

While there is a role for the hand at every stage of product design from concept to completion, mass production is only possible with the aid of machines. Until artificial intelligence takes over, however, machines are just tools. According to Yanagi, 'Kawai Kanjirō used to often say that the machine is an extension of the hand.'[14] Even Yanagi Sōetsu was not entirely opposed to them. Although he felt that the machine-made could not be as beautiful as handwork, he acknowledged that 'so long as man does not become enslaved to machines he may use them freely'.[15] The use of machinery may be an obvious difference between Mingei and modern design but it is not necessarily conflictual.

Though Yanagi Sōri's design work depended on machine production, his ideology was not so far from that of Yanagi Sōetsu. '[Sōri] learned design but his soul was influenced by his father', explains the Tokyo-based designer Fukasawa Naoto (b.1956).[16] Occupying a unique position, Yanagi Sōri straddled the worlds of Mingei and design. Fifteen years after Yanagi Sōetsu's death, the two came together when Yanagi Sōri was appointed the director of the Mingeikan. He recognised the importance of the museum's artefacts to designers, including Charles and Ray Eames and Charlotte Perriand, as well as more contemporary practitioners such as Arai Junichi (1932–2017), who co-founded the Tokyo textile design consortium Nuno. Part artist and part alchemist, Arai often sought inspiration from folk objects and traditional fabrics. But he entirely transformed that visual information, be it the look of a resist-dyeing technique or the construction of shiny silk strands, with the help of conventional photocopiers, cutting-edge technology and, of course, his own hands (fig. 11).

Following in Yanagi Sōri's footsteps, Fukasawa became the director of the Mingeikan in 2012, once again bringing modern design and Mingei together. At that point, the designer's practice, which started in 2003, was well established and his products, many of them collaborations with European and other foreign companies, had already gained international prominence. The author of a wide range of works from tableware to home appliances, furniture and more, Fukasawa is as much an innovator as an inventor. Instead of wowing the consumer with novelty, his products blend effortlessly with daily activity. Like a pair of well-loved blue jeans, they simply fit. But it takes a consciousness of unconscious behaviour, which Fukasawa defines as 'without thought',[17] to create objects with this remarkable compatibility. It is as if the physical form was already there, just waiting to be discovered – a process not dissimilar from making a wooden bucket or an earthenware bowl by hand. Explains Fukasawa: 'Design isn't something that I generate, so much as something that already exists "in situ"; all I do is give it concrete form.'[18]

That process starts in the designer's model shop. Located on the lower level below his studio, this tidy room holds assorted prototypes on its shelves, though without a stray scrap of Styrofoam in sight. As in Yanagi Sōri's studio, it is here where ideas become three-dimensional forms. 'We make models by hand first. Even for big sofas', explains Fukasawa.[19] Only after the design is resolved in model form is the data entered into the computer and then eventually sent on to the manufacturer.

For Fukasawa, form-finding stems in part from what he calls 'discontinuity in behaviour'.[20] Take the common rice cooker (fig. 12). Almost every home in Japan has one, and yet transferring cooked rice to a bowl can be a challenge. Since utensils that touch food are not placed directly on a counter or tabletop, figuring out where to put the *shamoji* scoop can involve a bit of juggling. Having

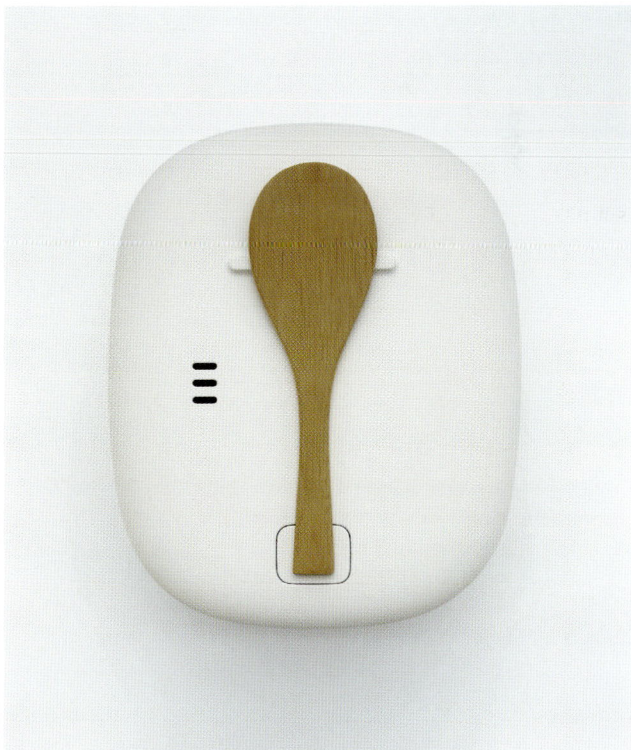

FIG 12 Fukasawa Naoto for Muji, Rice cooker, 2014

identified this 'discontinuity in behaviour', Fukasawa mitigated the awkward movement sequence by designing a rice cooker with a flat top and a built-in scoop rest. This approach yields a pure shape – nothing more, nothing less – and a perfect marriage of form and function. The economy of means and the primacy of the user's needs as the driver of the appliance's shape echo the craftsperson's handmade, household goods, a legacy of Mingei in the most modern of designs.

This quality, which designer Satō Taku (b.1955) calls *hodo-hodo* or 'just enough', can describe both traditional and modern items. As Satō explains, in contrast to the knife and fork, an all-purpose pair of chopsticks can cut, lift and place food in the mouth.[21] There is no need for anything more. This economical approach characterises every product sold by Muji, one of Japan's best-known brands, where Fukasawa is a member of the design advisory board. Distinguished by their neutral colours, clean shapes and conspicuous lack of decoration or overt branding, Muji wares, which include furniture, tableware and appliances, are easy to use and sit comfortably on the counter or in the closet (see p. 95). Conspicuously absent are the bells and whistles that adorn the vast array of merchandise hawked by electronics superstores. Be it a blender or a body scale, every Muji product is intended to fulfil a single task. Conceived by anonymous designers, they are unadorned, utilitarian and offered at an affordable price – qualities traditionally shared by Mingei wares. More than a mere marketing strategy, the Mingei ethos is embedded in many Muji products, even though these machine-made items may not look or feel like traditional, handmade objects.

Another initiative of Fukasawa which probed the question of how design and Mingei are related was the exhibition he curated in 2018 for the Tokyo gallery 21_21 DESIGN SIGHT, where he is a director. Uniting past, present and future, *MINGEI – Another Kind of Art* featured 146 items selected by Fukasawa from the Mingeikan collection. Presenting hand-crafted ceramics and traditional woven goods in the context of this important design venue emphasised their connection. 'It is impossible to make Mingei', says Fukasawa. But it has been, and can continue to be, a guide. In 1983 Yanagi Sōri wrote: '[W]e must not stay nostalgic or sentimental about the past beauty of Mingei. We must learn from that beauty and apply it to our future creations.'[22] The qualities that his father identified so long ago – the union of form and function, the bond between the object and its owner and making these goods affordable to all – remain today as pertinent to the artisan as they do to the designer. And in this shared sensibility the distinction between the two becomes comfortably unclear.

## NOTES

1. Yanagi 2015, 241.
2. Ibid., 269.
3. Kikuchi 2004, 97
4. Fisher 1994, 13.
5. Yanagi 2015, 277.
6. Ibid.
7. Ibid., 113.
8. Kikuchi 2004, 101.
9. Ibid., 218.
10. Ibid.
11. All quotations from Tendo Co. employees are taken from interviews with the author, conducted in March 2023.
12. Yanagi 2015, 49.
13. Ibid., p. 60.
14. Ibid., 125.
15. Kikuchi 2004, 55.
16. From an interview with the author, conducted in March 2023.
17. Fukasawa 2007, 6.
18. Ibid.
19. From an interview with the author, conducted in March 2023.
20. Fukasawa 2007, 34.
21. Satō 2022, 16.
22. Yanagi 2015, 52.

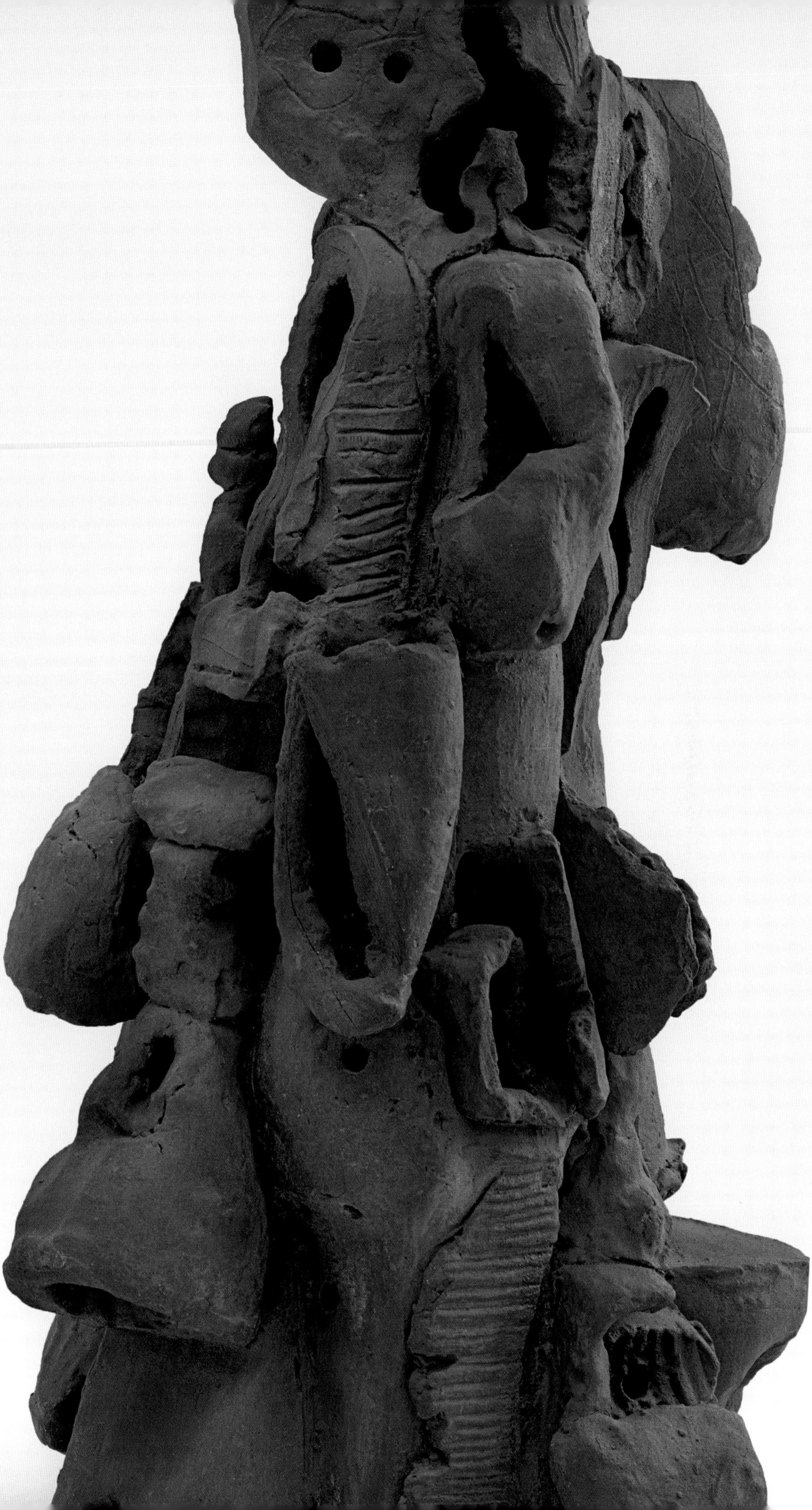

AARON ANGELL

# Ceramics and the Craft Problem

Towards the end of his life, the foundational Mingei theorist Yanagi Sōetsu (1889–1961) set about crystallising an aesthetic theory of the craft object at its most mystic. Putting aside the taxonomies and histories of folk craft at the level of regional varieties, nationalist artistic rejuvenation and trans-Oriental consumerism, Yanagi now wanted to get at the core: combining the divine 'thingness' of the Mingei object (which had lured him in the first place) with an ambitious new plan to reveal in Occidental minds a practical pathway to 'ultimate' beauty through craft. This was to be 'the great gift the East could make to the West'.[1] In his 1957 essay 'The Vow of Non-Discrimination between Beauty and Ugliness' (*Muu kōshū no gan*) Yanagi defined the spiritual kernel of the sublime craft object as containing an 'other-power' (*tariki*), usable as a form of 'outside help' to achieve enlightenment. Yanagi understood *tariki* via his engagement with the Pure Land school of Buddhism, where it is distinct from 'self-power' (*jiriki*), which is a path only available intrinsically and randomly to a few special monks. *Tariki* is enlightenment for the people, which Yanagi believed could be transmitted by encounters with particular objects made by unknown craftsmen, as they are the most 'pure and ethical of all objects'.[2]

This chapter discusses the alleged power of the 'humble' and mysteriously endowed craft object, which I shall call the divine craft object, and its digestion by, and confusing position within, the contemporary art world in Britain and Europe. I am writing with specific experience of ceramics, but I feel the points are applicable to other 'craft' objects, along with the nature of a 'craftesque' sensibility within art practice in general. As the most ubiquitous craft object of current times, ceramics may be said in this context to act as a stand in for craft, and vice versa. We are living through an era of intense interest in craft objects, and in their transformation into high-status commodities within the art world. I believe that here we are witnessing an aesthetic moment of anti-irony in which the current popularity of the divine craft object is symbolic of a novel contemporary lifestyle: a rusticated domestic programme, which in the extreme solemnness of its composure and its unconvincing prescriptions for spiritual living veer towards a form of high camp – a self-conscious and performative style, internationalistic in historical outlook, where the divine craft object is pre-eminent and talismanic.

The 'vow' of Yanagi's title refers to the irrelevance of contrasting states of beauty within the pure land of the Buddha field, where all is aesthetically equal and judgeless under ecstasy. For Yanagi, folk-crafts were 'already accepted into heaven'.[3] This vow has the potential to be paradoxical, constructed as it is around non-discrimination regarding form, aesthetic quality and perhaps taste, so long as the elusive spiritual charge of the divine craft object remains integral. This basic equivocation seems manifest today in the art/craft world not just in terms of a blending of the statuses of the handmade, the digitally augmented commodity and the academic art object (an outlook which is relatively new). It also makes for a more damaging position with regard to judgement, quality and the proper sorting of information with regard to the connoisseurship of craft within the art-world economy.[4]

In the art world, the ambiguous use-value of the divine craft object is rationalised and luxuriated by its proximity to the accepted commodity fashions of painting and sculpture. The market appeal of craft has been particularly apparent in the case of ceramics, where the romantic archetype of the free and idiosyncratic artist-potter has increased in its seduction exponentially, especially in opposition to the artistic personalities associated with the increasingly asinine forms of mechanical and digital production we see in the age of artificial intelligence and the 3D printer. This 'freedom' is related to the prevailing possibilities of easy disjunction within the medium: taking a material intrinsic to the everyday utilities of the dinner plate and the toilet, and contorting it into art, is still treated by the art world as inherently arch and iconoclastic upon the 'traditional' use of clay. This means that disruptive gestures that are completely commonplace, even pat, in other art media are treated as saucily rambunctious within ceramics, despite a multifarious formal history as probably mankind's earliest medium. There is also an inconclusive and unevenly distributed acceptance of ceramic sculpture within the Western canon as a liberated material (one that is free from functional necessity), something that feels especially true in Britain, but less so in North America, which had its mid-century 'clay revolution' in a way more pervasively modernist than contemporaneous movements in Europe.[5]

In this context, the inclusion of the divine craft object often takes the form of an all-too-readily deployable 'humble' foil for those mysteriously valuable and dubiously divine art objects in other media, which perhaps contain a more superficial or ambiguous measure of labour and construction. Curatorially, too, craft can represent a moment to inject a different sort of creative essence into a programme. It can be a cipher for a form of joyous anti-intellectualism, a symbol of hermetic obsession, and useful as a performatively anti-bourgeois sleight of hand.

The craft objects to be found in this sphere are extremely varied in terms of quality: sometimes they display knowledge of the great, delicate and sensual things craft can do for art: for example, Yasunaga Masaomi's (b.1982) discoveries from picking up stones at Nonaka-Hill Gallery in Los Angeles in 2022 (fig. 1). More often, however, they exhibit a position of ignorance and inexperience with regard to obvious cliché and juvenilia. This ignorance is obvious where a paucity of basic craft skills is concerned but also, more surprisingly, in terms of the fundamental aesthetic terms one sees applied to the rest of the art-object economy. The use of poor materials, basic and unintended construction problems, and pure, undivine ugliness are accepted in a way that is not usual within other forms. Craft seems to do something strange to the art consumer's brain. With its assumed righteousness, the divine craft object (or merely its associated 'meaningful' materials) often blinds the art world to problems that would probably cause work in more familiar media to be dismissed. Commercial art galleries that are new to craft remain somewhat satisfied with the ceramic object as a rapidly deployable signifier for creative honesty, a conscious and more ethically acquired 'outsideresque' style or some combination of the two, often with little attention paid to actual quality, or the sorting of genuine, considered novelty from the 'craftesque', or the lazy and unjustifiably naive.

In the craft world, the problem is reoriented. The art world's strange logic of processual non-discrimination – where the unskilled and laissez-faire is equal to the refined and craft-rich – is often extremely hard for craft practitioners to accept. For some, too, the well-made craft object should not be made too divine by the art world, lest it get ideas above some ill-defined station and lose its skeleton of usefulness entirely. This was reflected in a recent conversation I had with an elderly potter, at the deconstruction of studio potter Richard Batterham's (1926–2021) studio, about the ceramic artist Edmund de Waal (b.1964). On discussing De Waal's successful transition from the world of quasi-functional pottery into that of a gallery context, where his works are shown as artworks, the potter simply stated: 'I don't like being lied

FIG 1 Yasunaga Masaomi, *Empty Creature*, coloured glaze and slip, 2023 Courtesy Nonaka-Hill, Los Angeles and Lisson Gallery, London

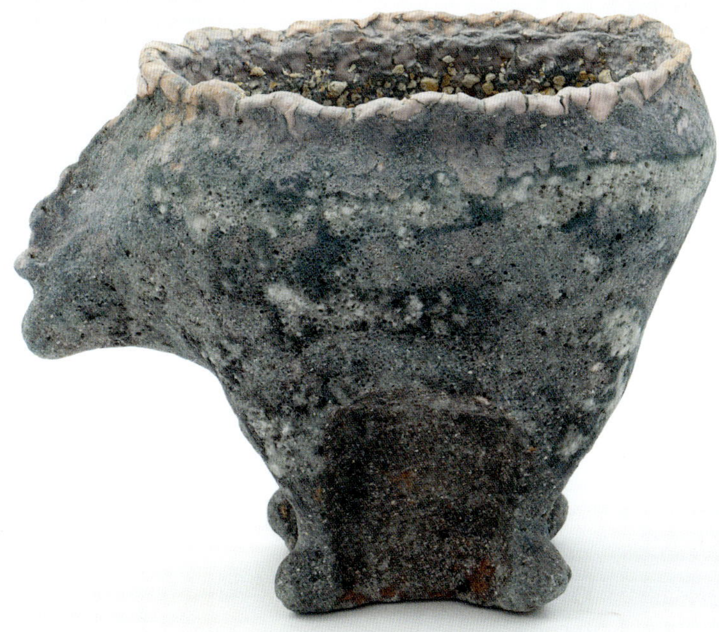

to.' This attitude, as it emanates from the traditional craft sphere, is somewhat understandable – the selection of craft phenomena for cultural and monetary elevation within the art world can be quite arbitrary, with bad making shown without consequences, and with little regard for the sincere and equitable philosophies of making that strongly pervade the world of craft. Though this outlook – a rejection of the art world's supposed confidence tricks – does elicit some sympathy, it is often also an extremely reactionary position. It is my feeling that gestures and ideologies that reject skill and right methodologies of making do not necessarily reject craft, and can be meaningfully playful upon its mores, but this approach is often treated by the craft world as a form of low cunning by interlopers.

In recent years, the craft object within the art world has proved a perfect and novel type for new adventures in retail.[6] But art remains a confusing zone for craft to land in, especially for the vessel-type object or that which references the functional. In the art world, any possible functional midlife of the object is completely elided, leaving us with only the beginning and end of the work's narrative: namely the divine and eternal spark of primal creation, and an eccentric connoisseurship of the humble sublime which would have been familiar to Yanagi.[7] This strange abstraction of humble utility is symbolic also of a shift in the lifestyle fashions of the collecting class, and part of the wider trend for what is broadly termed 'quiet luxury': an approach to design that favours the use of historically freighted materials and exquisite (though inexplicit) craftsmanship to produce subtle, muted, elegant things – often marked by some discreet detail or patina recognisable only to the initiated few.[8] Collecting for the non-speculator class is still firmly a matter of interior decoration, and the turn here seems to be away from the vividly ostentatious, and towards an earth-toned, ascetic mode of faux paucity and a Westernised 'Zen' domestic programme. We see here an appropriation of the concept of *wabi* – a quality of austere and serene beauty expressing a mood of spiritual solitude.[9] One of the primary promoters of this Western *wabi*, which I have previously called 'the materials taste', is Axel Vervoordt (b.1947), the Belgian interior designer and antiques dealer who works in a style that originates in the *wabi-cha*[10] culture of sixteenth-century Japanese Zen monasteries, transmogrified for a modernist European architecture to swooningly brown effect (fig. 2). Glass coffee tables are replaced with death-metal hunks of granite or worm-eaten wooden slabs; country bygones are upsold as dharma gates to the silent sublime.

Collectorship of the divine craft object itself, and the recognition of this spirit within other modes of art, has something in common with the eccentric warrior-aristocrat collectors of *chadōgu* (implements for the tea ceremony), who emerged in the 1500s in Momoyama-period Japan. As early as the ninth century aristocrats in China had begun collecting and preserving tea bowls explicitly associated with the life of the Buddha, but the new turn was towards wares of anonymous provenance and lineage, and of a rustic style and rugged beauty. So too we see this self-effacing performance proliferate among the moneyed and spiritually bereft connoisseur class of today, through the fetishisation of wear, ruin and superficial allusions to peasant life.[11] It is as seductive as it is ultimately unconvincing. As the sixteenth-century Zen teacher Murata Jukō proclaimed, the taste among contemporaneous monks for the 'chill and withered' rough teaware from Bizen and Shigaraki kilns[12] (in opposition to finer Chinese wares), and the assumption that this aesthetic choice alone was enough to elevate their praxis and ennoble their lifestyle, was 'unspeakably absurd'.[13]

In her seminal essay 'Notes on "Camp"' (1964), Susan Sontag (1933–2004) made the important point that 'pure camp is always naïve. Camp which knows itself to be camp . . . is less satisfying.'[14] The *wabi* interior, the sober use of meaningful materials, the appreciation of decay and the ruralised aesthetic are all things that recently have been the default signals of those wishing to exhibit the maxims of good taste. However, this concentrated turn against our irony-poisoned cultural moment reveals a strange reversal: in transmitting an ardent engagement with certain serious states of feeling, and attempting to inhabit a gnostic relationship with the natural world via consumerism, we see an inevitable collapse into a sort of highly determined lifestyle-camp. Here, the solemness of this carefully arranged aesthetic collapses under the impossibility of, and unwillingness to, *really* live like a rustic. It contains the 'process of aging or deterioration [which] arouses the necessary sympathy',[15] but fails the moment one steps back onto the street, or has to pick up one's iPhone to call the broadband people again.

Here we find the divine craft object contorted into a quasi-religious luxury good, and camp as the grotesque

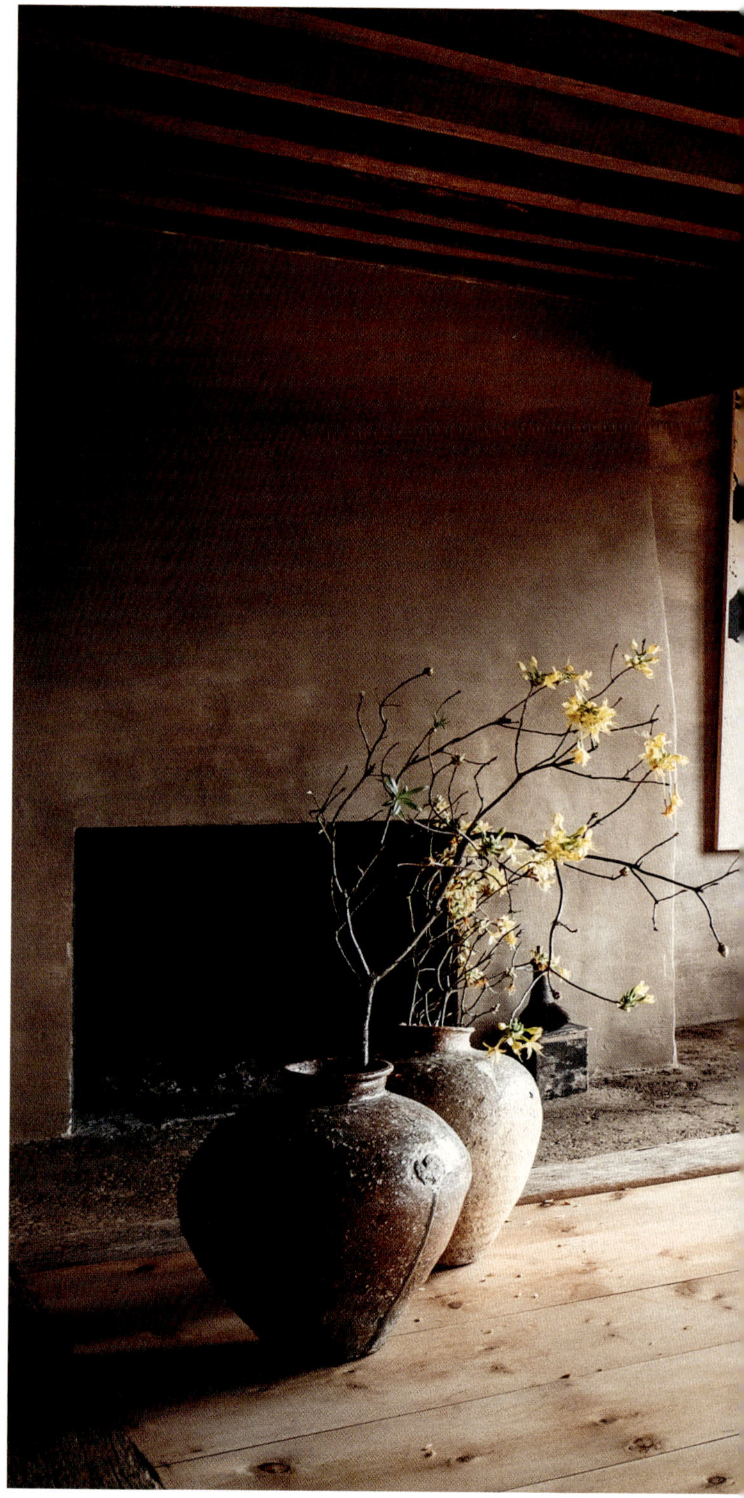

**FIG 2** The '*wabi* room' in Axel Vervoordt's castle, 2021
© Karlijne Geudens

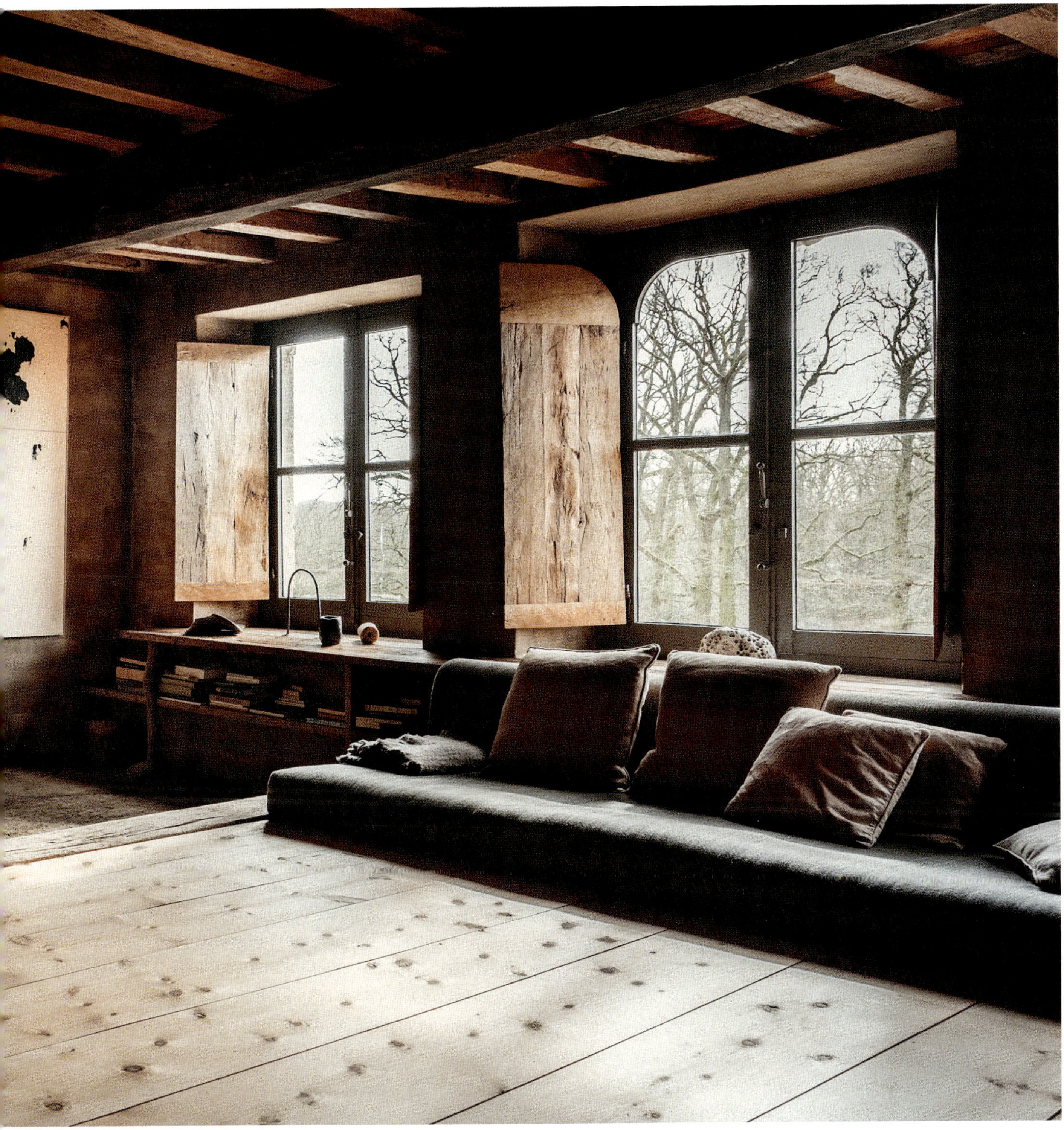

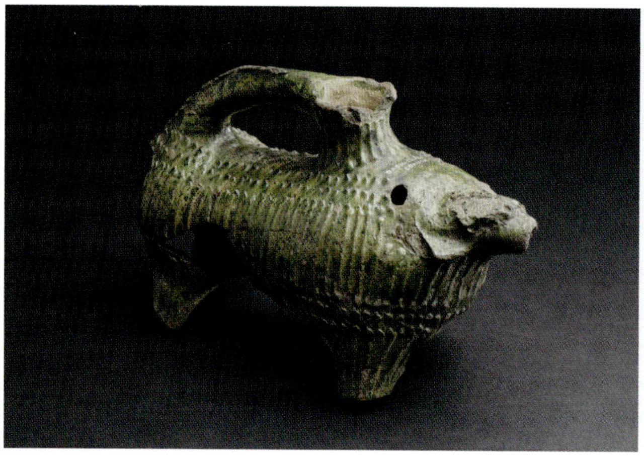

FIG 3 Pottery aquamanile in the form of a ram, green lead glaze, British, thirteenth century, British Museum

endgame of leisured boredom: a portable echo of the eighteenth-century dandy who paid an 'ornamental hermit' to stare at a skull for seven years in an artificial cave.[16] In the *wabi* interior, then, camp becomes a third way, a path between seriousness and satire that is only reachable by those emerging from a privileged society oversaturated with culture and taste options. Perhaps this mentality can account for the divine craft object's uninhibited rise to popularity within the shopping heavens of the blue-chip gallery and the international art fair. It is a hybrid mode of lifestyle design: a specious admixture of conspicuous consumerism with artificial humility and a pick-and-mix of pseudo-spiritual aesthetics. Sontag saw the origins of camp in eighteenth-century Britain, with the craze for sham ruins and stone benches carefully painted to look like gnarled wood. Today we can perhaps see parallels in our appreciation of the divine craft object and the *wabi* interior: the projection of rustic modesty and sincere aspirations collapse into failed gravitas and a risibly hypocritical social context.

How then, can the divine craft object be appropriately homed within the art world in a way that is neither patronising in its deployment nor throwaway in its quality? If it is unconvincing as an 'honest' and grounding presence among oscillating commodified trends of, say, formalism and figuration in painting, then what could be its right purpose? Craft in its 'proper' sense, with its implied use-value (however vestigial), doesn't need the veneer of art to justify its making. All legitimate art needs the spirit of craft, however abstracted, to build genuine power. As the sculptor Richard Slee (b.1946) once remarked to me, 'to make great cinema, Hitchcock needed to have great craft'. Being able to do something well, to the level of minutiae not completely visible in the finished work, is the gift that craft practice, and some of its philosophies, give to the true artist, and therein perhaps lies a future of craft as a tool for improving workmanship in painting and sculpture. By this I do not mean 'craft' in the sense of a 'necessary' rediscovery of the skilful handling of materials within, for example, painting, but 'craft' as an embodied mode of self-knowing and self-commitment to one's chosen processes, however non-technical that process or rude the results. Craft can also be successfully explicit as an aesthetic reference for artists, but they must be careful neither to deploy this as a throwaway gesture, nor to fall victim to the occasionally circumscriptive excesses of the contemporary high-craft object itself.

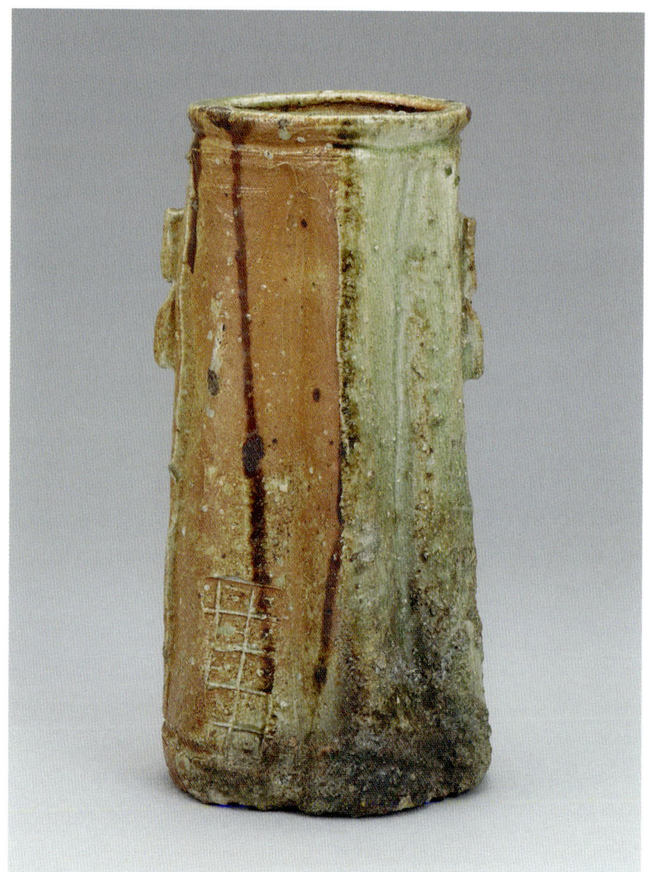

FIG 4 Iga *hanaire* (vase), Edo period, seventeenth century
Credit: Itsuo Art Museum

**FIG 5** Peter Voulkos, *Tientos*, 1959, clay with iron glazes, San Francisco Museum of Modern Art, Purchase through a gift of Phyllis C. Wattis and gift of Gregory LaChapelle © Estate of Peter Voulkos

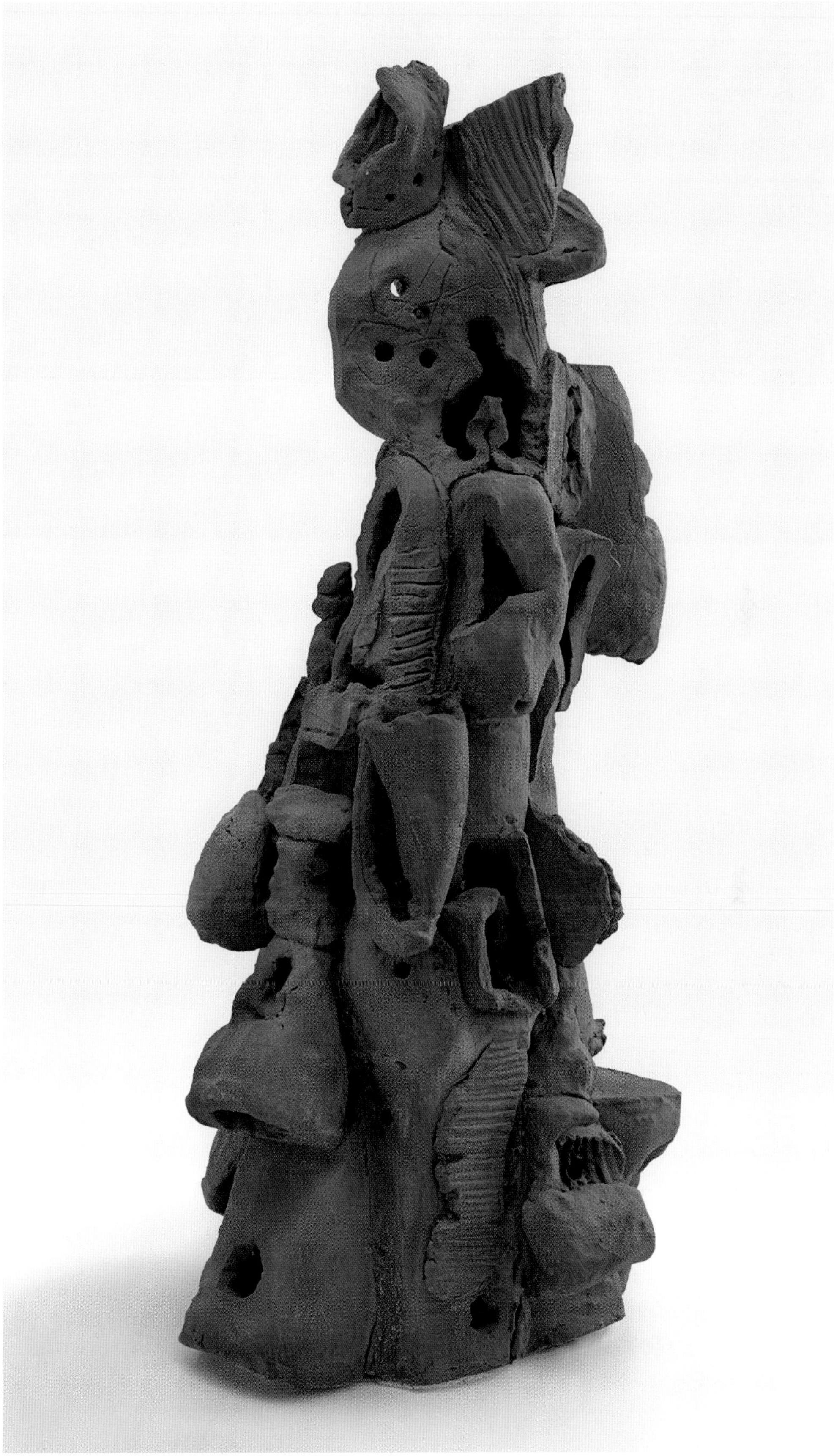

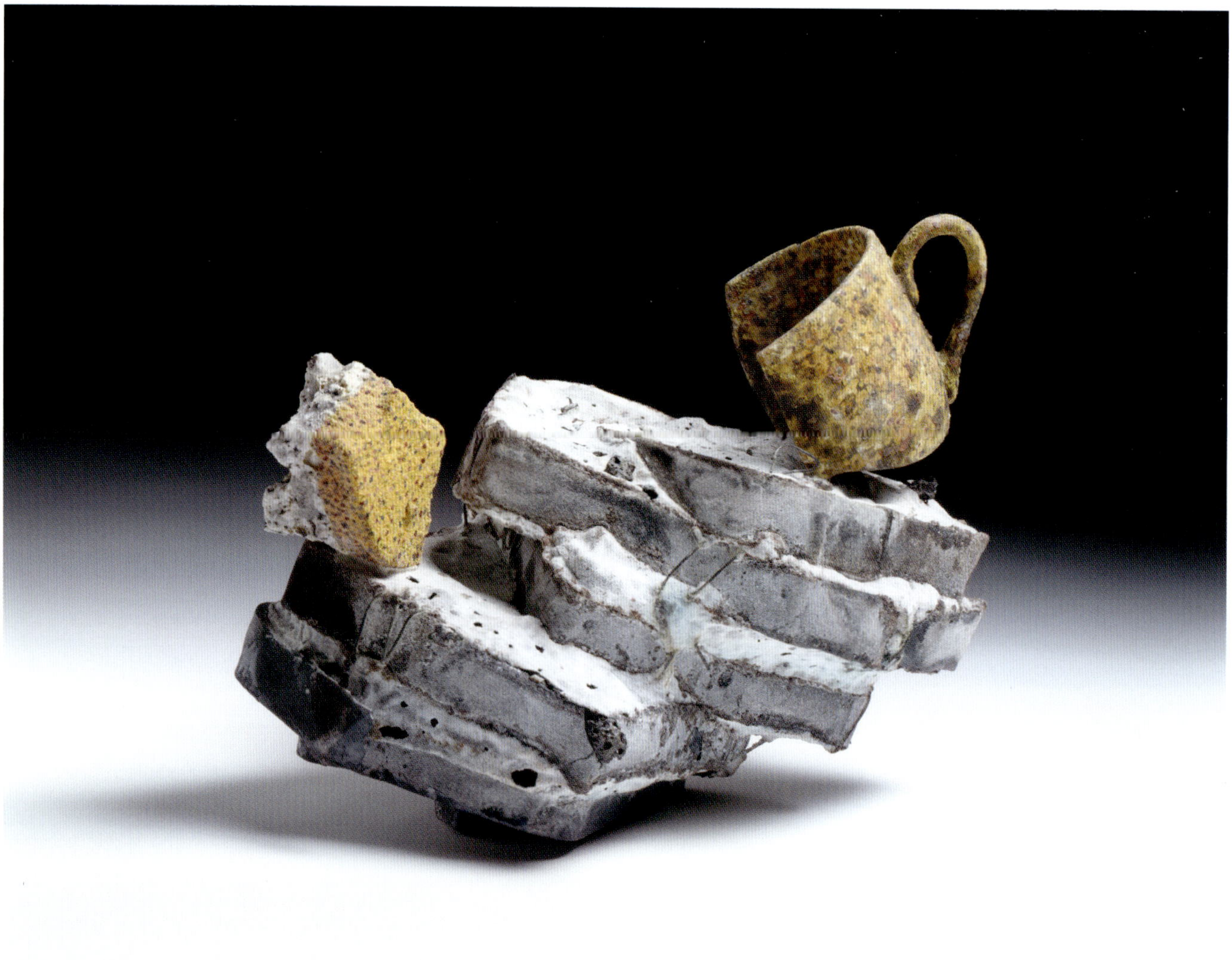

FIG 6 Gillian Lowndes, *Form*, stoneware, c.1986, Victoria and Albert Museum

Indeed, craft 'proper' seems to be taking something of an anti-rustic turn, as opposed to those forms currently popular in contemporary art. Perhaps this is in part a reaction against the ubiquity of the often wrongheaded and amateurish deployment of the craftesque gesture in the art world. For example, much, though by no means all, of the work that has appeared in recent iterations of the Loewe Craft prize[17] (much of which has been excellent) tends towards an obsessive formal complexity. As opposed to the divine and broad formal gestures associated with Yanagi's celebrated old tea bowls,[18] this occasionally projects an image of claustrophobic self-imprisonment within one's chosen medium. The mode here is one of baroque, repeated prayer for enlightenment, not the divine gestural revelation of the unlettered peasant.

This odd situation of craft-world introspection and art-world neophytism perhaps owes something to the complex history of studio ceramics in Britain. My belief is that in the early to mid-twentieth century, the parameters of studio ceramics were unduly narrow owing to Bernard Leach (1887–1979) and Hamada Shōji's (1894–1978) primary interest in importing and marketing the sensibilities of Mashiko ware, while largely ignoring a multiplicity of older, regional types of Japanese ceramic traditions. Mashiko ware as developed and promoted by Hamada and Leach is a complex and beautiful thing, and it is easy to forget that the merging of its associated glazes and forms with the rediscovery of a medieval British ceramics typology was a radical act of aesthetic synthesis. However, Mashiko ware must have been at least reasonably apposite to existing British tastes: its shapes and surface treatments are an important step away from industrial porcelain and towards a more 'folkish' and 'honest' mode of production, but in its cleanliness and clear colours it still has something in common with the popular ornamental Japonesque products designed in the late nineteenth century by Christopher Dresser (1834–1904) and the Martin Brothers. The rougher, more fantastic elements of native British pre-industrial techniques are also largely absent from this combining of Eastern and Western antique forms. The harmonious 'pulled' handles of medieval jugs were celebrated and included, but what of the grimacing face carved on the other side? What of the grotesque aquamanile in the form of a ram, the green lead glaze swamping around combed pellets of clay in a pathetic imitation of wool (fig. 3)?

This somewhat polite and careful approach of historical contiguity is in sharp contrast to the history of sculptural ceramics in the United States. When in the 1950s Peter Voulkos (1924–2002) and others began machistically stacking together lopsided hunks of coarse clay and wood-firing the results (latterly under the influence of pioneering Americana *anagama* artist Peter Callas), their eye seems to have been on the rude, undecorated ceramics of Bizen, Shigaraki and Iga, rather than 'finer' ornamental types (figs 4, 5).[19] This is important for understanding the earlier and easier integration of ceramic objects within the accepted canon of sculpture in the United States: the coarse, aleatory forms of Iga teaware and medieval Shigaraki food jars lent themselves much more easily to strains of abstract and expressionistic sculpture and painting (types that were, broadly, gestural and anti-decorative) from the same period than do wares from Mashiko or the brushwork of Ogata Kenzan (1663–1743). Any attempt, of which there have been many,[20] to join the Leach–Hamada ceramic avant-garde of the 1930s with more obviously radical movements of the time therefore seems somewhat doomed.

In Britain, the 'radical' British ceramicists of the 1970s, including Alison Britton (b.1948), Richard Slee (b.1946) and Gillian Lowndes (1936–2010), took a deliberate turn against Leach, manipulating clay into an art object on terms divorced from functionality and away from 'craft' as a mantra of historical reverence (fig. 6).[21] This is quite a late juncture for true ceramic sculpture to announce itself, and therefore a retrograde aura of novelty applied to the abstracted use of clay has long been present within the British discourse, as is the sense of the divine craft object, ceramic or otherwise, as a cipher for something unknowable, old or slyly unreconstructed. Leach himself, his attraction to this divine spirit, and his nature as a dilettante who never 'really' learnt good craft have been much discussed.[22] While Yanagi praised Leach for the 'naïve power' of his work, Leach complained that 'everywhere in Japan manual dexterity has become the criteria of the applied artist'.[23]

In their lifelong reaching for the humble sublime, then, we have in both Leach and Yanagi an early showing of the idea of the divine craft object as a fundamental human creative lodestone within an increasingly complex world. The appropriation of these aesthetics is something that was of course at odds with their respective class privileges, and this performative compulsion for a spiritually attuned bourgeoisie to appropriate a sense of bucolic tradition and continuity has cycled back again in our present age. Leach was 'categorical' that the power and heritage of folk crafts should be passed into the hands of self-asserting artist-craftspeople, rather than being re-energised in a prelapsarian working class of makers, seeing this as ineffectively unconscious and culturally inert.[24] I feel that the trend now is more towards an anonymising style – the current preference (especially where interior trends are concerned) veers towards the use of coarser, undecorated wares possessing a style of ambiguous authorship and historicity. The 'other power' of the divine craft object, then, has been returned in a sense closer to Yanagi's ideas of *tariki* aesthetics – a spiritual shortcut to the rude energies associated with the historical archetype of the unknown craftsperson. There is also, in the preference for rougher styles of ceramic, and their multiplication with crude wooden furniture and gravitas-laden stone materials, a turn towards something even further removed from the individual spirit of the heroic artist-craftsperson: a reference to the unstoppable and unknowable progression of natural forces, where explicit craftsmanship is concealed by results that strive towards an ambiguously crafted inhumanity. In a globalised visual culture increasingly denuded of meaning, this unegotistical approach to materiality allows the curators and consumers of this style to express a tuning-in to egalitarian channels of natural forces, crude necessity and, perhaps, melancholic feelings of a permanently degraded planet.

## NOTES

1. Porcu 2019, 590.
2. Kikuchi 2004, 199.
3. Yanagi 1976, 24.
4. By 'art world', I mean the sphere of galleries and institutions internationally accepted as being permitted to endow artefacts and phenomena with the status of a high-quality art object with a corresponding price tag, far removed from the realm of functional objects.
5. See Kaplan 2011.
6. See Hauser & Wirth's expansion of their *Make* galleries: Eileen Hanser, 'Hauser and Wirth Is Opening a New Space Dedicated to Craft and Design in the Hamptons', Artnet, 27 May 2022, https://news.artnet.com/market/hauser-and-wirth-make-southampton-2122368 (accessed 7 August 2023).
7. However, of course Yanagi did also consider the use of an object – in both a physical and aesthetic sense – to be a fundamental aspect of its beauty (Yanagi 1972, 197).
8. Thom 2023.
9. *Wabi* is the word most commonly used in the West, although Yanagi actually argued that *wabi*, as a formless spiritual concept, was insufficient for describing the appearance of objects and that the adjective *shibui* was more appropriate to convey an aesthetic quality of laudable restraint (Yanagi 1972, 184).
10. 'Forlorn tea' – a conspicuously rustic 'peasant' style of tea ceremony developed by tea master Sen no Rikyū in the sixteenth century.
11. For a detailed overview of this tendency as it appears in the commercial sphere as well as the domestic, see Tom Wilkins, 'Life in Ruins:The Fetishization of Decay in Contemporary Architecture', https://tmowilkinson.files.wordpress.com/2023/03/life-in-ruins.pdf (accessed 7 August 2023).
12. Rough, wood-fired teaware hailing from medieval peasant kilns centred around Shigaraki Valley and Imbe, Japan.
13. Pitelka 2017.
14. Sontag 2018, 6.
15. Ibid.
16. 'Ornamental Hermits of Eccentric Modern England', https://www.hermitary.com/lore/ornamental_hermits.html (accessed 7 August 2023).
17. An annual prize organized by luxury Spanish fashion brand Loewe, to 'acknowledge and support international artisans … who demonstrate an exceptional ability to create objects of superior aesthetic value'.
18. Cort 1992, 7–30.
19. Oral history interview with Ron Nagle (2003), Archives of American Art, Smithsonian Institution, https://www.aaa.si.edu/collections/interviews/oral-history-interview-ron-nagle-13019 (accessed 7 August 2023).
20. For example, the *Modern British Sculpture* exhibition at the Royal Academy, London, 2011; and *A Rough Equivalent: Sculpture and Pottery in the Post-War Period*, an exhibition held at the Henry Moore Institute, Leeds, in 2010–11.
21. I have heard Alison Britton in particular refer to Leach as a sort of 'blob' – a blockage in dialogue for later British makers who wanted to work with ceramic material as a teleologically liberated material. Britton writes admirably of the contrasting post-war situation in the United States, where clay practice was revealed as 'unproblematically sculpture'. See Britton 2016.
22. For example in De Waal 1998.
23. Ibid., 15.
24. Ibid., 23–4.

ADAM SUTHERLAND

# Making Everyday

## Mingei in practice for a sustainable environment

This chapter looks at the idea of a people's art and the meaning of functional things in everyday use. Written from a personal perspective and drawn from a lifetime of Mingei's insidious influence, it is based on my experiences of working with rural Japanese and English communities under the auspices of Grizedale Arts, an arts organisation based in the English Lake District. Central to Grizedale's ethos is the pursuit of valuable function for art, which is explored through commissioning, curating, making and education. This means that many of our projects foreground craft skills, collaborative production and the expertise of non-artists. The ambition is to develop creative self-determination: the use of creativity as an essential skill, used by everyone in everything; that is to say, an art of the everyday drawn from the resources at hand (fig. 1).

There are a couple of things that I find uncomfortable about the concept of Mingei and that remain difficult to square with my ideas about making. Firstly, the celebration of labour, of unconscious graft, by the non-worker or a person that has chosen to labour, a perverse notion expressed by Eric Gill's bon mot 'the Ecstasy of Drudgery' (fig. 2).[1] It is perhaps an ecstasy that is most deeply enjoyed by the middle and upper classes, eschewing the reality of the relentless grind and utter anonymity of the labourer. This view also implies that the maker is as a beast of burden, with their product only recognised by the educated and sophisticated eye, which feels like such an arrogant idea. The second issue that stands out for me is the bigger concept of valuing raw untutored creativity, an idea of 'realness' in which the authentic is represented by tradition, unquestioning and undeveloped. This concept is a construct of the modern world, a nostalgia that again belongs to the educated class. It seems to me to be reactionary, perhaps a cloaked kind of nationalism. All in all, this is an expression of ideas that would otherwise be unacceptable to the liberal-minded aesthete, unacceptable to me, hence my ambivalence about Mingei, or at least what I understand of its ambitions. I find Mingei a conundrum. As much as I might deride many of its principles, the artefacts draw me in. I recognise the impulse to embrace the aesthetic but understand that as a reactionary response to the modern world. I enjoy the idea of the anonymous maker, and the implied attack on the idea of individual genius and the Western Romantic tradition. These notions sit comfortably with my own vision for an art of the everyday. Yet I have never adopted the ideas behind Mingei, ideas I rejected while still at school.

I was educated at Dartington Hall School, a dynamic experiment in the Arts and Crafts legacy, driven by ideas

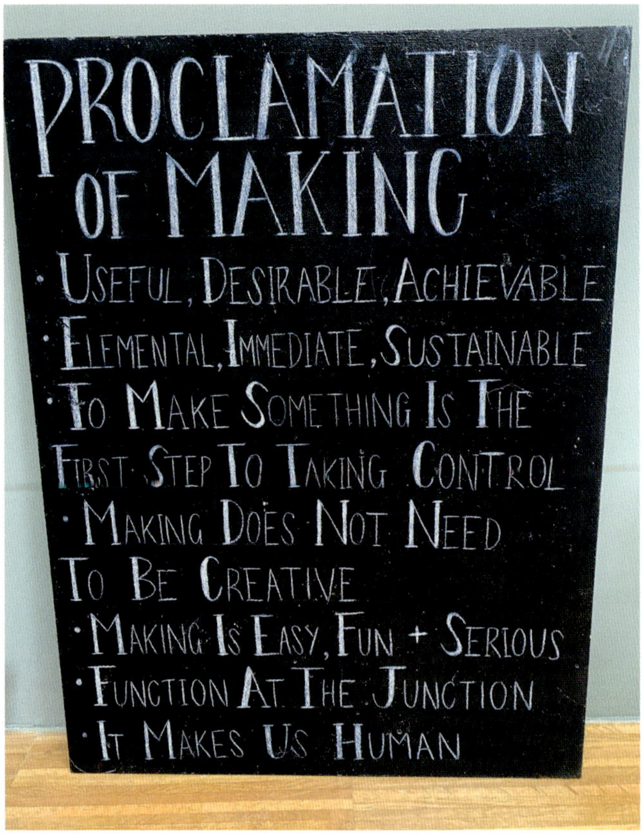


FIG 1 'Proclamation of Making' at Grizedale Arts
Credit: Adam Sutherland

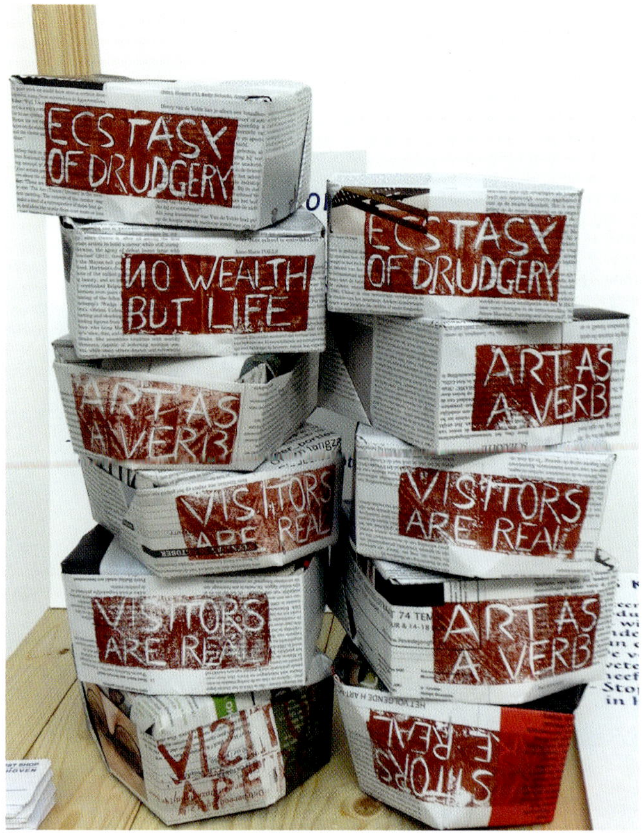


FIG 2 Newspaper carpenter's hat as worn by Eric Gill, from Grizedale Arts exhibition for Arte Útil at the Van Abbe Museum, Eindhoven | Credit: Adam Sutherland

derived from the writings of John Ruskin (1819–1900). Founded in 1926, it was based on a free-flowing openness to input, curated by serendipity and the connectedness of interesting thinkers of that time. Bernard Leach (1887–1979) played a significant role (and by default so did Ruskin, too) in the development of the Mingei ideas he brought back from Japan to Dartington. Prior to his involvement in pottery, Leach had been taught etching by Frank Brangwyn (1867–1956), a celebrated self-taught artist of the period who had himself worked for William Morris (1834–1896). Brangwyn's influence is very apparent in Leach's early ceramic work and ideology (figs 3, 4).

Leach taught pottery at Dartington and the school was in many ways in tune with his ideas, including the search for authentic makers and recreating the past as a backdrop for the construction of a modern future. I was at the school in the early 1970s and even then, despite the loss of momentum of many of its bigger ideas and ethos, we were still exposed to the ideas of Mingei. A quote attributed to Hamada Shōji (1894–1978) on the wall of the school pottery read 'A good pot is like walking down a gentle slope in a warm breeze'. My response at the time was, to say the least, not positive. I was confused as to why we made such small tea bowls for our shredded wheat and why we attached 'lugs' (small, ineffectual handles) to vases (fig. 5). I came to despise the sameness, the brownness, the tastefulness: all affectation, as I understood it, or rather misunderstood it. The Leach influence created a straitjacket of conformity; if you stepped away from it, you would be ostracised. One of my teachers was Bernard Forrester (1908–1990), one of Leach's early apprentices, who subsequently swore that he would never make two pots alike again. Forrester's departure from the conformist studio pottery world (the English manifestation of Mingei ideology) and the adoption of a kind of rough-hewn Byzantine aesthetic saw him demoted – or at least that is how I saw it – at Dartington from the pottery to being the jewellery teacher. A kind of Puritan's curse, a punishment for not towing the party line, for indulging in the decorative?

Much of the ethos of Dartington was unexplained to the pupils. We wandered among the Gerald Summers furniture, leant against the Rabindranath Tagore paintings, rolled cigarettes in the Gropius cinema, snogged behind the Henry Moores, oblivious to their meaning. It was only in later life that I started to understand where the ideas were coming from and what they all really meant in a wider context. But the fundamental ideas of learning, usefulness and the politics of making remained embedded in my thinking about society, education and ways to live. This idea – if it ever really was intended – of learning through osmosis came equally to inform how Grizedale Arts approached the vexed issue of education.

The idea of an authentic, unconscious raw art, a kind of stripped-down fantasy of good functional design, was and remains very attractive. It relies on the natural power of materials; they do the work, with the maker merely a conduit. Yet this return to a 'form follows function' aesthetic, however attractive, seems to me to be a construct of the educated, a sophisticated take on non-design that ignores the socio-economic and political framework that in fact has always dictated the majority of production. It seeks out and celebrates the 'real' maker, a person who produces things unconscious of art history, fashion or industry and instead makes things for the 'real' reason that what is being made is essentially, primarily useful.

Anything we now make in craft is not from this position. Craft is not needed; the production of essentials has long been overtaken by machine production. Making has instead moved to being a celebration of individualism. I remember as a teenager in the early 1970s travelling through rural Spain and being invited to lunch in farmers' homes. All the beautiful, raw folk pottery would be removed from sight and brightly coloured plastic versions of the same things would proudly replace them (albeit, as it turns out, these would be less functional: a plastic *botijo* does not cool water as much as warm it). This reinforced my own ambivalence about enjoying the rustic; the fetishisation of something that was not valued by its actual users coalesced with the abhorrence of plastics, synthetic colours and other prejudices of the educated mind. I would suggest that the lauding of outsider art is in effect appropriation of another culture. It is the spoils of war, the identity theft of the vanquished by an educated middle class whose cultural world now dominates society.

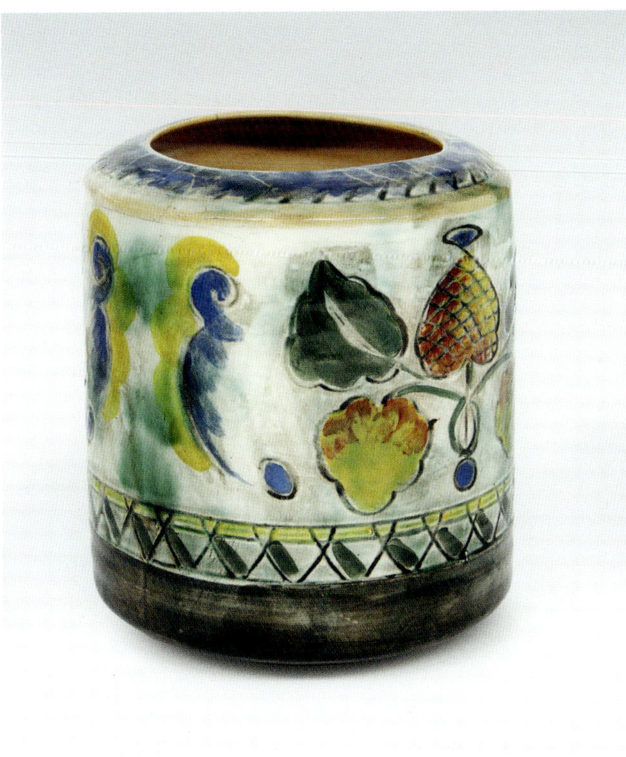

**FIG 3** Frank Brangwyn, pot, earthenware, 1930, William Morris Gallery, London Borough of Waltham Forest

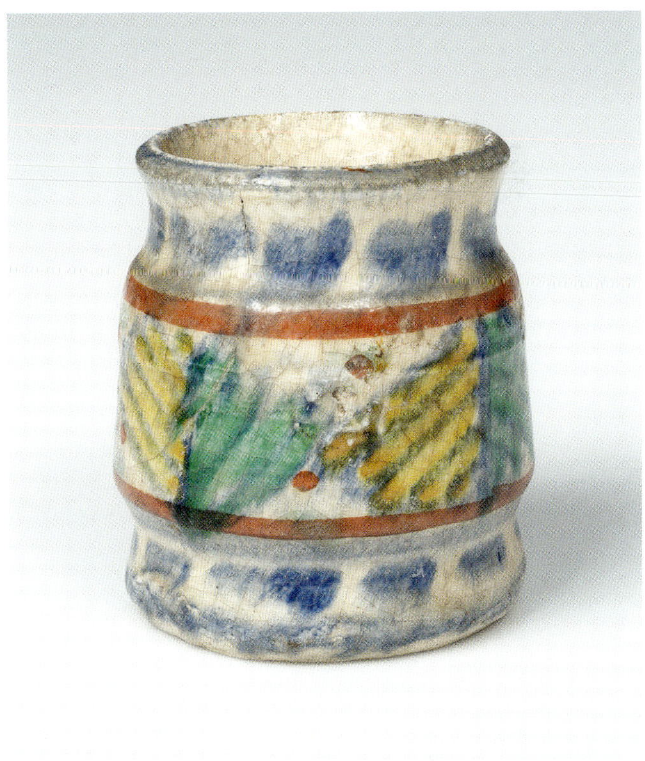

**FIG 4** Bernard Leach, small vase or *unomi* tea vessel, Raku ware, 1920s Credit: P.75.75 © Crafts Study Centre, University for the Creative Arts

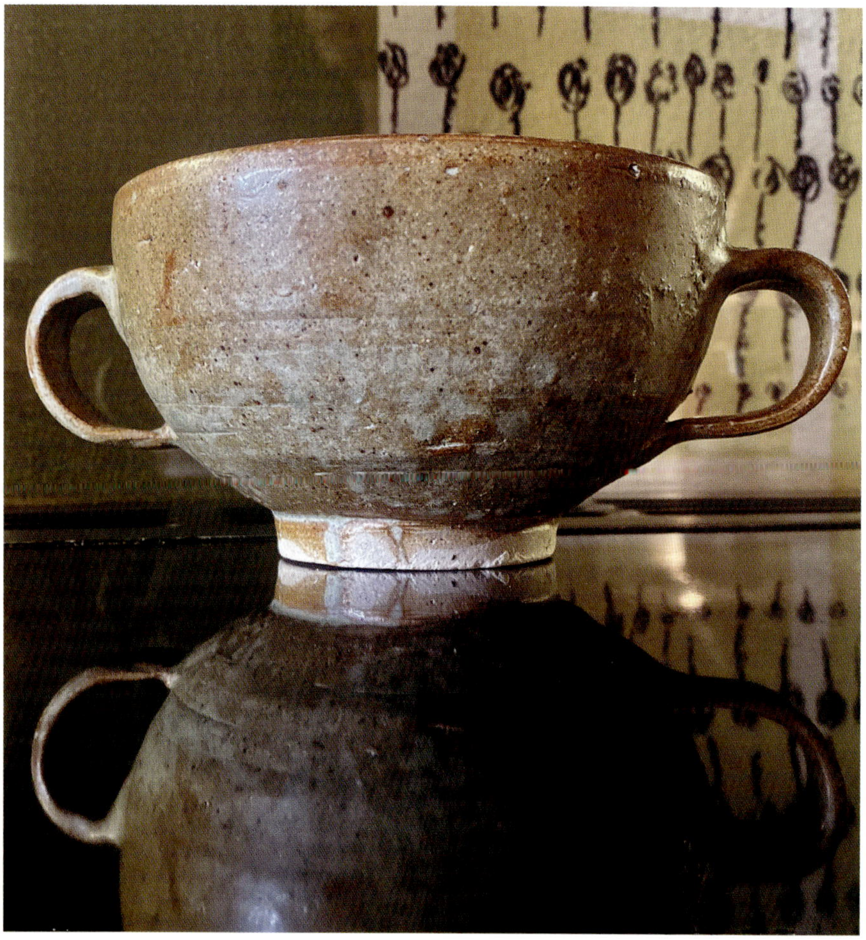

FIG 5 Shredded wheat bowl made by the author aged 14, still in everyday use Credit: Adam Sutherland

The appreciation of 'raw' creation is not new; it recurs over and over through the history of art and culture. A very early example would be the reassessment of the wine jar or *meiping* vase from the Chinese Tang (618–907) and Song (960–1279) dynasties. 'Humble' administrators, the intellectuals of the period, 'discovered' the *meiping* vase as an object of beauty; they appropriated its use for the display of wild plum blossom and it became valued as antique, embedded as a signifier of class and divorced from its former function as a wine vessel. A similar fate befell the celebrated Korean moon jar, where the dimensions of the ware reflect its symbolic value: the bigger the jar, the richer the owner and the more food it would store, despite the fact that it has long since lost any food-related function. It was the moon jar and similar wares that Yanagi Sōetsu (1899–1961) and Leach searched for in Korea, such refunctioned functional objects that they identified as Mingei: wares that were used almost as a weapon in the promotion of their ideals. It was a moon jar from Korea that Leach gave to Lucie Rie (1902–1995) as a criticism of her thin throwing and her modernist aesthetic, and, perhaps, as an act of love (fig. 6).

Rie's moon jar is now in the British Museum. This habit of housing the humblest of objects in the grandest of buildings is a somewhat absurd practice. It reflects the overblown nature of the value of making, which, in the end, is just making. There is no mystique; anyone can do it, and that should be the joy of it, but it is in a way the very thing that is so quickly denied, pushing the idea of making into a mystical place where the 'expert' once again holds forth. Hamada's famous, albeit anecdotal, quote that it took him 60 years and 10 seconds to decorate a plate is very much part of that fantasy. If anything, making is more about the acceptance of chance, a confidence and ease of creation, something Hamada also believed. To all intents and purposes anyone could have made those decorative marks. The absolute beginner would be indistinguishable from those with a lifetime of learning. It is these conundrums that complicate and devalue the ethos of an art of the people, given an arbitrary, gentrified value by the elite, and it is these aspects that I rebelled against and have sought ways around (fig. 7).

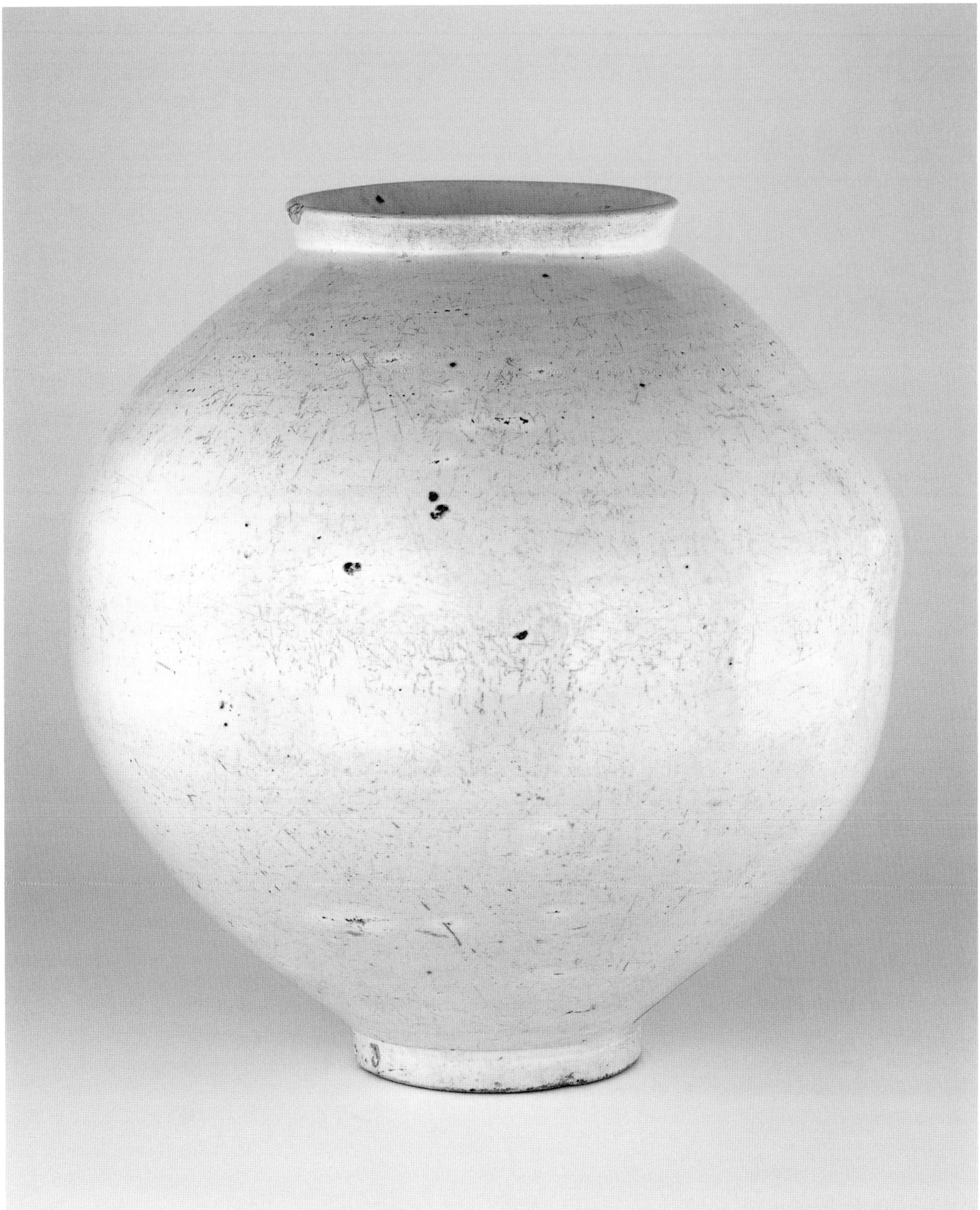

**FIG 6** Moon jar, Korean, glazed white porcelain, eighteenth century, given to Lucie Rie by Bernard Leach, British Museum

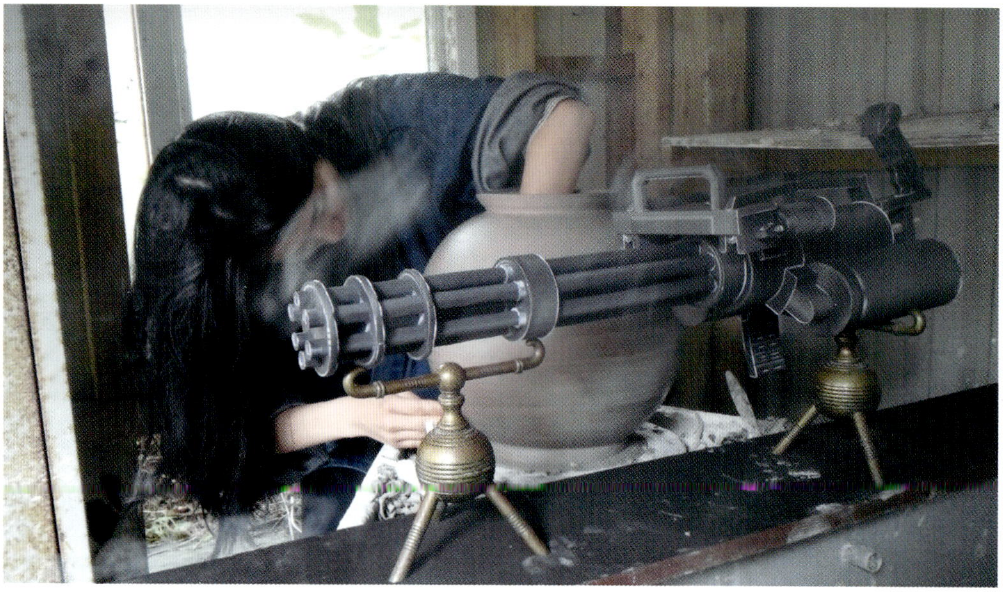

FIG 7 *The Moon Vase and the Machine Gun*, from Grizedale Arts exhibition *After Ford 151: The Politics of Craft* Credit: Adam Sutherland

In more than 20 years working for Grizedale Arts I have tried to approach the world of making in a non-hierarchical way, sitting the making of the amateur alongside the work of the art school version of making. In the early days, this approach was fairly uncomfortable, and neither party was happy. But as the art construct of socially engaged practice began to emerge in the late 1990s, the divisions were recontextualised. A difficulty emerges, however, as I feel that while this non-art art was instrumentalised to support the idea of engagement, it was not really valued in itself, or its appreciation was on a different level than originally intended, for example for its failings or ineptitude. The people's art became a symbol and an indicator of the more complex ideas behind the art construct. One example of such art is Jeremy Deller (b.1966) and Alan Kane's (b.1961) folk archive project, which they developed between 1998 and 2005, focusing particularly on Egremont, a 'lost' community on the west coast of Cumbria. On one occasion Jeremy and Alan were staying at Grizedale during a kind of faux festival we had constructed which focused on everyday making (*A Different Weekend*, 2000). They had enjoyed a huge cake made collectively by a number of local women, a composite that illustrated the valley and its perceived values and highlights. Jeremy and Alan were considering the cake for the folk archive. It fitted the rules, having been made by local people, yet had been brought about by the intervention of an artist, Karen Guthrie (b.1970). They decided that the proximity of that artist ruled the work invalid for the archive, as it was not authentic, being potentially sullied by the whiff of an art education.

At Grizedale we have worked with several 'outsider' artists, perhaps most notably Peter Hodgson (b.1950; fig. 8). We have done our best to expose Peter to as much 'art' as he could bear. He has worked with artists such as the Turner Prize winner Laure Prouvost (b.1978), whom he credits as a great influence and with whom he particularly enjoys collaborating. We have also encouraged him to join classes and learn how to do things 'properly'. His response was that it was 'OK', but that learning to do things properly really did 'take the fun out of it'. The lesson we learnt was that Peter was unchanged by the exposure as he already had a philosophy of making and had thought it through, even if he had not written it down. He has always retained functionality in everything he makes: even drawings are on blank postcards for sending. Yet his work only sells to what might be termed the 'educated' class, not to his local peers. The loss of personal identity through the evolution and artistic development of the maker is one of Mingei's most vexed issues. What is evolution and what is gentrification may not be so different. It is necessary to recognise that education cannot be used as a blunt instrument and that the relationship between artist and consumer is complex and multi-layered.

In the Grizedale Arts project *The Coniston Institute* (2009–19) we put art and ourselves into the service of the community, reacting to invitations from community and special-interest groups. The idea was to accept these invitations and expand on them, demonstrating the value to communities of creative thinking in everyday life. This philosophy was centred around an acceptance of the power of territory and ownership, and that whatever happened with the project was within the ownership of the inviter-host, in this case the community or communities. It's a somewhat obvious shift, from delivering art to the people to responding to the people with art, albeit art that is pre-set to perform a clearly defined function, that of being useful. It is also a kind of hybrid of the ideas behind Mingei, which from the outset combined the 'art of the people' with the 'educated' version of what it meant to be creative.

The other key aspect of this way of working is the adherence to the use of local, immediately available resources, people and materials, thereby making the most of what is around you. This idea echoes Yanagi's theories and some of the ethos of Dartington. Over a period of ten years, Grizedale and its collective of people worked with a number of different groups on projects set out by the aesthetics and ambitions of those groups. The objective at the time was to be anonymous, a collective of people working together using the ethos of making everything. It encouraged a do-it-yourself process even up to making things by hand that were available in industrial form, for example handmade spaghetti hoops (fig. 9). The project aimed to prove that everyone could make, and that through making the individual engendered a sense of the possibility to control and shape the world around them: I can make this, it's useful, I use it. This political message seems to me the principal value in making: it is a vital tool for understanding control and self-determination. One of the most revealing incidents occurred while I was running a house-building workshop with our youth club on a visit to Lawson Park (Grizedale Arts's base in the Lake District). One of the younger members of the club looked around the interior and exclaimed in wonder that it was 'almost as if someone had thought about everything in the building'.

The application of these ideas internationally, including in Japan and Korea, is at least twofold. The process of working as a mixed collective of what I find myself referring to as 'real people and art people' seems to me to benefit both parties. It often involves finding solutions to embedded issues and also releasing ways of working from the straitjackets we have ourselves created. This presents opportunities to see outside our usual working lives, gaining some perspective on how we do things well or badly. Be it shining examples or dire warnings, we all need exposure to both. Aside from the personal benefits of a more expansive perspective, these working experiences also seem to have generated a renewed interest in being active in the immediate community, creating programmes for the performing arts, taking roles in societies and special-interest agitation: in effect an expanded notion of self-determination, community future planning and a richer, more vibrant way of living.

In 2006 we received an invitation from the Echigo-Tsumari Triennale and a subsequent invitation from the remote mountain village of Tōge, Yamagata prefecture. The project

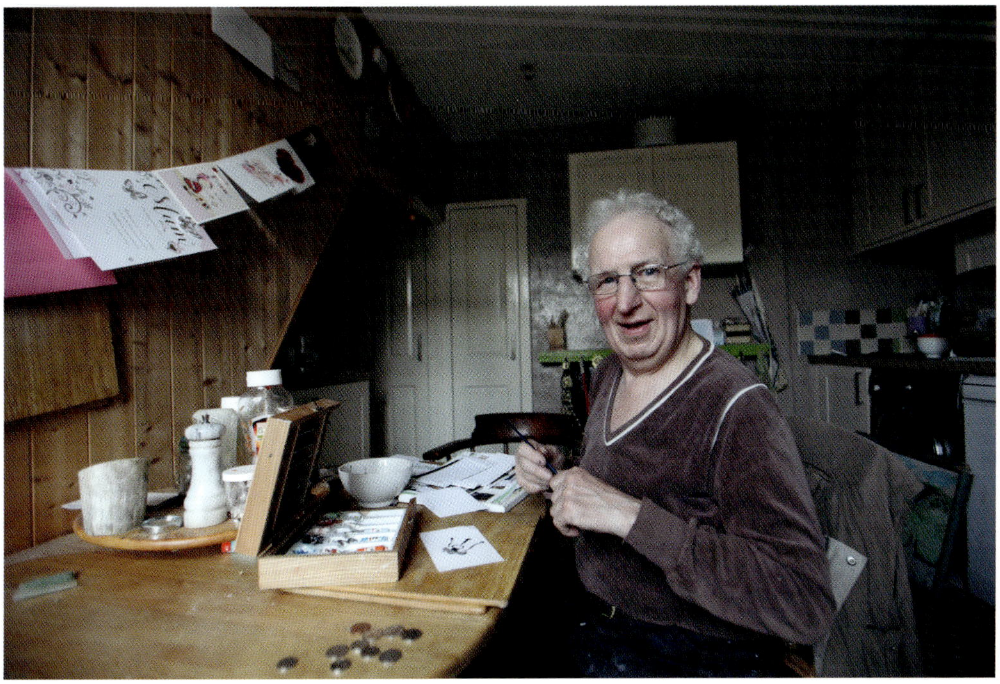

FIG 8 Peter Hodgson painting at his home in Ambleside, 2017 Credit: Karen Guthrie

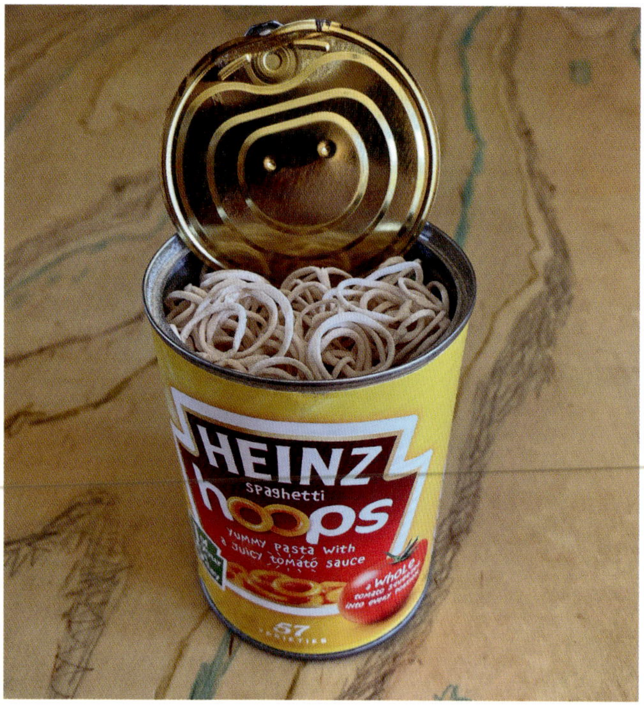

FIG 9 Spaghetti hoops for *Crap Italian*, Francesca Ulivi

attempted to assist the village with its ambition to better understand tourism and to help to generate self-determination, now scarce in its ageing community. Seven artists lived and worked in the village on functional projects before taking part in an art festival in Tokyo. The villagers joined the artists there as performers and in the presentation of a village market dedicated to their artist-rebranded rice. The programme continued in 2007 with a return visit to the UK by seven of the Tōge village farmers, who helped develop the farm at Lawson Park (creating a series of terraces now called 'The Paddies') and ran a wild-food cookery workshop attended by chefs from top local restaurants. The visit concluded with a successful one-day Japanese country café in Coniston village, focusing on local wild food, in particular bracken, the ubiquitous wild fern of the Lakeland fells. Each part of the project was highly influential on both communities and remarkably successful, with nearly all the artist-initiated projects being adapted and continued to this day.

In 2017 we were honoured to be invited to lead an initiative to connect the Japanese village of Kiwanosato (in Shimonoseki, western Japan) to a viable future. The project was a 'ten-year dream' as conceived by an 87-year-old local farmer, Okamoto Tadashi (1930–2023; fig. 10). The ambition of his project was to bring younger people to the farming way of life, to his small village with a rapidly ageing population. Working with the Fairland, a group of artists, designers and practitioners, we built and ran a bread oven, an antiques shop and a café, as well as taking part in pickle-making, soba noodle-making, bamboo harvesting, a ceramics workshop and basket-making. As a result of these research projects we developed the idea of an entire village as a school, one that could exchange skills (social and craft) with other villages in different parts of the world. We are growing this project as part of a worldwide initiative called 'The Confederacy of Villages'. We aim to learn from each other's approaches to similar issues, including housing, population and infrastructure. The project is set to become an ongoing host for a series of 'schools' in architecture, craft, hosting, collective working and reinvention, each led by different groups from across the globe. A recent manifestation of this in the Lake District has been a hands-on residential workshop to collaboratively build a small off-grid cold store. Led by architect Hayatsu Takeshi (b.1970), the project explored the use of local, natural materials and traditional Japanese and British building techniques.

It is striking that in Japan in particular there is a notion of collective working that is absolutely expected, and from the outside looks ideal. However, it is also clear that it can be very restrictive and demoralising for some people. Grizedale's experience of working in Japan has been educative: we have seen examples of functional working rural communities, diversification, and people living apparently rich, fulfilling lives. However, this rural life is not attractive to a younger generation and villages are being abandoned across the country; something is not working. For all the apparent valuing of craft and rural skills, these skills often only survive in a government-supported form, as signifiers of national identity. In Japan, as elsewhere, the reality of the 'art of the people' is on the whole centred around affordable practical solutions, as it has always been, yet this increasingly now means the adaptation of waste from mechanised production. The art of the people marches on: Mingei maybe needs to change its rules if it is to keep in step.

## NOTE

1. For a comprehensive account of Gill's life and work, see MacCarthy 1990.

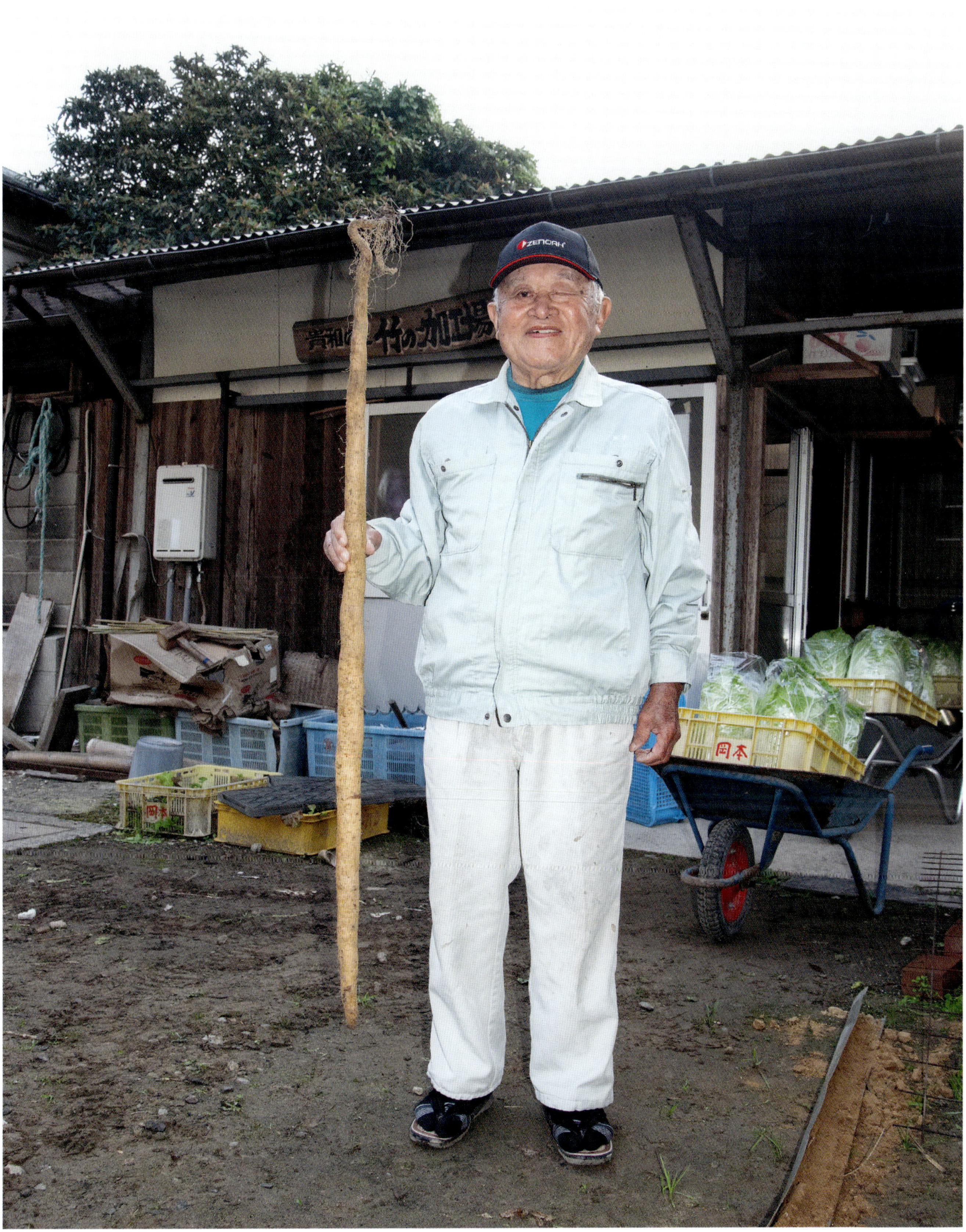


**FIG 10** Okamoto Tadashi, originator of 'The Dream of Kiwanosato' project, 2017
Credit: Photograph © Motoko Fujita

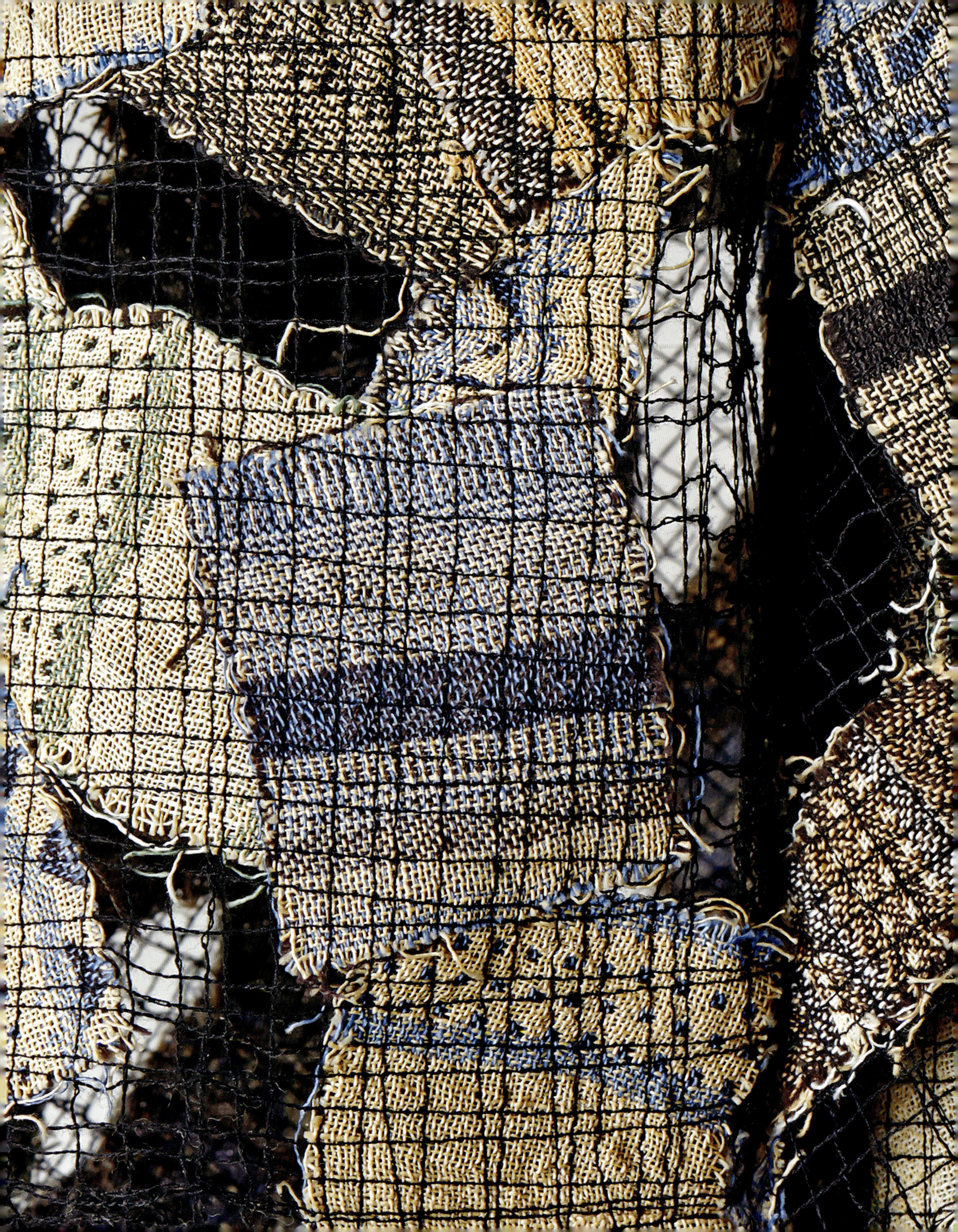

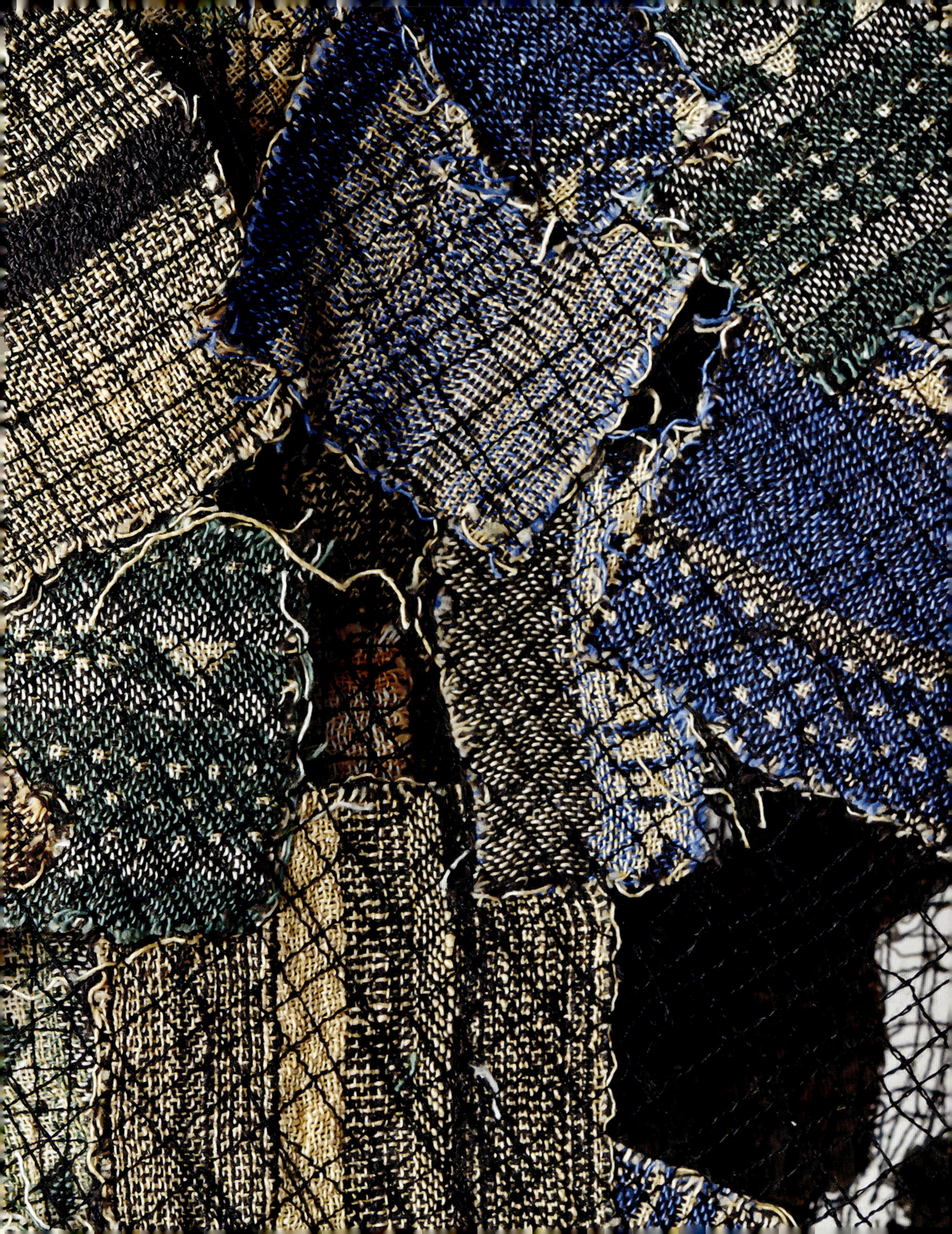

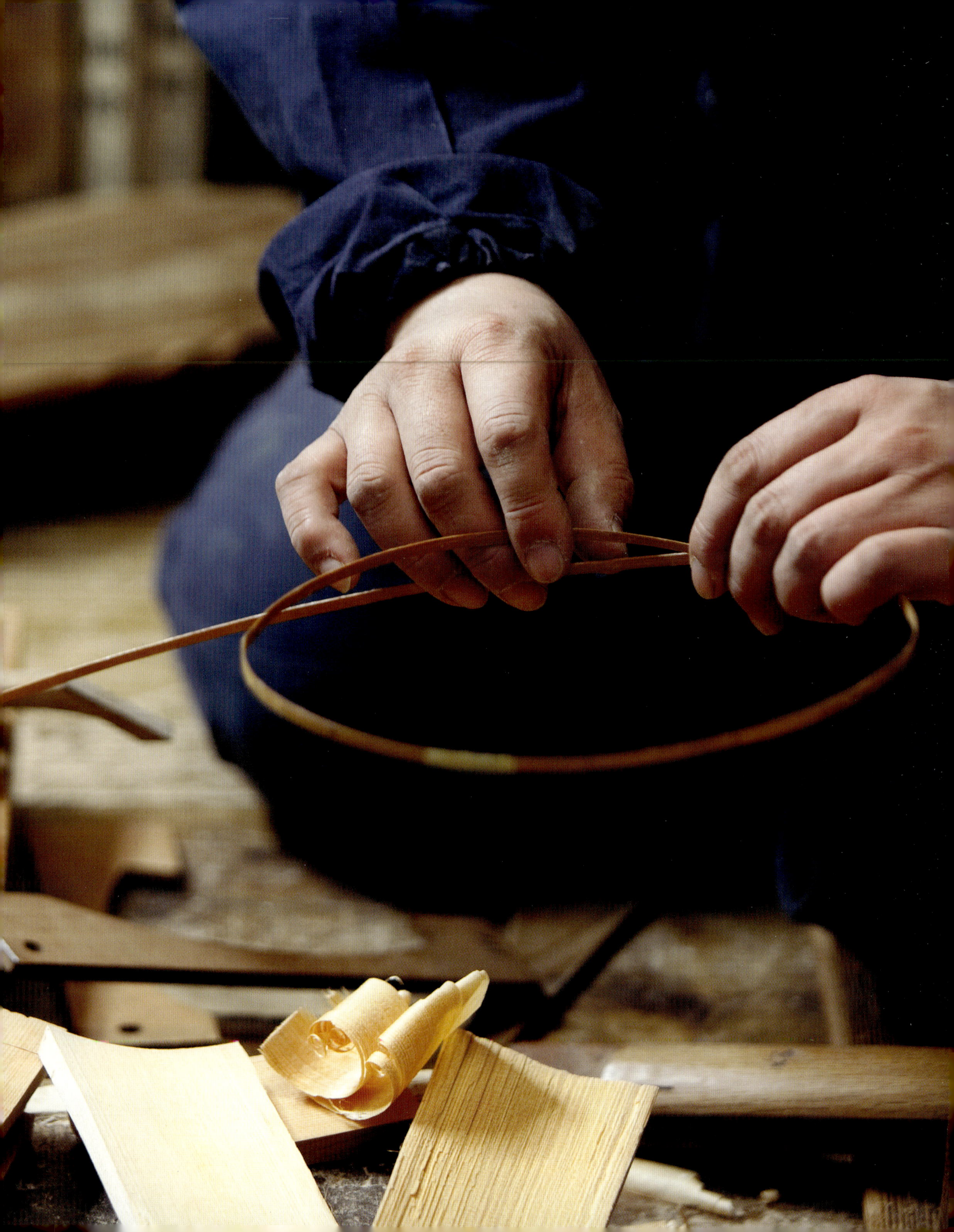

# Maker Profiles

PROFILE BY YOSHIZAWA TOMO

# Fukasawa Naoto

'I used to design "cool" products . . . coolest of the coolest. But at some point, I started questioning that.' This is how Fukasawa Naoto (b.1956), the internationally renowned designer and director of the Japan Folk Crafts Museum since 2012, talks about his trajectory. 'The cool, when it's reached its extreme, doesn't invite people into the space: there is no intimacy nor closeness. It wasn't something I wanted at my core.'

In Fukasawa's opening address to the Japan Folk Crafts Museum he described the allure of Mingei as *kawaii*, a term that attracted criticism for its associations with cuteness, but which he suggests translating to English as a feeling of warmth. 'If you had a dog, you'd pat it. In the same way, I can't help patting these *komainu* (lion dog statues)', he says, showing photos of the carved stone creatures that he found when travelling through Asia. The simple lined statue, possibly carved by an amateur craftsperson, still resembles the square chunks of stone from which it was shaped. 'When I'm referring to *kawaii*, I am looking at the personality held within the shape. Shape and personality are inseparable.'

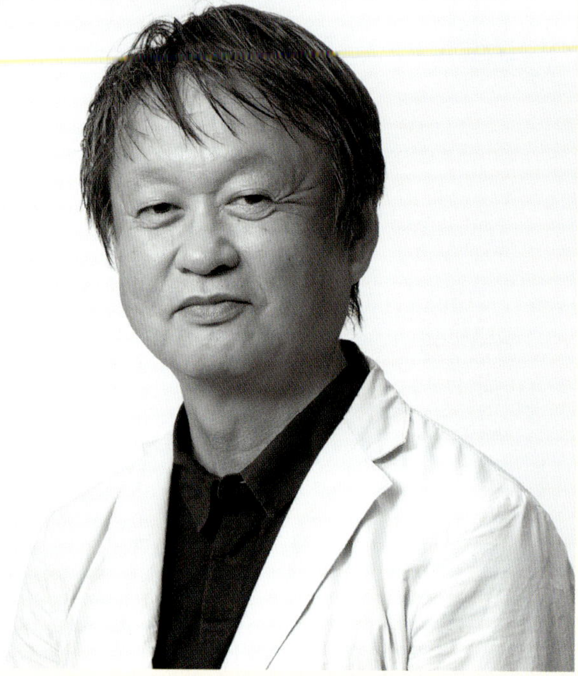

In the subsequent decade, this perception has deepened. 'The sense of closeness and openness is something Yanagi was drawn to, which also manifested in his pursuit of and call for humanity and peace. It is still the essence that moves me every time I encounter Yanagi's collection.'

As a designer, Fukasawa considers himself lucky. 'I was able to work with real artisans – for example, a leather craftsman in Italy – and saw how he would realise the meticulous curve on the back of the chair by a touch of his hands.' This sense of human contact is the essence that he incorporates into his designs.

The alienation of people from the products they create, accelerated today through modern technology, troubles Fukasawa. He gives the example of someone designing a house without being physically present. 'That's not interesting. Ideally, to fully appreciate an object, you must be in that space, directly feeling the entire surroundings, ambience and the air.'

Mingei objects provide an antidote to this sense of alienation. Made from regionally available materials, by local people, in accordance with seasonal routines, they are 'the product of the surroundings, ambience, and environment.'

This sense of appropriateness to surroundings stretches across time as well as space. 'The world has entirely changed from a century ago, which makes it difficult to live with Mingei objects in today's setting. But the soul of Mingei can still be alive today. How Mingei fitted into and was needed in the everyday life of people then; the same spirit can or should be found today.' Fukasawa himself lives with handmade objects, such as a woven basket by Nakagawara Shinichi which fits perfectly into the contemporary space designed by Fukasawa himself.

'The changes [in today's world] are too drastic and I see many people are searching for a sense of groundedness. They want to know where they stand. That's why people visit the Japan Folk Crafts Museum: they instinctively know what Mingei offers.'

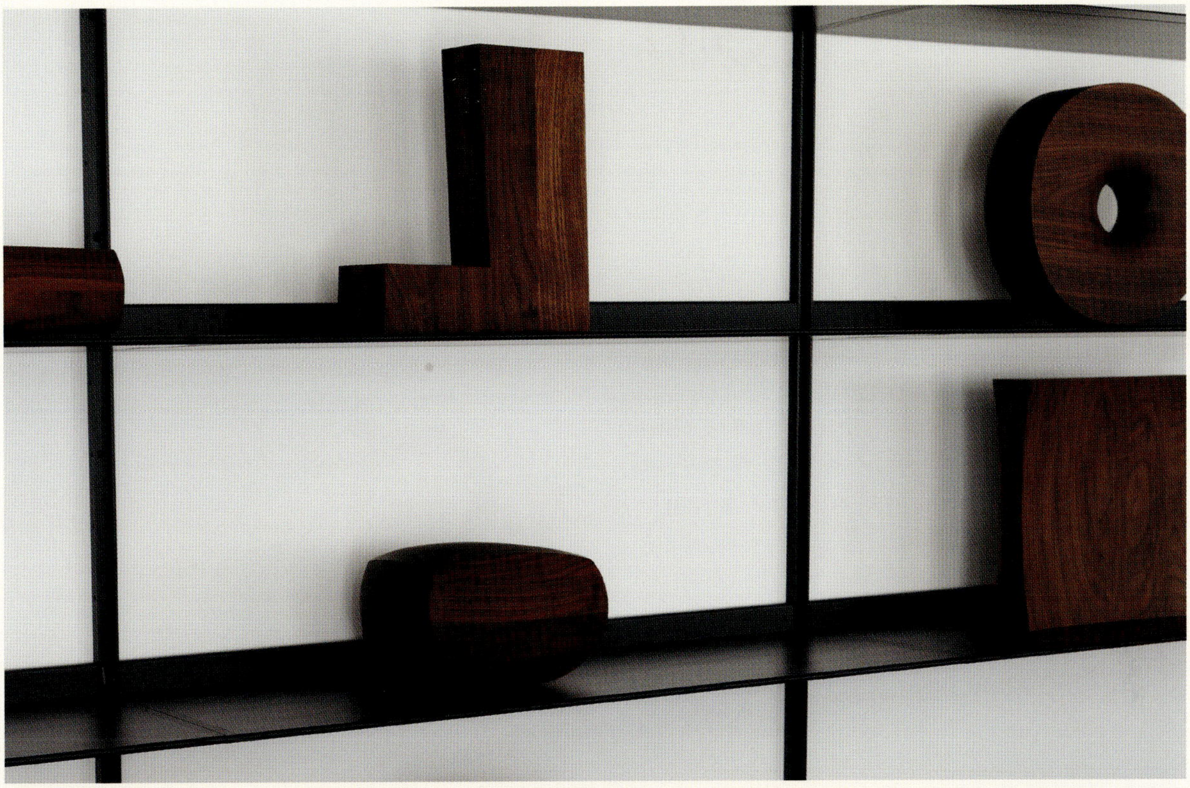

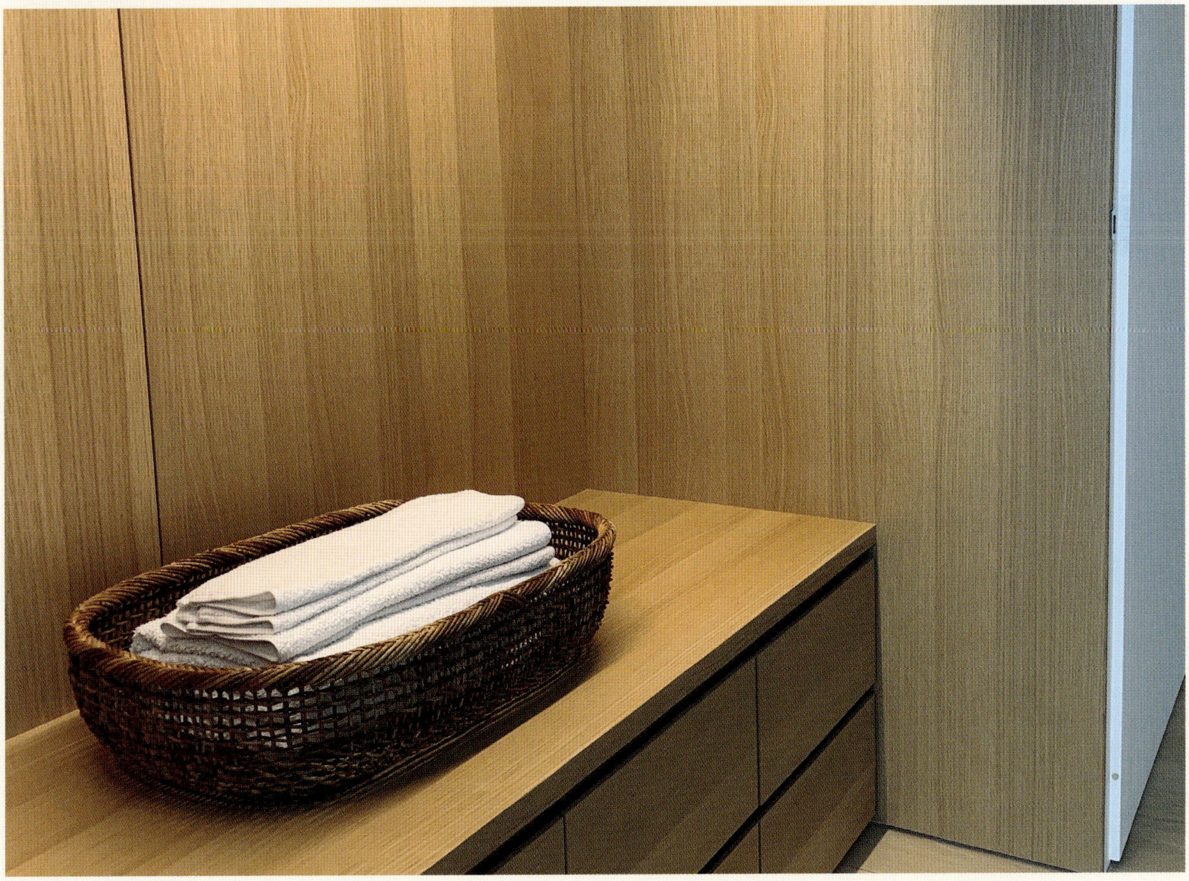

PROFILE BY YOSHIZAWA TOMO

# Hamada Tomoo

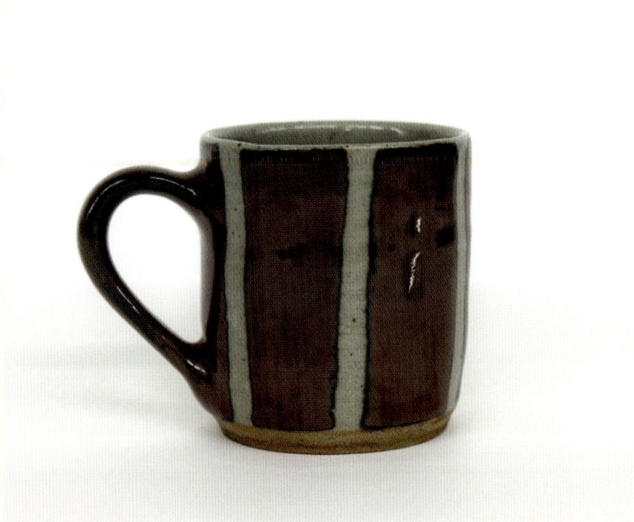

'They wanted to make Mingei internationally popular, so they shortened *minshūteki kōgei* to Mingei. And it was successful, possibly too successful.'

This is the view of Hamada Tomoo (b.1967), a grandson of Hamada Shōji, ceramic artist at the Hamada-gama Pottery, and Director of the Shōji Hamada Memorial Mashiko Sankōkan Museum. 'The term was catchy and spread quickly. In the 1950s and 1960s, there was a Mingei boom in Japan, when every corner shop in the countryside had "Mingei" souvenirs.' In Hamada Tomoo's words, both Yanagi Sōetsu and Hamada Shōji showed some concerns about this saturation of the concept of Mingei. He laughs, 'Maybe it should have been kept at the lengthy and hard-to-remember *minshūteki kōgei*.'

'I think it's good to be reminded that Mingei, the term born in 1925, was referring to the objects that were a century old then, which were almost disappearing. Take ceramics for example, kettles, sake containers, water vases . . . daily necessities that used to be made with clay were about to be replaced with metal, glass and water taps.' The Mingei movement, then, was already about redesigning objects so they could be used in the present-day context. 'Mingei is about being relevant in today's everyday life.' With this in mind, how has he kept the aspect of tradition, in adjusting and innovating for current production? 'It has to be 100 per cent handmade and good design.'

In today's Hamada-gama kiln, *shokunin* (artisan) potters make standard wares that are simple and can be 'mass-produced' by hand. Hamada Shōji, his son Shinsaku (1929–2023) and Tomoo himself have designed these standard wares, which are in line with Mingei aesthetics and principles. Bernard Leach also visited, on one occasion teaching them how to make mugs. 'They are selling more than teacups today', says Hamada. Separately from these everyday objects, Hamada and his father and grandfather have, as artists, also been creating art pieces that cannot be mass-produced.

'Shōji lived and worked in the countryside in the UK 100 years ago. What he saw then was the ideal country life, a beautiful and healthy way of living. The buildings might have looked old from the outside but they were refurbished and comfortable inside, and beautiful crafts were born from this lifestyle. And he wanted to recreate such surroundings when he returned to Japan. He knew neither Tokyo nor Kyoto would do; it had to be either Okinawa or Mashiko. And he chose Mashiko.'

Hamada Shōji bought and transferred more than ten old farmhouses from Mashiko and nearby areas. They are now maintained by Hamada Tomoo and his family, and open for visitors and people from the Mashiko community as the Shōji Hamada Memorial Mashiko Sankōkan Museum. While today's working kiln is now located nearby, the potters' studio and ascending kilns within the museum remain functional for demonstrations and special occasions. The essence of country life Shōji saw in the early twentieth century can still be felt and touched here in Mashiko.

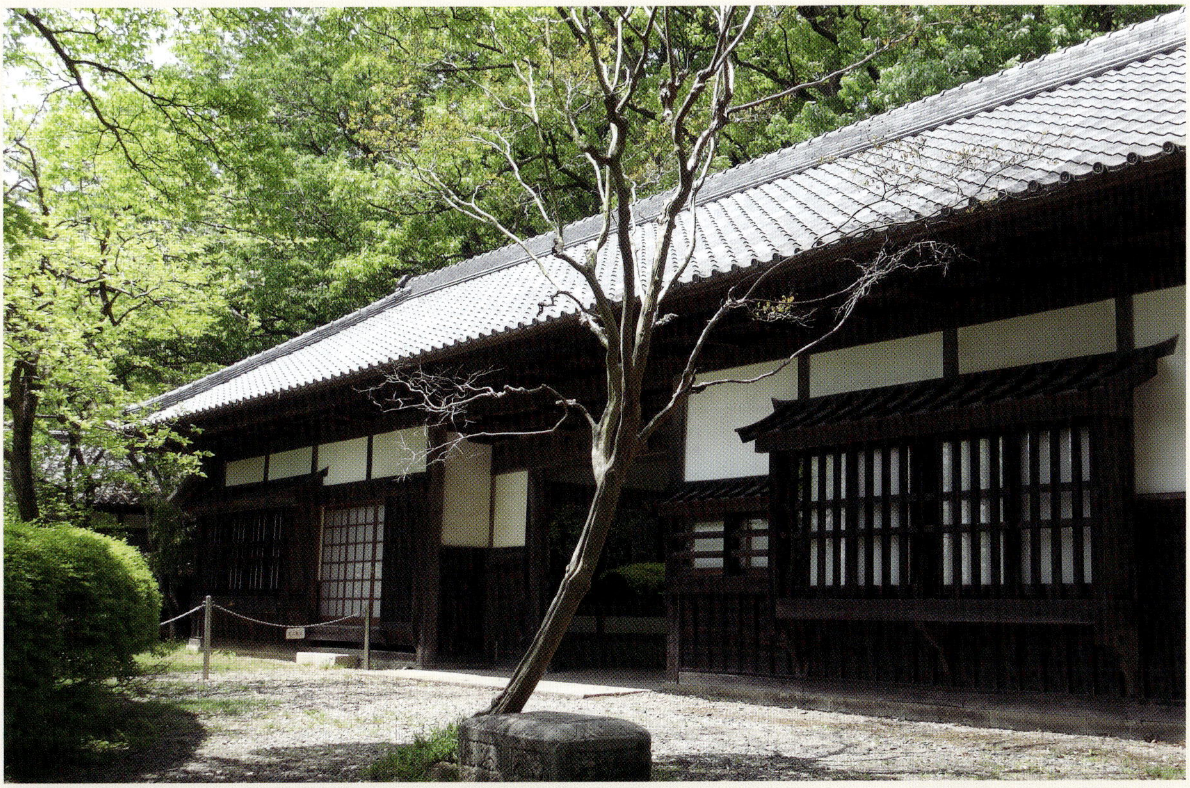

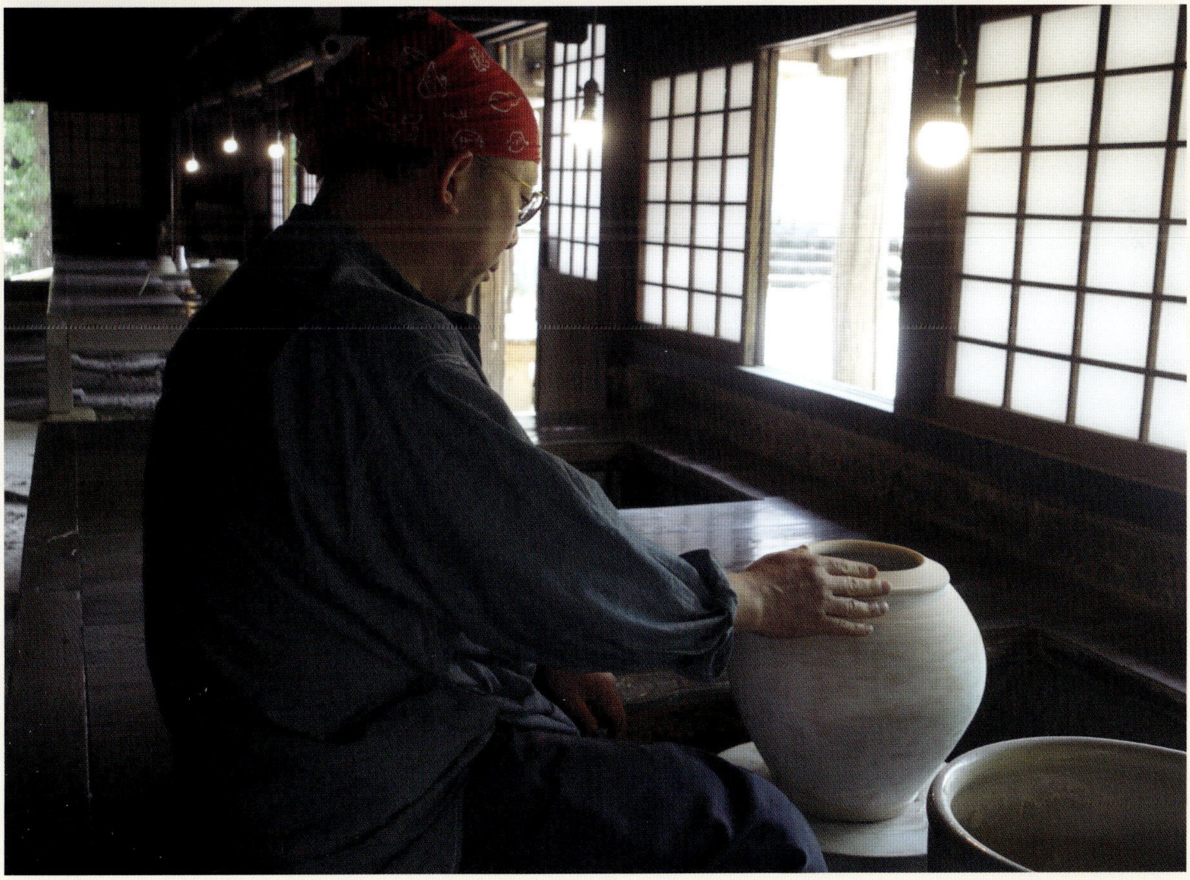

PROFILE BY YOSHIZAWA TOMO

# Oikawa Waka

Kōgensha, today one of the most prestigious retailers of folk craft products in Japan, is located in Morioka, Iwate prefecture. It has been the northern hub of Mingei for close to a century. The founder, Oikawa Shiro (1896–1974), was one of the most passionate supporters of Yanagi Sōetsu and the Mingei movement, although Kōgensha originally started as a publisher for the work of Miyazawa Kenji (1896–1933), a novelist, poet and author of children's literature. The publishing house had little success, and out of necessity in around 1935 Oikawa decided to reorient his business. He started to produce and sell local crafts, such as lacquerware and ironware, and later increased the shop's capacity to accommodate contemporary handmade crafts from all over Japan and beyond. Kōgensha also provided workshops for craftspeople to practise their skills.

Oikawa Waka (b.1944) grew up in Tokyo, close to the Japan Folk Crafts Museum. She studied law before marrying her university classmate Ryūji, grandson of Shiro, after graduation. Before long, they both moved to Morioka to help run Kōgensha. In Oikawa Waka's words: 'My husband was called to help them. I wasn't told to do anything, but then again, everyone else in the family was there working together so I naturally joined. It was also Shiro, my grandfather-in-law... there was something about him that made me think, "I want to work close to him."'

During this time Shiro, his four daughters, Waka and her husband used to gather in the living room daily to review handmade crafts sent to their shop. 'They would exchange candid, honest opinions. It's not like Shiro had the final say, either. In most cases, one of his daughters [her aunts-in-law] said something to differ', she smiles. Oikawa Waka believes the process helped cultivate her aesthetic sense: 'Shiro told me to see objects as they are. Leave my logic behind. Forget by whom or where they'd been made. It's not even about whether I like it or not. See if it's good or not.'

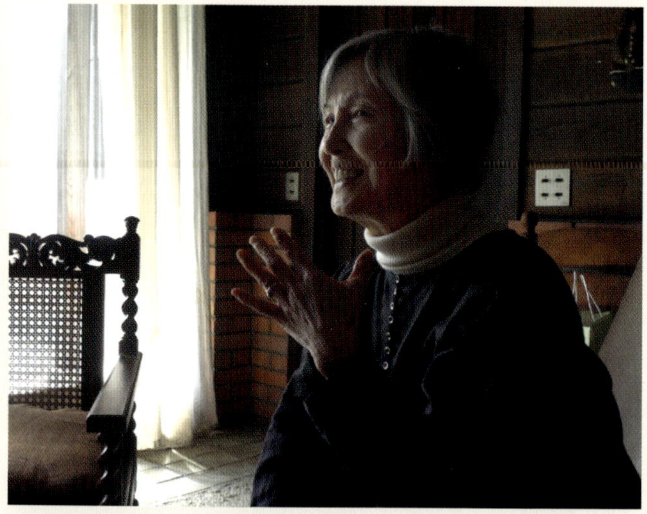

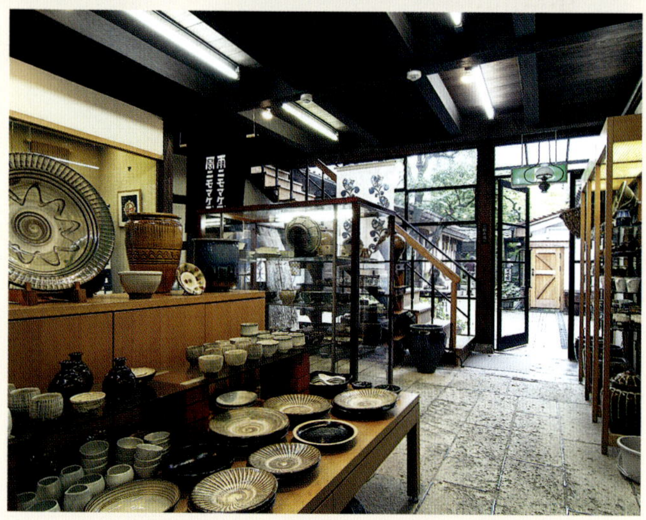

Oikawa Waka's husband Ryūji passed away in 2015 and she took on the responsibility of running the space, which includes a café and attractive courtyard overlooking the Kitakami River. Over the decades she has been involved in Kōgensha, Waka has witnessed many changes. 'I wonder if the current resurgence of Mingei in Japan has the same essence as the time when it started. Mingei is considered to be about objects. But we cannot bypass the human aspects involved in it. To me, Mingei encompasses the whole.'

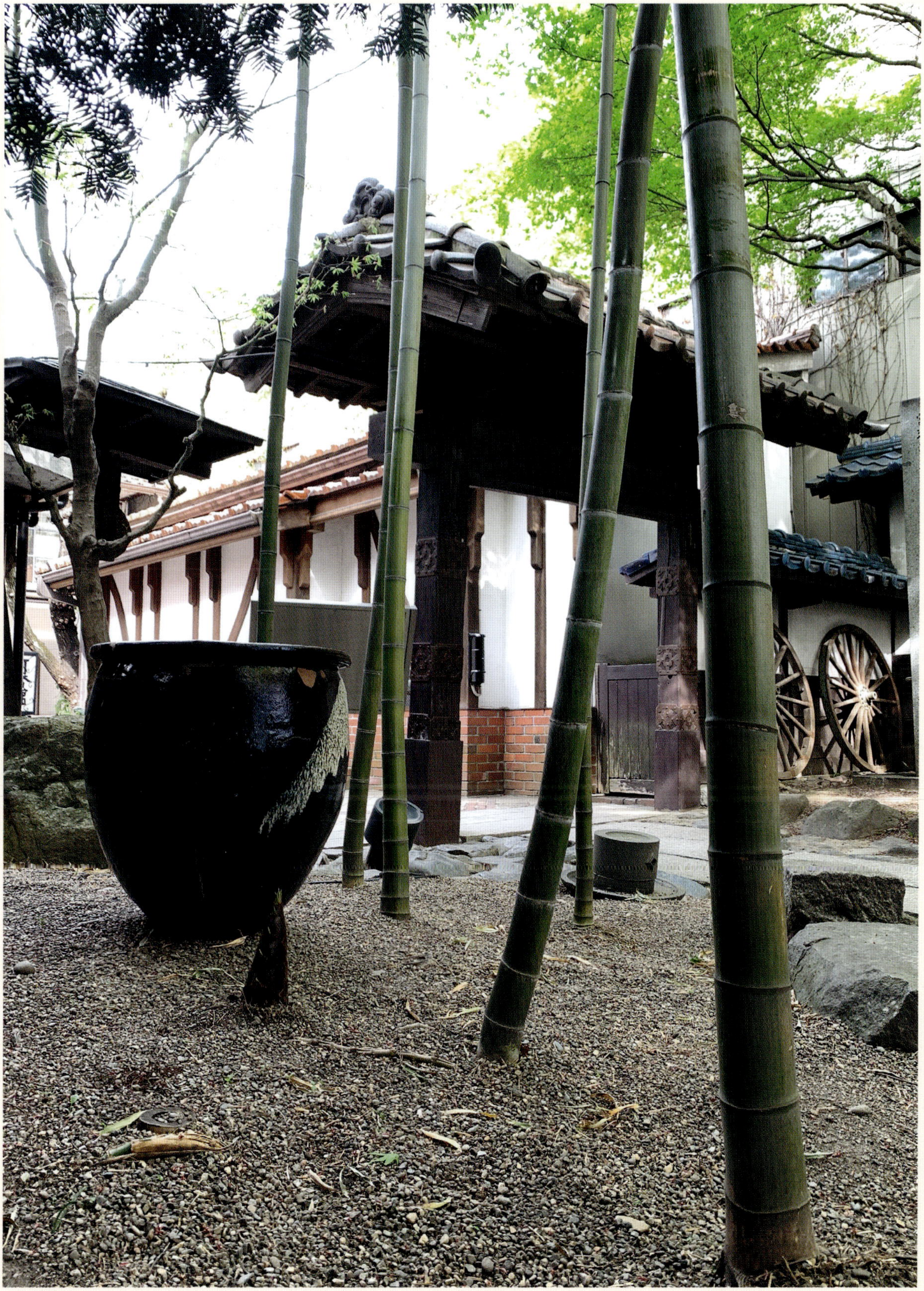

PROFILE BY YOSHIZAWA TOMO

# Higeta Tadashi

Higeta Tadashi (b.1939) is a master of weaving and indigo dyeing, the ninth generation of Higeta Indigo Dyeing Studio, established in the late eighteenth century in Mashiko, Tochigi prefecture. In today's workshop, there are 72 vats for indigo dyeing, which bubble with blue-purple 'flowers' on the surface, a sign of fermentation in progress.

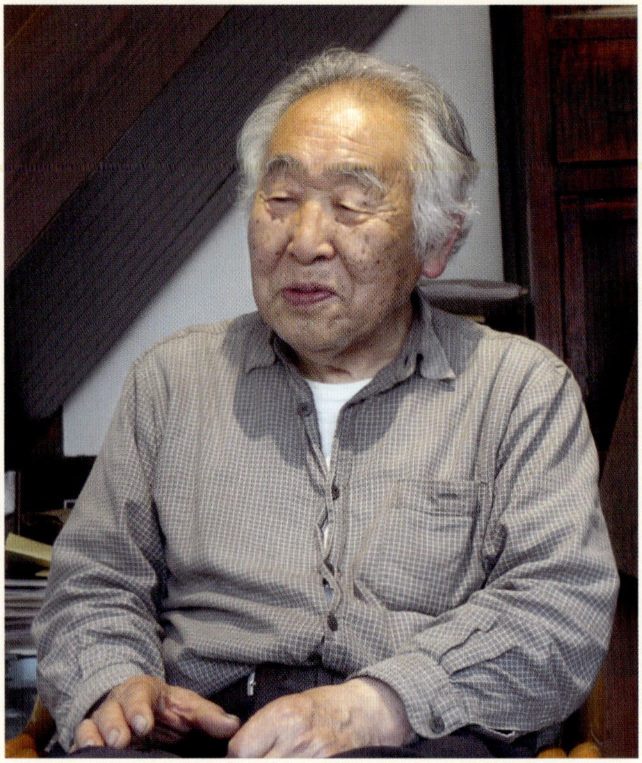

Higeta's father, Hiroshi, was a renowned *katazome* stencil-dye practitioner, but Higeta Tadashi opted to learn weaving from Yanagi Yoshitaka, Sōetsu's nephew. That's where he came into contact with the core members of the Mingei movement at an early stage. As a young man living in Mashiko he remembers Hamada Shōji walking around the town in his fashionable brown suit.

'I used to get called to help rearrange objects on display in the Japan Folk Crafts Museum. It was sixty-something years ago', he recalls. 'There was usually someone telling us where to place certain objects. I remember feeling nervous about carrying heavy ceramics. Mr Yanagi would walk out of his house with his cane and just sit there smiling. We shared tea and talked together during the tea break. Such a luxurious time I had.'

Higeta didn't drop any of these precious ceramics, but damaged a brand-new pillar in the director's office, he says. 'The museum didn't seem to have much in the beginning: there was no director's room nor proper storage space. At one point, they made an extension to the main building which became the director's office. I was carrying a heavy desk to the room and chipped the pillar a little. The scar should still be there.' He smiles like a child at this youthful memory.

Higeta witnessed the time when people, full of enthusiasm for the cause, started gathering under the torch of the Mingei movement. He says that Mingei was, above all, a social movement. Yet its relevance today is harder to explain. 'That is a very difficult question ... I always think, we have to go back to the origin of Mingei, to the phrase *minshūteki kōgei*, and ask what that meant.' He adds, 'I would also love there to be more connections made with William Morris's Arts and Crafts movement as there haven't been enough discussions about this, or so it seems to me.'

In Higeta's studio, there is a vast collection of his past works and the archival records of the business, which include the designs of weaving structures, the ratio of dyeing materials and thread samples for each piece. 'These are records of trial and error. So the next generation has something to refer to.'

Higeta has been pursuing his craft for over 60 years. Yet he doesn't describe his creative process as enjoyable. He turns a critical eye towards his own creation, somewhat contrasting with the otherwise gentle presence that he exudes. 'I'm hardly ever satisfied [with his work] ... There is still a long way to go until I can make the fabric of my ideal. And there is a huge pressure on my shoulders.'

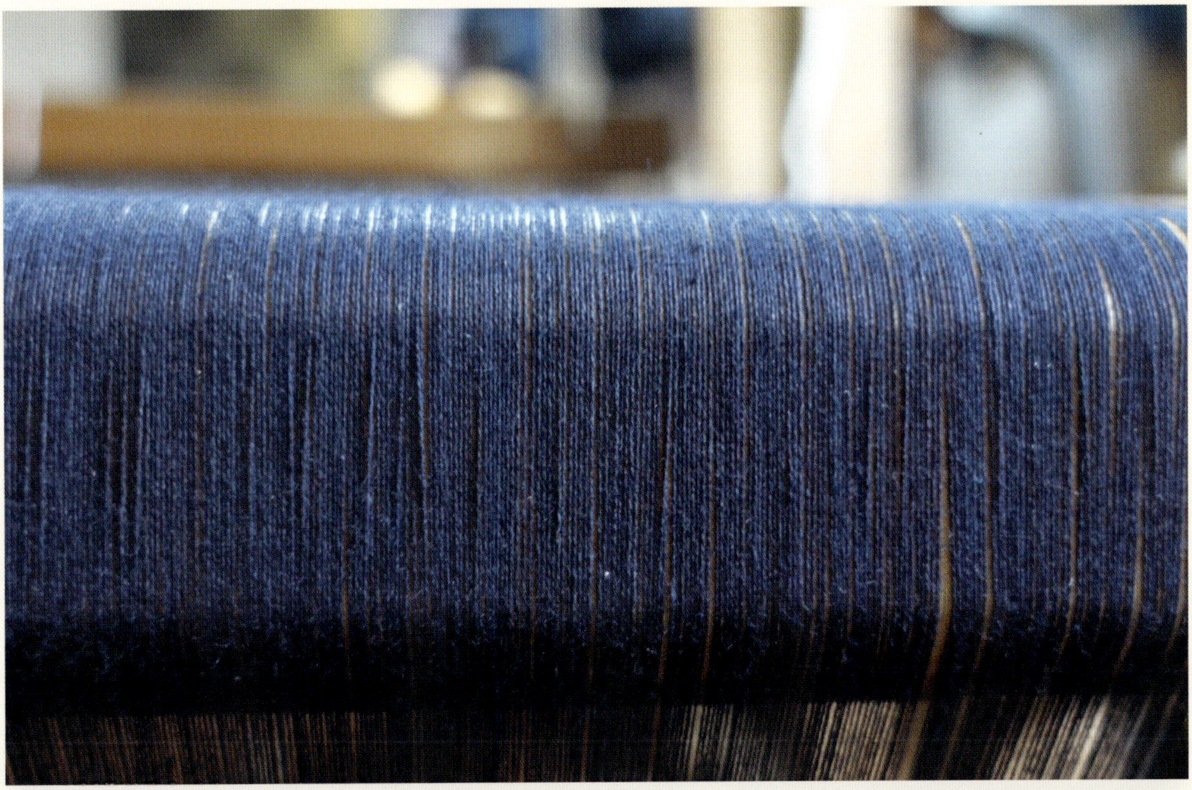

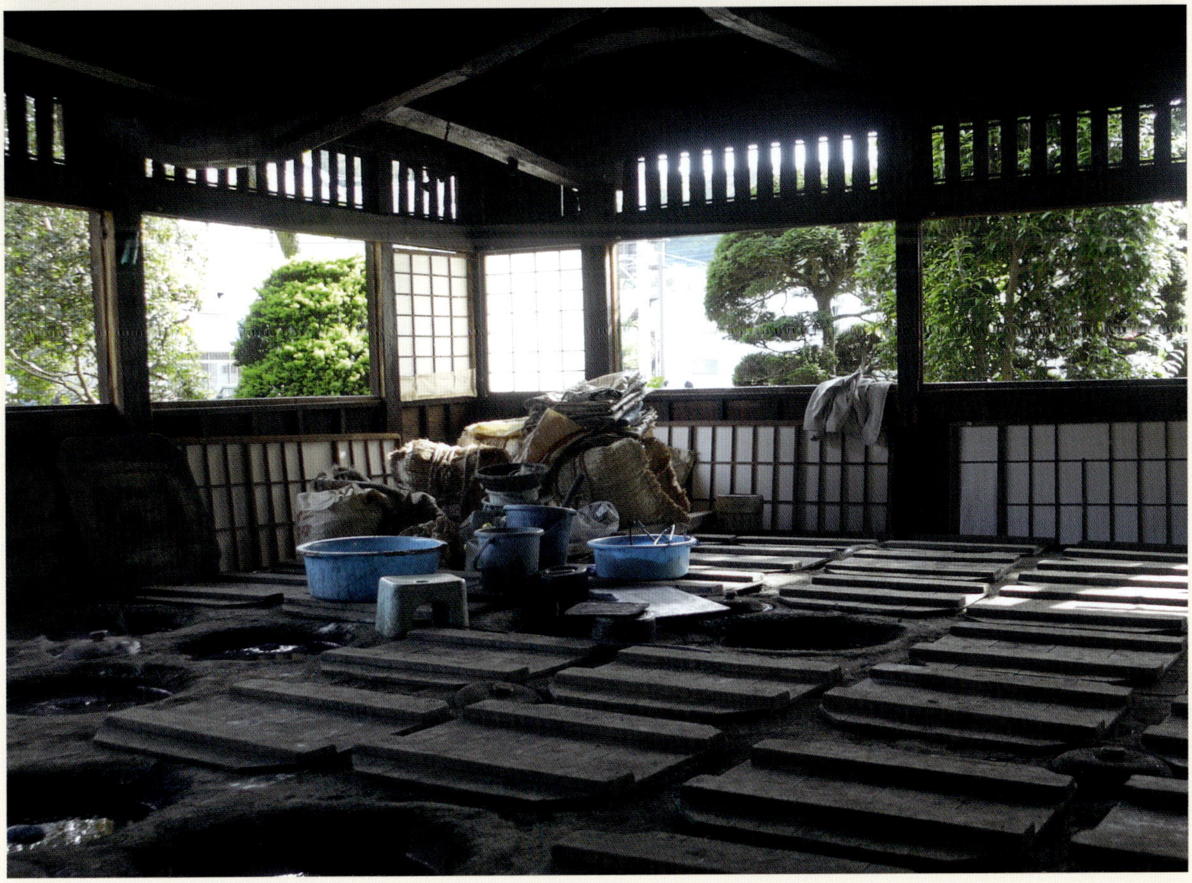

PROFILE BY YOSHIZAWA TOMO

# Hirano Kaori

Itoshiro village is a community of 220 people, high up in the mountains in Gifu prefecture. Over a decade ago, Hirano Kaori (b.1981) and her husband Akihide moved to Itoshiro and founded Itoshiro Yōhin Ten, an indigo dye studio, workshop and gallery, with the aim of learning and preserving the region's textile craft traditions.

Assisted by a handful of staff, some of whom have moved to the village as Local Vitalisation Co-operators, part of the Japanese government's scheme aimed at rejuvenating depopulated rural areas, Itoshiro Yōhin Ten is now part of the ecosystem of the area. As was done in the past, they grow vegetables to eat and to make natural dyes, they ferment indigo in their workshop, and they help clear the path to Hakusan, the sacred mountain that pilgrims access through Itoshiro village. To gain knowledge they search for historical photographs and learn through the oral histories of elderly villagers.

Itoshiro Yōhin Ten produces items of clothing using techniques of natural dye and pattern-making passed down in the community. The Mingei movement is not an explicit presence. Hirano trained as an ethnologist, and her perspective is that 'I like Mingei, though I'm no expert'. Implicitly perhaps, though, there is a strong overlap between some Mingei ideas and the work at Itoshiro. As Furuta Mari, one of the staff who dyes with indigo, explains: 'What I find amazing is that we are not making an art piece of an individual artist. Rather, I feel these colours are a gift from nature. We receive the colours and incorporate the wisdom passed on in this community, and bring them to life in a shape that is useful today. And the fact that our customers enjoy wearing it – that brings me joy.'

At first glance, their products look like any other items of modern fashion. But the secret is in the pattern, or 'the wisdom is in the shape', as Hirano describes it. Based on historical examples of everyday apparel, the straight lines of the clothes allow them to utilise every inch of textile they dye in the studio.

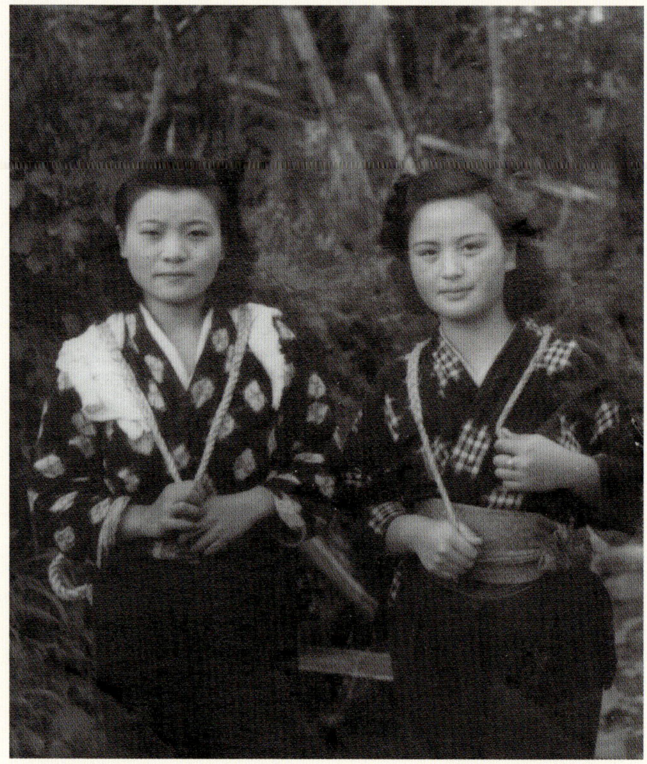

Yanagi Sōetsu's writings have helped Hirano see her work in a new light. She has recorded the stories of the villagers: how they treasured every fragment of textiles, which were more precious if brought from outside and they had patterns on, and how they creatively made full use of the fabric in their everyday workwear.

'When I read Yanagi's book, that Mingei was about the beauty that existed in the everyday life of people, I thought, "This is it!"' she says. 'Today, we dress up to go out for dinner, but for them, it was about making every day beautiful.'

Hirano tries to embody this way of thinking, passed on in the community, by creating things that are useful in their everyday wearability. 'It was the shape for me. I know textiles are a small portion of Mingei, and even then the focus tends to be on weaving, dyeing or stitching. But for me, it was the shape of Japanese textiles. It was the shape that held the wisdom within.'

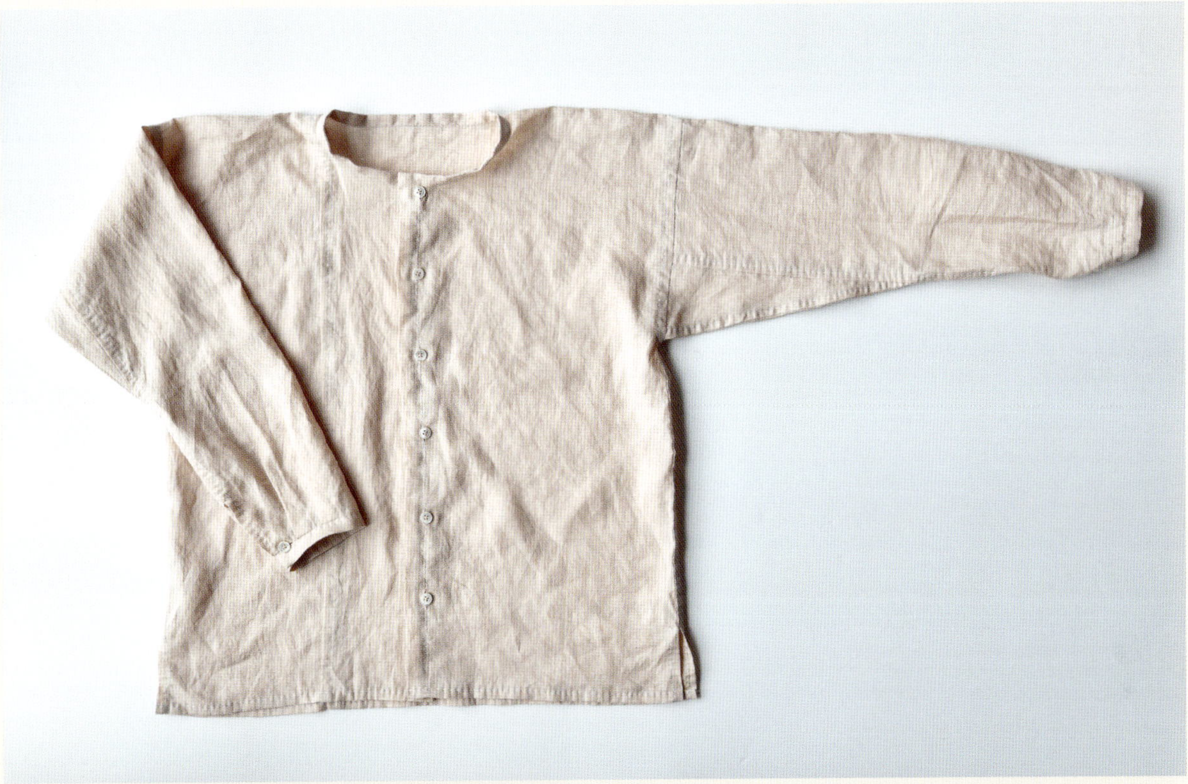

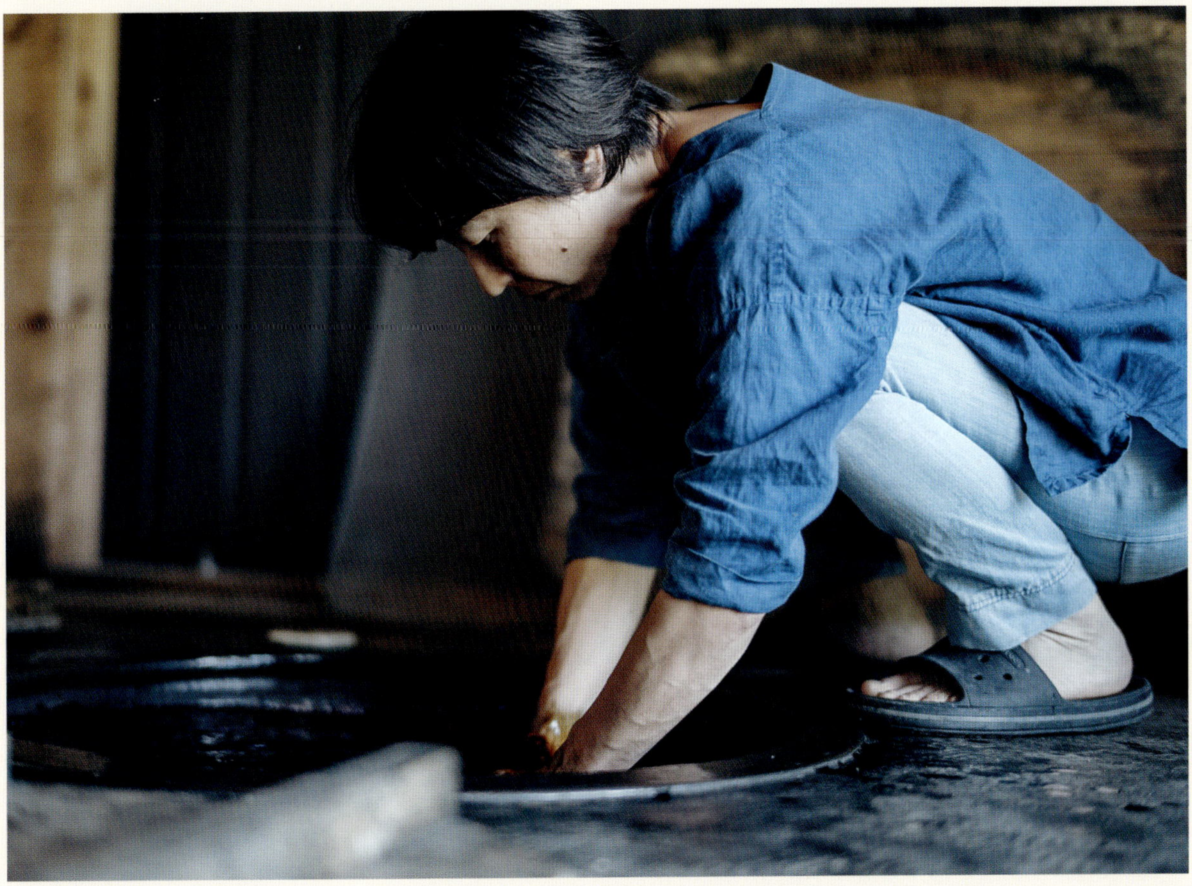

PROFILE BY RÓISÍN INGLESBY

# Akiko Hirai

Ceramicist Akiko Hirai (b.1970) moved to the UK from Japan in 1999 with the intention of continuing her studies in psychology. 'And then', she says, 'I met a potter.' Now based in Hackney, East London, for the past two decades Hirai has been developing her practice, which draws strongly on Korean ceramic traditions and focuses on the beauty to be found in the aged and the flawed.

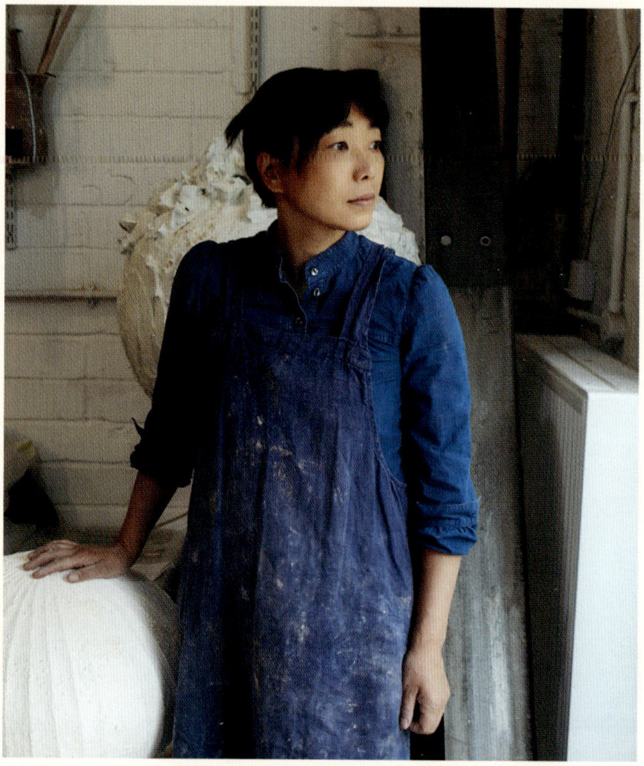

An encounter in the British Museum with Lucie Rie's moon jar (see p. 129), an eighteenth-century Korean porcelain vessel gifted to Rie by Bernard Leach, sparked Hirai's interest in the form for which she is currently best known. Attracted by 'how it is jointed, its indentations, pin holes and stains on the surface, little chips and small ageing marks', Hirai understood the moon jar to be 'really precious', more beautiful and special thanks to the wear accumulated through the ageing process. Hirai's own moon jars, of which she has made dozens in different sizes throughout her career, are an exploration of this character that objects and – as she points out – also people acquire through the stress, trauma and pleasure of lived experience. Her pieces, constructed as one vessel rather than two joined together as in traditional Korean moon jars, are created through a process of pulling and pushing, adding pressure and weight to reveal the beauty in deformity and imperfection.

Growing up, Hirai experienced Mingei as an embedded rather than explicit presence. 'In my family environment, we had a lot of handmade things ... we would enjoy selecting our own rice bowl [from among several possible options]; everything my grandmother served would be on different small plates. You didn't think about it, but you enjoyed it every day.' More recently, however, she has been reading Yanagi Sōetsu's writings. Yanagi's belief that true beauty is something to be found within objects that do not intend to be beautiful resonates strongly with Hirai's own practice. The beauty of the unexceptional, seen in relation to other things rather than standing out on its own terms, is one way in which she sees the presence of Buddhism in Japanese aesthetics, a stark comparison to the individualistic idea of beauty more prevalent in the West.

The influence of Korean ceramics remains strong in Hirai's work. 'Even though I started ceramics here [in London], I always come back to Korea.' This is evident in her continued interest in *kohiki*, a form of ceramic derived from Korean buncheong wares, typically involving an iron-rich clay body glazed in white slip. Over the years Hirai has repeatedly made bowls developed in her own way from a *kohiki* technique. The result suggests the ageing process of historical pots, evoking the long and complex relationship between people and the objects they make and use.

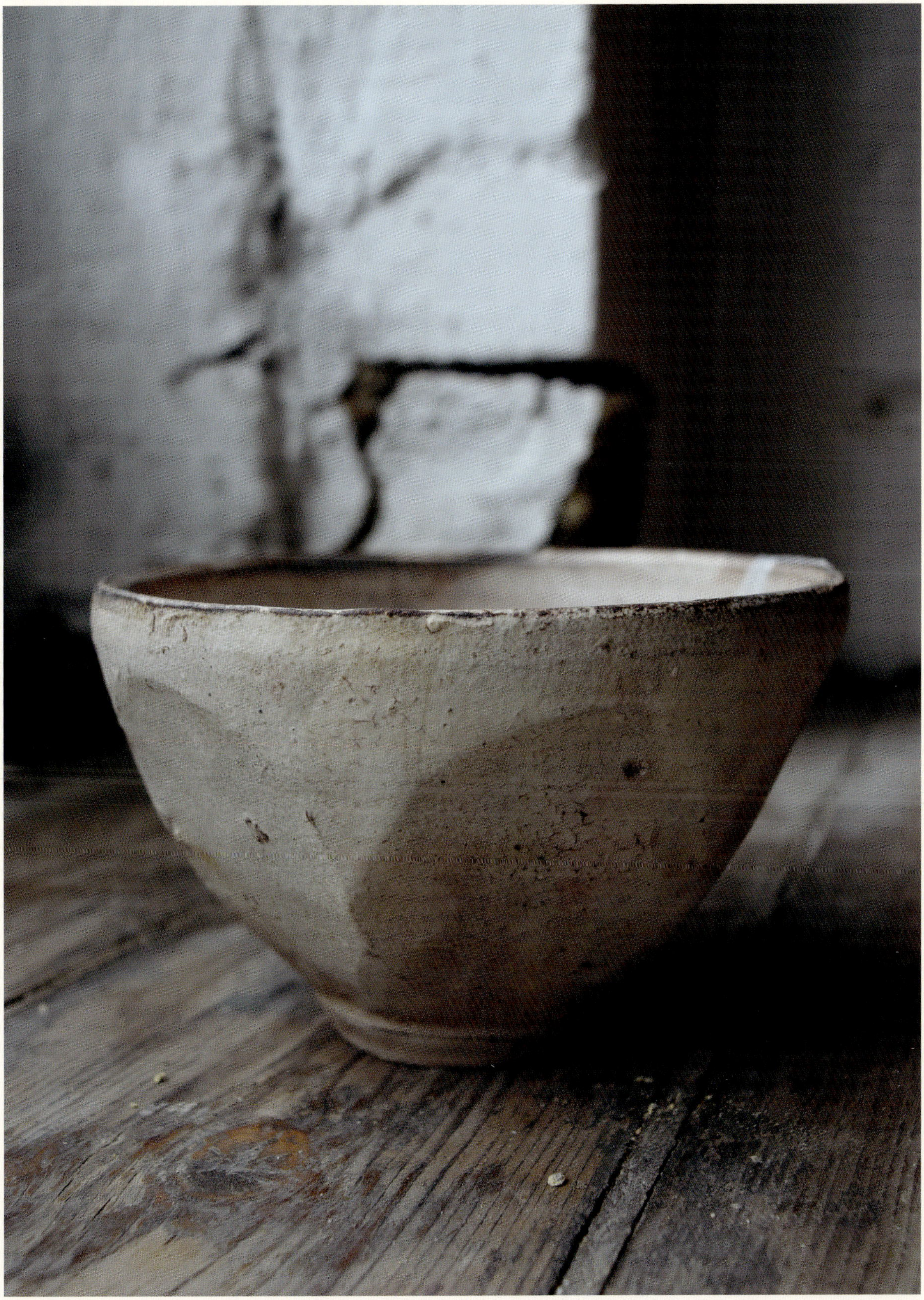

PROFILE BY YOSHIZAWA TOMO

# Nakagawa Shūji

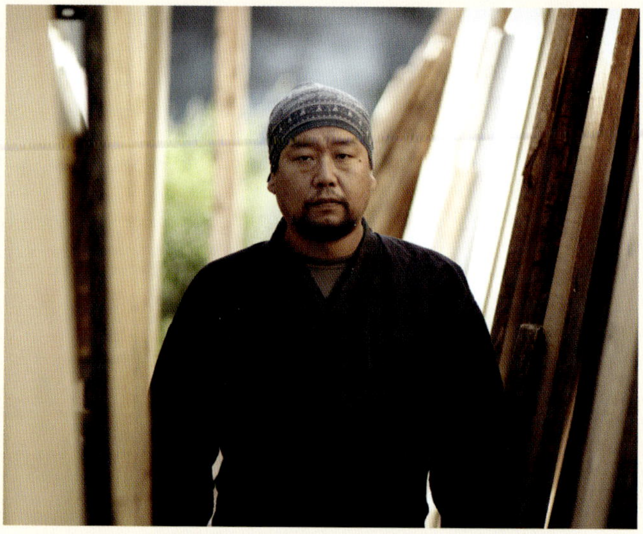

Nakagawa Shūji (b.1968) is a third-generation *kioke* wooden tub craftsman. His grandfather was a renowned wooden tub maker, said to be the best in Kyoto, and his father is a designated Living National Treasure. However, by the time Shūji took on the family craft, Japan had been through a phase of modernisation and the associated lifestyle shifts. Replaceable plastic boxes had become much more accessible than durable, repairable wooden containers, and 250 wooden tub makers in Kyoto were reduced to three.

A pivotal moment for Nakagawa came when he started working with designers both inside and outside Japan. They questioned basic principles that had never been probed within the community of wooden tub makers: 'Do the hoops to hold the wooden slats have to be two?' 'Can you make it in an oval shape, instead of round?' Each of these basic principles had well-grounded, practical reasons. But Nakagawa challenged them. Using digital design, as well as his knowledge of science, he made a wooden tub with only one hoop. And his oval-shaped champagne cooler has now become his signature work internationally.

Wooden tubs used to be a part of Japanese everyday life, used as containers for water and rice, buckets and much more. Nakagawa has taken new approaches to his crafts so they are relevant to today's living spaces. His craft practice seems to tick many of the boxes that could define it as Mingei: he works by hand, using natural materials to create objects within a long tradition while staying relevant to today's lifestyle. However, he says the question 'Are we Mingei?' has long been a topic of discussion among him and his fellow makers. And the conclusion he came to for himself is 'No.'

In trying to explain why, he recalls the time when he delivered his father's wooden tubs to an old farmhouse in Toyama. In this area by the Sea of Japan where deep snow covers the entire landscape in winter, these houses were built sturdily with thick pillars and beams, a style reminiscent of Hamada Shōji's house in Mashiko. 'And in that space, we all saw that my father's works didn't fit in. They were very much representative of Kyoto aesthetics: uncoated cedar slats showcasing fine grains, shaved as thin as possible. They would look perfectly fine in the Kyoto *machiya*-(wooden townhouse) styled building where the pillars and the entire structure were much thinner and finer.'

Despite that, 'I love looking at Mingei objects', Nakagawa says. 'But there's always some kind of distance between the objects and me as a maker.' For him, this is about his creative intention, in comparison with Mingei objects that are born free of it, or rather created by surrendering to something bigger. 'I don't think I can surrender fully... my creative intention gets in the way. So whenever I visit the [Japanese Folk Crafts] Museum there's a sense of sadness too.'

In an attempt to define what something is, it can also be helpful to understand what it is not. Nakagawa's insight, born of both daily practice and internal reflection, is of much value in examining what Mingei can be and offer to today's makers and users.

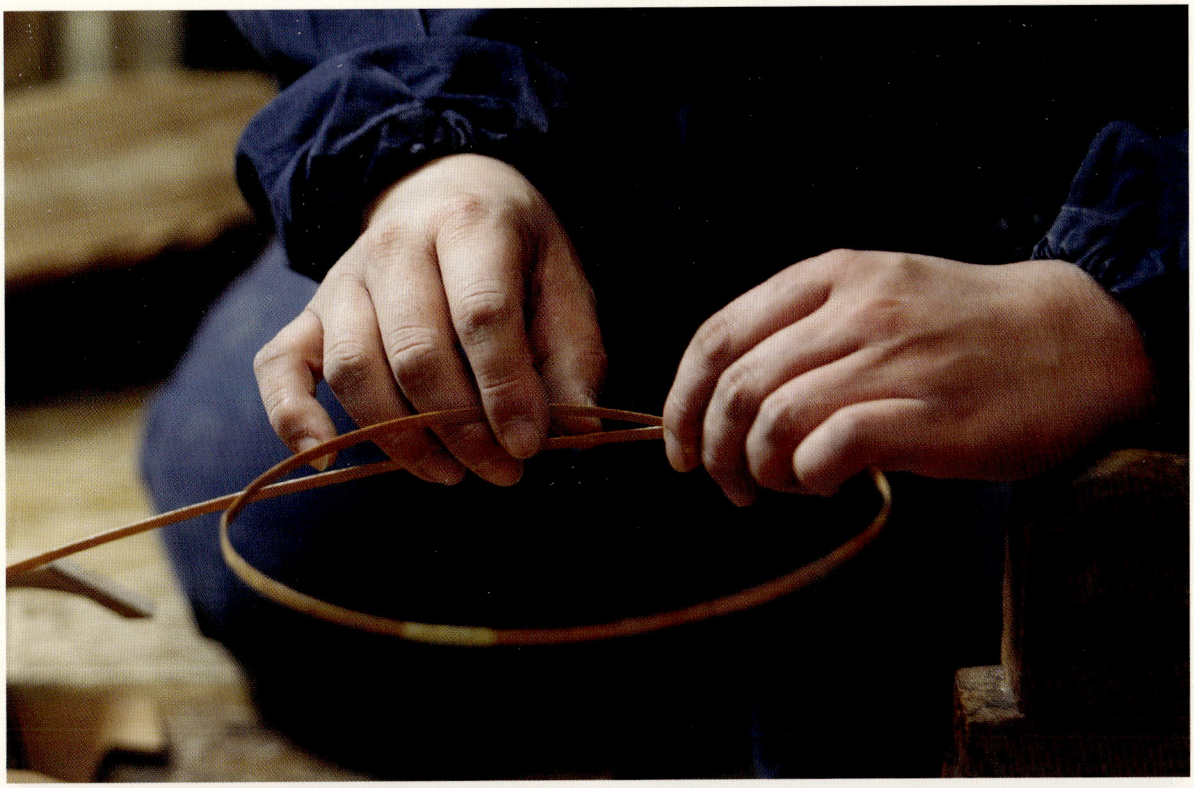

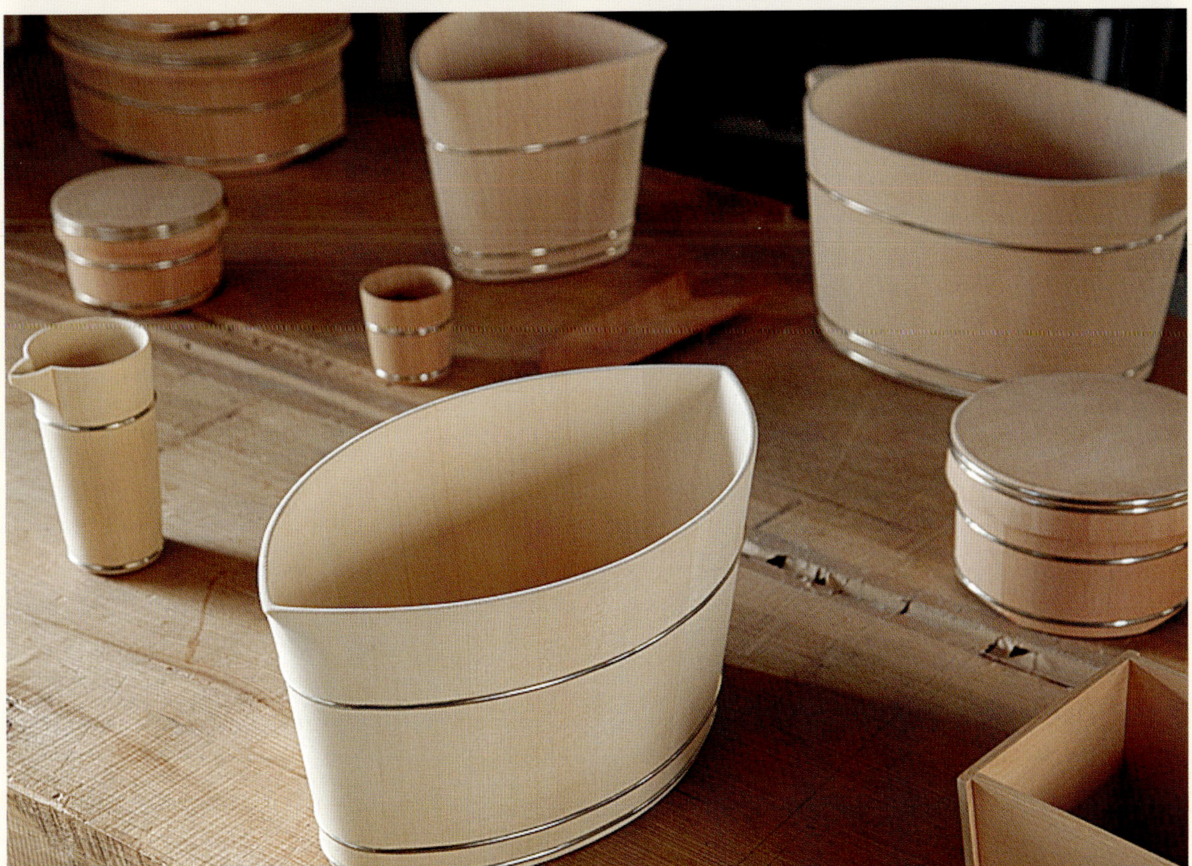

PROFILE BY OKAZAKI MANAMI

# Oki Izumi

Oki Izumi (b.1956) is a contemporary kokeshi maker whose work is in high demand due to her retro *kawaii* sensibilities. Her dolls sport cute clothes such as strawberry-covered hats, bathing costumes or a bear-shaped onesie suit, and have soft eyes akin to Showa-period manga characters. Gunma prefecture, where Oki is based, is the largest production area for creative kokeshi and represents a kokeshi culture that sits at the intersection of folk craft, kitsch and fine art.

After the Second World War, a culture of souvenir kokeshi flourished in parallel to the traditional kokeshi boom whereby items were manufactured as keepsakes for landmarks across Japan. Popularity for these spiked due to the trend for domestic travel during the 1960s and 1970s, and demand superseded output. Oki's father, the late Sekiguchi Sansaku (1925–2018), was a *nihonga* painter and was initially commissioned to design kokeshi by Usaburo, a manufacturer that produced mass quantities of souvenir kokeshi. As a formally trained artist, he was also part of a movement to make kokeshi fine art pieces that resembled large wooden sculptures and were sold in galleries and department stores.

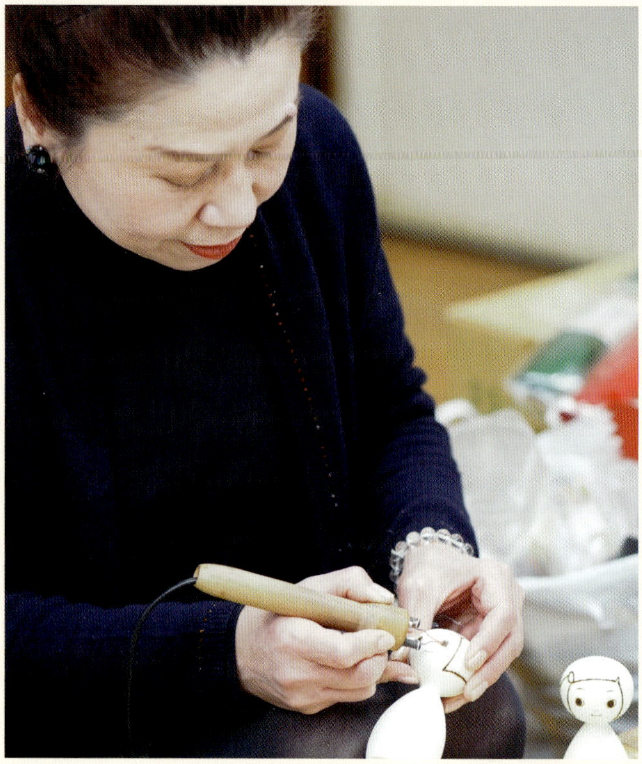

Oki also produces large artworks that are sold at a gallery in the affluent Ginza district of Tokyo. She explains that the main difference between the gallery items and those sold on the general market is not so much in the quality or the sentiment behind each piece, but rather that they are limited in quantity and are one-offs.

With both her cute souvenir kokeshi, which are typically sold at the nearby Ikaho Onsen shops, and her fine art kokeshi, Oki says that a sense of minimalism and negative space has to be present in the work. 'While kokeshi are my own creative expression, there is a margin for one's feelings and for people to construe the work as they wish. This blank space and simplicity is important. If the doll is too decorative, there is no leeway for interpretation.'

Oki admits that 'kokeshi are hard to categorise', particularly in Gunma. Rather than folk toys with a restrained, earthy aesthetic as in the Tōhoku tradition, they initially flourished in Gunma's kitsch mementos and were manufactured in the likeness of, for example, the Tokyo Tower building with girls climbing up its side, and *tanuki* racoons. However, no matter how *kawaii* the aesthetic is, the materiality and the qualities inherent in the wood itself are still central to creative kokeshi craftsmanship.

'One of the most important aspects, if not the most important characteristic, of kokeshi is that it is made from wood', Oki explains. 'I use dogwood, a natural material that is sourced from the local region. Fundamentally, people like wood, the tactile sensation, the smell. There is a basic knowledge that wood is beneficial for us humans. With kokeshi, you can hold it, feel the warmth of the wood and enjoy the tangible qualities – one's feelings are comforted, relaxed and calmed. I think people are exhausted and need these kinds of healing things. People want to be accepted and they imagine that kokeshi somehow understand them.'

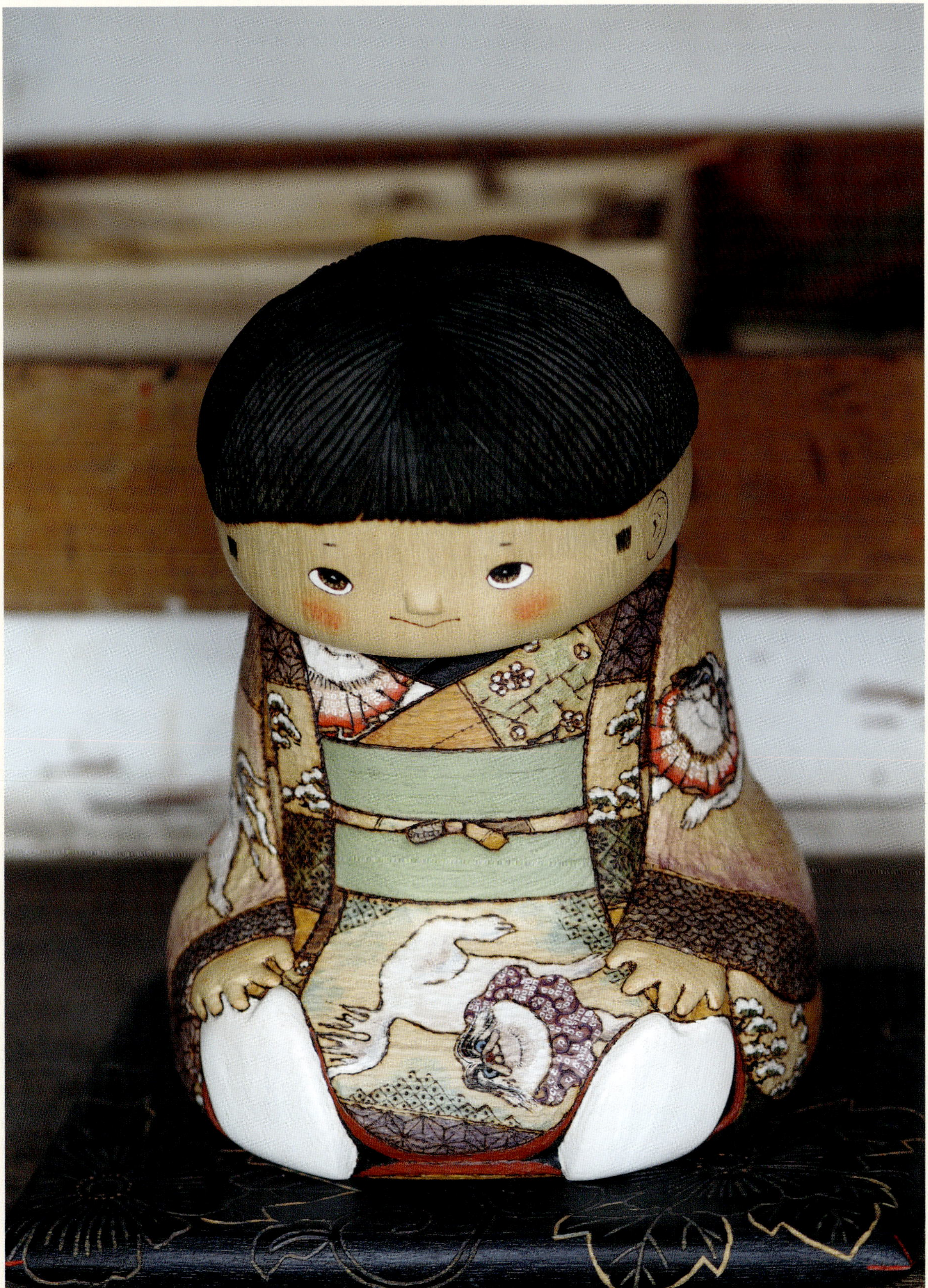

PROFILE BY YOSHIZAWA TOMO AND RÓISÍN INGLESBY

# Ōtsuchi Sashiko

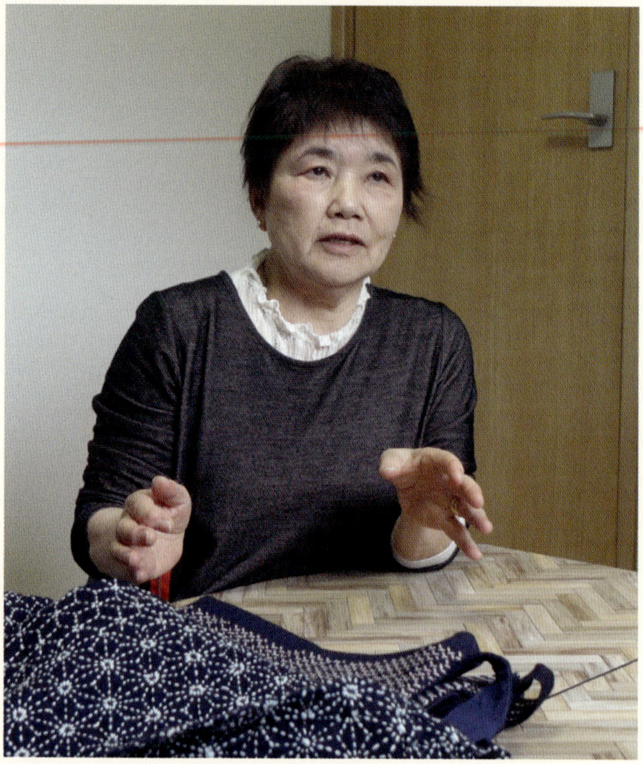

On 11 March 2011, the tsunami triggered by the Tōhoku Earthquake devastated the coastal town of Ōtsuchi: 1284 lives were lost, reducing the town's population by almost 10 per cent. Ninety-eight per cent of commercial property was damaged and thousands of people lost their homes. While the reconstruction effort was underway, they lived in tiny makeshift areas in the town's school gym. The floor was divided by sheets of cardboard to afford people a semblance of privacy; each space was just large enough to sleep in and to sit up in during the day. Amid this devastation, the Ōtsuchi Recovery Sashiko Project was born.

*Sashiko*, literally meaning 'little stabs', is a form of decorative stitching used to reinforce fabric and clothing. Although it is practised widely throughout the mountainous regions of northern Japan, there was no living tradition of *sashiko* in Ōtsuchi; the technique was reintroduced by a young aid worker who believed that the act of making might help members of the community with the psychological and financial trauma they were experiencing. *Sashiko* was an ideal craft form, needing very little space, no specialist equipment and only small amounts of inexpensive and readily available materials.

Over the years since 2011, dozens of women from Ōtsuchi have acquired the skills of *sashiko* and created pieces for sale. Learning from scratch, the group has received support from experienced *sashiko* makers across Japan, while also figuring out methods and techniques as they went along. Based in a small building constructed following the tsunami, members of the group are paid to create piecework, stitching to traditional patterns and leaving no individual traces within the finished product – at least to an outsider's eye. Their work includes collaborations with Muji and sustainable fashion brand KUON Tokyo. Presently 15 to 20 women, ranging in age from their forties to eighties, pop in weekly to drop off their complete works. Occasional gatherings called *ochakko* are for everyone to come together to chat over tea and sweets.

Kurosawa Kaori, Sasaki Kanako, Ōsawa Mieko and Kikuchi Hiromi have been members of Ōtsuchi Sashiko since the beginning. They do not consider themselves artists, nor do they explicitly see parallels between their work and the Mingei movement. Instead, for these *sashiko-san*, a respectful and affectionate way of referring to women who practise *sashiko*, their work is framed more by the mental independence and social benefits they gain than any self-conscious identification with a historical tradition. 'When I was handed threads and a needle, I felt the joy of being able to sew again', says Ōsawa. 'When I'm stitching, I find myself void of any thought, completely absorbed in what's in front of me.' She describes this experience as *mushin*, a word referring to a state of mental quietude. Other members of the group agree: 'Stitching is my "me time".' Their comments have interesting parallels with Yanagi Sōetsu's analysis of the beauty of *kogin*, a particular form of *sashiko*, which he believed derived from the makers' mental attitude: 'In this monotonous work,' he wrote in 1932, 'they forgot all monotony. They loved what they were doing.'[1]

1. Yanagi 2018, 134.

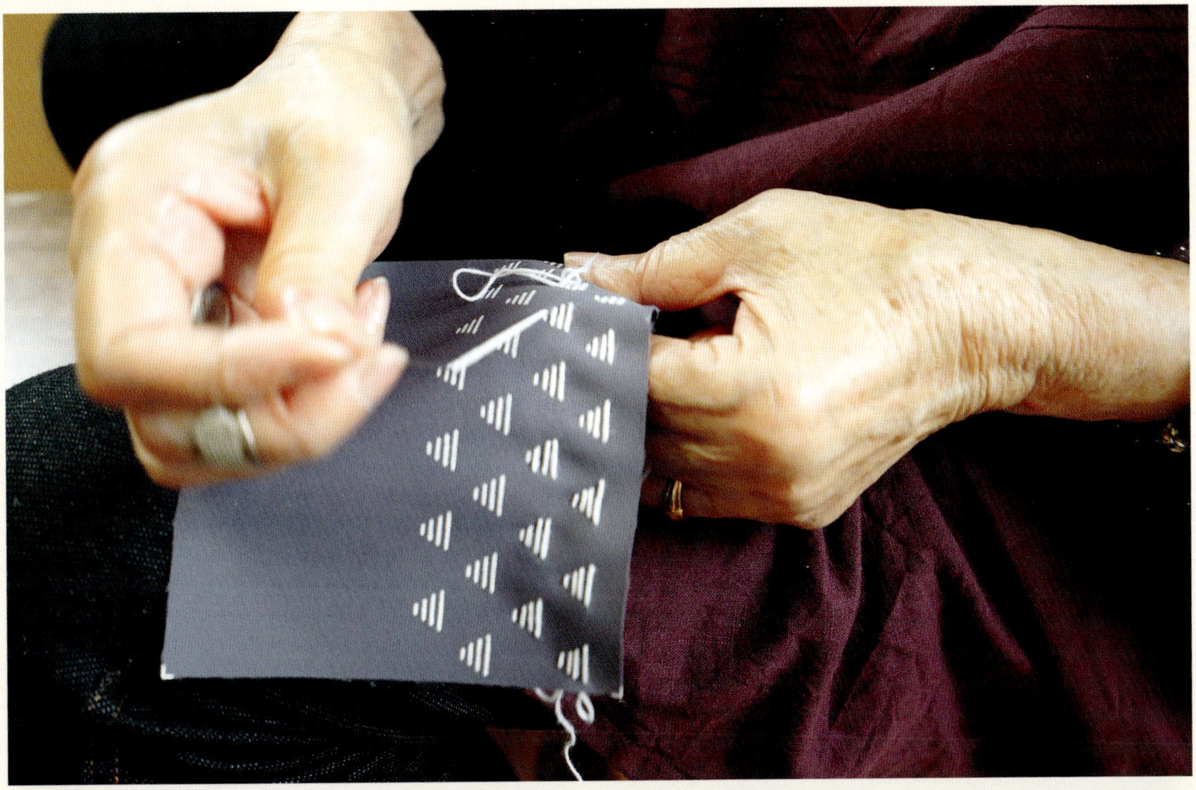

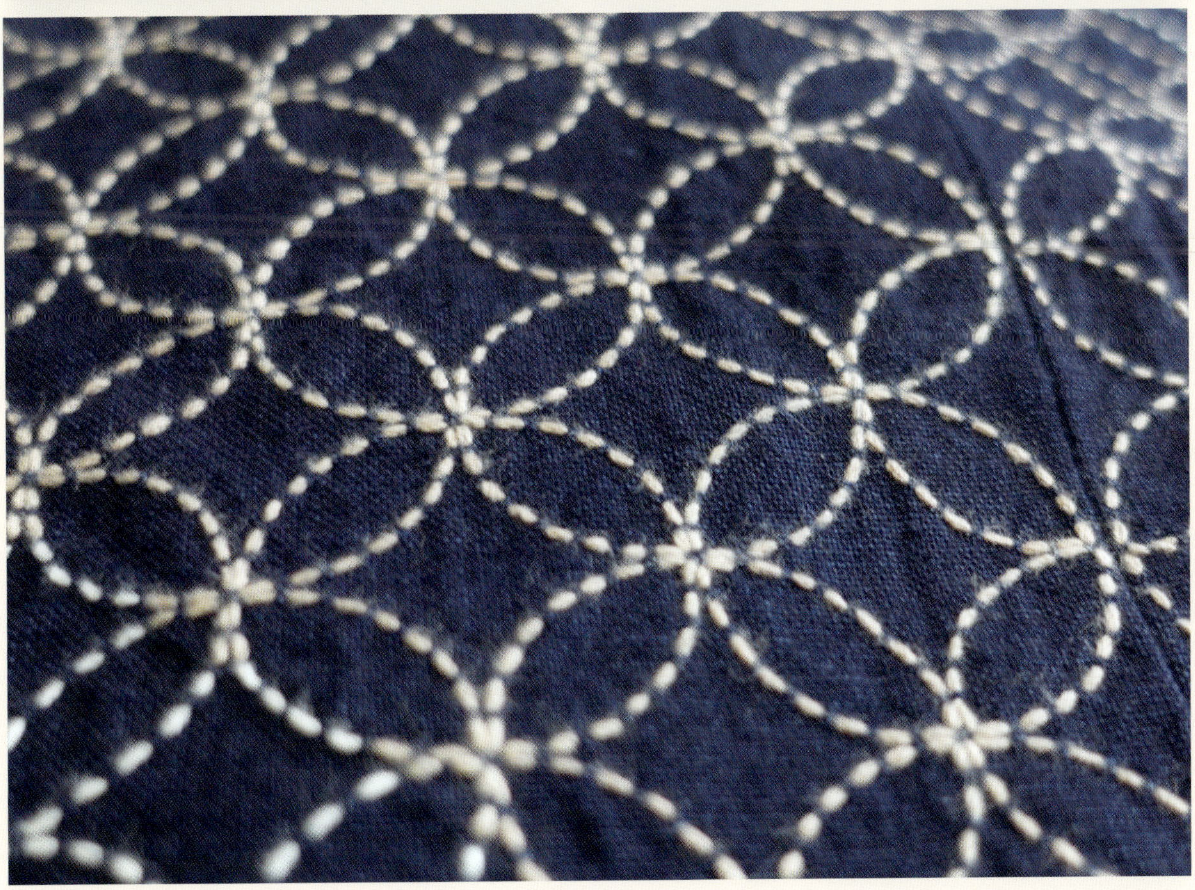

# Glossary

All words are Japanese unless stated otherwise.

**Aizome** Indigo dyeing

**Attush** Ainu robe made from fibres taken from the inner bark of the elm tree

**Bashōfu** Cloth woven from the fibres of the thread-banana plant

**Bijinga** A genre of Japanese art focused on beautiful women

**Bingata** Okinawan stencil resist-dyeing technique

**Boro** Patchwork fabric made from recycled or repurposed textiles

**Buncheong** [Korean] Also known as *punch'ong*, a form of stoneware with a blue-green tone achieved through application of white slip

**Chijimi** Lightweight, textured fabric made from hemp or ramie. The fabric is bleached through exposure to snow in direct sunlight

**Dentō** Tradition, convention

**Dingyao** [Chinese] Ding ware, historical ceramics, predominantly porcelain, produced in the prefecture of Dingzhou

**Futonji** Decorative textile used as the upper of the two pieces of fabric sewn together and stuffed with raw cotton to create the top part of *futon* (bedding)

**Getemono** Humble, everyday or low-value products, praised by Yanagi Sōetsu as exemplars of Mingei

**Ikebana** Japanese art of flower arrangement

**Jiriki** Self-power; in Buddhism, the ability to achieve enlightenment through one's own efforts

**Kasuri** A thread resist-dyeing technique in which sections of yarn are tightly bound or compressed to prevent the colour penetrating when the skein is dipped in the dye bath

**Kataezome** A form of *katazome* focusing on pictures rather than repeat patterns

**Katazome** Resist-dyeing technique using rice paste and stencils

**Kawaii** Aesthetic of cuteness

**Kijishi** Woodturner

**Kimono** Japanese straight-seamed garment worn by men, women and children of all social classes

**Kioke** Wooden barrel of variable size used for food preparation and storage, bathing buckets and water carrying

**Kirifuse** 'Cut and lay down' method of appliqué sewing

**Kōgei** Artisanal craft and contemporary art adopting 'crafted' aspects, often with a focus on high-quality and traditional techniques

**Kogin** A form of thread-count *sashiko* with patterns created by passing the stitch over a certain number of fabric threads

**Kohiki** Japanese ceramic technique derived from Korean buncheong ware, typically created through application of white slip over an iron-rich clay body

**Kokejo** Neologism used to describe female fans of kokeshi

**Kokeshi** Wooden dolls turned on a lathe

**Kurafuto** Japanese adaptation of the English word 'craft' used since the 1950s to indicate Scandinavian-inspired crafts. Now often associated with designer crafts, and crafts involving only partly handmade products

**Meibutsu** Famous or renowned local speciality or product

**Mingei** Folk crafts or art, an elision of *minshūteki kōgei*, usually translated as 'the art of the people'

**Mingeikan** Japanese Folk Crafts Museum, founded by Yanagi Sōetsu

**Miyadaiku** Carpenters specialising in shrine and temple construction

**Mottainai** Concept of minimising waste and appreciating resources

**Mushin** Mental state of being free of obstructive thoughts, associated with Zen Buddhism

**Nihonga** Japanese-style painting

**Noragi** Clothes for doing farm work or working in the fields

**Noren** Split curtain often used in doorways or entrances

**Obi** Waist sash that secures a kimono

**Oki nui** 'Placing and sewing' embroidery technique

**Onsen** Natural hot springs or hot spring resorts

**Raku ware** Hand-moulded, lead-glazed earthenware pottery fired at low temperatures, especially used in the tea ceremony

**Sasano Ittōbori** A one-knife carving technique from the Sasano area, Yamagata Prefecture

**Sashiko** Method of sewing together one or more layers of cloth with running stitch, initially used to reinforce fabric

**Sashimonoshi** Cabinetmaker

**Seikatsu kōgei** Everyday crafts; crafts for daily life

**Shamoji** Rice paddle used for serving or mixing rice

**Shibori** Tie-dyeing technique in which fabric is bound, stitched or clamped before being placed in the dye bath

**Shibui** Aesthetic of simplicity, elegance and subtle beauty

**Shibukawaii** Elision of *shibui* and *kawaii*, denoting a form of restrained cuteness

**Shingata** New or modern style

**Shōji** Sliding paper doors or screen

**Shojo** Manga genre aimed at young women and girls

**Soban** [Korean] One-person dining table

**Sofubi** Soft vinyl toys

**Tansu** Chest of drawers or storage cabinet

**Tanuki** Japanese raccoon dog, popular in folklore. Anthropomorphised *tanuki* statues, typically those of Shigaraki pottery, are commonly found outside restaurants and shops across Japan

**Tariki** Other power; reliance on a power outside of oneself to achieve enlightenment, often associated with Pure Land Buddhism

**Tategushi** Woodworker or joiner skilled at making frames for *shōji* and other sliding panels without nails or screws

**Tenmoku** Both a form of pottery and a dark black-brown ceramic glaze containing iron

**Tenugui** Thin cotton cloth often used as a hand towel

**Tōji** Taking to the baths, recuperating in hot springs

**Torii** Gate or archway often found at the entrance of Shinto shrines

**Tsumugi** Cloth woven from raw silk, or the thread itself. Utilises short staple silk fibre rather than the longer filament silk, and has an uneven, slubbed texture

**Tsunagi** Collage of fabric patched together

**Tsutsu** Paper tube used for *tsutsugaki*

**Tsutsugaki** Freehand resist-dyeing technique for creating patterns on fabric using rice paste squeezed from a *tsutsu*

**Uzukuri** Stiff brush, traditionally made from tightly bound organic fibres, used for scrubbing wood to give it texture

**Yogi** Sleeping coverlet in the shape of an oversize kimono

**Yukata** Cotton kimono used after the bath or as an informal garment in summer

# Bibliography


ADAMSON, GLENN, 2018, *Fewer, Better Things: The Hidden Wisdom of Objects*. London and New York: Bloomsbury.

ADAMSON, GLENN, 2021, *Craft: An American History*. New York: Bloomsbury.

AJIOKA CHIAKI, 2015, 'The Three Musketeers' Cross-continental Tour of the USA'. *Art Action History Newsletter*, 15: 1–12.

ANTONELLI, PAOLA, 2007, 'Design and Architecture'. In *What Makes a Great Exhibition?*, edited by Paula Marincola. London: Reaktion.

ASAKAWA, TAKUMI, 1996, 'Joseon ui Soban'. In *Joseon ui Soban: Joseon Doja Myeonggo*, translated by Sim Woosung. Seoul: Hakgojae.

AVITABILE, GUNHILD, Eleanor von Erdberg and Robert Moes, 1993, *Japanese Folk Art: A Triumph of Simplicity*. New York: Japan Society.

BAE, SUJUNG, 2018, 'Kawai Kanjiro and Korean Ceramics'. *Study of Ceramic Art*, 27.

BAE, SUJUNG, 2019, 'The Rethinking of Hamada Shōji's Style Changing: Focusing on the Influence of Korean Ceramics'. *Journal of Korean Modern & Contemporary Art History*, 37: 35–67.

BENEDETTA, MARY, 1936, *The Street Markets of London*. London: John Miles.

BENJAMIN, WALTER, 1982, *Passagenwerke: The Arcades Project*, translated by Howard Eiland and Kevin McLaughlin. Vol. 1. Cambridge, MA: Belknap Press of Harvard University Press.

BENNETT, TONY, 1995, *The Birth of the Museum: History, Theory, Politics*. London: Routledge.

BHABHA, HOMI, 1994, *The Location of Culture*. London and New York: Routledge.

BLACK, ANTHEA AND NICOLE BURISCH (EDS), 2021, *The New Politics of the Handmade: Craft, Art and Design*. London: Bloomsbury Visual Arts.

BRANDON, REIKO MOCHINAGA, 1986, *Country Textiles of Japan: The Art of Tsutsugaki*. New York: Weatherhill.

BRANDON, REIKO MOCHINAGA AND BARBARA B. STEPHAN. *Textile Art of Okinawa*. Honolulu: Honolulu Academy of Arts, 1990.

BRANDT, KIM, 2000, 'Object of Desire: Japanese Collectors and Colonial Korea', *East Asia Cultures Critique*, 8.3.

BRANDT, KIM, 2007, *Kingdom of Beauty: Mingei and the Politics of Folk Art in Imperial Japan*. Durham, NC: Duke University Press.

BRITTON, ALISON, 2016, 'American Potters Today'. In *That Continuous Thing: Artists & the Ceramics Studio, 1920–Today*, edited by Sam Thorne and Sara Matson. London: Tate Publishing.

BURDELSKI, MATTHEW, AND KOJI MITSUHASHI, 2010, 'She Thinks You're Kawaii: Socializing Affect, Gender, and Relationships in a Japanese Preschool'. *Language in Society*, 39.1.

CANCLINI, NÉSTOR GARCÍA, 1995, *Hybrid Cultures*. Minneapolis and London: University of Minnesota Press.

CERTEAU, MICHEL DE, 1984, *The Practice of Everyday Life*, translated by Steven Rendall. Berkeley, Los Angeles and London: University of California Press.

CHOI, HARIM, 1974, 'Introduction: Yanagi Sōetsu's Views on Korean Art'. In *Hangukkwa ku Yesul*, translated by Lee Daewon. Seoul: Jisiksaneopsa.

CHOI, SOON-WOO, 1993, *Choi Soon-woo Jeonjip*, vol. 4. Seoul: Hakgojae.

CLIFFORD, JAMES, 1992, 'Travelling Cultures'. In *Cultural Studies*, edited by Lawrence Grossberg, Nelson Cary and Paula A. Trichler. London and New York: Routledge.

COOPER, EMMANUEL, 2003, *Bernard Leach: Life and Work*. New Haven, CT and London: Yale University Press.

CORT, LOUISE, 1992, 'The Kizaemon Teabowl Reconsidered: The Making of a Masterpiece'. *Chanoyu Quarterly*, 71.

CRAWFORD, ROMI, 2022, 'Surface and Soul in the Work of Nick Cave'. In *Nick Cave: FOROTHERMORE*, edited by Naomi Beckwith. Chicago: Museum of Contemporary Art and Delmonico Books.

CWIERTKA, KATARZYNA J, 2020, *Branding Japan's Food: From Meibutsu to Washoku*. Honolulu: University of Hawaii Press.

DE WAAL, EDMUND, 1998, *Bernard Leach*. London: Tate Gallery Publishing.

EARLE, JOE (ED.), 2009, *Serizawa: Master of Japanese Textile Design*. New Haven, CT and London: Yale University Press.

*Eyes on Tōhoku*, 2022. *Tōhoku he no Manazashi 1930–1945*. Tokyo: Nihon Keizai Shinbunsha.

FISCHLI, FREDI, NIELS OLSEN AND ADAM JASPER (EDS), 2021, *Retail Apocalypse*. Zürich: GTA Verlag.

FISHER, FELICE, 1994, 'Japanese Design: From Meiji to Modern'. In *Japanese Design: A Survey since 1950*. New York: Abrams.

FISHER, JEAN, 2005, 'The Syncretic Turn: Cross-Cultural Practices in the Age of Multiculturalism'. In *Theory in Contemporary Art since 1985*, edited by Zoya Kocur and Simon Leung. Oxford: Blackwell.

FORRER, MATTHI, 1992, *Hokusai: Prints and Drawings*. London: Royal Academy.

FRANCK, KLAUS, 1961, *Exhibitions: A Survey of International Designs*. New York: Praeger.

FUKASAWA, NAOTO, 2007, *Naoto Fukasawa*. London: Phaidon.

GILROY, PAUL, 1993, *Black Atlantic: Modernity and Double Consciousness*. London and New York: Verso.

GLISSANT, ÉDOUARD, 2020 [1997], *Treatise on the Whole-World*, translated by Celia Britton. Liverpool: Liverpool University Press.

GORRILL, HELEN, 2020, *Women Can't Paint: Gender, the Glass Ceiling and Values in Contemporary Art*. London: Bloomsbury.

GUTH, CHRISTINE M. E., 2021, *Craft Culture in Early Modern Japan: Materials, Makers, and Mastery*. Oakland: University of California Press.

HAMADA, TAKUJI, 2006, *Mingei Undō to Chiiki Bunka [The Mingei Movement and Local Culture]*. Kyoto: Shibunkaku.

HAN, YOUNGDAE, 1997, *Investigators of the Joseon Beauty*, translated by Park Kyunghee. Seoul: Hakgojae.

HARA, KENYA, 2014, 'The Origins of Japanese Design'. In *Wa: The Essence of Japanese Design*, edited by Rossella Menegazzo and Stefania Piotti. London: Phaidon.

HARA, KENYA, 2018, *Designing Design*. Zürich: Lars Müller.

HAUSER, WILLIAM, "The Diffusion of Cotton Processing and Trade in the Kinai Region of Tokugawa Japan." In *Journal of Asian Studies*, Vol XXXIII, No.4, August 1974

HONG, SOONHYUCK, 1928, 'Proud of Joseon's Art; National Treasures'. *Byeolgeongon*, May.

JACKSON, ANNA, 1997, *Japanese Country Textiles*. London: Victoria and Albert Museum, 1997.

JACKSON, ANNA, 2002, 'Textiles'. In *Timeless Beauty: Traditional Japanese Art in the Montgomery Collection*, by Edmund de Waal et al. Milan: Skira.

IDEKAWA NAOKI, 2002, *Ningen Fukko No Kogei*, translated by Jung Heekyun. Seoul: Hakgojae.

JANELLI, ROGER L., 1986, 'The Origins of Korean Folklore Scholarship'. *Journal of American Folklore*, 99. 391.

JONES, CAROLINE A., 2017, *The Global Work of Art: World's Fairs, Biennials, and the Aesthetics of Experience*. Chicago: University of Chicago Press.

JUNG, IL-SEONG, 2007, *Yanagi Muneyosi ui tu olgul*. Seoul: Jisiksanupsa.

KAPLAN, WENDY, 2011, *California Design, 1930–1965: Living in a Modern Way*. Cambridge, MA: MIT Press.

KATO, RIE, 2012, 'Koreans' Research History on Yanagi Muneyoshi'. In *Yanagi Muneyoshi and His Thoughts on Korean Culture*. Seoul: Somyeong.

KAWABATA, YASUNARI, 2022 [1935–7], *Snow Country*, translated by Edward Seidensticker. London: Penguin.

KAWAI, KANJIRŌ, 1935, 'Straw Crafts and Their Makers'. *Kogei*, 51.

KIKUCHI, YUKO, 1994, 'The Myth of Yanagi's Originality: The Formation of Mingei Theory in Its Social and Historical Context'. *Journal of Design History*, 7.4.

KIKUCHI, YUKO, 2004, *Japanese Modernisation and Mingei Theory*. London and New York: Routledge.

KIKUCHI, YUKO, 2005, 'The Mingei Movement'. In *International Arts and Crafts*, edited by Karen Livingstone and Linda Parry. London: Victoria and Albert Museum.

KIKUCHI, YUKO, 2015, 'The Craft Debate at the Crossroads of Global Visual Culture: Recentring Craft in Postmodern and Postcolonial Histories'. *World Art*, 5.1: 87–115.

KIM, DAL-SOO, 1968, 'Chōsen Bunka nit suite' ['Concerning Korean Culture']. *Iwanami Kōza Tetsugaku*, 13.

KIM, HOYOUNG, 2020, 'A Study on the Artworks of Kawai Kanjirō'. Seoul: Korea University.

KIM, JUNG KI, 2011, *Joseon, the Nation of Beauty*. Seoul: Hanul Academy.

KIM, WON-RYONG, 1973, 'The Characteristics of Korean Art and Their Formulation'. *Hanguksasangdaegye*.

KIM, YANGGI, 1977, 'Yanagi Sōetsu no Kankoku no Bi' ['Yanagi Sōetsu's Beauty of Korea']. *Asahi Shimbun*, 26 January.

KIM, YOUNGWON, 2015, 'The Nature and Character of Korean Ceramics: Focusing on Exquisite Ceramics, Collection of the Japan National Museum of Fine Arts'. In *Arts of Korea: Highlights from the Japan Folk Crafts Museum*. Seoul: Overseas Korean Cultural Heritage.

KLONK, CHARLOTTE, 2009, *Spaces of Experience: Art Gallery Interiors from 1800 to 2000*. New Haven, CT: Yale University Press, 2009.

KO, YU-SEOP, 1931, 'Keumdong Miruk Bangasang ui Gochal' ['A Study of the Seated Figure of Maitreya']. *Gaebyeok*, 4: 153–64.

KO, YU-SEOP, 2007, 'Features of Ancient Korean Art and Their Transmissions'. In *Ko Yu-Seop Jeonjip*. Seoul: Yeolwhadang.

KOJIMA, TAKEHIKO, 2011, 'Diversity and Knowledge in the Age of Nation Building: Space and Time in the Thought of Yanagita Kunio'. PhD dissertation, Florida International University.

KOWOLIK, LEOPOLD, 2021, 'Craft as Property as Liberalism as Problem'. In *The New Politics of the Handmade: Craft, Art and Design*, edited by Anthea Black and Nicole Burisch. London: Bloomsbury Visual Arts.

KUNIK, DAMIEN, 2012, 'The Invention of "Folk Crafts": Yanagi Sōetsu and Mingei'. *Cipango: French Journal of Japanese Studies*, 1.

KURATA TAKASHI (ED.), 2012, *'Mingei' no ressun: tsutanasa no gihō* [*Lesson on 'Mingei': Skilful Clumsiness*]. Tokyo: Film Art.

LEACH, BERNARD, 1960, *A Potter in Japan: 1952–1954*. London: Faber and Faber.

LEACH, BERNARD, 1978, 'Korea'. In *Beyond East and West: Memoirs, Portraits and Essays*. New York: Watson-Guptill.

LEE, IN-BEOM, 1999, *Art of Joseon and Yanagi Muneyoshi*. Seoul: Sigongsa.

LEE, MAN-YEOL, 1974, 'Book review: Korea and Its Art by Yanagi Muneyoshi'. *Sukdae Sinbo*, 23 September.

LIONNET, FRANÇOISE, AND SHU-MEI SHIH (EDS), 2005, *Minor Transnationalism*. Durham, NC and London: Duke University Press.

LIVINGSTONE, KAREN, 2008, 'Morris to Mingei: The Arts and Crafts Movement in Britain, Europe and Japan'. In *Life and Art: Arts and Crafts from Morris to Mingei*. Tokyo: Asahi Shimbun.

MACCARTHY, FIONA, 1990, *Eric Gill*. London: Faber and Faber.

MAEDA, TAIJI, 1975, *Gendai no Kōgei: Seikatsu to no Musubitsuki o Motomete* [*Contemporary Crafts: Yearning for Connection to Living*]. Tokyo: Iwanami Shoten.

MATSUZAKI, YUKO, 2020, 'Shōji Hamada: The Eyes of a Brilliant Collector'. In *Bernard Leach: Discovered Archives*, edited by Simon Olding. Farnham: Crafts Study Centre.

MCCLELLAN, ANDREW, 2008, *The Art Museum: From Boullée to Bilbao*. Berkeley: University of California Press.

MERCER, KOBENA, 1994, *Welcome to the Jungle: New Positions in Black Cultural Studies*. New York and London: Routledge.

MEYER, RICHARD, 2013, *What Was Contemporary Art?* Cambridge, MA: MIT Press.

MILGRAM, LYNNE, 1993, *Narratives in Cloth: Embroidered Textiles from Aomori, Japan*. Toronto: Museum for Textiles.

MOERAN, BRIAN D., 1981, 'Yanagi Muneyoshi and the Japanese Folk Craft Movement'. *Asian Folklore Studies*, 4.1.

MOERAN, BRIAN D., 1997, *Folk Art Potters of Japan: Beyond an Anthropology of Aesthetics*. London and New York: Routledge.

MOES, ROBERT, AND AMANDA MAYER STINCHECUM, 1995, *Mingei: Japanese Folk Art from the Montgomery Collection*. Alexandria, VA: Art Services International.

MORRIS, WILLIAM, 1883, 'The Art of the People'. In *Hopes and Fears for Art*. London: Ellis & White.

MORRIS, WILLIAM, 1884, *Useful Work versus Useless Toil*. London: Socialist League Printery.

MORRIS, WILLIAM, 1888, 'The Revival of Handicraft'. *Fortnightly Review*, November.

MOON MYUNG-DAE, 1977, 'Art Movements in the 1930s'. *Studies on Folk Culture*, 12.

NAKANE, CHIE, AND SHINZABURŌ ŌISHI, 1990, *Tokugawa Japan: The Social and Economic Antecedents of Modern Japan*. Tokyo: University of Tokyo Press.

PRAN NATH MAGO, *Gurcharan Singh*. New Delhi: Lalit Kala Akademi, 1995.

NITTONO, HIROSHI, FUKUSHIMA MICHIKO, YANO AKIHIRO AND MORIYA HIROKI, 2012, 'The Power of Kawaii: Viewing Cute Images Promotes a Careful Behaviour and Narrows Attentional Focus'. *PLOS One*, 7.

OKAZAKI, MANAMI, 2013, *Kawaii: Japan's Culture of Cute*. Munich: Prestel.

PARK, JONGHONG, 1922, 'Joseon Misul ui Sajeok Gochal' ['A Historical Study of Korean Art']. *Gaebyeok*, 3.9: 13–26.

PARK, SOO-A, 2010, 'Tomimoto Kenkichi's Theory of Ceramics: A Methodical and Philosophical Research on Mass Production'. *Korea Society of Craft*, 13.2.

PARRY-WILLIAMS, Tim, 2016, 'Bashofu: The Traditional Banana Fibre Textile Culture of Okinawa'. *Selvedge*, 70: 60–3.

PETERSON, SUSAN, 1977, *The Living Tradition of Maria Martinez*. Tokyo, New York and London: Kodansha International.

PITELKA, MORGAN, 2017, 'Form and Function: Tea Bowls and the Problem of Zen in Chanoyu', in *Zen and Material Culture*, edited by Pamela D. Winfield and Steven Heine. Oxford: Oxford University Press.

POLLOCK, NAOMI, 2020, *Japanese Design since 1945: A Complete Sourcebook*. London: Thames & Hudson.

PORCU, ELISABETTA, 2019, 'Toward a Pure Land Buddhist Aesthetics: Yanagi Sōetsu on the Vow of Non-Discrimination between Beauty and Ugliness'. In *Pure Lands in Asian Texts & Contexts: An*

*Anthology*, edited by Georgios T. Halkios and Richard K. Payne. Honolulu: University of Hawaii Press.

RATHBUN, WILLIAM JAY, 1993, *Beyond the Tanabata Bridge: Traditional Japanese Textiles*. New York: Thames & Hudson in association with the Seattle Art Museum.

ROBERTSON, JENNIFER, 1998, 'It Takes a Village: Internationalization and Nostalgia in Postwar Japan'. In *Mirror of Modernity: Invented Traditions of Modern Japan*, edited by Stephen Vlastos. Berkeley, Los Angeles and London: University of California Press.

ROH, JUNIA, 2014, 'Study on the Craft Section of the Joseon Fine Arts Exhibition'. *Art History Forum*, Center for Art Studies Korea, 2014.

SAID, EDWARD, 1983, *The World, the Text and the Critic*. Cambridge, MA: Harvard University Press.

SATŌ, TAKU, 2022, *Just Enough Design*. San Francisco, CA: Chronicle Books.

SHIMAZAKI, MAKOTO (ED.), 2012, *Shoya Yoshida: A Remarkable Ancestor and Multiple Producer of Japanese Folk Crafts*. Tottori: Tottori Folk Crafts Museum.

SONTAG, SUSAN, 2018 [1964], *Notes on 'Camp'*. London: Penguin.

SPINOZZI, ADRIENNE, 2022, *Hear Me Now: The Black Potters of Old Edgefield, South Carolina*. New York: Metropolitan Museum of Art.

SUDO, REIKO, AND NAOMI POLLOCK (EDS), 2021, *Nuno: Visionary Japanese Textiles*. London: Thames & Hudson.

SUZUKI, D.T., 1935, *Manual of Zen Buddhism*. Available at: http://www.buddhanet.net/pdf_file/manual_zen.pdf (accessed 5 September 2023).

TAKASAKI, SOJI, 2005, *Becoming the Soil of Joseon: Asakawa Takumi*, translated by Kim Sunhi. Paju: Hyohyung.

TEASLEY, SARAH, 2022, *Designing Modern Japan*. London: Reaktion.

THIELEMANS, VEERLE, 2015, 'Beyond Visuality: Review on Materiality and Affect'. *Open Edition Journals*.

THOM, DANIELLE, 2023, 'The Class Signifiers of Quiet Luxury Are Nothing New'. *Art Review*, June.

TOMIMOTO, KENKICHI, 1912, 'William Morris no Hanashi' ['The Story of William Morris']. *Bijutsu Shinpō* [*Art News*], 11.5–6.

TOMITA, JUN, AND NORIKO TOMITA, 1982, *Japanese Ikat Weaving*. London: Routledge and Kegan Paul.

TOMITA, YASUKO, 2014, 'Modern Japanese Ceramists and "Korea"'. *Journal of Korean Modern & Contemporary Art History*.

URRY, JOHN, 1990, *The Tourist Gaze: Leisure and Travel in Contemporary Societies*. London: Sage.

VON HANTELMANN, DOROTHEA, 2019, 'Art Institutions as Ritual Spaces: A Brief Genealogy of Gatherings'. In *Theater, Garden, Bestarium: A Materialist History of Exhibitions*, edited by Tristan Garcia and Vincent Norman. Lausanne: ECAL/University of Art and Design.

YAMAGUCHI, MASAO, 1991, 'The Poetics of Exhibition in Japanese Culture'. In *Exhibiting Cultures: The Poetics and Politics of Museum Display*, edited by Ivan Karp and Steven D. Lavine. Washington, DC: Smithsonian Institution Press.

YANAGI, SŌETSU, 1921, 'About the Joseon Folk Craft Gallery'. *Yomiuri Newspaper*, 10 May.

YANAGI, SŌETSU, 1972, *The Unknown Craftsman: A Japanese Insight into Beauty*, translated by Bernard Leach. Tokyo, New York and San Francisco: Kodansha International.

YANAGI, SŌETSU, 1976, 'The Pure Land of Beauty'. *Eastern Buddhist*, 9.1.

YANAGI, SŌETSU, 1981, 'Kindai Bijutsukan to Mingei' ['Museum of Modern Art and the Japan Folk Crafts Museum']. In *Yanagi Sōetsu Zenshū* [*Collected Works of Yanagi Sōetsu*], vol. 16. Tokyo: Chikuma Shobō.

YANAGI, SŌETSU, 2006a, 'Art of Joseon'. In *Joseon and Its Arts*, translated by Lee Giljin, 81–103. Seoul: Singu Publishing.

YANAGI, SŌETSU, 2006b, 'His Visit to Joseon'. In *Joseon and Its Arts*, translated by Lee Giljin, 51–80. Seoul: Singu Publishing.

YANAGI, SŌETSU, 2006c, 'Seven Mysteries of Joseon Ceramics'. In *Joseon and Its Arts*, translated by Lee Giljin, 298–311. Seoul: Singu Publishing.

YANAGI, SŌETSU, 2006d, 'Thinking about the Joseon People'. In *Joseon and Its Arts*, translated by Lee Giljin, 30–50. Seoul: Singu Publishing.

YANAGI, SŌETSU, 2018, *The Beauty of Everyday Things*, translated by Michael Brase. London: Penguin Classics.

YANAGI, SŌRI, 2015, *The Philosophy of Design: Essays. Tokyo: Yanagi Design Office.*

YEE, LYDIA, AND CAMERON FOOTE (EDS), 2022, *Theaster Gates: A Clay Sermon*. London: Whitechapel Gallery.

YEOM, WOON OK, 2007, 'Yanagi Muneyoshi and Oriental Orientalism'. *History & Culture*, 14.

# Contributors

**Aaron Angell** is an artist, occasional curator and writer, and the founder and director of Troy Town, a pottery for artists in Hoxton, London. His practice absorbs hobbyist cultures, the antique teawares of Iga and Shigaraki and the underground hand-built ceramics of Britain from the 1970s and 1980s. He has undertaken residencies at Tate St Ives and the Leach Pottery, and in Korea and Japan, where he developed his interest in Mingei-style ceramics. His work is in the collections of Tate, the Victoria and Albert Museum and the Arts Council, and has been shown in numerous solo and group exhibitions, including at Studio Voltaire (London), GoMA (Glasgow), Kunstverein Freiburg and the Hayward Gallery's *Strange Clay* exhibition (2022).

**Róisín Inglesby** is Curator at the William Morris Gallery, where she focuses on Morris's global connections and international Arts and Crafts movements. Recent exhibitions include *Pioneers: William Morris and the Bauhaus; Distant Fellowship: Morris and South Asia;* and *Young Poland 1890–1918: An Arts and Crafts Movement*, which won the AAH Curatorial Prize. Following curatorial roles at the Victoria and Albert Museum and Historic Royal Palaces, Inglesby worked at the Teien Museum in Tokyo, where she assisted in creating greater accessibility for non-Japanese visitors.

**Anna Jackson** is Keeper of the Asia Department at the Victoria and Albert Museum. A specialist in Japanese textiles and dress, she is the curator of the 2020 exhibition *Kimono: Kyoto to Catwalk* and editor of the accompanying catalogue. Her other books include *Japanese Country Textiles* (1997), *Japanese Textiles in the Victoria and Albert Museum* (2000) and *Kimono: The Art and Evolution of Japanese Fashion – the Khalili Collection* (2015). In 2004 she was co-curator of *Encounters: The Meeting of Asia and Europe 1500–1800* and in 2009 lead curator of *Maharaja: The Splendour of India's Royal Courts*. In December 2020, Jackson was awarded the Foreign Minister's Commendation by the Japanese government for her contribution to the promotion of Japanese art and culture in Britain.

**Yuko Kikuchi** is Head of Academic Programmes at the Victoria and Albert Museum. In her positions as Professor of Craft History and Studies at Kanazawa College of Art, Japan, and Reader and founding member of TrAIN Research Centre at the University of the Arts, London, she has developed the area of post-colonial transnational theories in relation to 'crafts'. Her earlier scholarship examined the relationship between the Art and Crafts movement in Britain and Japan, and in 1997 she curated the travelling exhibition *Ruskin in Japan 1890–1940: Nature for Art, Art for Life*. This was followed by publication of the monograph *Japanese Modernisation and Mingei Theory: Cultural Nationalism and Oriental Orientalism*, which has recently been refreshed through a Korean translation (2022). Kikuchi has since focused particularly on the post-colonial conditions and sustainability of crafts in East Asia, including *Refracted Modernity: Visual Culture and Identity in Colonial Taiwan* (2007), and *The Craft Debate at the Crossroads of Global Visual Culture: Re-centring Craft in Postmodern and Postcolonial Histories* (2015).

**Okazaki Manami** is an author and journalist. Her articles have been featured in the *Japan Times, Wall Street Journal, Guardian, South China Morning Post, Tokyo Weekender, Tempura* and *Transit*. She has produced

15 books on Japanese culture, art, crafts and fashion, including *Japanese Kokeshi Dolls: The Woodcraft and Culture of Japan's Iconic Wooden Dolls, Japanese Mingei Folk Crafts, Kimono Now, Land of the Rising Cat* and *Kawaii, Japan's Culture of Cute*. She has curated kokeshi exhibitions for Sway Gallery (London, Stockholm and Paris) and Kyobashi Edogrand (Tokyo), as well as events at the Japan Foundation Los Angeles, Japan Foundation Rome and the Daiwa Anglo-Japanese Foundation. Okazaki owns Tonbi Books, a store that focuses on folk craft and rare, out-of-print books and printed matter located in a *nagaya* (historic row house) in Sumida, Tokyo.

**Naomi Pollock** is an American architect who writes about design in Japan. Her work has appeared in numerous publications on both sides of the Pacific, including *A+U, Dwell, Jutakutokushu, Kinfolk, Wallpaper** and *Architectural Record*, for whom she is a contributing editor. In addition, she is the author of several books, including *Modern Japanese House, Made in Japan: 100 New Products, Jutaku: Japanese Houses, Sou Fujimoto and Japanese Design since 1945: A Complete Sourcebook*. She was also the co-author of *New Architecture in Japan*, a contributor to *Architecture: The Whole Story and Shigeru Ban: Humanitarian Architecture* and the editor of *NUNO: Visionary Japanese Textiles*.

**Dasom Sung** is Assistant Curator of Korean Arts at the Victoria and Albert Museum. She was a lecturer at Seoul National University from 2020 to 2021 and is currently a doctoral candidate there, researching the design and material culture of factory-made porcelains in Korea. Her research interests lie in the history of materials, the government's craft export policies of Korea and Japan, and East Asian modern design history. Sung's recent publications include *Chilbo: Korean Traditional Enamelling* (2022).

**Adam Sutherland** is the Director of Grizedale Arts. Over the past 20 years he has developed Grizedale's programme of creative approaches to everyday life, working with major institutions and small communities across the globe. Since 2017 Grizedale has run a residency programme in a remote rural community in Japan that links artists, designers and the local community to projects concerning rural crafts in building and product development.

**Sam Thorne** is a writer and curator, and Director General and CEO of Japan House, London. He was formerly Director of Nottingham Contemporary, Artistic Director of Tate St Ives and Associate Editor of *frieze* magazine. His exhibitions include *That Continuous Thing* (Tate, 2017), which explored the relationship between Japanese and British studio ceramics, and he has curated shows by artists including Lara Favaretto, Denzil Forrester, Marguerite Humeau, Allison Katz, Elizabeth Price and Wu Tsang. Thorne was a co-founder of Open School East and is the author of *School* (2017).

**Yoshizawa Tomo** was born into a family of craftspeople and writes, translates and interviews in the fields of Japanese crafts and culture, with the aim of providing authentic understanding and universal relatability in a modern context. Following a career at MTV Japan and in retail within the Japanese craft sector, Yoshizawa was the Tokyo government's inaugural appointee as International Public Relations for Culture in the lead-up to the 2020 Olympics.

# Acknowledgements

RÓISÍN INGLESBY

This book, in keeping with the ethos of the *Art Without Heroes* exhibition project and of what I understand of the Mingei movement as a whole, has been an open and collaborative endeavour dependent on the generous support and expertise of dozens of people in both the UK and Japan. I am profoundly grateful to Yoshizawa Tomo for her boundless energy, knowledge, cultural diplomacy and friendship, which have enriched the project in more ways than I can mention, and to Munehiro Yosuke and Kuniko for opening so many doors – both literally through the warm welcome to their home, and also through their connections with the objects, people and ideas relating to Mingei in Japan.

The authors of this book and I would like to thank all those who made *Art Without Heroes* possible, including:

The Addyman family; Baba Junko; Greta Bertram; Louise Boyd; Everett Kennedy Brown; Rosina Buckland; Nicholas Coldicott; Jill Fanshaw Kato; Fujita Motoko; Fukasawa Naoto; Furuya Mayumi; Futatsuya Atsushi and Keiko; Marty Gross, Sato Chitose and Lissa Mateus at the Mingei Film Archive for their huge generosity in sharing their expertise and many fascinating hours of film footage; Hamada Tomoo; Akiko Hirai; Hirano Kaori and Akihide, Saito Mariko, Matsuo Yuka and Furuta Mari at Itoshiro Yōhin Ten; Higashikata Akane; Higeta Tadashi; Honda Akiko; Isaka Koichiro; Kato Naoki; Kato Setsuo; Fran Kazui; Matsuo Yuka; Mayunkiki; Miya Nobuho; Joan Mirviss; Moriyama Kaoru; Motohashi Naoko; Nagaoka Yuji; Nakagawa Shūji; Nakamoto Michiyo, Naohito Shikama; Oikawa Waka; Ōtsuchi Sashiko Recovery Project, especially Yoshida Mai, Kurosawa Kaori, Sasaki Kanako, Ōsawa Mieko and Kikuchi Hiromi; Iona Penrice; Gwen Robinson; Suzanne Perrin; Serizawa Keiko; Sudo Reiko; Sugiyama Motoshi; Taira Meiko; Tamura Kanoko; Tatsumi Kiyoshi; Karun Thakar; David Wertheim and Masami Yamada.

Sincere thanks are due to the Friends of the William Morris Gallery for funding various aspects of the publication, and to the Daiwa Foundation and the Art Fund's Jonathan Ruffer grant, without whose support much of the research that contributed to the maker profiles would not have been possible. I am especially grateful to The Great Britain Sasakawa Foundation, who have generously supported the exhibition as a whole.

I am grateful to all the authors who have contributed their time and expertise to this book, and I can only apologise for any occasions on which, in the words of Bernard Leach's editors, in poking about the linguistic coals I have put out the fire altogether. I'm particularly grateful to Anna Jackson and Yuko Kikuchi for their additional support and kindness, which gave me the confidence to pursue various elements of the *Art Without Heroes* project. Thanks also to Sarah Mercer for her invaluable detective work and organisational skills in sourcing and reproducing images and to my colleagues at the William Morris Gallery for their support and belief in the project. I am extremely grateful to Mark Eastment, Rachel Hughes and Daphne Fordham-Smith at Yale University Press for making the book a reality, to Robert Davies for providing such a thoughtful copyedit and to Aniela Gil for the book's design.

Finally, my profound thanks go to Ōta Junko and Ogawa Eri (1951–2019) for the warmness of their hospitality and generosity in sharing their lived understanding of Japanese beauty; to Jimbo Kyoko and her colleagues at the Tokyo Metropolitan Teien Museum; to Kajiwara Akiko for her continued assistance, friendship and care parcels from Japan; and to Chris, who by making everything, makes everything possible.

## MAKER PROFILE IMAGE CREDITS

All images in the Maker Profiles section are © Róisín Inglesby / Yoshizawa Tomo unless stated below.

**Fukasawa Naoto**: Profile image © Fukasawa Naoto; maruni / Wooden Objects / Design Fukasawa Naoto
**Oikawa Waka**: Interior view © Hagihara Kentaro
**Hirano Kaori**: © Itoshiro Yōhin Ten
**Akiko Hirai**: Profile image © Philip Sinden; *kohiki* bowl © Akiko Hirai
**Nakagawa Shūji**: All images © Nakagawa Shūji
**Oki Izumi**: All images © Okazaki Manami
**Ōtsuchi Sashiko**: Close-up of *sashiko-san* working, Photo by Yamamoto Kōhei

# Index

Page numbers in *italic* refer to the illustrations